& TREES
in
BRITISH
COLUMBIA

Mike Fenger, Todd Manning,
John Cooper, Stewart Guy, Peter Bradford

LONE
PINE.

Lone Pine Publishing

The Publisher: Lone Pine Publishing

10145 – 81 Avenue　　　　　　　　　202A, 1110 Seymour St.
Edmonton, AB T6E 1W9　　　　　　 Vancouver, BC V6B 3N3

Website: www.lonepinepublishing.com

Library and Archives Canada Cataloguing in Publication

Wildlife & trees in British Columbia / Mike Fenger ... [et al.].

Includes bibliographical references and index.
ISBN-13: 978-1-55105-071-3
ISBN-10: 1-55105-071-4

1. Forest management--British Columbia. 2. Forest ecology--British Columbia. 3. Wildlife habitat improvement--British Columbia. 4. Habitat (Ecology)--British Columbia. 5. Trees--British Columbia. 6. Animals--British Columbia. I. Fenger, Mike, 1949- II. Title: Wildlife and trees in British Columbia.

SD146.B7W53 2006　　　　　　333.7509711　　　　C2006-902707-2

Editorial Director: Nancy Foulds
Project Editor: Gary Whyte
Editorial: Carmen Adams, Volker Bodegom, Genevieve Boyer, Nicholle Carrière, Linda Kershaw, Roland Lines, Wendy Pirk
Photo and Illustration Database: Carol Woo
Production Manager: Gene Longson
Book Design: Elliot Engley, Heather Markham
Book Layout: Elliot Engley, Heather Markham, Curtis Pillipow
Cover Design: Gerry Dotto
Chart Design: Curtis Pillipow
Range Map Design: Willa Kung, Volker Bodegom
Scanning & Digital Film: Elite Lithographers Co.

Front cover photo by Mark Nyhof
Back cover photo by Anna Roberts
See page 6 for all photo and illustration credits.

We acknowledge the financial support of the Government of Canada through the Book Publishing Industry Development Program (BPIDP) for our publishing activities.

PC: 13

Table of Contents

TABLE OF CONTENTS

List of Figures, Tables and Maps

Photo and Illustration Credits

(All photos, illustrations and maps used with permission. Numbers refer to page numbers and location on the page).

PHOTO CREDITS

B.C. Ministry of Agriculture and Lands, Integrated Land Management Bureau: 51
B.C. Ministry of Forests and Range (MoFR): 26b, 42a, 42b, 50, 53, 57a, 61, 62, 63a, 63b, 65, 69a, 72a, 73, 74, 77, 84, 88, 89a (inset), 89b, 92a, 92b, 93, 94b, 94d, 95b, 97a, 101a, 101b, 101c, 101d, 101e, 103b, 103c, 103d, 104a, 104b, 104c, 104d, 105b (inset), 105c, 105d, 105e, 106b (inset), 109a (top inset), 109c (bottom inset)
Ken Bowen: 31, 278a
Evelyn L. Bull: 13, 72b, 130a, 142, 185a, 188, 204a, 205, 242, 283a
Rob Butler: 263
R. Wayne Campbell: 25a, 184, 189, 210a, 265, 278b
Dick Cannings: 187
S.R. Cannings: 154
Fred Chapman: 17
John Cooper: 127a, 137
John Deal: 76a, 76b
Dave Dunbar: 280
Mike Fenger: 11a, 40b, 78, 85, 87, 90a, 90b, 91a, 91b, 94a, 94c, 96a, 96b, 96c, 97b, 97c, 98a (inset), 98b, 99a, 99b, 99c, 100a, 100b, 100c, 103a, 105a, 106a, 107, 108a, 108b, 108c, 110a, 110b, 110c (inset)
Jeff Foott (Valan Photos): 283b
David F. Fraser: 10a, 12, 38a
Tony Hamilton: 40c
Stefan Himmer: 256
Jared Hobbs: 122, 139b, 149b (inset), 150b (inset), 227, 243, 279, 281
Mark Hobson: 254, 275
Alex Inselberg: 69b
Linda Kershaw: 95a, 109b
Thomas Kitchen (Valan Photos): 169
Aubray Lang (Valan Photos): 193
Robert Lankinen (First Light): 133b (inset), 250
Wayne Lankinen (Valan Photos): 183
Douglas Leighton: 199, 262
Dion Manastyrski (earthpics.ca): 30b
Irene Manley: 276
Tim Matheson: 30a
Mark Nyhof: 1, 10b, 10c, 11b, 14, 16b, 20, 25b, 25c, 25d, 26a, 26c, 27a, 27b, 27c, 38b, 39, 41, 47, 57b, 67, 79, 80, 81, 111, 119, 124a, 124b, 125, 126, 127b (inset), 129, 130b (inset), 131, 132, 133a, 134a, 134b, 135a,

135b (inset), 136, 138, 139a, 140, 141b, 143a, 145a, 145b, 146, 147a, 147b, 148, 149a, 150a, 151, 153, 155a, 155b, 157a, 157b, 158, 159a, 162, 164a, 164b, 165, 166a, 166b, 168a, 168b, 173, 175, 179, 182, 186, 190, 191, 192, 194, 195, 196, 197, 198, 200, 201, 202, 203, 204b (inset), 206, 207a, 207b (inset), 208, 209a, 209b, 210b, 212, 214a, 214b, 215a, 215b, 216a, 216b, 241, 244, 246, 247, 248, 251, 261, 266, 268b, 273, 335, front cover
Mike Pirnke: 141a, 171, 178b, 267, 268a, 272a
Anna Roberts: 123, 144, 156, 160, 219, 221, 237, 229, 231, 239, back cover
Esther Schmidt (Valan Photos): 178a, 181
Andy Stewart: 180
Mike Stini: 40a, 269, 270
Bill Swan: 264, 272b
Merlin D. Tuttle (Bat Conservation International): 223, 233, 235
Maarten Vonhof: 16a, 18, 217
Ole Westby: 167, 277
Brian K. Wheeler: 185b (inset)
Michael Wigle: 121, 159b
Tim Zurowski: 143b (inset), 163, 172, 174, 177, 213, 274, 282

ILLUSTRATION CREDITS

Mark Nyhof: 14 (fig.1, 2), 15 (fig. 3, 4), 17 (fig. 5), 18 (fig. 6, 7), 19 (fig. 8), 20 (fig. 9), 21 (fig. 10), 22 (fig. 11), 23 (fig. 12), 32 (fig. 14), 33 (fig. 15), 36 (fig. 16, 17), 37 (fig. 18), 43 (fig. 19), 44 (fig. 20), 52 (fig. 23), 57 (fig. 25)
Gary Ross: 220, 222, 225, 228, 230, 232, 234, 236, 238, 240, 245, 249, 252

TREE SILHOUETTES: B.C. Ministry of Forests and Range

MAP CREDITS

Tree range maps: Adapted from Agricultural Handbook #654 "Silvics of North America," Russell M. Burns and Barbara H. Honkala, Technical Coordinators. U.S. Department of Agriculture, Forest Service, Washington, DC, 1990.
British Columbia's Terrestrial Ecoprovinces map: B.C. Ministry of Environment
Biogeoclimatic Zones of British Columbia map: B.C. Ministry of Forests and Range
Animal species range maps: original compilation by the authors

Foreword

It was the American poet, Joyce Kilmer, who penned the lines that almost every school child associates with trees:

"I think that I shall never see
A poem lovely as a tree."

Kilmer's poem leaves no doubt that his "lovely" tree was verdant, symmetrical and healthy—the best that Nature had to offer.

Like many things, as we grow older we realize not everything measures up to our childhood image. Kilmer probably would not have had the same glowing words for trees that were old, damaged, deformed, diseased and decayed. Ironically, these types of trees are often among the "loveliest" from an ecological point of view. Had Kilmer the information in this book available to him, I like to think he would be the first to agree.

In a society that values youth, beauty and physical perfection above all else, Nature frequently reminds us that this judgement is mostly superficial and that the old, ugly and deformed can be equally desirable and perhaps more valuable. Wildlife trees are a case in point.

Our perception of what is valuable changes with increased research, knowledge and experience. When I began my career in government, we routinely took to court those logging companies who felled or dragged large logs into fish-bearing streams. Research later showed that "large organic debris" was one of the essential contributors to fish habitat and stream stability and that a moderate amount of it was beneficial, if not critical.

Similarly, for years the principal focus in wildlife management was almost exclusively the protection of living old-growth stands to provide winter range for ungulates. Dead or dying trees were simply felled as they posed a safety hazard to forest workers. Since then, we have learned that other components of a forest are equally valuable if we want to retain the full range of biodiversity. Wildlife trees are near the top of that list.

The fight to generate a more enlightened approach to the protection of wildlife trees in British Columbia was a long and often adversarial one. For years, any such tree was simply regarded as a safety threat and was summarily removed. After much argument, based on research, saner heads prevailed and the Workers Compensation Board regulations now permit certain trees to be retained. We make progress in tiny steps.

Traditionally in this province, foresters managed trees for the mill and biologists managed the wildlife habitat that was left. We are, hopefully, moving toward the time when all forest managers realize that they must work together collaboratively and consider all the values of the forest if they are to retain the "social license" to log. This is especially true when government has abrogated much of its role in forest management and relies on the professionalism of foresters and biologists. Recognition of this new obligation is happening, but not fast enough or universally enough and often with unfortunate retrogressive steps prompted by changes in policy by both government and industry. This book will help to accelerate the pace of positive change by providing more tools for the responsible manager and needed information for those who lobby and pressure the not-so-responsible ones. The fact that this book is a collaboration by several biologists and foresters is itself a good sign.

One of the authors remarked to me that there is nothing in this book that is new. That may be true for the practicing biologist or forester, but the interested public is often unaware of even old information, since it may not be easily accessible to non-professionals or available in understandable language. This book contains a wealth of information in a readable and usable format—for example, the tables regarding the stages and classification of wildlife trees. And the text moves logically from what constitutes a wildlife tree to the role of wildlife trees in ecosystem management, then focuses in considerable detail on individual trees and animals. For those who want a quick course on the ecology of the forest and how harvesting can affect it, "Part 2: Wildlife Trees & Ecosystem Management" is a good current summary.

The information on wildlife trees in the urban landscape is understandably not as well developed as that for forest stands. Only recently have local governments begun to realize that, for more and more people, a truly livable subdivision means the retention of natural elements. It is still a challenge to convince homebuyers, developers and local governments that an old, decayed and damaged tree can be a more interesting addition to their subdivision than the "nice" trees usually pictured in real estate ads. However, British Columbians are among the most environmentally aware people on the continent and increasingly, news stories tell of public efforts to protect such trees. This book will provide even more material for letters to the editor or arguments before the local council.

At the end of his poem Kilmer says:

"Poems are made by fools like me,
But only God can make a tree."

Fortunately, with respect to wildlife trees, Kilmer is again only half right. Once a tree has become established, "Creating Wildlife Tree Features" in Part 2 outlines practical suggestions that can be implemented to help convert an old tree into a wildlife tree and speed up its ecological usefulness. It will probably never be as good as what Mother Nature would have done, but there is much here for local stewardship groups.

"Part 4: Knowing the Trees," on the classification and attributes of wildlife trees, and "Part 5: Knowing the Wildlife," on the 66 species that are currently known to use them, are admittedly works in progress, but they contain a surprising amount of detailed information. As our knowledge increases, new animal species and new trees will undoubtedly be added to the list, as will more knowledge of their contributions to biodiversity.

The authors stress repeatedly throughout this book that it takes years to create a wildlife tree. Unfortunately, we do not have the same luxury of time to protect many of them. As population increases, forestry and resource extraction accelerates and urban growth occupies more and more land, wildlife trees are fast disappearing. Equally distressing, so are many of the younger trees that would be candidates to become wildlife trees in the future.

In a country and a province that lauds itself on its enlightened approach to diversity, we need to remind ourselves as Canadians that if we are to be a truly sustainable and unselfish example for the world, our concern for protecting diversity must extend to other species, not just humans.

This book is a small but positive and practical step in that direction and will prompt us to do more than just talk about it.

Jim Walker
April, 2006

Jim Walker offers a unique inside-of-government view on the evolution of scientific understanding of our natural environment and its integration into government policy, legislation and standards of practice. A former career civil servant, Jim knows wildlife management and habitat protection from the ground up as he progressed from field biologist to Assistant Deputy Minister in charge of Fish and Wildlife for the B.C. Ministry of Environment.

Acknowledgements

The concept for this guide first took shape over a decade ago. The authors recognized a need to share understanding of how forested ecosystems work and how to manage for wildlife species that depend on specific types of trees for their life history requirements.

Once the concept and structure of the guide had been developed, sections were parcelled out to several biologists to provide early drafts. We gladly and gratefully acknowledge the contributions of Frances Backhouse (introductory sections), Linda Guy (owls, waterfowl and bats), Susan Holroyd (bats), Marlene Machmer (woodpeckers, birds of prey and bats) and Chris Steeger (introductory sections and woodpeckers).

During the ensuing years, additional research, better understanding of ecosystem management and improved knowledge of species and their management resulted in restructuring and new emphasis, entailing significant changes, to arrive at the final guide.

We are also truly grateful to the people who conducted technical reviews of the many versions of the chapters and species accounts and those who responded to our many questions. They are Greg Ashcroft, Mike Badry, Robert Barclay, Louise Blight, Mark Brigham, Evelyn Bull, Alan Burger, Rob Butler, Wayne Campbell, Syd Cannings, Mike Chutter, Sharon Clifford, Ted Davis, John Deal, Craig Delong, Dennis Demarchi, Orville Dyer, Tom Ethier, Laura Friis, Pat Gregory, Tony Hamilton, Bill Harper, Lisa Hartman, Ed Hennan, Jared Hobbs, Rick Howie, Dave Jones, Dave King, Eric Lofroth, Dave Low, Andy MacKinnon, Fred Marshall, Kathy Martin, Erica McClaren, Katie McGregor, Scott McNay, Ian McTaggart-Cowan, Del Meidinger, Ken Morgan, Dave Nagorsen, Kari Nelson, Brian Nyberg, Mark Nyhof, Stan Orchard, Kathy Paige, Jim Pojar, Anna Roberts, Dale Seip, Tory Stevens, Susan Stevenson, Doug Steventon, Richard Thompson, Maarten Vonhof, Michaela Waterhouse, Richard Weir and Lisa Wilkinson.

Mark Nyhof was involved from the beginning and throughout the project. He provided many of the photographs and coordinated acquisition of the remaining images. Mark also illustrated most of the figures for the guide.

Thanks also to Robert Barcley for his help with the bat images and to Paul Nysted and Rick Scharf for their help with the tree silhouettes.

Assistance in word-processing was initially provided by Gail Harcombe and then by Christine Ensing, who also provided encouragement and editorial comments during the next draft versions. Sheilagh Ogilvie completed the first complete review of the initial draft, and Frances Backhouse completed a thorough edit of the final draft with attention to consistency in content and style. Rod Davis and Rod Silver must also be thanked for their ongoing commitment to the completion of this book.

Many thanks to Lone Pine Publishing for their patience and confidence in this project. Thanks to their staff for putting this guide together: Carmen Adams, Volker Bodegom, Genevieve Boyer, Nicholle Carrière, Gerry Dotto, Elliot Engley, Nancy Foulds, Shane Kennedy, Linda Kershaw, Willa Kung, Roland Lines, Gene Longson, Heather Markham, Curtis Pillipow, Wendy Pirk and Gary Whyte.

Financial assistance in the production of this book has been provided by B.C. Ministry of Forests and Range and by B.C. Ministry of Environment.

About This Guide

A collaboration between biologists and foresters, this guide integrates conservation biology principles with tree management practices. It is intended for anyone who wants to know more about his or her natural surroundings, especially people who are interested in how to maintain the biological diversity of forests—such as foresters, biologists, naturalists, land-use planners, arborists and others who regularly make decisions about trees. Its focus is "wildlife trees," an important and threatened part of forest biodiversity, and 66 species of birds and mammals, some of them provincially designated as threatened or endangered, for which wildlife trees provide essential habitat.

Although the parts of this guide are linked, each one can stand alone, so it is not necessary to read sequentially.

PART 2, WILDLIFE TREES AND ECOSYSTEM MANAGEMENT reviews concepts of ecosystem management. It discusses where, when and how many wildlife trees occur in ecosystems under natural conditions and how their natural occurrence relates to wildlife tree retention in managed forests. It outlines the difference between managing for wildlife trees in general and providing for the habitat needs of individual species. Wildlife trees are then considered in both the landscape-level context and the stand-level context. Finally, this section offers techniques for creating and enhancing single wildlife trees.

PART 1, INTRODUCTION TO WILDLIFE TREES AND THEIR DEPENDENT SPECIES defines what a wildlife tree is and then describes the features to look for that make these trees valuable to wildlife. An overview of the wildlife tree-dependent species and the roles they perform in their ecosystems follows. This section also offers tips for finding wildlife trees with existing use.

PART 3, WILDLIFE TREES AND THE MANAGEMENT OF URBAN AND RURAL LANDS looks at the conservation of wildlife trees in urban and rural areas, including parks and private lands. The lessons learned from the authors' experience, primarily in forested ecosystems and forestry management, can also be applied to rural and urban settings.

PART 4, KNOWING THE TREES is a species-by-species description of the characteristics of conifers and hardwoods and how they grow to become wildlife trees. It provides information about where they are found (both their broad geographic distribution and their microsite preferences), conditions for germination, growth rates, relationship to other tree species, longevity, size and decay factors, as well as details about each species' contribution as a wildlife tree and some of the wildlife species that use them.

The final section, **PART 5, KNOWING THE WILDLIFE** is devoted to accounts of each of British Columbia's 66 featured wildlife tree-dependent species.

They have been divided into three groups:
primary cavity excavators,
secondary cavity users
and open nesters.

A map shows the provincial range of each species. Each species account has one or more photos and a physical description of the species to assist with identification in the field. Photos also illustrate feeding and breeding habitats. Information about territory and home range size and breeding biology are also provided. Accounts conclude with stewardship provisions that provide more detailed species habitat preferences,

when known, to supplement the generic practices outlined in Part 2. (In some cases, this information is supplied in the preceding overview for a grouping of species.)

Following the glossary and a list of references is an appendix that addresses questions of risk to human safety and property and legal liability. The final two appendices provide tabular summaries of the species and habitat information given in Part 5. Consult these tables to learn which species might depend on habitats on property in your care.

List of abbreviations and symbols used in this guide

See also: Knowing the Trees (p. 88), Ecoprovinces (p. 113), Biogeoclimatic Zones (p. 114), and the Glossary (p. 284).

>	greater than
<	less than
cm	centimetre
dbh	diameter at breast height
g	gram
ha	hectare
kg	kilogram
km	kilometre
km²	square kilometre
m	metre

PART 1

WILDLIFE TREES & THEIR DEPENDENT SPECIES

WHAT MAKES A TREE A WILDLIFE TREE?

A wildlife tree is any standing dead or living tree with special characteristics that provide vitally important habitat for the conservation or enhancement of wildlife. These characteristics, such as large trunks (sometimes hollow), large branches, deformed and broken tops, internal decay and sloughing or loose bark, are becoming increasingly scarce as old forests are harvested for forest products or cleared for agriculture and other types of land development. Without these key features, the bird and mammal species that depend on them cannot survive as part of our forested ecosystems. As their habitat disappears, certain species will become increasingly endangered.

No single feature or characteristic determines which trees are best for wildlife, but the most important wildlife trees are usually large, old, damaged, deformed, diseased or decaying trees— a legacy of forests that have developed through natural disturbances and aging. Relative size (height and diameter), branch characteristics, bark condition, a hollow trunk, the type and stage of decay and the location are all important wildlife tree features that are discussed below. The distribution (scarcity) and likelihood of remaining standing (persistence) also affect a tree's potential value to wildlife.

Although almost all trees have the potential to become wildlife trees, only a relative few will eventually perform this vital ecological role. The genetic information stored in the seed from which a tree sprouts determines how long it can live and how large it can grow. Under favourable conditions, a seed germinates, becomes a tree, survives long enough to produce its own seed crops and then, with age, loses vigour and dies.

However, the actual fate of a tree depends on many physical and biological influences:
- moisture availability, temperature and available light
- competition with neighbouring plants for water and nutrients
- viral, bacterial and fungal diseases
- insects and other animals that feed on its needles or leaves, bark and wood
- disturbances such as fire, landslides, ice storms, wind and flooding.

Collectively, these factors determine how individual trees and stands of trees develop over time, and they create a wide variety of wildlife tree types from the assortment of trees in a locality.

It is important to remember that, under natural conditions, a tree remains part of the forest ecosystem long after its death. Its rate of decay varies according to the species, cause of death, climate and other factors. If left undisturbed by humans, a dead tree may remain standing in the forest for up to half the time it stood while alive. A tree's ecological importance continues as it breaks apart and falls to the ground or after it topples, and eventually all its nutrients are cycled back into the soil to be taken up by new plants.

For a tree to grow to this size takes well in excess of two centuries. Internal decay also takes time to create a chamber large enough for a nest site. The prominent ear tufts, size and fuzzy appearance mark this youngster as an unfledged great horned owl.

13

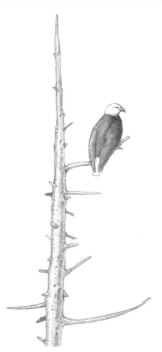

Figure 1. Perching in a spike-topped snag. Birds of prey hunt from and rest on high perches. These vantage points need to be in trees old enough to have developed both sufficient height and the stiffness to afford a good perch, even on windy days.

Figure 2. A broken-topped larger diameter Douglas-fir snag. After death, a Douglas-fir can persist for centuries, providing cavities, perches and open nest sites for a variety of species, such as this owl. Over time, the sloughing-off of the bark makes the site more secure from climbing predators. Surrounding overstorey trees also enhance security from nest predation, as well as improving shelter from wind and rain for open nesters.

SIZE

The greater the diameter and height of a tree, the greater the number of species and individuals that can potentially use it. Large trees have a greater trunk volume, a greater bark surface area and, generally, more numerous large branches—which all add up to more habitat in a single tree. The largest trees allow the biggest cavities and offer more security and better lookout posts, providing the most benefits to the widest range of species. Old trees are often larger than younger ones and are also more likely to have some form of decay, making cavity excavation easier. Trees that have lived many decades, or even centuries, surviving various natural disturbances over time, tend to be windfirm and more likely to remain standing, providing long-term habitat when they are retained.

Witches' brooms add structurally diverse habitat that is used for shelter, resting, nesting and denning.

Figure 3 Witches' brooms. These dense branch clusters are the result of certain pathogens, particularly dwarf mistletoe. Large brooms provide resting areas for the marten and fisher, and nest platforms for some large owls, the northern goshawk and the northern flying squirrel.

Figure 4. Large branching habitat in mature and older black cottonwoods. For species such as the great blue heron, bald eagle and osprey, which build nests close to their feeding waters, large branches provide secure anchoring.

BRANCH CHARACTERISTICS AND WITCHES' BROOMS

Young trees have small, flexible branches. As trees age and reach their full size, their branches increase in diameter and strength, with those of many species becoming large enough to support the heavy open nests of bald eagles, ospreys and great blue herons. These nesting platforms are also used by some hawks and owls. The marbled murrelet, though it is a small bird, needs large, moss-covered branches as platforms on which to make its nests in our coastal forests.

A mature tree with dense foliage can provide good cover and shed rain, helping to reduce an animal's energy loss in wet, cold conditions. On the other hand, dead treetops or branches with no foliage make good observation posts and hunting perches.

Some trees can develop dense clumps of swollen stems and branches— referred to as "witches' brooms" or simply "brooms." The cause is often dwarf mistletoe, a parasitic flowering plant that absorbs nutrients, water and carbohydrates from its host tree. Although the brooms are a deformation of the tree, they provide habitat for some wildlife species. The elevated platforms provide sites for safe resting, nesting and denning, as well as vantage points from which predators such as the fisher can see and smell prey. Western hemlock, western larch, lodgepole pine and Douglas-fir can all produce large witches' brooms that are beneficial to wildlife.

15

BARK CONDITION

Bark characteristics change as trees age. Young trees generally have smooth bark, which increases in thickness and roughness with age; this change is more pronounced in some species, such as Douglas-fir and ponderosa pine, than in others. Furrowed bark provides habitat for insects, which are an important food source for many wildlife species, such as woodpeckers. After a tree dies, the bark begins to loosen and pull away from the trunk. The protected space under the sloughing bark becomes valuable habitat sought by bats and some small birds, such as the brown creeper.

Furrowed Douglas-fir bark. *A brown creeper has built a nest behind a thick section of bark that has pulled slightly away from the trunk, affording a sheltered, hidden, safe space for a nest.*

Loose bark. *Loose bark creates significant hidden cover for bat roosts and foraging opportunities for insectivores.*

VETERAN TREES

In forests where natural fire regimes control the regeneration of the stand, a few trees may escape being killed, whereas others burn and die. In forest inventories, these trees are referred to as veterans ("vets" for short), a fitting name for these survivors. Vets stand out above the forest canopy and may be centuries old.

Vets occur in species that develop increasingly thick bark over the years, providing ever-increasing protection against fire. Their ability to survive fires helps them to achieve full size before dying from old age or the effects of insects, disease and fungi. By the time they die, vets have usually developed deformities and dimensions that attract many wildlife tree-dependent species. Douglas-fir, ponderosa pine and western larch are the most common vets.

A ponderosa pine veteran. *This open-grown ponderosa pine vet has survived over the centuries in a landscape with natural disturbances, such as fire and insect infestation. Black scars are testimony to the fires that frequently kill young trees before they develop bark of sufficient thickness. The top may have been killed by insects or disease.*

Figure 5. An enlarged cavity in a ponderosa pine. Over time, a primary cavity that was used by a small owl will undergo sufficient natural decay and become large enough for other nesting species. The wood duck will use nest trees up to half a kilometre from water.

Vets are naturally scarce and are always susceptible to being felled because their size and condition means they are classified as danger trees and are slated for felling to protect worker safety. In addition, they may attract the attention of some timber cutters, but they typically make poor grades of lumber and their irregularities, such as spiral grain, large knots and pitch cracks, cause milling difficulties. Because vets make the best wildlife trees in their areas, they need to be protected and retained during regular forest harvesting, and they need continued protection over time from salvage loggers and firewood cutters. They are good candidates for wildlife tree signs (see p. 77). Anyone who buys firewood or wood from salvage harvesting should ensure that it does not come from these rare and vitally important trees (see p. 75).

A large natural cavity in a hollow western red-cedar. *This large, natural cavity was formed when extensive internal decay hollowed the trunk over time. A split in the trunk allows secondary cavity users access to shelter from the elements and predators.*

HOLLOW TRUNKS

Generally uncommon and often rare, trees with hollow trunks are highly sought after by wildlife, both when standing and after they fall, making them an important present and future habitat resource. A tree with no internal decay present before its death will not develop a hollow core, which forms when fungi attack the inner heartwood of a live, standing tree, but not the outer part of its trunk. Western red-cedar, yellow-cedar and black cottonwood are the three tree species most likely to develop hollow trunks. In these two conifers, because of the decay resistance of the heartwood, this process takes a very long time, even longer than in the cottonwood.

Hollow trunks provide large cavities that offer safety and shelter to many species. They are used as colonial roost sites by bats and Vaux's swifts, as hibernation dens by black bears, as nest and roosting sites by large owls and as temporary

Figure 6. A secondary cavity user in a ponderosa pine. This old northern flicker cavity is a suitable size to provide a secure nest site for a small owl, such as this saw-whet. Large ponderosa pine snags persist in the landscape for many decades and are exceedingly important for many species. Unfortunately, open ponderosa pine forests with large trees are in dwindling supply. Only through coordinated, sustained effort and commitment will there be a future supply of this habitat.

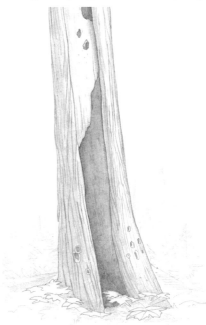

Figure 7. A hollow trunk in a western red-cedar. Created by brown cubical rot and pocket rot, these extremely valuable large cavities are used by bats and swifts for their colonial roost sites.

rest sites or maternal dens by medium-sized mammals, such as martens.

Because a hollow trunk takes a long time to develop and generally does so infrequently, it is extremely important to retain hollow trees. Shake cutting and salvage logging pose a significant and persistent threat to this scarce and vitally important wildlife tree feature. Therefore, hollow trees are good candidates for wildlife tree signs (see p. 77). In addition, because hollow trees have reduced stability, it is important to protect them from blowdown, most importantly by leaving adjacent trees to act as a windbreak (see p. 65, Selecting Windfirm Trees).

TYPES OF DECAY

Like the broom-producing organisms described earlier, decay fungi serve the purposes of wildlife tree users by converting healthy trees into potential

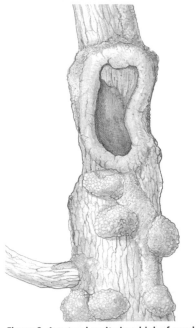

Figure 8. A natural cavity in a bigleaf maple.
Cavities like this one form when a large branch breaks and fungi invade the damaged tissues of the tree. A cavity in a living tree will last longer than a cavity in a dead tree.

special habitats. Trees that are sick or stressed are generally less capable of defending themselves from insects and are therefore more attractive to them. Insect-inhabited trees become foraging sites for a host of woodpeckers and other wildlife species.

Decay fungi can be divided into three main categories based on the part of the tree that they affect: roots, sapwood or heartwood. (The sapwood is the living outer portion of the trunk or branch that carries water and nutrients from the roots to the leaves, and the heartwood is the inner part that is no longer active in this way.)

Root Decay

Root diseases kill the living parts of tree roots and decay the woody parts. They can advance several metres up the trunk and will weaken a tree, making it susceptible to other fungi, bark beetles and windthrow.

A root-rot centre is a cluster of trees infected with root rot. High concentrations of insects found in these centres are a source of food for many birds. These clusters are particularly inviting to woodpeckers, which also use these trees for nesting.

Root decay fungi sometimes enter through wounds on the roots or lower trunk, but they usually spread from tree to tree where healthy roots come in contact with diseased roots, resulting in groups of infected trees with thinning, yellow crowns. Infected trees typically grow more slowly than normal, and conifers under stress will produce smaller yet more numerous cones than usual. Some root decay fungi produce visible "conks" (fruiting bodies also commonly known as bracket fungi).

Sapwood and Heartwood Decay

The sapwood is surrounded by a layer of reproducing cells known as the cambium, which is in turn surrounded and protected by the bark. Damage to the bark (and possibly the sapwood) allows specialized fungi to invade, and some decay fungi can progress beyond the wound site and cause decay in the heartwood. Physical damage that creates such a wound can occur when trees fall against each other, when they are scorched by fire or when extreme frost causes splitting. The resulting decay produces dead tops, hollow basal cavities and localized deterioration of the wood. Decayed trees are prone to breakage, especially at the site of infection. However, sapwood- and heartwood-rot fungi do not necessarily kill their hosts, and some of them attack only dead wood.

Trees with sapwood or heartwood rot usually display conks on the trunk or branches. Scars, broken tops, branch stubs, frost cracks, forks and crooks are also indicators of possible decay, because they may have served as entry points for decay fungi.

Fungi that cause decay in the heartwood perform an important role in creating wildlife trees. Rotten wood that is still firm on the outside attracts birds that dig out their own chambers for nesting and roosting (the primary cavity excavators), and the natural cavities that form in trees with sufficient heart rot provide homes for species that use existing cavities (the secondary cavity users).

External conks indicate internal decay. *The conk (bracket fungus) near the bottom of the photo indicates that this tree has internal decay. The four entrance holes near the bend in the trunk testify that primary excavators have found the wood excellent for cavity excavation.*

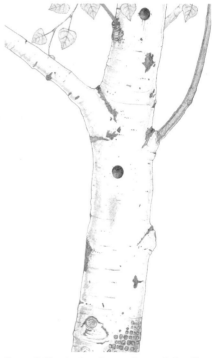

Figure 9. Heart rot and sapsucker wells in a live hardwood. Trunk-rot fungi invade only the heartwood, and so do not kill the tree because the sapwood remains intact. This condition is ideal for strong primary cavity excavators such as flickers, sapsuckers and other woodpeckers. Sapsuckers create sap wells by making neat punctured rows in the cambium of live trees. They then drink the sap and feed on the insects that it attracts once it begins to flow.

Figure 10. Tree defect and mortality agents

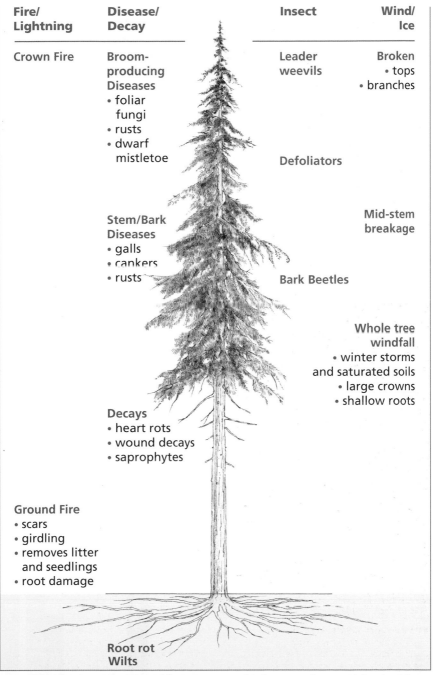

Fire/ Lightning	Disease/ Decay		Insect	Wind/ Ice
Crown Fire	Broom-producing Diseases • foliar fungi • rusts • dwarf mistletoe		Leader weevils	Broken • tops • branches
			Defoliators	
	Stem/Bark Diseases • galls • cankers • rusts			Mid-stem breakage
			Bark Beetles	
				Whole tree windfall • winter storms and saturated soils • large crowns • shallow roots
	Decays • heart rots • wound decays • saprophytes			
Ground Fire • scars • girdling • removes litter and seedlings • root damage				
	Root rot Wilts			

Depending on the circumstances, any of these agents may affect just a part of a tree or bring about the death of the whole tree.

Figure 11. Classifying conifers on form and degree of decay

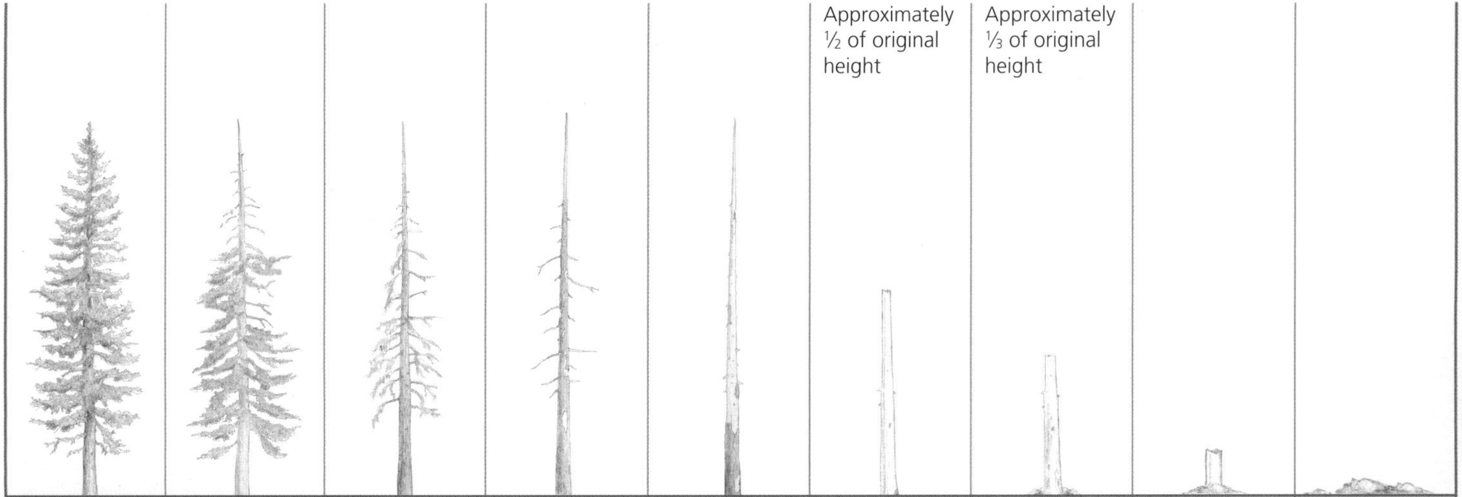

GENERAL DESCRIPTION OF TREE:								
Live/healthy —no decay	Live/unhealthy —internal decay or growth deformities	Dead —hard —fine twigs	Dead —hard —few branches	Dead —spongy —fewer branches —bark deteriorating	Dead —soft —height loss	Dead —soft —more height loss	Dead —soft —more height loss	Debris —trunk fallen
					Approximately ½ of original height	Approximately ⅓ of original height		
CLASS:								
1	2	3	4	5	6	7	8	9
LIVE		DEAD						DEAD FALLEN

Figure 12. Classifying hardwoods on form and degree of decay

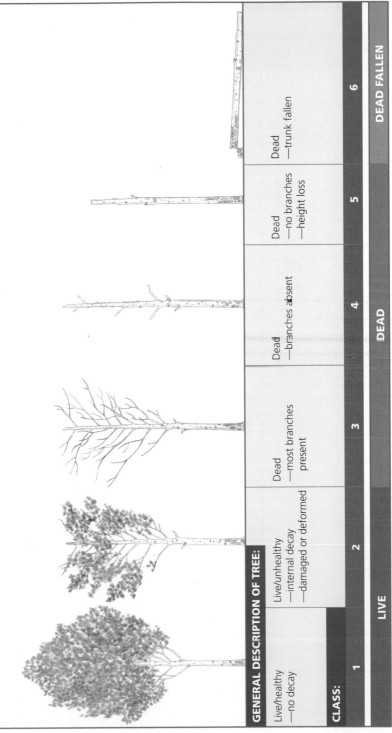

GENERAL DESCRIPTION OF TREE:					
Live/healthy —no decay	Live/unhealthy —internal decay —damaged or deformed	Dead —most branches present	Dead —branches absent	Dead —no branches —height loss	Dead —trunk fallen
CLASS:					
1	2	3	4	5	6
LIVE		DEAD			DEAD FALLEN

Figure 13. Decay classes of conifers and hardwoods and their characteristics

Decay Class		Characteristics	
Conifers	**Hardwoods**	**Status**	**Wildlife Uses**
1	1	• alive and healthy	• large branches, or branches that are clustered or gnarled, provide nest platforms for large birds of prey and herons • large, mossy branches that are flat on top become nest sites for marbled murrelets
2	2	• alive, but typically unhealthy, damaged or deformed	• dead tops provide hunting perches for birds of prey and platforms for open nesters • soft depressions created by top breakage and decay sometimes become nest sites for great horned owls • trees with heart rot are used by strong primary cavity excavators • insects attracted to trees in distress become food for insectivorous birds
3 and 4	3	• dead, in the early stages of decay • class 3 conifers still have fine twigs, whereas class 4 conifers have few branches	• a hard outer shell of sapwood surrounding a softer, decaying heartwood attracts all nesting woodpeckers and other primary cavity excavators • abandoned nest holes and natural cavities are used by many different birds and mammals • abundant insects attract a variety of insectivorous birds
	4 and 5	• advanced stages of decay • class 5 hardwoods show considerable height loss; branches are mostly gone	• the soft wood of class 5 conifers is suitable for weak cavity excavators • abandoned nest holes and natural cavities are used by many different birds and mammals • abundant insects attract a variety of insectivorous birds
5 and 6	-	• increasing deterioration • branches and bark are mostly gone • some height loss	• still structurally sound enough for nest cavity excavation by woodpeckers • abandoned woodpecker nest cavities and natural holes and hollows are used by various birds and mammals • abundant insects attract a variety of insectivorous birds
7 and 8	-	• trunk is very soft; much of it has fallen to the ground, contributing coarse woody debris to the forest floor	• abandoned woodpecker nest cavities and natural holes and hollows are used by various birds and mammals • abundant insects attract a variety of insectivorous birds

Note: A fallen conifer is class 9, and a fallen hardwood is class 6. Although these downed trees are important for many wildlife species, coarse woody debris is beyond the scope of this book and only passing mention will be made of downed wood.

The system of decay classes summarizes the condition of a tree based on external evidence. A tree's decay class provides insight as to how long it is likely to persist and its potential utility to wildlife tree dwellers. Hardwoods are described with fewer decay classes than conifers because they generally decay faster. When a tree trunk falls it begins to recycle into the forest floor and is called coarse woody debris.

Hardwood in Decay Class 1. *One of these live, healthy black cottonwoods is supporting five nests in this heron rookery. Because they are generally within riparian ecosystems, cottonwoods are ideally situated for many wildlife tree species that require aquatic feeding sites.*

Conifer in Decay Class 1. *Ponderosa pine*

Hardwood in Decay Class 2. *The conks indicate that this live trembling aspen has internal decay, and the entrance for a yellow-bellied sapsucker's home is visible near the top of the photo. Over time, natural decay will enlarge such cavities, thus providing opportunities for successively larger secondary cavity users until the tree eventually dies and finally falls down.*

Conifer in Decay Class 3. *This recently deceased conifer has not yet lost its fine branches. The lack of foliage enhances its usefulness as a vantage point from which raptors can watch for prey.*

25

Conifer in Decay Class 3. *This dead conifer in decay class 3 houses a northern flicker nest cavity.*

Conifer in Decay Class 4. *This decay class 4 ponderosa pine houses a Lewis's woodpecker nest. Dead trees retain their branches much longer in dry climates.*

Conifers in Decay Class 5. *These conifer snags in decay class 5 retain their full height, but are missing all their branches.*

Conifer in Decay Class 6. *This decay class 6 conifer shows a loss of height.*

Conifer in Decay Class 7. *Even though, because of the dry climate, this large ponderosa pine with loose bark has maintained its limbs, its significant loss of height makes it a better fit for decay class 7 rather than 6.*

Conifer in Decay Class 8. *This conifer is in the final stages of decay.*

27

DECAY CLASSES

Death and decay are dynamic processes, but they do not necessarily occur rapidly. Unless a tree is killed by a single, sudden event (such as a fire or avalanche or the actions of beavers or humans), trees age and die gradually, over many years. As a tree ages and becomes less vigorous, it becomes more susceptible to damage, rot pathogens and tree diseases. It is common to see old trees with dead tops or branches, fungal fruiting bodies and witches' brooms—all evidence of disease or decay. These features provide the habitat that makes a tree a wildlife tree.

Pathogens and trees in various stages of decay are important natural components of forest ecosystems. Both conifers and hardwoods (broad-leafed, deciduous species) go through a similar series of decay stages. Each decay stage provides conditions suitable for a different assortment of wildlife tree users. For example, strong primary cavity excavators—most woodpeckers are in this category—prefer to nest in trees that have live sapwood, but with heartwood that has been softened by rot. The weakened inner wood of these trees offers less resistance when the birds are excavating their nest cavities at the centre of the trunk, whereas the firm sapwood provides strong walls and secure entranceways. Weak primary cavity excavators, such as chickadees and nuthatches, can excavate only in trees in advanced stages of decay.

Tree decay stages can be classified according to various external and internal features. The system for classifying conifers and hardwoods based on form and decay provides a visual guide to identifying the various stages of decline before and after death. Because hardwood trees typically remain standing for a significantly shorter time once dead, they are described with fewer decay classes than conifers.

LOCATION

Location is an important factor in determining the value of a wildlife tree. At the site level, wildlife trees located near special habitats, such as wetlands, open water or grasslands, provide the additional benefit of being near important food sources and so have enhanced value.

On a broader scale, the biogeoclimatic zone (see p. 111, Ecoregion and Biogeoclimatic Ecosystem Classification) in which the tree stands is also important. Different zones have different average numbers of frost-free days, hours of sunshine, depth and duration of snow and amount of growing-season precipitation, all factors that affect ecosystem productivity and biological diversity in both plant and animal communities.

Biogeoclimatic zones at lower elevations generally have longer growing seasons, and the activities of most animal species there also begin earlier and end later. Ecosystems in these zones tend to be more diverse and more productive than those at higher elevations. However, low-elevation land is often the most attractive for forestry, agriculture, transportation, hydroelectric development and urban settlement. As a result, ecosystems at lower elevations are the most altered and have far fewer wildlife trees than in the past.

Because of their scarcity compared to pre-settlement days, the remaining low-elevation wildlife trees in the Bunchgrass, Interior Douglas-fir and Coastal Douglas-fir biogeoclimatic zones and in the major valleys of the Coastal Western Hemlock and Interior Cedar–Hemlock zones are especially important.

SPECIES DEPENDENT ON WILDLIFE TREES

Some wildlife species depend completely on wildlife trees to complete their life cycles. This dependence may be tied to reproduction (nests and dens), feeding, shelter from the elements, protection from predators or a combination of these needs. The degree of dependence was a key factor when deciding which species to include in this guide, but note that the dependence levels for many species are not yet fully known.

The emphasis in this guide is on vertebrates that are not known to successfully shift to alternative *natural* habitats when wildlife trees and their special features are absent. Some wildlife tree users may accept artificial structures, such as nest boxes, when available. Despite their adaptability, these species are discussed in this guide because of the near impossibility of providing and maintaining enough manufactured habitat to entirely meet their needs in this way. Other species, such as woodpeckers and marbled murrelets, do not have the behavioural flexibility to accept artificial substitutes. For them, wildlife trees are absolutely vital habitat.

We have intentionally omitted a number of vertebrate species that successfully use both wildlife trees and alternative habitats. Salamanders, for example, in spite of their use of wildlife trees when available, are more typically associated with fallen decaying wood. Similarly, the opportunistic raccoon often raises its young in a tree cavity but seems equally at home denning in a cave, an old badger burrow or the crawlspace under a porch. We also left out the species whose dependence on wildlife trees is best discussed within the broader context of their reliance on extensive areas of old-growth forest; an example is the mountain caribou, which eats the lichens found in old-growth forest.

This guide also omits the many named and unnamed invertebrates (insects, spiders, etc.) and the lichens and fungi that depend on old trees and that are also present in wildlife trees. Although we recognize the importance of these species within forest ecosystems, we also acknowledge that information

about them is very limited and that the presence of dead and decaying wood may be sufficient to retain these species in the forest. In time, we expect that there will be a better understanding of the myriad ways in which biodiversity is linked to wildlife trees and old-growth forests.

Based on available research, the species in this book were classified as either highly or moderately dependent on wildlife trees for breeding, feeding or other needs (such as roosting, denning or perching while hunting). These rankings can be found in Appendix 2. We may have erred on the side of including species that may in time be found to be less dependent than indicated, but we may also eventually find that we have omitted species whose wildlife tree needs we did not fully understand.

According to their similar reproductive or functional habitat requirements, the species selected for inclusion in this guide have been divided into three "guilds": the primary cavity excavators, the secondary cavity users and the open nesters.

Primary cavity excavators are birds that excavate their own nest holes in trees; this guild consists of the woodpeckers (including the sapsuckers and flickers), the chickadees and the nuthatches. Secondary cavity users are animals that use either the abandoned nest holes of primary cavity excavators or natural cavities formed by trunk breakage, branch loss and other damage and decay; among the members of this guild are some species of ducks, owls, bats and squirrels and the black bear. The open nester guild consists of birds such as eagles, ospreys and herons that construct massive, open, platform-style stick nests on strong tree limbs or in sturdy treetops, as well as the marbled murrelet, which nests on the large, moss-covered branches of certain old

FOREST INSECTS: PREY AND OTHER ROLES

Except for a few charismatic species, such as butterflies and ladybugs, most people don't like insects very much. We fear their stinging and biting abilities and their cyclical population fluctuations, especially when we see their legacy of defoliated and dead trees, trees for which we may have had plans.

Many species of wildlife, however, see these invertebrates as food. Some wildlife species, such as bats, swifts, woodpeckers, bluebirds, nuthatches and chickadees, are wholly dependent on a supply of forest insects. Bats can consume one-half their body weight in insects nightly. Some species of woodpeckers have been estimated to consume 14,000 bark beetles in a year. By exerting constant pressure on insects

Tussock moth caterpillar

at their various life stages— from egg through larva and pupa to adult—wildlife species regulate their numbers, thus providing natural insurance against more frequent and larger-scale insect epidemics.

Moths, wasps, butterflies, ants, bees, termites, beetles and mosquitoes—to name just some of the more familiar groups—are among the many types of insects that inhabit our forests, and there are other invertebrates as well, such as spiders, centipedes, millipedes, sow bugs, worms and slugs. As natural components of forest ecosystems, these creatures perform important functions beyond feeding wildlife. Some are essential in the pollination of many plants, others, such as certain ants and spiders, are themselves predators of various insects, and still others are essential to the recycling of nutrients in the decay process. And, along with fire, disease and extreme weather, insects are important natural disturbance agents that help maintain complexity in forest

Mountain pine beetle (actual size similar to a grain of rice)

stands. The complex roles of insects and other invertebrates in forest ecosystems and their relationships to wildlife species in general and to the wildlife tree dwellers in this guide in particular are still being deciphered.

trees, and several owls. All of the guilds are described in greater detail in Part 5.

Nineteen of the species in this guide are known to have at least one sub-species or population *at risk* (threatened or vulnerable) in British Columbia. Therefore, species dependent on wildlife trees represent approximately 14 percent of the 131 species of birds and non-marine mammals that are officially designated as having at least one subspecies or population *at risk* within this province. The risk status of each species and subspecies is listed in the individual accounts (Part 5) and in Appendix 2.

THE ECOLOGICAL ROLES OF WILDLIFE TREE SPECIES

Wildlife tree-dependent species, like all wildlife, are members of a complex ecological web. The important roles that they collectively play within natural ecosystems include the creation of cavity habitat for other species, the control of insect and small mammal populations and the dispersal of mycorrhizal fungi and plant seeds.

Primary cavity excavators, especially members of the woodpecker family, are referred to as "keystone" species because of their role in creating habitat suitable for other forest wildlife, namely the many secondary cavity users. Abandoned woodpecker nest holes provide homes for, among others, Vaux's swifts, American kestrels, several species of small owls and northern flying squirrels. Over time, as these cavities are enlarged by weathering and decay, they may be occupied by large species of owls, cavity-nesting ducks, martens and bat species. Figure 14 shows the relationship between tree diameter, cavity entrance size and users, as well as the dependence associations between primary cavity excavators and secondary cavity users.

Many wildlife tree-dependent species help maintain a natural balance in their ecosystems by eating invertebrates,

Like the truffles of Europe, certain North American mycorrhizal fungi produce nutritious fruiting bodies underground. In order to propagate, they rely on small mammals to find these bodies by smell, dig them up, eat them and deposit the undigested spores in new locations (see Figure 17).

primarily insects, or small mammals that would otherwise have the potential to rapidly increase their populations.

Most primary cavity excavators and many secondary cavity users specialize in eating insect adults, eggs, larvae and pupae. Insect-eating birds forage by gleaning from the foliage or bark, drilling, probing or "hawking" (catching insects while in flight). Skilled aerial hunters, bats eat large numbers of insects in order to maintain their high metabolic rates, and the plants in bat-populated areas benefit from the very rich nitrogen content of the droppings. Conserving populations of all these insectivores is a forest health insurance policy that protects against more severe and frequent insect irruptions.

Many small mammals, as well as providing a prey base for hawks and owls, are also critical in promoting the growth of forests. A number of species of mice, voles and squirrels (including the wildlife tree–dependent Keen's mouse and northern flying squirrel) play a key role in the dispersal of beneficial mycorrhizal (root-inhabiting) fungi.

31

Figure 14. Primary and secondary cavity species webs

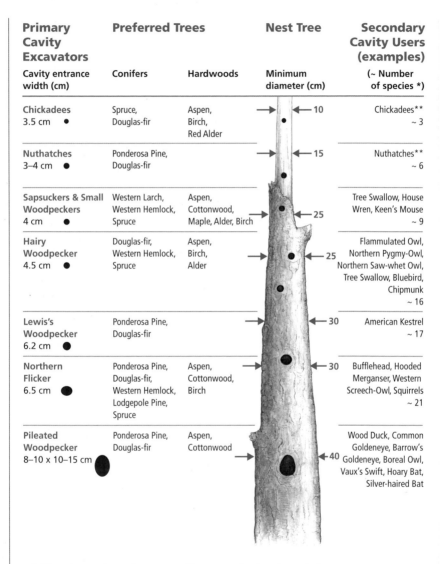

Primary Cavity Excavators	Preferred Trees		Nest Tree	Secondary Cavity Users (examples)
Cavity entrance width (cm)	Conifers	Hardwoods	Minimum diameter (cm)	(~ Number of species *)
Chickadees 3.5 cm ●	Spruce, Douglas-fir	Aspen, Birch, Red Alder	10	Chickadees** ~ 3
Nuthatches 3–4 cm ●	Ponderosa Pine, Douglas-fir		15	Nuthatches** ~ 6
Sapsuckers & Small Woodpeckers 4 cm ●	Western Larch, Western Hemlock, Spruce	Aspen, Cottonwood, Maple, Alder, Birch	25	Tree Swallow, House Wren, Keen's Mouse ~ 9
Hairy Woodpecker 4.5 cm ●	Douglas-fir, Western Hemlock, Spruce	Aspen, Birch, Alder	25	Flammulated Owl, Northern Pygmy-Owl, Northern Saw-whet Owl, Tree Swallow, Bluebird, Chipmunk ~ 16
Lewis's Woodpecker 6.2 cm ●	Ponderosa Pine, Douglas-fir		30	American Kestrel ~ 17
Northern Flicker 6.5 cm ●	Ponderosa Pine, Douglas-fir, Western Hemlock, Lodgepole Pine, Spruce	Aspen, Cottonwood, Birch	30	Bufflehead, Hooded Merganser, Western Screech-Owl, Squirrels ~ 21
Pileated Woodpecker 8–10 x 10–15 cm ●	Ponderosa Pine, Douglas-fir	Aspen, Cottonwood	40	Wood Duck, Common Goldeneye, Barrow's Goldeneye, Boreal Owl, Vaux's Swift, Hoary Bat, Silver-haired Bat

* Although secondary cavity users may fit, some species do not occur in the range of the primary excavators.

** Chickadees and nuthatches can be either primary or secondary.

On this generalized tree, nest records have been used to show the cavity entrance size, favoured trees and minimum diameter at entrance height for each primary cavity excavator. On the right it shows which secondary cavity users in this guide are able to use each kind of cavity for nesting, denning or roosting when abandoned. This dependency on them by other species for secure nest sites makes the strong primary excavators keystone species in forested ecosystems.

Figure 15. Small mammal–root fungus relationships

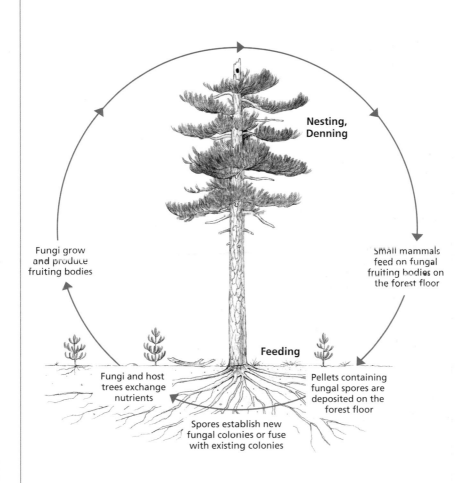

Nesting, Denning

Fungi grow and produce fruiting bodies

Small mammals feed on fungal fruiting bodies on the forest floor

Feeding

Fungi and host trees exchange nutrients

Pellets containing fungal spores are deposited on the forest floor

Spores establish new fungal colonies or fuse with existing colonies

Near the top of this conifer is a woodpecker cavity now available and occupied by a small mammal such as a squirrel or a chipmunk, which relies heavily on fungi for food, especially in winter. The fungal spores pass through the animal's digestive tract intact and are excreted in the fecal pellets, often in a different location where they can start a new fungal colony. Fungal colonies benefit trees by essentially extending the trees' root systems and increasing nutrient uptake.

These fungi are found as nodules on the roots of most trees and shrubs and are essential for nutrient uptake and exchange between soil and roots. When rodents eat the fruiting bodies of mycorrhizal fungi, they ingest fungal spores that pass through their digestive systems intact. The spores are later deposited on the forest floor in fecal pellets that contain all the nutrients necessary for the development of new fungi. Meanwhile, the digging activity of these rodents and other forest mammals enhances soil aeration, the flow of soil moisture to plant roots and nutrient uptake, all of which improve forest growth (see Figure 15).

WILDLIFE TREES AND BIOLOGICAL DIVERSITY

Biological diversity (biodiversity) refers to the multiplicity of plants, animals and other organisms in all their forms and levels of organization. Biodiversity includes the diversity of genes within a single species as well as the diversity of species and ecosystems within a landscape and the various evolutionary and functional processes that link them.

Wildlife trees make a vital contribution to biodiversity by providing protective cover as well as nesting, denning, feeding, roosting and perching sites for a wide variety of species. It takes many decades—in some cases, centuries—before a tree can serve as a wildlife tree. There is not enough time for wildlife trees to develop within the prevalent commercial timber harvest cycle, in which clear-cut harvests are scheduled every 40–120 years. If biodiversity is to be maintained, some individual trees must be retained and allowed to follow their natural cycle through death and decay. Some areas of old forest must also be allowed to follow their natural cycle. Part 2 of this guide describes how this goal can be

achieved through appropriate ecosystem management.

FINDING WILDLIFE TREES WITH EXISTING USE

Finding wildlife trees effectively, even ones that are being actively used, requires a knowledge of the local species and their activity patterns (including both their daily cycles and their annual cycles). It also requires observation skills (visual and auditory), time spent in the field and some luck or intuition. Some species are easier to detect than others, but knowing what, when, how and where to look and listen will make your search more effective. Our focus in the following paragraphs will be on finding the sites of greatest importance to species survival, particularly the ones involved with breeding.

Most species have a reproductive cycle that involves courtship, mating and, finally, tending their young until they are no longer confined to the home tree. During the breeding season, species that are active by day can often be spotted, but nocturnal species, such as most owls and bats, are less obvious. Consulting the information regarding breeding season "windows" in the species accounts in this guide will help you to know when species are "at home" in their wildlife trees. Even when "at home," many species are secretive, a behavioural strategy to avoid predators and thus increase reproductive success.

Many wildlife trees, because of their use for breeding, remain vacant for most of the year, though abandoned nest cavities are often used as roost sites by winter residents. A bear den in a hollow cedar, which might be easily missed when the entrance is 10 metres up the trunk, is another example of a wildlife tree with seasonal use only. Sap wells (small perforations in the bark made by sapsuckers) are another sign of wildlife tree use that is not directly related to reproduction. Careful observation of wildlife activity is important for understanding habitat use.

Large stick nests are easily spotted year-round, even by casual observation. The winter absence of foliage makes the spotting of stick nests in deciduous forests even easier than in summer. The presence of the birds themselves may be necessary for the unskilled observer to identify the species, but the structural characteristics of the nest can help with identification. For example, osprey nests are always at the top of a tree, eagle nests often have some part of the tree structure protruding above the nest, and heron nests are usually in colonies, with "whitewash" typically abundant (i.e., herons are messy nesters relative to eagles and ospreys).

The increased feeding activity in the vicinity following the hatching of the young also helps to locate nest trees, and sometimes the "begging" calls of the young (at least for diurnal species) can be heard. These calls are sometimes the most noticeable sign that a nest is nearby. Wildlife trees featuring both large stick nests and large juvenile birds making loud noises are the easiest nest trees to find and positively identify.

Finding owls and their nests, large or small, requires skill and experience—casual daytime observation is not likely to result in the detection of any nests, even at the right time of year. Although some owls use open stick nests (i.e., platform nests), the nocturnal habitats and secretive ways of great horned owls and long-eared owls make their nests more difficult to locate than those of most platform nesters. The majority of owl species use cavity nest structures, which offer very few external clues to alert the observer to the presence of an active nest.

The most successful method used to locate nest trees for any of the owls is by using call-playbacks during the courtship period. To work, call-playback techniques need to be done on owl time—at night—and for each species separately. If a resident male owl is in the area, he will often respond to sounds from a perceived rival (a female will sometimes also respond). The response rate depends on the species; for example, the great gray owl is unlikely to respond regardless of survey timing or breeding activity, whereas the barred owl (the most responsive and territorial owl) has at least a 50 percent likelihood of responding. Getting a vocal response tells you that an owl nest territory is nearby, which is the first step to locating the nest tree.

Finding an owl nest tree is a real skill helped by patient observation. Owls are typically more secretive than usual when sitting on eggs, so even when a nest site is found and the season is right, confirming nest activity requires the observation of adults entering and leaving the structure or cavity entrance—typically only at dusk or at night. An owl sitting on eggs is unlikely to flush from the nest even if the tree trunk is tapped, but a lot of disturbance may lead to nest abandonment. The best time to find an active nest is when the adults are bringing food for their nestlings.

The northern goshawk is a secretive open-platform nester, but once the young have hatched, the adult goshawk will typically swoop and attempt to drive intruders (people included) from the nest area. Highly aggressive swooping and "dive-bombing" behaviour by an adult may indicate that you are near an active nest. Nestling goshawks are usually quite vocal. You may hear them "begging" for food, and they will often respond vocally to call the playback of "begging" calls.

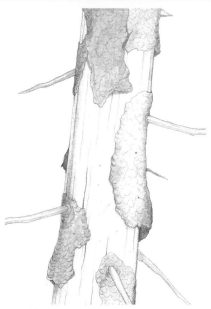

Figure 16. Loose bark. Loose bark provides a favourable microclimate for insects that attract insectivores such as wrens, nuthatches and chickadees. Loose bark can also provide roosts for bats.

Figure 17. Heart rot and loose bark in a grand fir. Loose bark provides nest sites for brown creepers and nuthatches and roost sites for certain bats. Bracket fungi indicate well-developed internal decay. Once insects have access to the inner part of the trunk, strong woodpeckers will excavate for them.

Another species group, the woodpeckers, are strong primary cavity excavators. They can be heard hammering (drumming) on tree trunks during feeding or as part of their courtship or territory establishment and defence. The sound of woodpeckers drumming should alert the observer to the potential for nesting activity in the area. Excavating the nest tree is also a noisy occasion, but it is finished relatively quickly. Once sitting on their eggs, woodpeckers are silent. However, the noise generated by excavating for insects or drilling sap wells can also disclose the presence of a woodpecker.

Newly active woodpecker nest cavities can be identified by the "freshness" of the excavation (old cavities tend to have darkened wood around the inside of the cavity opening). However, old cavities may be reused by some species (and are often reused by other species), so no likely looking cavity should be ignored. Some species will flush from their nests when approached or when the tree trunk is rapped with a stick, but others will sit tight.

The easiest time to find woodpecker nest trees is once the young have hatched, but before they fledge. Near the nest, their "begging" calls can be heard, and the frequent comings and goings of the adults can be seen. Young woodpeckers also return to the nest tree for safety even after they fledge—whole woodpecker families create more chances for observation.

Chickadees and nuthatches are small, weak cavity excavators, and unlike the noisy woodpeckers, they do not give vocal clues to their nest locations, although excavating birds can be heard for a short distance through the woods. Only a keen observer at the right time will be able to detect the nest trees of these species. The easiest method for locating an active nest for these species—at the right time of the year—is to know the cavity size for the species, and when you observe a cavity that appears appropriate, rap on the tree with a stick. If no bird emerges, observe the cavity for at least 30 minutes. Small birds have a fast metabolism, so prey delivery to the gestating female, and even more so in the case of the developing young, is very frequent and usually very obvious.

The nest trees of large secondary cavity users such as wood ducks, goldeneyes, buffleheads, and common and hooded mergansers are also difficult to detect even when birds are incubating their eggs. Once hatched, the young leave the nest promptly for the nearest water body. Feathery down caught on the edge of the cavity entrance is a clue that the cavity may contain a nest.

In the wettest forested areas of British Columbia and the U.S. Pacific Northwest (i.e., coastal forests and the Interior western red-cedar–hemlock forests), black bears often hibernate in tree dens. These dens are easier to detect than those of martens, fishers or flying squirrels because of the opening size and the presence of hair and bedding sign (moss, fine twigs, etc.) left inside. Claw or bite marks, usually found near the den entrance on recently used dens, are a good indication of potential use.

Most black bear tree dens are "basal entry"—they have the opening at the tree base at ground level. Less commonly, bear dens are arboreal, with an aboveground entrance either on the side of the tree trunk or where the top has broken off. Pregnant females prefer arboreal dens because of the added security and protection they offer the cubs. In all cases, bear den trees must have enough internal decay and hollowing in order to accommodate the body of a single hibernating bear or a pregnant female preparing to birth her cubs inside. Entrance openings 25–45 centimetres wide are favoured for the best protection from predators and the weather.

Figure 18. Forest insect suppression. Constant feeding by insectivorous birds such as this black-capped chickadee keep insect populations in check. Their well-distributed presence is thought to be "insurance" that can reduce the frequency of insect outbreaks. However, if insect populations do reach epidemic levels, it usually takes additional factors, typically dwindling food supplies or adverse weather, to bring them back into the normal range.

Nesting on a broken cottonwood. *Sturdy branching structure or a broken trunk in the right location are requirements sought by species such as this osprey, which has constructed a large stick nest on this broken black cottonwood trunk. Such large stick nests are the easiest wildlife tree features for untrained observers to spot; finding the hidden nests of the more secretive open-nesting large owls is much more challenging.*

seabird definitely requires expert knowledge and skill. The birds leave the sea at dusk, they are rapid in flight, and their breeding success depends on a secretive, dispersed nesting strategy. They usually nest on a flat, mossy branch platform in the forest canopy. They incubate in silence and leave the nest at the first light of dawn. Researchers have been using radar in some areas to get counts of dawn and dusk flights in and out of watersheds. Because this little bird will fly long distances inland, sometimes up to 50 km, its nest trees have largely eluded detection.

The wildlife trees used by the 11 species of bats that need them for maternity and

A northern saw-whet owl's nest cavity. *This hardwood's state of decay (class 3) is the first clue that it may have wildlife use. The old woodpecker cavity entrance provides additional support for this premise, but being here at the right time of year is the only way to be sure which species is currently in residence.*

Large-diameter, hollow-butt western red-cedars are the preferred den trees in coastal and wet Interior forests. Tree dens have also been discovered in western hemlock, spruces and black cottonwood.

Some of the most difficult nest trees to find are those of the marbled murrelet. Nest detection for this diminutive day and night roosts are possibly the most difficult ones to find. As a group, bats are challenging to study, but they do emit echolocation signals for navigation and hunting. These ultrasonic cries, which can be detected with specialized equipment, can be used to distinguish some bat species.

Once you've determined which bat species are present, finding their colonies is a more difficult task. Where mechanized harvesting is being done in relatively gentle terrain, some forestry equipment operators have learned to recognize which trees might house bats (that is, ones that appear to have some

A red-breasted sapsucker at sap wells. *Once the sap begins to flow, this bird will return repeatedly to drink it and to eat the insects attracted by the sap.*

rot or damage or loose bark). Before felling, the knowledgeable operator should give these trees a hard knock with the cutting head and wait to see if any bats emerge. This practice may dislodge some bats in daylight and has led to some spared roost sites, but it is not foolproof, because, if the bats are in torpor, they will be sluggish and unlikely to be alert enough to take flight and abandon the site.

Finding a few bat roost trees in a forest stand may mean that a colony of bats is using additional trees in the stand to meet their various roosting needs. Bats are social creatures, and a colony will return to a series of suitable trees on a regular basis and over a number of years, so retaining the full range of roost trees is important to the survival of the colony.

Although we are not aware of any studies in which infrared surveillance equipment (e.g., cameras and night-vision scopes) have been used specifically for finding occupied wildlife trees, the use of such tools for nocturnal searches is worth investigating.

Finding the active nests and dens or residences of the species in this guide can be difficult and requires a sufficient lead time; sometimes an entire year or more in advance of logging activity or development is needed to do a survey to inventory standards. It is particularly important to do a thorough job of finding the residences of any endangered and threatened species likely to be present. Given the complexity of the task, professionally assisted, species-specific surveys are the best means of finding the essential habitat and residences of these species. And, because some habitats and sites are used only at certain times of the year, sufficient preplanning is essential.

Pileated woodpecker cavity entrances. *Large, oblong to rectangular cavity entrances, such as the one in this lodgepole pine, are the work of the pileated woodpecker, the largest and strongest of the primary cavity excavators.*

Woodpecker feeding sign. *The significant number of chips at the base of this conifer and the missing bark indicate the amount of woodpecker feeding that has taken place here.*

High-entry black bear maternity den. *A casual observer may miss this bear den entry high in a western red-cedar. Closer observation reveals the claw marks that confirm it as a den tree.*

PART 2

WILDLIFE TREES & ECOSYSTEM MANAGEMENT

WILDLIFE TREES IN FORESTED ECOSYSTEMS
Natural Disturbance and Forest Succession

As a forest ages, the mix of species within it and the condition of its trees change. Every forest goes through a series of ecological phases over time, as one plant community is replaced by another, in progression from young forest to old-growth. This process of change is called "succession," and the phases are known as "seral stages."

Early-seral species are often referred to as "pioneers." These plants are capable of establishing on sites where the soil

41

Wildfire. *Historically, forest fires have been the primary natural disturbance agent that "reset the successional clock," the frequency, intensity and extent depending on the ecosystem. In dry ecosystems, frequent low-intensity ground fires periodically remove accumulations of litter and kill many regenerated trees, thus maintaining more open forests, but more than half a century of successful fire suppression has changed forest stem density and composition in many areas.*

Wildfires and beetle outbreaks, unlike conventional logging practices, leave significant dead, woody structures. Many insects are drawn to these dead trees, as are woodpeckers and other insectivorous birds.

has been freshly exposed (e.g., by flooding or landslide) or where most of the competing vegetation has been removed (e.g., by fire or harvesting). If left undisturbed, mid-seral species eventually replace the pioneers and are replaced in turn by late-seral (or "climax") species. In general, pioneer tree species require full light for germination and establishment, whereas the seedlings and saplings of climax species are more shade tolerant.

In one sense, a climax forest represents the final stage of natural forest succession for a particular locality. However, succession is a cyclical process that has no real beginning or end. Old trees will always eventually be replaced by new seedlings, and the current stage in the successional process varies from forest to forest. In some forests, all of the trees may be very similar in age, but others may consist of trees of a wide range of ages.

The age structure and complexity of a forest stand are influenced by natural disturbances, including fire, insects, wind, disease and human activities. Wide-ranging, severe disturbances, such as major fires and insect outbreaks, can kill a majority of the trees over an extensive area of forest. Isolated disturbances, such as lightning strikes, root rot and other pathogens, often affect individual trees or small groups of trees, leaving surrounding trees untouched. Thus, gaps in the forest and opportunities for new trees to grow are created in a variety of ways, from the loss of a single tree in a stand of live, healthy trees, to the simultaneous death of thousands of trees in one catastrophic event. Individual old trees that remain after a severe natural disturbance—whether live or dead, standing or fallen—perpetuate part of the biological legacy of the preceding older forest.

Operating within a framework of the relatively permanent physical features in a landscape—rivers, lakes, wetlands and rock outcrops—succession and

Figure 19. Changes in species diversity at different stand ages (seral stages)

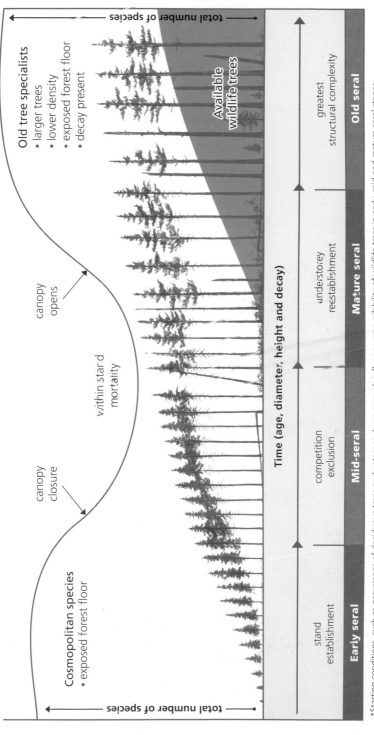

total number of species

Old tree specialists
- larger trees
- lower density
- exposed forest floor
- decay present

Available wildlife trees

canopy opens

within stand mortality

canopy closure

Cosmopolitan species
- exposed forest floor

total number of species

Time (age, diameter, height and decay)

Early seral	Mid-seral	Mature seral	Old seral
stand establishment	competition exclusion	understorey reestablishment	greatest structural complexity

*Starting conditions, such as occurrence of deciduous trees and veterans, have enough influence on availability of wildlife trees in early, mid and mature seral stages. Species diversity is highest during a forest's very early and late seral stages. Some species, particularly certain wildlife tree specialists, are restricted to late seral forests. Shrubs and forbs are initially present, but, by the mid- and mature stages, the competing trees dominate to such an extent that understorey plants may be absent. Consequently, stand structure distribution affects plant and animal diversity.

Figure 20. Life stages of a single conifer

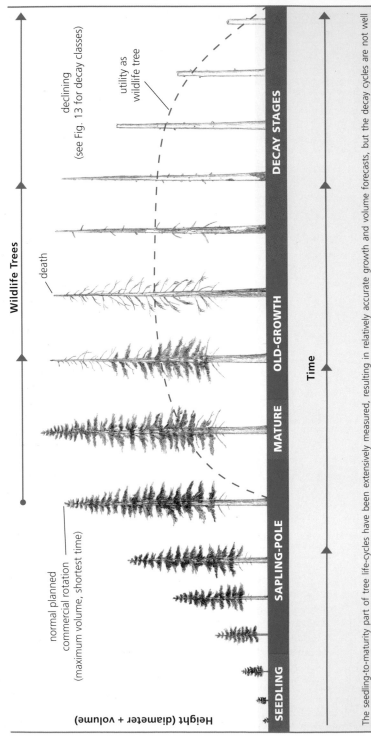

Height (diameter + volume)

Time

SEEDLING · SAPLING-POLE · MATURE · OLD-GROWTH · DECAY STAGES

Wildlife Trees

normal planned
commercial rotation
(maximum volume, shortest time)

death

declining
(see Fig. 13 for decay classes)

utility as
wildlife tree

The seedling-to-maturity part of tree life-cycles have been extensively measured, resulting in relatively accurate growth and volume forecasts, but the decay cycles are not well documented. Function as a wildlife tree typically begins at maturity and continues until the trunk returns to the forest floor; a tree's usefulness to the species in this guide generally increases with size and state of decay. The time taken for a tree to shed its top, limbs and bark, and to decay to ground level can be significant.

disturbance create the complexity and diversity of seral stages that make up the forest mosaic. The frequency, severity and extent of disturbances determine which sections of forest are returned to the early phase of the successional cycle, and which are allowed to reach an old-growth phase. Acting together over time, succession and disturbance play a critical role in influencing species composition and stand structure within a forest. They are instrumental in creating a shifting mosaic of various types of wildlife tree habitat, thereby strongly affecting wildlife species distribution.

Some species of plants and animals are generalists that persist throughout the successional cycle, but many are specialists, adapted to only one seral stage. As is shown in Figure 19, a greater diversity of plant and animal species occur in young and old forest stands than during mid-seral phases.

Today, forest harvesting, stand-tending and fire prevention, along with agriculture and other land development, have heavily modified the natural processes of disturbance and succession. Therefore, to maintain habitat suitable for the old-forest specialists that are associated with wildlife trees while managing forests for commercial harvest, one must understand natural patterns of disturbance and succession. This knowledge of natural variation in forested ecosystems is also applicable when converting forests to agricultural land or managing trees in rural and urban areas (see Part 3). If our activities are within the range of natural variation, ecosystem processes and the diversity of species of the natural forest will presumably be sustained. An adequate supply of wildlife trees is one component of an ecosystem for which we can manage. Though there will be fluctuations in the supply of wildlife trees over time, we can sustain wildlife species if we maintain a supply of suitable habitat within the natural range of variation. The life stages of a single tree—and when it achieves utility as a wildlife tree in relation to its age and forest harvest planning—are shown in Figure 20.

Old Forests

Because many of the features that give wildlife trees their value—such as great height, a large diameter or a large-limbed crown—take many decades or even centuries to develop, wildlife trees more commonly occur in forests that are dominated by old trees. Decay and death, which are such important factors in wildlife tree development, are also a product of time.

Because local climate largely determines the frequency and severity of natural disturbances, the amount of naturally occurring old growth varies from one ecological zone to the next. In wet climates, the dominant natural disturbances include windthrow, insects, disease and landslides. These factors generally affect only small groups of trees or a few trees within a stand, and where trees have been killed, the gaps thus created allow young trees to establish.

Ecologically similar areas with wet climates on the coast and in the wettest portions of the Interior rarely experience disturbances that kill the majority of the trees in a forest, such as major fires. Therefore, prior to the current scale of human influences, the proportion of the landscape covered with old trees in these areas was naturally high. The boreal forests of British Columbia's northern and central Interior experience frequent, severe, widespread wildfires and beetle epidemics, and have, therefore, historically had a relatively smaller component of old forest. The province's dry Douglas-fir and ponderosa pine forests experience frequent understorey fires that result in forests with trees of many ages and structural differences

Figure 21. Relative size, life and decay expectancy of B.C. hardwoods

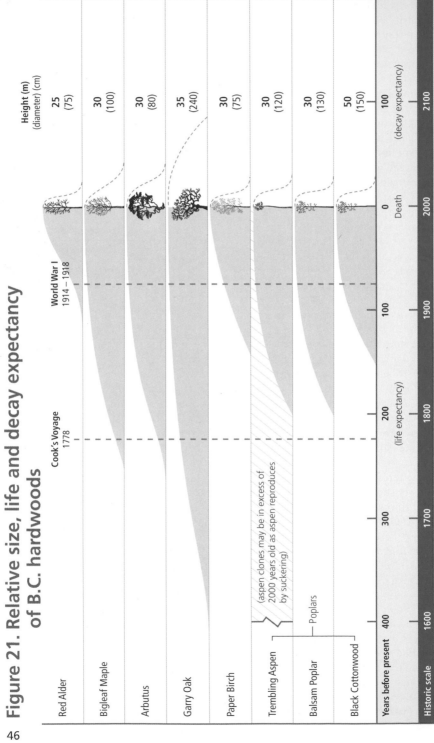

	Height (m) (diameter) (cm)
Red Alder	25 (75)
Bigleaf Maple	30 (100)
Arbutus	30 (80)
Garry Oak	35 (240)
Paper Birch	30 (75)
Trembling Aspen	30 (120)
Balsam Poplar	30 (130)
Black Cottonwood	50 (150)

Cook's Voyage 1778

World War I 1914 – 1918

(aspen clones may be in excess of 2000 years old as aspen reproduces by suckering)

Poplars

Death

(life expectancy)

(decay expectancy)

Years before present   400   300   200   100   0   100

Historic scale   1600   1700   1800   1900   2000   2100

(refer to "Dry Southern Interior Forests: Unique Pressures on a High-value Habitat," p. 125). As with wet forests, these dry forests have old trees distributed across the landscape.

Long-term Distribution of Old Forests

Maintaining the unique diversity of flora and fauna associated with old growth in the context of the managed forest requires that we set aside some areas with high conservation value.

When large and small protected areas have an old-growth forest component, they play a vital role in conserving old-growth diversity in the surrounding managed forest landscape. They do so both by providing a greater range of habitats and a supply of seed for natural restocking. However, unless these old-forest remnants reflect the quality and productivity of the original forest and contain a full complement of old-growth ecosystems, their contribution to sustaining old-growth diversity may have limited conservation value.

Note that setting aside large, widely dispersed protected areas will likely be insufficient for many wildlife species to survive, because areas of suitable habitat must be close enough to allow barrier-free travel to search for mates and for dispersal and migration. Unless there are enough suitably placed protected areas to maintain old-growth ecosystems and their diversity, management for old-growth forest has to be integrated with timber harvesting objectives outside of designated protected areas as well.

Protected areas and old-forest reserves outside of protected areas do contribute significantly to the conservation of biological diversity, but the management of the forest outside of these long-term reserves, the so-called "managed forest matrix," is also critical to retaining biodiversity. Although the focus of the managed forest matrix is on

Old-growth forest. *In order to develop, old-growth forests require an extended time period without a major stand-replacing disturbance. These forests have large stand structures, including a high proportion of dead wood.*

the extraction of commercial products, this area also needs to provide a sufficient quantity and quality of habitat to reduce the effects of forest fragmentation and to provide connectivity for the successful movement of organisms between the older forested reserves. Because long-term reserves are likely to be a small component of our future forests, the success of conservation depends on sufficient conservation provisions in the managed forest matrix; from it must come most of the ongoing supply of wildlife trees.

Figures 21 and 22 show the relative size, life and decay expectancy for hardwoods and conifers.

Figure 22. Relative size, life and decay expectancy of B.C. conifers

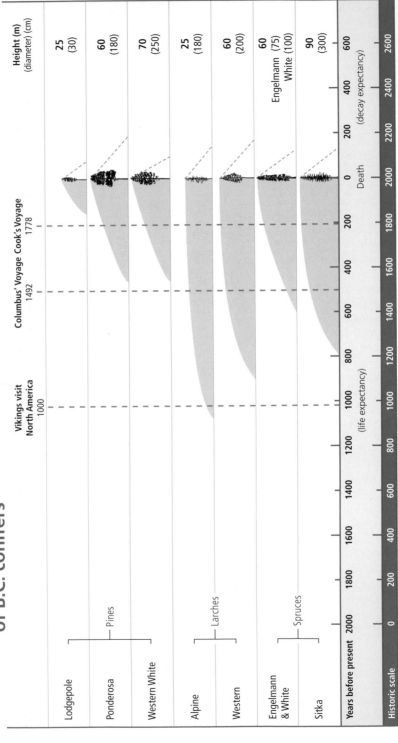

Figure 22 (continued). Relative size, life and decay expectancy of B.C. conifers

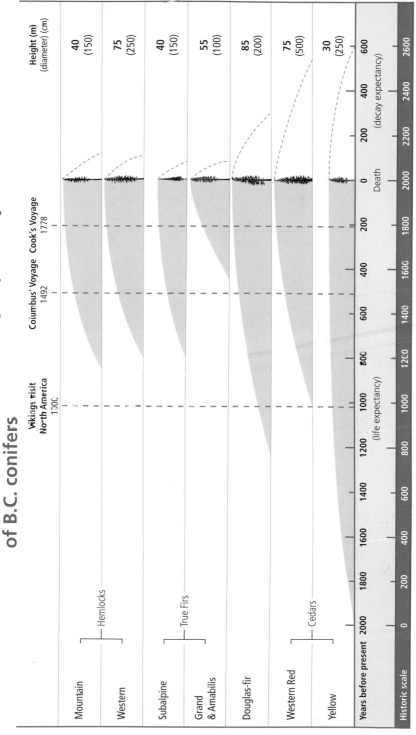

	Height (m) (diameter) (cm)
Mountain	40 (150)
Western	75 (250)
Subalpine	40 (150)
Grand & Amabilis	55 (100)
Douglas-fir	85 (200)
Western Red	75 (500)
Yellow	30 (250)

Hemlocks
True Firs
Cedars

Vikings visit North America 1300
Columbus' Voyage 1492
Cook's Voyage 1778

Death
(decay expectancy)
(life expectancy)

Years before present

Historic scale

Natural edge habitat. *The edge habitat where a forest adjoins an avalanche track, grassland or riparian ecosystem provides extra benefits to many species. Here they can meet needs such as feeding in one habitat yet having security or a home in the other.*

Edge and Interior Forest Habitat

Where the edge of a forest gives way to a more open, natural ecosystem, such as a meadow, wetland or a recent clear-cut, there are very different habitats than those found deep within the forest interior. Interior forest and edge habitats differ in microclimate (temperature, sunlight and relative humidity), protective cover and shelter (security from predators and weather) and food sources. Certain songbirds, small mammals and ungulates thrive along forest edges and use open, early-seral habitat in preference to mature or old-growth forest. Others, including many wildlife tree–dependent species, need undisturbed, mature or old-growth forest interior habitat instead. Interior conditions generally begin at a distance of several tree heights from the outer edge of an old forest. Wildlife trees located in openings or along forest edges are of little or no use to interior forest species, such as the marbled murrelet and the spotted owl.

Natural openings and clear-cuts are both surrounded by edge habitat, but the effect is not necessarily the same. A clear-cutting pattern that results in many openings and small patches of forest will result in an excess of edge habitat and a scarcity of interior old-forest habitat. This scarcity exposes old-growth-dependent species to unfavourable conditions, such as increased predation, and eliminates the interior forest conditions vital to their existence. A resulting overall increase in the number of species in an area can obscure a decline in the number of specialist species that need interior old-forest conditions.

To avoid creating a disproportionately large ratio of edge habitat to interior forest habitat, the size ranges of harvest areas that produce early-seral forests and old-forest leave areas should closely resemble those resulting from naturally occurring disturbances. This approach creates a mosaic of large and small patches of disturbed and undisturbed land rather than the checkerboard of uniformly sized, relatively young stands that have originated from typical cut-block harvesting plans. Some of the undisturbed old patches will include old forest with interior habitat conditions. Even patches disturbed through logging, if they are left long enough, will eventually recover and again be able to provide old forest with interior habitat conditions. Allowing a sufficient number of wildlife trees to remain during and after logging greatly enhances post-harvest ecological recovery and enables many wildlife species to remain and continue their ecological function, even within a landscape that is dominated by relatively young trees.

Historically, in the dry Southern Interior and wet coastal and interior forests, natural disturbances did not often create distinct, even-aged patches of various sizes. Instead, continuous, structurally complex forest with young and old trees in the same stands extended over large areas. Even-aged patches would occur only when the successional "clock" was turned back on a single stand through infrequent natural events, such as crown fires or outbreaks of insects or disease. In general, edge habitat in earlier days on the wet coast and interior, also in the dry interior, was restricted to the areas where the forest gave way to more permanent features, such as avalanche tracks, wetlands, rock outcrops and grassland openings.

Certain partial-harvest systems, such as variable retention, can result in a situation that more closely resembles natural forest conditions. They do so by retaining a complexity of stand structures within and adjacent to harvest

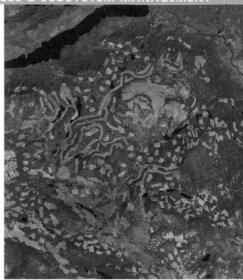

Satellite image of forest fragmentation. *This harvest pattern leads to uniformly sized, early-seral stages without an older stand structure to provide wildlife trees. Whereas natural disturbances, such as fire and insect infestations, create stands of varying sizes with a significant legacy of structural elements, here a current and future supply of wildlife trees can occur only in the remaining pockets of natural forest. Significantly greater stand structures and a variety of harvest sizes and larger old-forest areas will more closely mimic natural disturbances and allow wildlife tree–dependent species to be well-distributed in the forest mosaic.*

blocks in a way that more closely resembles the distribution of these habitats as they would have occurred under natural successional forces. Under these systems, retention focuses on patches of trees, dispersed individual trees, riparian management areas and coarse woody debris left scattered on the cut-block.

Forest Fragmentation and Landscape Connectivity

A species will not survive over the long term if there is not enough suitable habitat to meet its needs for food, shelter, protective cover and breeding habitat. Nor will a species be able to persist if the remaining suitable habitat becomes too fragmented and the fragments too isolated. Habitat fragmentation and lack

Figure 23. Cross-section and plan view of riparian management area

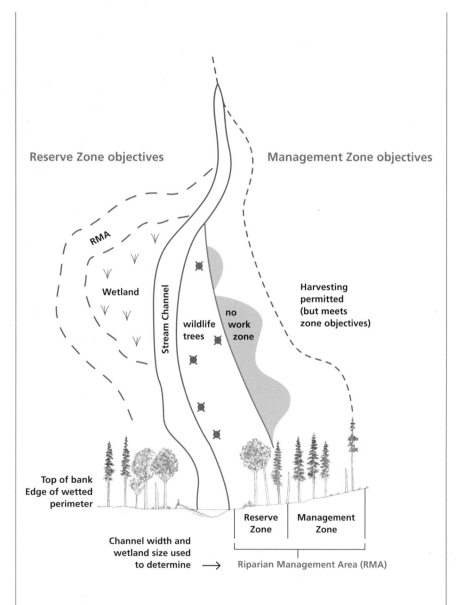

A reserve and management zone is a means of giving priority to conservation objectives in the biologically productive diverse areas adjacent to streams, lakes and wetlands. Wildlife trees retained here ensure access to more of the insects, fish, aquatic invertebrates and amphibians sought by species such as herons, ospreys, eagles, ducks and bats in this guide.

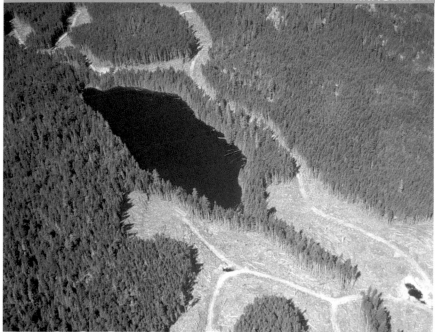

Riparian reserve in a cutblock *Riparian ecosystems, although a very minor component of the landscape, support a significant proportion of its biological diversity. When maintained intact, they provide natural travel corridors for many species and assure an ongoing distribution of wildlife trees across the landscape.*

of connectivity can prevent some animals and plants from moving or being transported from one area of suitable habitat to another. Fragmentation also segregates members of the same species from each other, thereby reducing breeding opportunities, resulting in smaller, less successful populations. As a general rule, the closer together "islands" of suitable habitat are situated, the more likely it is that an animal will be able to move between them. However, the size, mobility and natural behaviour of each species determine how far individuals can disperse.

Retained wildlife trees within young forests provide variation in stand structure and help to reduce the negative effects of forest fragmentation by supplying patches of suitable habitat to assure some habitat connectivity between patches of old forest. Maintaining a distribution of stands with varied structural features across the landscape (through partial cutting or long-term planning that defers or removes a portion of mature and older stands from harvesting) is crucial to maintaining connectivity and biological diversity.

Riparian Ecosystems

Riparian ecosystems—those adjacent to streams, lakes and wetlands—are most easily distinguished from the surrounding uplands by their lusher vegetation and greater diversity of plant species, with the contrast being greatest in dry ecosystems. Riparian ecosystems are critically important because of their greater biological diversity and productivity relative to nearby areas. Many wildlife species are attracted to riparian habitats by the feeding opportunities provided by the varied and abundant plant life, or by the fish, insects and amphibians that live in the water bodies. Trees provide nutrients to the aquatic ecosystems through leaf litter and other debris, and their shade modifies stream temperatures. The root systems of large trees stabilize the banks of streams and rivers. When large trees, such as wildlife trees, fall into streams, they create pools and riffles for fish habitat. During peak flows, downed trees help stabilize stream channels by slowing the flow of water and debris and capturing sediments.

Forest plans, in many cases, may choose a no-harvest zone along streams, lakes and wetlands to clearly communicate how their practices protect riparian ecosystems and the many conservation objectives that intact riparian ecosystems perform. This can also be achieved in some riparian ecosystems by partial harvest and other restrictions that maintain ecosystem function (see Figure 23). Because of a riparian forest's diverse structural nature, long-term retained riparian forest significantly contributes to the pool of wildlife trees in a given area. These leave areas and partial-harvest areas together will be important as sources of wildlife trees across managed landscapes.

WHAT ARE COARSE AND FINE CONSERVATION FILTERS?
Managing for Habitat Diversity: The Coarse Filter Approach

We can greatly reduce the risk of losing genetic, species and ecosystem diversity by choosing forest harvesting and regeneration practices that result in managed forests that resemble naturally established forests as closely as possible. Conversely, the less the forest resulting from our practices resembles that which nature would supply, the greater the chance of losing species and functions from an ecosystem. Thus, to protect biological diversity while harvesting our forests, it is necessary to understand the range of natural variability and to maintain forests within this natural

range. Achieving the desired result means that areas of old and very old forest, as well as specific stand structures, such as wildlife trees, need to be retained when planning harvest areas. This general approach to maintaining portions of natural ecosystem diversity is termed "coarse filter" management.

We have only limited knowledge about most forest-dwelling species and their functions in the ecosystems of which they are a part. Many previously unknown species—especially invertebrates—are still being found on the forest floor and in the forest canopy. Coarse filter management compensates for the gaps in our understanding by assuming that the more a managed forest resembles a natural one, the more likely it is that native species and ecological processes will be maintained. Coarse filter management increases the chances of effectively maintaining habitats for a majority of species by retaining the full array of habitat diversity. Retaining some old forest stands and old-growth stand structure within a watershed or landscape also, to some degree, maintains the numerous small habitats associated with old forests.

The habitat needs of many of the species in this guide and others that form the bulk of forest species complexity can be met through the coarse filter approach. The success of this approach depends on the quantity and quality of habitat maintained. If the filter is too coarse and only small amounts of riparian areas, old-forest stands and stand structure are retained in a natural condition, the habitat needs of many forest species will either not be met or will be met in a very limited area and only for a limited time.

Determining the parameters that a coarse filter must have for successful conservation begins with research and monitoring to establish the existing habitat needs of selected specialist

Figure 24. Coarse and fine filter conservation concepts

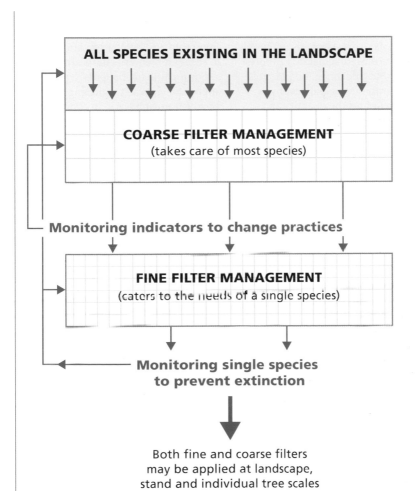

In this analogy, our current management practices, guidelines and plans collectively provide a coarse filter to safeguard all the species in a landscape. If our current practices do provide an effective safeguard, then all the species will remain in the landscape; none will become threatened or endangered. Monitoring of selected habitats, such as wildlife trees (and the wildlife described in this guide), will indicate how well we are sustaining this segment of biological diversity.

The fine filter approach refers to the management for a single species whose needs are not met by the coarse filter approach. The population trends and habitats of these species require careful monitoring. If too many species are in need of special management, then the coarse filter needs to be adjusted to provide a more effective safeguard.

wildlife species as well as the quality, quantity and distribution of selected forest attributes, such as dead wood and old trees. Based on the best available information, it is then possible to develop guidelines for current habitat requirements that are broadly applicable and likely to sustain a majority of forest species. These guidelines and practices need to be monitored and adaptively managed to adjust the quantity and quality of habitat being retained. The presence of wildlife species in a managed forest is a good indicator of the success of filter parameters and the adjustments required.

Managing for Individual Species: The Fine Filter Approach

Management for individual species is called "fine filter" conservation management. This approach is required when a broad-brush, coarse filter approach does not meet the habitat needs of a particular species, as is the case with many species that are known to be *at risk*. Figure 25 shows the relationship between coarse and fine filter conservation concepts. In the case of wildlife tree management, even when the coarse filter practices leave large-diameter wildlife trees in riparian areas and other reserves, this level of retention may still be inadequate for some species of wildlife tree users.

The endangered white-headed woodpecker, for example, needs large-diameter ponderosa pines for nesting and feeding, so retaining large-diameter Douglas-fir will not provide this species with its habitat requirements. An appropriate fine-filter strategy for the white-headed woodpecker focuses retention on mature and older forests where ponderosa pine is dominant (see p. 143 for further details). This strategy aims to arrest the decline in the white-headed woodpecker population by halting and reversing the decline of old ponderosa pine forest, which has been reduced to less than

one-third of its historic extent. To sustain this woodpecker in the long term, an adequate number of young ponderosa pines will need to develop into wildlife trees. Continued monitoring of the white-headed woodpecker's population trend and habitat condition are key to seeing if recovery efforts are effective.

For the fine filter approach to work appropriately when managing for biodiversity, it must be used in conjunction with the coarse filter approach. There are too many species in the forest for each one to be managed for on an individual basis. Furthermore, the habitat requirements of different species can vary widely, and an emphasis on management practices that specifically benefit one species may be detrimental to another. A need for single-species recovery efforts indicates that the conservation provisions to date (coarse filter approach) have been inadequate and need revising.

Based on current forest management practices, the following species in this guide are known to require fine filter habitat management:

Primary Cavity Excavators:

Lewis's woodpecker (p. 126)
Williamson's sapsucker (p. 130)
hairy woodpecker, Queen Charlotte
    Islands subspecies only (p. 140)
white-headed woodpecker (p. 142)

Secondary Cavity Users:

hooded merganser (p. 181)
flammulated owl (p. 187)
western screech-owl (p. 190)
northern pygmy-owl (p. 195)
northern saw-whet owl (p. 201)
western bluebird (p. 213)
Keen's long-eared myotis (p. 223)
northern long-eared myotis (p. 227)
western red bat (p. 233)
red-tailed chipmunk (p. 248)
fisher (p. 252)
black bear, glacier bear only (p. 254)

Figure 25. Crossing scales: subregional, landscape, stand, tree and tree feature

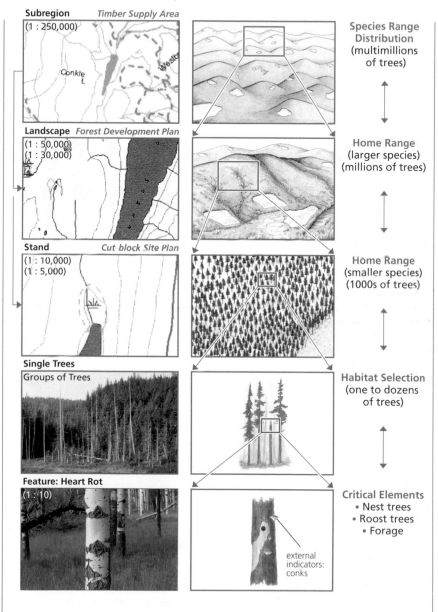

Subregion *Timber Supply Area*
(1 : 250,000)

Conkle L.

Species Range
Distribution
(multimillions
of trees)

Landscape *Forest Development Plan*
(1 : 50,000)
(1 : 30,000)

Home Range
(larger species)
(millions of trees)

Stand *Cut-block Site Plan*
(1 : 10,000)
(1 : 5,000)

Home Range
(smaller species)
(1000s of trees)

Single Trees
Groups of Trees

Habitat Selection
(one to dozens
of trees)

Feature: Heart Rot
(1 : 10)

Critical Elements
• Nest trees
• Roost trees
• Forage

external
indicators:
conks

*Even with many trees available only a small fraction may become wildlife trees or are suitable.

For a given species, migration may occur at a regional or continental scale, and the breeding territory at a stand or landscape scale, whereas day-to-day activities involve the features of individual trees within the home range.

Open Nesters:

great blue heron (p. 261)
northern goshawk, coastal subspecies
  only (p. 269)
marbled murrelet (p. 274)
spotted owl, northern subspecies (p. 279)

A fine filter icon is used to identify these species in their individual accounts in Part 5 of this guide.

MANAGING FOR WILDLIFE TREES ACROSS THE LANDSCAPE

The cumulative effects of past forest management practices, land clearing and urban development have produced incremental changes in habitat through time. When the supply of a particular habitat, such as a certain kind of wildlife tree, falls significantly below the range of natural availability, species become absent, or extirpated, from parts of their historic range. Each species has its own threshold. The higher the degree of departure from the natural habitat condition, the higher the risk of losing a species. As a result, to mimic natural conditions appropriately, one must compare the supply of wildlife trees in a managed landscape against the supply that would have been available naturally.

Coarse filter management uses a variety of planning and time scales. Figure 22 shows the most common planning scales used in forestry—the subregional, landscape and stand levels—and how they relate to wildlife needs. The subregional scale is used for land-use planning and for timber supply forecasting to set harvesting levels. The same data can be used to forecast the expected future supply of specific habitats. This scale addresses large areas and is important in management for wide-ranging animals, such as fishers, and for forecasting trends in habitat supply and the likely accompanying species population changes.

The landscape level deals with an area that is smaller than the subregion, so is used for harvest planning and the planning of developments that have the potential to affect wildlife trees. Landscape-level plans are appropriate for showing where natural forests are scheduled to remain many decades into the future, where past harvesting has already removed mature or older trees, where there may be an absence of wildlife trees and where opportunities exist for immediate harvesting.

Forest planning at the stand level can address conservation values and minimize the risk to high-value habitats through the appropriate placement of individual cut-blocks away from these areas. Then, as ground crews walk, measure and finalize cutting boundaries before harvesting (or when a new road is being surveyed, land is about to be cleared for urban use, or agriculture development is being proposed) they can identify high-value features associated with individual trees or groups of trees. In many instances, these features can be retained through modification to the cut-block (or project) design.

As was indicated in Figure 25, the landscape scale is considered appropriate for providing the context for determining how much area or how many wildlife trees to retain at the cut-block level. When planning a harvesting operation and determining how much area should be managed to supply wildlife trees, it is necessary to consider an area in the range of 10,000–100,000 ha, such as an entire watershed or series of watersheds. The size of the landscape to be considered for a supply of wildlife trees should be large enough that a single natural event, such as a wildfire, would be extremely unlikely to affect the entire area. In a dry ecosystem with frequent disturbances, the area that needs to be taken into account will be larger than in a wet ecosystem.

Topography also influences the type and scope of many natural disturbances

Figure 26. Amount of area recommended available for wildlife trees in a cut-block after harvest

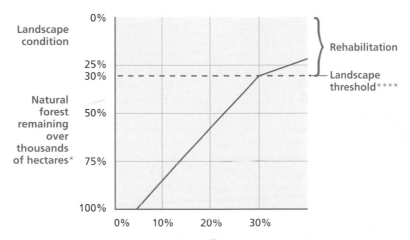

Area to leave for wildlife tree supply**
when planning harvests over hundreds of hectares***

     * Native forests supply current wildlife trees.
   ** As harvesting progresses wildlife trees will remain only by design.
  *** The trees retained need to be functionally appropriate. Monitoring and research will adjust the amount and condition over time.
**** When there is less than 30% of the natural forest remaining (the original forest is in remnants) consideration to retaining all the remaining may be appropriate as a conservation measure.

Leaving stand structure within each cut-block ensures that stand structures are left distributed across the forest. Where there is sufficient knowledge, it may be possible to specify a number of wildlife trees per hectare for a single species; however, leaving an area of natural forest undisturbed has the additional benefits of retaining soil, shrubs and understorey remnants of the natural system. Bear in mind that the utility to wildlife depends also on the quality of trees retained, not just the overall area.

• The X-axis shows the percentage of natural forest scheduled to remain in long-term reserves and that can be relied on to supply wildlife trees through natural successional processes. Outside of these areas of natural forest, as harvesting progresses, wildlife trees will be provided by areas left by design.

• The Y-axis shows the area to be left in wildlife trees as a percentage of the planned harvest area. The trees retained in this area will be of most benefit and provide the greatest safeguards if they are the best available from the natural stand. The higher the planned removal of the original forest, the greater the need to retain areas as harvesting continues.

• The estimation of an appropriate size of area to accompany each cut-block needs to be considered separately for each major ecosystem in the harvesting area, e.g., valley bottom, mid-elevation and high-elevation.

• In areas where harvesting is entirely second-growth and little natural forest remains from which to choose functioning wildlife trees, selected areas should be left to go through natural succession so as to be able to rebuild old-forest features and restore habitat function.

and hence affects the size of the area required to provide the context for stand management decisions. Thus, a rolling plateau with no natural barriers requires a larger context area than a mountainous landscape with alpine ridges, even if the climate is similar.

Because not all of the wildlife trees in a landscape area provide habitat of equal value or type, the supply of wildlife trees should also be considered separately for each biogeoclimatic zone within the area under consideration. Accordingly, the supply of wildlife trees in high-elevation ecosystems needs to be considered separately from the supply of wildlife trees in nearby low-elevation ecosystems. Low-elevation western red-cedar forests, for example, provide different wildlife trees than subalpine fir forests within the same drainage.

Once an appropriate area has been determined to provide the ecological context, it is necessary to consider both the long-term management of the forest and the area's harvest history. The following simplified example illustrates this point.

Consider a 100,000-ha forested area with two major biogeoclimatic zones of 50,000 ha each. One of these zones has topography favourable for forest harvesting, where long-term planning calls for the logging and reforestation of 70 percent of the 50,000 ha. So far, only 30 percent of the available harvest area has been harvested. Because the importance of wildlife trees was unknown during prior harvesting, we can assume that few if any suitable trees were retained in the first harvest passes and that, as a result, few wildlife trees remain in most of the second-growth forest. Therefore, for many decades into the future, the only wildlife trees available will be in the forest that has not yet been harvested and the 30 percent of the parcel that will not be harvested (long-term reserves).

In this parcel, the distribution of wildlife trees has been compromised by past practices. By retaining wildlife trees in the cut-blocks planned today and into the future, we can eventually compensate for the harvest history that removed all stand structures and address the adequacy (quality, location and size) of long-term reserves. These factors (harvest history, future plans and the adequacy of long-term forest conservation areas) determine how much area is appropriate to retain in wildlife trees during current and future harvest entries. In general, the longer the harvest history and the larger the area previously harvested, the greater the proportion of wildlife tree areas that need to be retained during further harvesting entries.

In the second zone from the above example, harvesting is just commencing. Here, 30 percent of the 50,000 ha is scheduled to become second-growth forest—the remaining 70 percent will definitely not be harvested. The need to retain specific areas for wildlife trees here is much lower than in the first zone, with more options in the distribution of wildlife tree leave areas. Because of the 70 percent that will never be logged, most of the wildlife tree needs in this landscape will be supplied by the natural forest area. However, wildlife tree management needs to be integrated with the areas planned for harvest nevertheless, because these areas are likely the ones with the highest biological productivity and may already be providing most of the habitat for local wildlife tree dwellers in the entire area.

Clearly, how much area to set aside during each harvesting operation is influenced by the expected supply of wildlife trees at the landscape level over time. Watersheds that have had little harvesting typically offer a good opportunity to retain many high-value wildlife trees in an even distribution across the landscape, but watersheds with a history of intensive harvesting will likely have wildlife trees in short supply. These latter areas thus require that more of the remaining natural stand structure (particularly wildlife trees) be retained when any old-growth forests are harvested. Figure 26 shows how to establish conservation goals for the retention of wildlife trees at the cut-block or forest stand level in relationship to the overall landscape condition.

It is currently thought that retaining somewhere between 5 and 30 percent of each proposed harvest area will sustain the biological functions for most of the complement of native species within our forested landscapes, provided that the retained portion is chosen to include the trees that are most suitable for conservation. The exact area needed for retention within an area planned for logging is determined by the context of the proposed harvesting, the history of harvesting in the area, the quality of the trees and wildlife needs. Continued research on species' needs and the monitoring of the effectiveness of wildlife tree retention practices are necessary to adjust the number and quality of trees retained until we have confidence that an adequate area with a supply of suitable trees sufficient to sustain our wildlife tree–dependent species has been conserved.

MANAGING FOR WILDLIFE TREES IN FOREST STANDS

The previous section discussed how to place harvest planning into an ecological context and integrate it over an extended time period in order to determine appropriate sizes for wildlife tree management areas. The next step is to decide which stand of wildlife trees to retain.

The selection of wildlife trees for retention needs to be both at a coarse-filter level and for any individual tree-using species being managed. When the number of currently functioning wildlife trees in an area is known, it becomes more apparent whether it is easiest to retain trees singly or in groups. Other considerations when selecting areas for conservation include maintaining the diversity of plant species, a complex stand structure and fallen trees and other woody debris, as well as their proximity to special habitats such as open water or grassland. Integrating wildlife tree retention with harvesting will ensure that forestry operations maintain these trees and so will not completely disable the functions they provide in forested ecosystems. The characteristics of suitable wildlife trees and each of these stand-level elements that contribute to maintaining biodiversity are discussed in more detail below.

Wildlife Tree Selection

The first priority for protection are the trees that have current wildlife use or significant wildlife tree features (see p. 12). In general, the more of these features a wildlife tree has, the more valuable it is to wildlife. For example, a very tall, large-diameter tree is further increased in value when it has internal decay and

Single tree retention. *Trees left individually across a harvest block provide a distribution that is often close to that found in forests that have developed through natural disturbance. The distribution of wildlife trees is, however, highly variable, and wildlife will shift to areas of suitable habitat.*

Groups of wildlife tree reserves provide areas where natural succession can continue and where current and future wildlife trees can develop. Reserves often provide more windfirm conditions overall than singly retained trees under the same conditions, and, as an additional benefit, the natural forest understorey is also left undisturbed.

downy woodpeckers, chickadees, nuthatches, tree swallows and bluebirds. There should be a mix of solid and rotting trunks, representing all the wildlife tree decay classes initially present on the site. The intention is to retain trees that provide immediate habitat value as well as those most likely to develop suitable features for future use.

If no trees currently appear to have high value, the retention priority should be those areas where trees will develop suitable characteristics in the shortest time. Trees selected to be future wildlife trees should be the most suitable choices available, with a reasonable expectation that they will remain in the long term, be windfirm and pose a low risk to safety in the future.

Retaining Trees Singly and in Groups (Wildlife Tree Patches)

Each proposed harvest area has a different complement of trees from which to choose wildlife trees. The identification and assessment of existing wildlife trees is best done early, well before landings and harvest boundaries are planned. At this time, current wildlife use, the presence of "vets" (veteran trees) and the locations of the areas with the most valuable wildlife trees can all be noted and integrated with harvesting (refer to "Finding Wildlife Trees with Existing Use," p. 34).

In addition to early searches for wildlife trees, the people actively engaged in harvesting need to be vigilant for wildlife tree potential and any current use, and they should be given sufficient direction to allow them to designate additional trees with high value for retention should any be encountered during harvest. In areas that use mechanical harvesters, educating the operators as to which trees have the highest value may maximize both the conservation value of the retained trees and operational efficiency.

existing use, usually indicated by a large nest. Features of all types, including raptor perches and witches' brooms, need to be represented. Local wildlife requirements will affect the number of trees with each feature type and help select which tree species to retain. If high-value wildlife trees are to be removed, the onus rests with whoever removes them to ensure that they are not vital habitat for species *at risk.*

Retained trees should be as large as possible for the site. Large birds such as eagles and large tree-using mammals generally require trees that are 50 cm in diameter at breast height (dbh) or greater, and at least 15–20 m tall. Trees with a dbh as little as 10–30 cm can provide habitat for smaller users, including

Single tree retention in conjunction with wildlife tree reserves. *A combination of singly reserved trees and groups of wildlife trees creates habitat structures that enable species to move across the landscape more easily.*

A strategy that is based on capturing existing habitat elements and selecting the best future wildlife trees may mean retaining single wildlife trees as well as groups of trees ("wildlife tree patches"). Live, healthy (decay class 1) trees retained singly or within wildlife tree patches, as well as individuals kept as seed trees and shelterwood trees, have the potential to develop into other, more valuable classes of wildlife trees if allowed to remain standing and go through the entire natural cycle of growth and decay, which may mean retention over several commercial harvest rotation periods. Wildlife tree patches also help to protect biodiversity by providing areas of undisturbed understorey and forest floor.

Trees selected for retention should be assessed for danger to forest workers during harvesting and to the general public (see Appendix 1). Retaining dangerous wildlife trees also requires pre-planning and a knowledgeable work force. Features such as split trunks,

Progressive clear-cut. *Although this large clear-cut will regenerate in trees, the absence of stand structure and the removal of all wildlife trees means that the new forest will not be able to provide for any of the species in this guide for many decades.*

dead tops or limbs, advanced decay or thick, sloughing bark can make some of the best wildlife trees potentially dangerous. Nevertheless, many of these trees are capable of standing for decades and withstanding natural disturbances, such as wind or fire, and can be safely maintained.

63

A potentially dangerous wildlife tree can be retained throughout harvesting operations if a safety ("no-work") zone of sufficient size, such as a wildlife tree patch, is established around it to ensure protection of the workers from potential hazards. In certain situations, additional measures may be required to protect the public (see Appendix 1). It is especially important to retain high-value wildlife trees, and they are worthy of the extra precautions that may be necessary.

The degree to which harvest area boundaries are adjusted to accommodate wildlife trees depends on a combination of factors: the ease with which a tree or group of trees can be retained during harvesting operations, the relative scarcity of high-value wildlife trees and species use and status. These decisions require judgements on the current and future value of particular trees, their likelihood of persistence and operational efficiency considerations.

When a forest stand is relatively homogeneous and no area of the stand or no individual trees have obviously higher wildlife tree value than others, then some of the largest available trees and a representative sample of the natural species mix of the stand being logged should be retained.

Where possible, retain hardwood trees such as paper birch, cottonwood, trembling aspen and bigleaf maple, particularly large ones with visible decay, because of their importance to primary cavity excavators. Hardwood species are often found in valley bottoms and riparian areas, but they are especially valuable to wildlife where they are naturally scarce, such as in up-slope areas. However, hardwood species should not be relied upon exclusively to meet the needs of wildlife tree users, because these trees have shorter life spans than conifers and decay more quickly, limiting their long-term value as wildlife trees. Also, they are not ecologically appropriate for all wildlife tree–dependent species.

By retaining wildlife trees within each cut-block, we assure that they will be distributed across the landscape, from valley bottoms to up-slope areas. Retained wildlife trees need to remain standing within the new stand. The objective is to leave these trees to go through their natural decay cycle, so they should not be cut or salvaged. When the next harvest entry in this area occurs, appropriate new prospective wildlife trees need to be identified for retention at that time. Some wildlife trees will persist through one or more rotations and provide long-term conservation benefit before completing their natural decay cycle.

The authors believe that wildlife tree–dependent species will be able to persist in the remnant forest structures associated with retained wildlife trees, and that they can disperse across landscapes dominated by second-growth forest, if suitable wildlife tree structures are well distributed in these forests. Wildlife tree–dependent species will be at lower levels than in forests influenced only by natural disturbances, but at least they will be able to persist as part of the forest ecosystem. In addition to providing habitat, retained wildlife trees also contribute to reforestation (e.g., for natural reseeding and as a reservoir of beneficial fungi) and visual aesthetics. Monitoring and evaluation of the number and quality of wildlife trees and research on their use by wildlife are needed to adapt coarse and fine filter management strategies to specific ecosystems. It is important to identify whether our practices are providing sufficient retention and replacement of wildlife trees and whether the full natural complement of species are able to continue as part of the managed forest.

Selecting Windfirm Trees

When selecting single wildlife trees for retention or laying out wildlife tree patches, consider the ability of the retained trees to withstand strong winds. Some tree species normally develop long tap roots, which anchor them firmly into the ground. (The relative wind-firmness of individual tree species is discussed in the tree accounts in Part 4.) However, susceptibility to windthrow is generally more dependent on factors such as location with regard to strong winds, soil conditions, crown size and previous wind exposure patterns. Regardless of species, any tree's ability to withstand wind is greatest if it has been exposed to frequent high winds throughout its growth. Trees in exposed areas and those that dominate the upper canopy are typically quite windfirm. The amount of foliage in the upper canopy and the degree to which trees become exposed as a stand is logged are important considerations. Trees in areas with a high incidence of root rot, and those growing on shallow, hardpan or wet soils, are generally more prone to windthrow.

If the windthrow risk is high, designing wildlife tree patches to have windfirm boundaries (i.e., generally oriented parallel to the prevailing winds and on the leeward side of cut-block openings) will result in reduced loss of valuable habitat to windthrow. Wildlife trees to be retained singly should be resistant to blowdown; dominant, well-rooted trees are good choices in this regard. In situations where the best wildlife trees would be prone to windthrow if retained singly, a patch of trees left to surround them will provide a buffer to the wind, significantly reducing the potential for

Windthrow. *Windthrow occurs naturally, even in closed canopy forests, so the blowdown of some trees left as wildlife trees is to be expected. However, selecting windfirm trees or areas of windfirm trees as part of harvest planning greatly reduces windthrow, thus helping to maximize the effectiveness of wildlife tree habitat retention.*

blowdown. Windthrow can be minimized through judicious tree selection and harvest design as well as by topping (see p. 72) to reduce the amount of crown exposed to wind. If topping is done, it is best carried out prior to when the moist soils and storms of autumn and winter place newly exposed trees at their greatest risk of windthrow.

Species Composition

Greater vegetation diversity generally supports greater wildlife diversity. As was indicated earlier, the diversity of tree species and understory vegetation in a forest vary naturally over time as stands age and disturbances occur.

Following harvest, with the intention to maximize timber production, cut-blocks have most often been replanted with early-seral species that are well adapted to regeneration after clearcutting. In some biogeoclimatic zones, up to 10 conifer species and three hardwood species might be harvested from a single cut-block, but replanting has rarely been done with as many species. The resulting second-growth forests generally have much lower tree-species diversity and little structural complexity compared to mature or older forests developed by natural disturbance.

When an area is being harvested and replanted, forest tree species diversity can be maintained and even increased relatively easily by not cutting any tree species that have become scarce in that area, as well as by deliberately planting those species. In addition, if any old-growth stands remain nearby, some of the species complexity will eventually return to the replanted area through natural seeding with a complex seed mixture that includes late-successional species. For this returning complexity to fully develop, however, stand treatments, such as brushing and spacing, would need to be tailored to promote tree species diversity.

Over time, planting sufficient numbers of any scarce or absent tree species and retaining any minor, shade-tolerant species during spacing operations can restore the species composition, stand diversity and complexity of a second-growth forest. However, it is a slow process to change the tree species composition of a forest and return areas with a history of stand simplification and tree species conversion to a condition closer to that created by natural disturbance and succession. It also takes a long time for reintroduced trees to develop wildlife tree characteristics, such as large diameters and heart rot.

Knowledge of the differences between tree species is vital to deciding what to plant and which trees to leave during harvesting or spacing. Part 4 describes the characteristics of the different species of trees that serve as wildlife trees in the ecosystems for which this guide can be applied and the importance of certain tree species to particular wildlife tree users.

Stand Structure and Wildlife Trees

The term "stand structure" relates to the variation in height, diameter and distribution of the trees in a forest stand. Vertical and horizontal variation in stand structure are provided by multiple canopy layers (understorey and overstorey), canopy gaps and a range of tree diameters and crown shapes. Wildlife trees, both live and dead, are elements of stand structure. Succession and natural disturbances cause ongoing changes in stand structure.

Forest stands that develop after natural disturbances differ significantly from those that originate after logging. Trees may be killed, downed or converted to charred wood and ashes by a natural disturbance, but their biomass remains on-site. Harvesting removes most of a stand's biomass and, in the case of clearcutting, all of the stand structure.

Natural disturbances tend to increase the number of wildlife trees in a forest, but harvesting tends to deplete the supply of current and future wildlife trees. Because wildlife trees are such an important structural element, it is vital to include them as a significant structural component in the management of second-growth and succeeding forests.

After Wildlife Trees Fall

Wildlife trees do not cease being useful when they fall. Downed trees (often referred to as "coarse woody debris") and other forest floor litter (small branches, leaves and other organic material) provide habitat for small mammals, amphibians, reptiles, invertebrates, lichens, mosses, fungi and bacteria. One of the most important ecological functions of decaying logs and forest floor litter is nourishing the forest and maintaining site productivity by recycling nutrients,

retaining moisture and building up the soil. And, as noted earlier, fallen trees are also important in regulating the flow of streams. Even in this final stage of a tree's existence, it contributes to the health of the ecosystem. Coarse woody debris often contains large populations of insects such as carpenter ants, which are a primary food source for pileated woodpeckers and black bears, as well as many other species.

Dead wood in our forests may appear to be wasted wood, but it provides a tremendously important material contribution to ecosystem function and diversity. The amount of coarse woody debris within a naturally developed forest stand varies widely and depends on the amount of time that has elapsed since the last disturbance, the stand condition and composition of trees in the stand when disturbed, the type and severity of the disturbance and the rate of decay (the

Coarse woody debris. *Fallen trees are an essential component of the forest ecosystem; they provide habitat for many species, from ants to salamanders to mice.*

latter being linked to tree species and climate). After a major disturbance, such as a wildfire or insect-kill, nearly the entire volume of the affected forest will be recycled as the dead trees fall and decay. Areas prone to these types of natural disturbances commonly receive large periodic inputs of coarse woody debris.

It is important that a managed forest landscape retain the range of variability in the amount and size of dead and downed wood that would result from natural disturbances. Some areas of the landscape need to be left alone and allowed to go through natural disturbances (e.g., fire or insect-kill), with the resulting dead and downed wood left in place. To retain this wood on the forest floor, the salvaging of dead wood must be restricted from these portions of the landscapes.

As with the management of wildlife trees, the appropriate amount and distribution of coarse woody debris to leave after harvesting requires an understanding of site ecology and a knowledge of long-term harvest plans. An approach of varying woody debris quantities based on site-specific conditions (e.g., tree species, stand age, topography and fire or disease concerns) is preferable to setting uniform ecosystem targets for coarse woody debris retention to be applied on each cut-block. (The latter approach would eventually reduce the range of natural diversity in coarse woody debris to a homogeneous level.) If, in a particular area, a high percentage of the forested landscape is expected to be harvested, then some parts of it will need to be managed over time for significantly more dead wood in order to meet the objectives of maintaining a full range of coarse woody debris levels.

In general, long, large-diameter logs are more valuable for retention than small logs. Because they decay more slowly and hold more moisture, they are useful to a wider array of organisms for a longer time. Dead wood left distributed over a site better emulates natural distribution than does piled woody debris. Maintaining logs in a full range of decay classes, from hard to crumbling wood, will help maintain habitat for the array of organisms linked to various decay stages. Conifer wood persists longer than hardwood, but all tree species should be represented.

Without adequate planning, it may be difficult to ensure a supply of dead wood at the end of the first managed forest rotation (and subsequent ones), because what was originally on the ground will now be largely decayed, and the natural input may be solely from the fallen trees left as wildlife trees. Decisions and practices related to maintaining wildlife trees will thus influence the future supply and distribution of coarse woody debris. So as not to overly deplete the supplies of coarse woody debris, salvage operations will need to be restricted or foregone in certain cut-blocks.

Special Habitats

Habitats such as riparian areas, gullies, meadows, seepage areas, avalanche tracks and rock outcrops are considered "special," particularly in forested landscapes where they are uncommon. These uncommon habitats make a significant contribution to biodiversity, because their microclimates, flora and fauna differ from those of other habitats in the surrounding stand and landscape. When harvesting, in addition to leaving high quality wildlife trees as usual, it is particularly important to maximize the conservation benefit of wildlife trees adjacent to these special habitats so that they will be easily accessible to species, such as ospreys, bats, and owls, that use both kinds of habitats.

CONSERVATION PRACTICES FOR FOREST HARVESTING

Based on the information presented above in the sections on managing for wildlife trees across the landscape and within forest stands, this section provides a set of practices for managing and conserving the ecological values associated with wildlife tree habitat using a coarse filter approach. These practices provide a generic approach to managing for wildlife trees that is the basic recommendation suitable for all the species in this guide. Additional stewardship provisions for more carefully tailoring habitat management are given in the individual species write-ups in Part 5 of this guide. These additional provisions are essential for supplying the specific needs of the 20 species identified with a fine filter icon and for catering to the needs of these individual species as we best understand them.

In general, logging systems that preserve much of the existing stand structure, including suitable wildlife trees, will be the most beneficial for wildlife tree–dependent species. Clear-cutting, for example, traditionally leaves no trees behind after harvest, but modified clear-cutting with reserves can result in significant retention of stand structure in a cut-block after harvest. Partial-cut harvesting produces more complex stands, but if over time, all the old trees in the block are removed through multiple entries, the net effect will be the same as with clear-cut harvesting—without deliberate wildlife tree retention in patches or as single trees, all the standing dead trees will be eventually removed. The array of partial-cut harvest systems currently in general use have a focus on reforestation and need to be modified to meet conservation objectives through the retention of wildlife trees.

Floodplain habitat such as this mixed spruce and cottonwood stand provide significant, well-distributed older forest stand structures.

Retaining mature and older trees singly or in groups after harvest enables many species to persist in predominantly younger forests.

A SUMMARY OF CONSERVATION PRACTICES FOR MAINTAINING ECOSYSTEM VALUES ACROSS FORESTED LANDSCAPES

- **Locate harvesting areas and salvage activities outside of areas needed for the retention of representative, rare and high-conservation-value, old-growth forest ecosystems.** A certain amount of old forest to be retained in the long term will be within protected areas, riparian zones and elsewhere in forested areas that are uneconomic to log or salvage. If these long-term reserved forest areas are too limited in area, poorly represent the diversity of natural forest or are too fragmented or too distant from one another to reasonably sustain the old-growth biodiversity, then the retention of additional representative old-growth forest is strongly recommended.

- **Ensure that proposed harvest areas do not convert a disproportionate amount of the landscape to young forest.** The acceptable range for the ratio of young to old forest should be based on natural seral stage distribution. Maintaining a mosaic of young, mature and old forest lowers risks to ecosystems and species. To achieve a natural mix and maintain ecosystem function and conserve biodiversity across forested landscapes, it may be necessary to refrain from harvesting or schedule the harvesting of certain areas for dates decades in the future and shift the immediate planned harvest to other areas within the surrounding landscape or to other watersheds.

- **Identify the habitats of wildlife species and plant communities that are known to be _at risk_ (threatened, endangered or vulnerable) and sensitive to harvesting and road building and avoid harvesting or disturbing these.**

- **Integrate harvesting goals with conservation values by indicating on operational plans a sufficient ecologically appropriate area of suitable wildlife trees that will be left within each cut-block or harvest planning area.** (Check back to "Managing for Wildlife Trees Across the Landscape," p. 58, for guidance).

- **Use a harvest system that most closely retains stand structures resembling those normally found in forests established after natural disturbances.**

- **Plan the location, size and shape of harvest areas and roads to minimize the effects of forest fragmentation.** Examine the range of natural forest patch sizes to be retained and consider whether past harvesting has already significantly fragmented the natural ecosystem and whether additional harvesting can achieve a more natural distribution of early seral patch sizes or whether harvesting should be shifted to other portions of the forest landscape.

- **Plan to retain or plant tree species or stand mixes that were historically common across the landscape, but are currently scarce.** The natural range of tree species composition can be determined using a knowledge of ecosystems, natural succession and forest inventory. Before harvesting, assess the area's tree species composition and note where certain species or stand mixes are becoming scarce.

A SUMMARY OF CONSERVATION PRACTICES FOR MAINTAINING ECOSYSTEM VALUES WITHIN FOREST STANDS

- **Ensure that the cut-block design will meet the overall goal for the amount of area to be retained.** In order to retain adequately distributed stand-level biodiversity across the managed forest landscape, wildlife tree retention must occur on every harvest block. (Check back to "Managing for Wildlife Trees Across the Landscape," p. 58, for guidance.)

- **Assess wildlife trees in the proposed harvest area.** Allow sufficient lead time. Any wildlife tree with species *at risk* in residence must be retained. Also, mark and take note of trees for retention with special features, such as osprey or bald eagle nests, heron rookeries, bear dens, bat maternity and hibernation roosts, nest holes and other signs of existing wildlife use. Local knowledge can make an important contribution to building an inventory of currently used wildlife trees. Also consider tree size and decay class when selecting trees for retention. (Check back to "Wildlife Tree Selection," p. 61, and "Finding Wildlife Trees with Existing Use," p. 34, for additional guidance.) It is helpful to mark some trees with these features with wildlife tree signs (see p. 77).

- **Identify for retention on the harvest plan any riparian zones and unstable soil areas, as well as high-value wildlife trees and currently used trees, within the initially proposed harvest area and adjust harvest plans for their retention.** The plan should allow for the retention of sufficient appropriate overall area to meet stand-level conservation objectives over the long term. Decide which individual high quality wildlife trees or groups of trees to leave and adjust the roads, landing placements and cut-block boundaries as necessary. The final selection of trees to be cut is a most important conservation decision that dictates how well the new forest will sustain wildlife tree–dependent species over the next century. Therefore, this decision should be made by knowledgeable individuals.

- **Review the cut-block design in advance of harvest to ensure minimum windthrow risk for the retained trees.** In areas prone to windthrow, design cut-block shape and reserve areas to help the most suitable wildlife trees withstand winds. In less wind-prone areas, choose leave trees that are more windfirm and that are located toward the leeward edges of cut-blocks. Consider topping windthrow-prone leave area trees during the harvest entry. (Also see "Selecting Windfirm Trees," p. 65, and "Topping," p. 72.)

CREATING WILDLIFE TREE FEATURES

In areas where there are currently few or no natural wildlife trees, various techniques can be used to create, restore or enhance wildlife tree habitat or simulate certain wildlife tree features, such as cavities. Designed to attract species back to areas lacking wildlife trees, these practices are not intended as a substitute for retaining high-value wildlife trees and other mature trees that will develop into wildlife trees as the existing ones decay and die. They can, however, provide immediate benefits in areas with few current wildlife trees and supply bridge habitat that meets the needs of wildlife during the time it takes for wildlife trees to naturally develop.

Topping

The primary use of topping is to windproof trees that are retained so that they will remain standing and subsequently age rather than blow down. Topping does not usually kill the tree, and it can promote laterally spreading branching near the top that over time can support large open nests.

In stands with few wildlife trees, live trees (including ones without defects) can be topped to create future wildlife trees. Ideally, these trees should retain some live branches and be cut with a rough, jagged edge at the top to simulate natural breakage and to facilitate subsequent weathering and decay.

Live trees with aerial hazards, such as a large, dead, forked top or large, dead limbs, can also be topped to remove the overhead hazard to people or facilities (for example, when trees are near buildings, trails or power lines). However, if possible, it is better for wildlife if this type of tree can be safely cordoned off within a no-work zone (thereby reducing exposure to the hazardous part), instead of topping the tree.

Only highly experienced, trained people should climb and top trees.

Artificial Cavities in Live Trees

If natural cavities and abandoned woodpecker holes are in short supply, live trees can be excavated with a power saw to create nest and roost cavities for secondary cavity users. The artificial

Topping to windfirm retained trees. *Topping effectively improves the windfirmness of trees by reducing the amount of crown area exposed to wind as well as by moving the tree's centre of gravity downward.*

Cross-section of a woodpecker cavity. *Woodpeckers generally prefer trees with heart rot. The reduced firmness of the interior wood requires less effort to create the relatively large nest cavity where the young will remain until fledged.*

HIGH-CUT STUMPS ("STUBS")

A certain number of trees in a given cut-block will have visible defects in the lower bole, such as butt rot, scars or cracks, or show fungal conks, which indicate decay. These characteristics reduce their timber value, but enhance their habitat quality. It is best for the wildlife to leave these defective stems standing in their entirety as leave area trees, rather than fell them, but where they cannot be retained, it is better to leave a piece of the trunk as a high-cut stump or "stub" rather than cut the whole tree.

Stubs are easily produced during mechanized forest harvesting operations using a feller-buncher, which can safely reach 4–6 metres up the trunk. Defective stems suitable for stubbing can be marked by ground crews during cruising or layout. Alternatively, feller-buncher operators can be trained to recognize good candidates and then decide whether to retain the whole tree or to move the cutting head up the bole and harvest the sound wood portions only.

Wildlife that use cavities relatively near the ground, along with insectivores of all kinds, will benefit the most from stubs being retained. However, trees normally develop heart rot only when they are alive, so do not use this technique with the expectation of creating hollow-tree features in the stubs. Stubbing should, by the way, be used as a complement to the retention of entire wildlife trees and groups rather than an alternative.

"Stubs." *"Stubs" (intentionally created tall stumps) retain some vertical structure and give certain wildlife species a place to nest or feed during the early seral stage of the new forest. On-the-ground personnel can choose trees, preferably ones of sufficient size and with some internal decay or structural defect, to be stubbed and left to develop into decay class 5 (and beyond) stumps over time.*

Artificial cavity creation

thickness of 4 cm or more (also dependent on crown and wind considerations) is required after artificial cavity excavation. Trees should be chosen to ensure that the artificial cavity provides habitat for the longest time possible and trees selected should not put members of the public at undue risk in the future. This type of in-tree cavity can have greater longevity than a nest box and will appear more natural.

Only highly experienced, trained people should select and climb trees to create nest cavities.

Inoculation with Heart-rot Fungi

Heart rot can be promoted in selected live trees by inoculating them with naturally occurring decay fungi. This technique greatly accelerates the natural process of decay in the wildlife tree cycle—decay can be achieved in as little as 5–10 years, as opposed to 100 or more years through natural decay dynamics. Because inoculation does not kill the tree, this technique has the advantage of retaining a relatively sound, live tree that still has its full height and foliage but has the primary wildlife tree attribute of heart-rot decay, making it suitable for cavity excavation. Inoculated trees usually present few worker safety problems, and because they are live and relatively healthy in appearance, they are at low risk of being felled by firewood cutters.

Fungal inoculation is readily applicable to stands where wildlife trees are scarce, especially where partial-cutting silvicultural systems are used in managed second-growth forests. It is also suitable for other locations lacking in old forests or old-growth structures and in wildlife habitat areas where an increase in the abundance of wildlife trees is desirable. Consequently, fungal inoculation may be of particular significance as a habitat recovery tool for cavity-dependent wildlife that is designated *at risk*.

cavity is created by removing a slab or faceplate from the side of the tree, then routing out a hole or cavity with the end of the power saw.

Where possible, the size and shape of the excavated hole should be designed for a specific wildlife species. (Not much is known about the preferences of various species, however, but larger or deeper cavities are usually preferable to smaller ones, because the users will line the cavities to suit their needs.)

An entrance hole is then drilled in the slab, which is reattached to the trunk by nailing it in place. Figure 14 (p. 32) and the individual species accounts in Part 5 provide information on the entry hole sizes needed by different species and the minimum trunk diameters required. When done appropriately, this technique can be used to benefit any of the secondary cavity users.

The tree will be weakened and more prone to breakage at the excavation site, so if the intention is to restore habitat for bufflehead or hooded mergansers, a tree greater than 30 cm in diameter at the cavity entrance is needed. To reduce the chance of stem breakage on this size of modified tree, a remaining wall

FIREWOOD AND SALVAGE CUTTING

Firewood cutting and salvage harvesting are a much greater threat to wildlife trees than most people might guess. In our highly productive valley-bottom lands, urban and rural development, agriculture and forestry operations have already significantly reduced biodiversity. The additional loss of wildlife trees to any additional cutting further reduces the habitat available to wildlife tree users. Aggravating the situation is a widely held misconception that salvaging dead wood for firewood or other forest products benefits forests and is better than removing live trees. Because of their large size and dry wood, some of the best and rarest wildlife trees are targeted for firewood. Wildlife trees occurring along the edges of forest roads near settled areas are the most vulnerable.

Large trees found in ecologically important areas, such as grasslands, riparian areas, wetlands and lakeshores, and trees with high wildlife habitat value (for example, trees showing active wildlife use and trees with form and condition suitable for nesting, denning, perching or feeding) need to be protected wherever possible. Only live trees and standing dead trees with limited wildlife value should be felled for firewood.

Firewood cutters themselves need to be educated about wildlife tree issues, and officials issuing permits to cut firewood or to salvage timber can help by ensuring that wildlife trees are not included within these permits by omitting old-growth trees from the permits, but increasing market pressure is vital to changing the situation. This market pressure can come from you if you buy firewood. Do your best to ensure that your firewood does not come from high-value wildlife trees. In addition to asking the vendor where the wood came from, you can recognize old-growth wood, which is likely to have come from a wildlife tree, by its dense growth rings and thick bark. Refuse to buy wood that has these old-growth characteristics. There are ample supplies of second-growth wood and commercially thinned wood to offer responsible, ecologically sound alternatives. Commercial firewood cutters will change their practices when there is sufficient consumer preference against the use of firewood from wildlife trees.

Heart-rot fungi are specific to certain tree species, so expert advice from a forest pathologist is essential for the selection of appropriate fungal species, tree species and condition and inoculation techniques.

Nest and Roost Boxes

Properly designed, installed and maintained nest boxes can provide localized, short-term artificial nest sites for secondary cavity users such as bluebirds, wood ducks and small owls or roost sites for bats. Nest and roost boxes are especially useful in areas with few trees or few trees with natural cavities, such as in urban areas.

However, nest boxes cannot replace wildlife trees. They do not provide habitat for the insects that sustain many wildlife tree users. Nor do they provide nest habitat for most primary cavity excavators—these birds will only use holes that they themselves have excavated.

Installing, maintaining and monitoring nest boxes on a large scale is costly and labour intensive, but involving volunteers in these tasks creates a valuable opportunity for environmental education and learning about habitat stewardship.

"Planting" Wildlife Trees

"Planting" wildlife trees with an excavator has been done in a number of areas. The excavator picks up large logs from the ground and sets them upright like posts, burying their bases in a previously dug short trench, to a sufficient depth that they will not fall over (1 m of trench depth for each 3 m of log length is recommended). This technique can provide immediate habitat structure, especially in disturbed areas such as power line rights-of-way, and on deactivated forestry roads and landings. Large-diameter cull logs with some internal decay, which would otherwise be piled and burned, are ideal candidates for this purpose.

These planted snags can benefit primary cavity excavators by providing food sources and suitable sites for the excavation of cavities. Additional monitoring of current planted sites, as part of forest management, is needed to learn which species are using these structures as habitat and to discover the true utility of this practice.

Snags being planted with an excavator. *These are class 6 or 7 conifer logs that were left at roadside after harvesting. This habitat enhancement activity was coordinated with road deactivation.*

Planted snags located in small groups within a cutblock opening. *These can provide habitat for cavity-excavating birds, as well as perch sites, immediately after harvesting and throughout stand development.*

HANGING WILDLIFE TREE SIGNS

Posting wildlife tree signs is an effective and valuable way to help protect trees for wildlife by alerting people to their importance. It can be done by practically anyone with a basic knowledge of what makes a wildlife tree important to wildlife, including people in the forest industry, government employees and contractors, researchers, natural history clubs, conservation groups, landowners and the general public.

The highest priority are wildlife trees with current use by wildlife and that are believed to be in danger of being cut down, but any tree with one or more of the wildlife tree features described in the introduction of this guide can be a candidate for a sign. The signing of wildlife trees helps to prevent increases in the number of species at risk. Signs can be placed on both private and public property, as long as permission has first been obtained from the land's owner or the agency responsible for its management. For public forest land, contact the Ministry of Environment or the Ministry of Forests and Range.

Wildlife tree signs should be positioned so as to be visible to any would-be faller before cutting begins. However, they should be placed so as not to detract from the visual landscape. That is, they should not, for example, be immediately visible to people travelling down highways or secondary roads. There can, however, be educational benefits to signs that can be readily seen in certain places, such as along trails. The quality of the sign and the context need to be considered.

Assess overhead hazards prior to any hammering or vibration that could bring down loose material. If in doubt, your safety comes first. Make sure that the nails go into solid wood.

Wildlife tree signs. *Signs like these serve to educate would-be fallers about the habitat value of wildlife trees.*

What you need to hang a wildlife tree sign:

- *sign*
- *hammer*
- *two nails*

Use legible lettering and wording something like: "Wildlife Tree. Do not disturb. Save for food, shelter and nesting." As far as practical, choose materials likely to last as long as the tree. Signs made of UV-resistant plastics appear to be holding the message well nearly two decades after installation. The nails need to be long enough to pass through the bark and penetrate at least 3 cm into the woody trunk. On live trees that have not yet reached their final girth, particularly with thin signs, do not fully hammer the nails in (leave a centimetre or two sticking out) to reduce the likelihood of nail-head pull-through.

Assess overhead hazards prior to any hammering or vibration that could bring down loose material. If in doubt, your safety comes first. Make sure that the nails go into solid wood.

Recording the locations of wildlife trees and other details about them is very desirable and can further help to protect them. For example, this information can be brought forward when plans for harvesting or land development are being devised or management options are being considered, and it can be used by researchers monitoring the activities of species and the residences of species *at risk*.

A coordinated signing program would ideally include as many people as possible who are in regular contact with trees, but in the absence of such a program, because of the many benefits to hanging wildlife tree signs, anyone interested is encouraged to start signing on their own.

KEEPING A WILDLIFE TREE INVENTORY

Desirable tools for keeping an inventory:
- *diameter tape or measuring tape*
- *stick about 1 m long*
- *map*
- *GPS (Global Positioning System) receiver*
- *camera*
- *notebook*

A thorough inventory record indicates:
- *a general descriptive location using landmarks or the names of roads or drainages and tributaries that would be enable other people to find the tree*
- *location in UTM (Universal Transverse Mercator) coordinates or latitude and longitude*
- *the year the sign was hung*
- *tree species (record as "unknown" if unsure)*
- *diameter at breast height (measured or an estimate)*
- *height (measured or an estimate)*
- *decay class*

- *observations of wildlife tree features and wildlife use, including the species (record as "unknown" if unsure)*
- *the name of the person who posted the sign*

Note that a diameter tape will give the diameter directly when you wrap it around a tree; if using a regular tape, divide the circumference by 3.14 to get the diameter. One of the simplest ways to estimate a tall tree's height is to position yourself at a distance from the tree that you think is about equal to its height and hold a stick upright in one hand at arm's length. Your feet should be at about the same elevation as the base of the tree and the length of stick above your hand should equal the distance from your hand to your eyes. Walk toward or away from the tree until the part of the stick above your hand appears to be as tall as the tree—your distance from the tree equals its approximate height.

Signing for safety in high-use areas. *For public safety, signage can be used to caution recreational users to avoid hazardous wildlife trees on windy days or when camping.*

PART 3

WILDLIFE TREES IN URBAN & RURAL ENVIRONMENTS

MAINTAINING WILDLIFE TREES IN SETTLED AREAS

The conservation framework outlined in Part 2 can also be applied to urban and rural environments. The terminology may be different, but the process also involves considering the broad forested landscape context and then narrowing the focus, first to groups of trees (stands) and then to individual trees and the features used by wildlife tree–dependent species.

Although the terms "landscape-level," "stand-level" and "single tree retention" are commonplace in forestry, they have no widely accepted parallels in the lexicon of the municipal and rural planners, councils, boards and individuals who make the decisions that affect the trees on urban and rural lands. Perhaps an appropriate parallel to "landscape-level" would be the "urban forest" or "rural forest," depending on the administrative jurisdiction. An urban forest encompasses all the trees within the boundaries of a town or city, and the rural forest comprises all the trees on the interurban lands and the rural surroundings of an urban area, out to the boundary with publicly owned provincially or federally controlled lands. In an urban or rural setting, an area such as a treed park or private land where trees dominate can be treated as a forest stand. As in forest conservation management in commercially based forestry, rural and urban decisions concerning the retention of single trees or groups of trees need to be based on their features, wildlife use and safety.

In the urban (or rural) forest, decisions regarding the retention of individual trees or small groups of trees (forest stands) are made by maintenance workers, arborists and anyone who decides which trees to leave or cut on public land or in their own private yard. Over the past 200 years, countless such decisions have shaped the current distribution, abundance and availability of wildlife tree habitat, particularly in densely populated areas. As the human population increases, the expansion of housing, roads, industrial complexes and commercial centres will likely continue to diminish natural ecosystems and their habitat elements. However, the urban landscape, though highly fragmented, often retains some important isolated remnants of wildlife habitats. The intent of this section is to provide general knowledge regarding the importance of wildlife trees and how it is possible to retain some of them safely.

A cavity dweller at home in an urban setting.
Homeowners can choose to retain trees like this one that are suitable for cavity dwellers if the tree is assessed by a trained individual to not present a danger or liability.

The management of wildlife tree habitat in urban and rural areas poses a number of challenges. All settled areas have a history of habitat removal, alteration and fragmentation, and in many areas, the management of natural habitats continues to be a low priority for rural, municipal and urban planners. In addition, on both public and private land, wildlife trees are targeted for removal because of the perception by untrained persons that all standing dead trees are automatically a liability and therefore must be felled. This belief is compounded by the general lack of awareness that these trees have significant wildlife value. Furthermore, many arborists and firewood cutters are unaware of wildlife habitat needs, so many trees that could be retained are needlessly removed.

Another challenge is that green spaces in settled areas often contain only remnant populations of native vegetation and animals, intermixed with growing numbers of domestic (or feral) animals and invasive nonnative plant species. Introduced plants and animals compete with native species, including wildlife tree–dependent animals, for food, water, shelter and space. For example, European starlings and house sparrows, both introduced, often aggressively compete with a number of native primary cavity excavators, ousting them from their nests and destroying eggs or killing hatchlings. Similarly, introduced gray squirrels and fox squirrels use cavities required by native species.

Although it is not possible to retain (or reintroduce) all the original wildlife tree–dependent animals in developed environments, many species described in this guide can successfully inhabit rural and urban environments where sufficient habitat is available. Much of this habitat is controlled by regional governments and private landowners, who, through education and extension, can become more aware of their roles as wildlife tree managers.

To maintain wildlife tree–dependent animals in rural and urban settings, the primary recommendation is to retain large trees with large limbs and cavities in locations where they do not pose a risk to people, structures or infrastructure. As well, ongoing access to appropriate food, water, shelter and space for these wildlife species needs to be ensured.

Functioning wildlife trees in remaining treed fragments in settled areas, trees that would otherwise be cut as a public safety measure, can often be retained. However, to do so will also require appropriate tree hazard assessment procedures (see Appendix 1 for a discussion of human safety and liability). With this approach, people who work with trees can learn to remove only the specific portion of a wildlife tree that poses a hazard to overhead lines, park facilities or buildings, rather than felling the entire tree. When trees in settled areas are managed for wildlife, and some trees with wildlife tree features are maintained—or even created (see p. 72)—a number of wildlife species that depend on these trees can be expected to remain in, or even return to, our highly fragmented urban and rural forests.

Regional districts, municipal councils and other local groups can help to conserve wildlife trees and other natural habitats by establishing policies, requiring the training of staff and offering public education programs.

Education and extension will lead to the changes that are needed to integrate cost-effective wildlife habitat conservation practices with other management objectives. When the knowledge of how to safely retain wildlife trees is available to all planners, engineers, developers, arborists, educators and citizens, and this knowledge is applied, we will all be able to enjoy a more diverse and natural urban and rural forest, as will some of the wildlife species that were at home in these places before we arrived.

A number of additional specific actions and strategies can be used to help maintain wildlife trees in settled areas. An inventory is the normal first step in such planning.

A natural areas inventory will show where the remaining rare and scarce habitat elements and species are and indicate which areas offer the greatest opportunities for conservation. Knowing the areas with the greatest

When this tree died, the owner of the field left it to go through its natural decay cycle. Now at decay stage 3, it has been chosen by this osprey as a nest site.

natural species richness and where rarity exists will point to conservation priorities, suggest possible mitigative measures and reveal opportunities to restore lost habitat.

An inventory of existing forested habitats, the different tree species, sizes, classes and conditions, along with the land tenure, is basic to the understanding of any urban forest. It will provide a starting point for determining opportunities and options that can integrate conservation provisions into policy, zoning, covenants, training, education and extension programs. This inventory will show where young trees can be expected to reach maturity and the areas where there will be continued loss of older trees. As a critical component of the urban forest, wildlife trees must be an integral part of this inventory.

On a broad scale, an inventory should record the locations and extent of several different classes of urban forest, for example:
• large, relatively intact ecosystems with mature forest habitat (such as are often found in parks);
• more modified but still dominantly natural treed areas (such as those found in some people's yards, lands managed by public institutions and certain privately held lands);
• treed roadways and power-line rights-of-way with relatively undisturbed vegetation that link natural areas.

The inventory should also record the age classes of different trees species so that the current and future supply of wildlife trees can be estimated.

More locally, a natural areas inventory needs to include currently functional areas of wildlife trees and note whether they are recognized and included as objectives in the urban or rural landscape and where they may be at risk. Trees with high wildlife value can be identified. The locations of trees and their surrounding habitat with existing use by any of the primary cavity excavators, secondary cavity users and open nesters in this guide help show where suitable habitat still exists and which species are still at home in our urban and rural forests. In many cases, local residents will be glad to share their area knowledge by indicating the locations of wildlife trees and areas frequented by wildlife species.

If a localized inventory is being undertaken in response to a specific proposed development, it should include an assessment of the wildlife trees, the impact of their removal on identified wildlife habitats and species, and options for retention. The conservation value of such an area can be placed in a broader context if there is an existing inventory of the surrounding jurisdiction. This broader understanding of conservation priorities can be used to negotiate improvements to development where they most affect conservation priorities.

In general, the results of an inventory are recorded largely in tables or on maps or a combination of the two. Increasingly, computers with GIS (geographic information system) software are being used.

After an inventory has been done, the opportunity for maintaining natural habitat for wildlife tree–dependent species becomes more obvious. Often, the best opportunity lies in ecologically sensitive areas that may contain rare plants and scarce remnants of the former natural ecosystem, such as riparian areas, wetlands, ravines and major gullies. In this way, it is possible to focus conservation efforts on areas with high wildlife tree values and to minimize the effects of development and tree maintenance on these trees in both the short and long term.

In many cases, informing the public of the results of an inventory will lead to greater support for (and involvement in) follow up conservation measures. Some ideas for outreach are mentioned below in the section about training and extension.

Because of the large number of groups currently doing groundbreaking work in the inventorying of urban and rural situations, we recommend that the interested reader seek additional information regarding recording methodologies and presentation ideas and so on from local or other sources.

POLICY AND ZONING

The existing urban forest is likely already regulated by civic policies that support certain activities within defined zones while prohibiting others. A review of either zones or policies, or both, is an important part of addressing wildlife tree retention. Zoning and policy can be used to maintain native vegetation buffers along waterways, keeping portions of them in a condition where wildlife trees can be retained.

These tools can also be used to soften the impact of new developments on wildlife by ensuring the retention of wildlife trees and the dedication of green spaces. Zoning can be used to protect wildlife tree habitat and provide direction for new housing, golf courses and industrial developments, to maximize areas of natural land so that wildlife trees can be part of the developments' design. Many recent developments have included the dedication of green space as a condition of the approval of the final plans.

Conservation covenants are another mechanism that can be used to set some private land in trust for conservation. A conservation covenant is made at the owner's discretion. It is a legally binding statement that can be placed on the land title that ensures some designated portion of a property, such as a treed riparian area, will be maintained in perpetuity with conservation as a priority.

Training and Extension

Once zones and policies are clearly laid out and the maintenance of trees, including wildlife trees, is an official objective in various zones, then training will need to be made available to ensure that this retention is done effectively and safely. At the civic or municipal level, engineering, maintenance and parks staff normally would be the people most involved. In-service programs and extension courses offered through various continuing education outlets can be used to educate public employees as well as utility service company workers, private-sector arborists, other involved professionals and interested members of the general public about these issues. In many places, such training and education concerning wildlife trees and safety are already available.

In addition to topics such as recognizing wildlife trees, hazard assessment and tree-trimming paradigms, this training can deal with matters such as reducing the disturbance of wildlife during breeding and nesting seasons (usually late April to mid-July) by the appropriate scheduling of activities. It can also address strategies to limit human activities in areas with high concentrations of wildlife trees, both to ensure public safety and to help retain wildlife tree habitat. Along with explaining the benefits and pleasures of living with a diversity of species, education and extension can disseminate the skills for safely retaining wildlife trees within settled areas and instill the confidence to do so.

For best results, it is necessary to inform and involve the community at large in habitat protection planning, maintenance and enhancement activities. To reach a broad audience, ads or features on radio and TV and in local publications, websites, open houses, information tables at malls and public buildings and household leafletting are some avenues that might be employed.

A course on wildlife trees and safety. *People working with trees today need to be able to identify which ones are used and needed by wildlife and which ones are potentially dangerous. Training for arborists, maintenance staff and private landowners helps integrate human activities with the needs of wildlife in the management of trees in urban and rural environments.*

Local volunteers will often be willing to monitor the use of wildlife trees. Civic officials can approach local naturalist groups or contact nearby residents to request their assistance. These volunteers can be asked to watch for potential threats to certain trees and record any changes in usage, with reporting to occur on both a scheduled and an as-required basis. The benefits of such a volunteer program include not only the capacity to monitor wildlife trees more effectively but also greater public awareness and "ownership" of the area's wildlife trees. Many jurisdictions will have existing volunteer recruitment and recognition programs in other sectors that can potentially be extended to the monitoring of wildlife trees.

MANAGING FOR INDIVIDUAL TREES IN THE URBAN AND RURAL FOREST
Urban habitat managers, municipal and rural forest managers, park naturalists and maintenance staff, participants in outdoor recreational activities, landowners and others all share responsibility for the long-term maintenance of individual wildlife trees in settled areas. Knowledge of the value of deformed or damaged trees means that a landowner can instruct arborists to leave features for wildlife or choose to hire arborists who indicate that they are willing to integrate wildlife dependence with tree care.

Long-term planning, proactive management, knowledge and training coupled with appropriate policy and zoning will collectively ensure that wildlife trees and their dependent wildlife can coexist with people. When and where this integration occurs, both wildlife and humans will be better off.

Wildlife tree habitat in British Columbia is provided primarily by 17 conifer and eight hardwood species. Other native species, such as western yew, whitebark pine, Rocky Mountain juniper, western flowering dogwood, bitter cherry and several willows, will only rarely achieve the size needed to function as wildlife trees, so they are not profiled in this chapter.

Nest records and other biological observations provide insight into the species of trees that wildlife select for use. A review of the 66 wildlife species

Figure 27. Relative tree sizes

SPECIES	Upper limits of ht (to nearest m)	Relative Size (to nearest 0.1)
Subalpine fir	50	0.5
Amabilis fir	47	0.5
Grand fir	75	0.8
Western red-cedar	59	0.6
Yellow-cedar	61	0.6
Western larch	61	0.6
Alpine larch	22	0.2
Engelmann spruce	53	0.5
White spruce	52	0.5
Black spruce	20	0.2
Sitka spruce	96	1.0
Lodgepole pine	46	0.5
Western white pine	62	0.6
Ponderosa pine	50	0.5
Douglas-fir, coastal	94	1.0
Douglas-fir, Interior	46	0.5
Western hemlock	76	0.8
Mountain hemlock	52	0.5
Bigleaf maple	49	0.5
Red alder	41	0.4
Arbutus	36	0.4
Paper birch (White birch)	28	0.3
Trembling aspen	35	0.4
Black cottonwood	58	0.6
Balsam poplar	30	0.3
Garry oak	33	0.3

accounts in Part 5 of this guide gives an indication of the relative popularity and level of use of different tree species.

Among the conifers, Douglas-fir and ponderosa pine appear to be the most sought-after wildlife trees by the greatest number of wildlife species, followed by western red-cedar, lodgepole pine, Engelmann spruce, white spruce and western hemlock. Western larch, Sitka spruce and western white pine are the next most popular, with the remaining conifers being used by the fewest species.

The most sought-after hardwood species are black cottonwood and trembling aspen, followed closely by paper birch, then by red alder, bigleaf maple and balsam poplar. Of the hardwoods discussed in this guide, arbutus and Garry oak receive the least use.

The results are informative but caution must be used in applying them because the ratings are based only on the number of bird and mammal species reported to make use of each tree species. They do not necessarily reflect frequency of use, the relative abundance of different tree species or the choices available in forests that are dominated by conifers, nor does this type of listing account for the strong association between some wildlife species and certain tree species or decay conditions. (See the individual wildlife species accounts in Part 5 for additional information regarding their tree preferences for particular purposes.)

Although hardwoods are usually a minor component in forest stands in many regions of the province, the most favoured hardwoods are chosen as often as the most sought-after conifers. Black cottonwood, in particular, is selected by a high proportion of wildlife tree users despite its restricted availability. Maintenance of black cottonwood habitat should be a priority, because this favoured wildlife tree species is naturally scarce and continues to be diminished through urbanization, agriculture and forestry practices.

Such characteristics as trunk and bark details, branching patterns, longevity, potential size (height and diameter), rooting traits, conditions needed for germination and growth, shade tolerance, requirements for nutrients and moisture, common associations with other trees and the results of disturbances can vary greatly from species to species. Being aware of these attributes is necessary in order to effectively select, identify, retain and protect the appropriate wildlife trees to provide the habitat required in any particular situation. Readers seeking more detailed field identification information are encouraged to consult other guides (see References, p. 306).

In the following accounts, tree diameters are the forest-inventory standard "diameter at breast height" (dbh) dimension, measured at 1.3 m above the estimated germination point of the seed (usually approximately 1.3 m above ground level). As much as possible, heights and diameters reflect trees found in B.C.; growing conditions in parts of the U.S. Pacific Northwest may yield larger specimens. Also note that the listings of wildlife species associated with each tree are not necessarily comprehensive.

Trembling aspen clones can reproduce through suckering and some clones are estimated to have survived this way for 2000 years.

Abbreviations for British Columbia's 13 treed biogeoclimatic zones:
See map on p. 114. These zones are discussed in more detail in Part 5 and the wildlife tree–dependent species in each zone are listed in Appendix 3.

BG: Bunchgrass
BWBS: Boreal White and Black Spruce
CDF: Coastal Douglas-fir
CWH: Coastal Western Hemlock
ESSF: Engelmann Spruce– Subalpine Fir
ICH: Interior Cedar–Hemlock

IDF: Interior Douglas-fir
MH: Mountain Hemlock
MS: Montane Spruce
PP: Ponderosa Pine
SBPS: Sub-Boreal Pine–Spruce
SBS: Sub-Boreal Spruce
SWB: Spruce–Willow–Birch

Conifers

Seventeen species of conifers function as significant wildlife trees in British Columbia. The province is extensively conifer-dominated, with a limited amount of mixedwood forest (conifers and hardwoods occurring together). The very few areas of pure hardwood forest are located primarily in the northeastern corner of the province.

TRUE FIRS
Subalpine Fir
(Abies lasiocarpa var. lasiocarpa):
abundant in ESSF, MS, SBS and SWB; common in BWBS, ICH and MH; uncommon or rare in CWH and SBPS.

Subalpine fir has smooth, thin, grey bark with resin blisters. The branches— short, extremely stiff and densely packed together—are well suited for shedding snow. This fir is distinguished

by a long, conical crown terminating in a prominent spike. The smallest of the true firs, this species typically has a height of 20–35 m and a dbh of 30–60 cm (an exceptional tree may exceed 50 m in height or have a dbh of 1.5 m), and it can live for up to 250 years. The thin bark, shallow roots and retained lower limbs make this fir susceptible to severe injury from fire.

Subalpine fir grows under a wide variety of stand conditions, from open to dense and in even- or uneven-aged

Subalpine fir

stands. It is very shade tolerant and is a climax species in many locations. Although subalpine fir can be found in pure stands, it is often found mixed with Engelmann spruce, white spruce, mountain hemlock, western hemlock, amabalis fir and western red-cedar.

Subalpine fir's primary value as a wildlife tree results from infection by a broom-forming rust. Large brooms are commonly used for nests and dens by northern flying squirrels in boreal and sub-boreal forests, as resting platforms by martens and fishers, as roosts by northern saw-whet owls and as nest platforms by great horned and great gray owls.

Amabilis Fir (Pacific Silver Fir)
(Abies amabilis): abundant in CWH and MH; uncommon or rare in ESSF and ICH.

Amabilis fir

Grand Fir
(Abies grandis): common in CDF, ICH and IDF; uncommon or rare in CWH and MS.

Amabilis fir (commonly known in the U.S. as Pacific silver fir) and grand fir have much in common ecologically and produce wildlife trees with very similar qualities.

Amabilis fir has a grey trunk with perpendicular branches and a cylindrical to cone-shaped or dome-shaped crown formed by densely packed flat branches that sweep downward and then level outward toward their tips. "Silver" refers to the shining undersides of the needles. This species can (rarely) attain a height of over 45 m and a dbh over 2.3 m on the coast, but it more commonly ranges between 25–40 m, with a dbh of 60–80 cm. Grand fir has a straight, greyish brown trunk, downward sweeping branches that turn upward and a blunt, asymmetrical crown. It can grow to over 70 m tall on the coast and 25–40 m tall in the southern Interior, with a dbh of 50–85 cm (over 2 m on exceptional trees). Both of these species live approximately 400 years.

They are very shade tolerant and are commonly associated with western hemlock and western red-cedar; grand fir is also found growing amongst western white pine and Douglas-fir. Amabilis fir is more susceptible to fire and windthrow than grand fir. Both of these true firs have smooth bark with resin blisters when young, but *amabilis* bark becomes scaly with whitish grey chalky patches with age, whereas *grandis* bark becomes ridged.

When dead or with advanced heart rot, these firs are frequently used by pileated woodpeckers, sapsuckers, nuthatches and chickadees for nesting. Hollow trees are also used by martens, bushy-tailed woodrats and flying squirrels for denning and resting. Martens, Keen's mice and other small mammals use hollow fir logs for dens and rest sites. Pileated woodpeckers and black bears forage on ants found in the decayed wood of these trees.

CEDARS

Western Red-cedar

(Thuja plicata): abundant in CWH and ICH; common in CDF and IDF; uncommon or rare in ESSF, MH, MS, PP and SBS.

Both on the coast and in the Interior, western red-cedar is a significant tree for wildlife tree species, but it takes a very long time to develop the special features needed. It is a large tree with thin, grey to reddish brown bark that tears off in long, fibrous strips, a tapered trunk (often buttressed at the base) and drooping, J-shaped branches with small, scale-like leaves. A western red-cedar growing in the open develops large branches throughout its height and a spreading crown, but old trees that form the forest overstorey often develop multiple tops. When they die, these tops become bleached by the sun and are referred to as "candelabras," "spiketops" or "cake

forks." Western red-cedar ranges in height from a maximum of about 40 m in the Interior to around 60 m on the coast, with a dbh that often exceeds 3 m. It is not uncommon for a western red-cedar to live for 1000 years or more and reach a height of over 40 m, with a dbh of over 5 m, with exceptional trees exceeding 6 m. Very able to withstand competition, western red-cedar can develop an extensive root system in full shade, giving it a strong capacity for surviving in the understorey. Understorey cedars often graft their roots to older overstorey cedars to gain sustenance from them.

Able to invade disturbed sites with its widely distributed seeds or regenerate

Western red-cedar

vegetatively in undisturbed sites, western red-cedar is found in association with many other trees. It can be present in all forest seral stages—its competition-hardiness and longevity generally make it part of any climax forest within its range—but pure stands are rare.

More than 200 fungi species can occur in western red-cedar. However, the species is less susceptible than other conifers to fungal invasion, partly because of its production of thujaplicin, a toxic oil that acts as a fungicide. During its long life, a western red-cedar tree may be subject to many fungal attacks, and eventually, the heartwood substances that provide decay resistance are detoxified by the invading fungi. Over time, butt- and trunk-rot fungi often create the large cavities and hollow trunks that are so highly valuable to wildlife. The western red-cedar can survive with a higher ratio of decayed wood to living wood than any other B.C. tree species, and relative to most tree species, hollow trunks are comparatively common in western red-cedars of sufficient age.

Western red-cedars as a species are extremely important wildlife trees not only because of their longevity and hollow trunks, but also because their wood provides better heat insulation than that of any other conifer species. In areas where western red-cedars grow, black bears seek out the hollow trees for use as dry, warm hibernation dens. Hollow western red-cedars are also used for roosting by bats and Vaux's swifts and for nesting by pileated woodpeckers.

The thick bark on old western red-cedars provides habitat for a variety of insects, which are eaten by insectivorous birds. Pileated woodpeckers forage extensively for carpenter ants on western red cedars. The habitat behind the loose bark of old trees also provides brown creepers with places to build their diminutive, hammock-like nests.

Yellow-cedar
(Chamaecyparis nootkatensis): abundant in MH; common in CWH; uncommon or rare in ESSF.

Yellow-cedar is a high-elevation tree with a tolerance for the cool, wet climate of coastal British Columbia. It can be distinguished by its buttressed trunk with dirty white to greyish brown bark, flattened branches that hang limply downward and a leader that droops similarly to that of western hemlock and western red-cedar. This slow-growing, long-lived tree (up to 2000 years or more) can grow to over 60 m tall (usually

Yellow-cedar

91

20–40 m), with a dbh of around 90 cm (with exceptional specimens exceeding 3 or even 4 m).

In climax forests, yellow-cedar is most often associated with mountain hemlock or, at lower elevations, with western hemlock and western red-cedar. It rarely grows in pure stands.

The full extent to which yellow-cedars provide wildlife habitat is unknown, but this species may have the greatest longevity of any tree in British Columbia, so the habitat that each tree does provide will potentially be available for centuries. Like western red-cedars, yellow-cedars produce natural fungicides: nootkatin, chamic acid and chaminic acid ward off the 80 species of fungi that attack yellow-cedars. As these trees become less vigorous with advanced age, blackstain fungi succeed in invading and heartwood decay sets in. Also like western red-cedars, yellow-cedars develop hollow trunks that black bears use for denning.

LARCHES
Western Larch
(Larix occidentalis): abundant in IDF and MS; common in ICH; uncommon or rare in ESSF and PP.

The largest of B.C.'s three larch species, all deciduous conifers, the western larch is sometimes incorrectly called "tamarack," a name that correctly belongs to *L. laricina* of the northern boreal forest.

The western larch has a long, clear trunk with deeply furrowed, reddish brown bark, short branches and an open pyramidal crown. Its needles turn bright yellow in autumn before being shed. It reaches a height of 30–50 m or even more, with a dbh of about 1 m (approaching 2 m on exceptional trees). Among the conifers, only lodgepole pine can match the 30 cm average annual height gain of this fast-growing species, which is twice the average rate at which Interior Douglas-fir grows. If western larch is overtopped and shaded, however, its growth rate rapidly declines.

In British Columbia, western larch grows only in the province's south-central and southeastern regions. This long-lived tree (up to 900 years) is often found growing with Douglas-fir, and it also grows with paper birch, trembling aspen, ponderosa pine, grand fir, western red-cedar, western hemlock, Engelmann spruce and subalpine fir.

Western larch develops a deep and extensive root system. These roots and the lack of foliage during winter storms make this species extremely windfirm. Nearly all windthrown larches are found to have been infected with root rots before being blown down.

Western larch

Mature western larches are the most fire-resistant of all conifers because of their thick bark, the low flammability of their foliage, their open branching structure and their habit of shedding lower branches.

Pileated woodpecker, black-backed woodpecker and sapsuckers all commonly nest in western larches. Abandoned woodpecker nest holes and natural cavities are used by a variety of birds and mammals, including barred owls, great horned owls, bats and flying squirrels. Witches' brooms in western larches are used by great horned owls and great gray owls for nesting, by martens as rest sites and by northern sawwhet owls as roosts. Decaying western larches frequently contain colonies of carpenter ants, which are eaten by pileated woodpeckers and black bears.

The size, longevity and windfirmness of western larches result in them meeting the ecological needs of many cavity nesters and open nesters. Veteran western larches—because they have large-diameter trunks, usually with heart rot, and large, strong limbs—are especially significant wildlife trees.

Alpine Larch
(Larix lyallii): common in ESSF.

As its name suggests, alpine larch grows in cold, exposed settings near timberline. This deciduous conifer, which can survive at or above the limits of evergreen conifers, marks the upper limit of tree growth in the Engelmann Spruce–Subalpine Fir zone. It is a

Alpine larch

slow-growing tree with a life span averaging 400–500 years. Alpine larch is distinguished from western larch by its gnarled branches, the dense, woolly hairs that cover its twigs, its irregular crown and its lesser height of about 10–20 m, with a dbh of 30–60 cm (over 1 m on exceptional trees). In autumn, its needles turn golden yellow before dropping.

Alpine larch needs full sun and does not compete well with other conifers, but it often grows together with subalpine fir and Engelmann spruce in mixed stands. It can form pure groves above the limits of all other conifers on north-facing sites in the B.C. portions of the Cascade Mountains and the southern Rocky Mountains.

The short growing season at the elevations where alpine larch occurs results in its limited use as a wildlife tree. However, where stem rot occurs, it can create natural cavities that are used by birds and mammals for hiding and shelter in an otherwise exposed environment.

SPRUCES

Engelmann Spruce

(Picea engelmannii): abundant in ESSF and MS; common in ICH; uncommon or rare in IDF and MH.

White Spruce

(Picea glauca): abundant in BWBS, SBPS and SWB; common in SBS; uncommon or rare in ESSF, IDF, MS and PP.

Engelmann spruce and white spruce have similar wildlife tree characteristics, and where the two species meet, they hybridize and become difficult to differentiate.

Engelmann spruce is the most prevalent tree in British Columbia's Interior mountains, where winters are cold, snowfall is heavy and summers are cool. It has a thin, purplish grey bark of loosely attached scales. Open-grown trees are heavily limbed, with thousands of tassel-like branchlets that hang down from the main limbs. The pyramidal crown is normally symmetrical. Engelmann spruce is a long-lived species (typically 500–600 years, but up to 1000 years for some individuals) and grows about 25–50 m tall, with a dbh of 30–90 cm (exceeding 2 m on exceptional trees). Often associated with subalpine fir, it is rarely seen in pure stands.

White spruce usually grows at lower elevations than Engelmann spruce and is found across Canada's sub-boreal regions. The trunk is slightly tapered and the thin, flaky bark is greyish brown. The branches, which often cover the entire trunk and extend to the ground, form a narrow to broadly pyramidal crown. White spruce grows 20–40 m tall (rarely over 50 m), attains a dbh of 40–70 cm and typically lives 250–400 years. It is commonly associated with subalpine fir, Douglas-fir and lodgepole pine.

Both species have shallow root systems and can develop extensive crowns because of their tendency to retain lower limbs as they mature. These two characteristics make them susceptible to windthrow. Their thin bark, shallow

Clockwise from upper left: White spruce tree, bark, needles; Engelmann spruce cones

roots and branching habits also make them vulnerable to fire damage.

Root and trunk rots create wildlife tree features in old spruce trees, particularly in stands with veteran trees that have been missed by fires. Woodpeckers nest in these trees, often foraging in and under the bark. The trunks of both species will appear orange where woodpeckers have recently flaked off the outer bark in their search for bark beetles and other insects. Witches' brooms growing in these trees may be used for nests and dens by northern flying squirrels in boreal and sub-boreal forests, as resting platforms by martens and fishers (especially in riparian areas), as roosts by northern saw-whet owls and as nest platforms by great horned and great gray owls.

Black Spruce
(Picea mariana): abundant in BWBS; common in SBS; uncommon or rare in ICH and SWB.

Black spruce has an extensive range in North America, but in B.C. it is found only in the northern and central Interior, where it is largely restricted to marshes, bogs and peaty areas. It has a slender, tapered trunk, scaly bark and a narrow, irregular (somewhat club-like) crown with drooping branches, the lower ones often reaching the ground. This small, slow-growing conifer can reach 10–20 m in height and 15–40 cm dbh. It generally lives for about 250 years and most commonly grows in pure stands.

Black spruce

Because of its small size, black spruce is not thought to play a significant role for cavity-dwelling wildlife, but its dense foliage is believed to offer thermal and hiding cover for many species.

Sitka Spruce
(Picea sitchensis): abundant in CWH; uncommon or rare in CDF and MH.

Sitka spruce, the world's largest species of spruce, grows in regions with moist maritime air, mild winters and cool summers. It is restricted to a coastal strip stretching from California to northern Alaska, where winter rain and summer fog provide abundant year-round moisture. Sitka spruce has thin, reddish brown to greyish brown bark and large, long, horizontal main branches that hang with moss, nearly reaching to the ground on open-grown trees. The needles are very stiff and sharp. The broad, symmetrical crown is not easily seen on mature trees. This spruce commonly grows up to 70 m in height, with a dbh of 2 m, and can live 700–800 years, but exceptional trees can approach 100 m in height or have a dbh over 4 m.

Sitka spruce usually grows in mixed stands with western hemlock, western red-cedar, amabilis fir, red alder, bigleaf maple and black cottonwood. Its longevity eventually gives Sitka spruce the dominant position in the canopy of spruce-hemlock stands.

Unlike some conifers, it can grow new branches along the lower trunk when the availability of light increases. As a result, exposed Sitka spruce trees are very heavily branched, and the dense, drooping branches can shelter wildlife from wind and rain.

Windthrow is probably the most damaging natural disturbance for Sitka spruce, but fallen trees are likely to have been previously weakened by root or butt rots.

The humid climate within the range of this species encourages the growth of mosses and epiphytes, and over time, the limbs of Sitka spruce often become thickly covered with moss. The mossy branches and dense foliage, which helps to screen nests from the view of predators, may provide the best breeding habitat for the open-nesting marbled murrelet, which does not build a nest but instead seeks naturally flat upper canopy sites on mossy branches. Great blue herons and bald eagles construct their immense nests in large Sitka spruce as well. On the north coast, red-breasted sapsuckers are especially attracted to this species.

PINES
Lodgepole Pine
(Pinus contorta var. *latifolia*):
abundant in BWBS, ESSF, IDF, MS, SBPS and SBS; common in CDF, CWH, ICH and SWB; uncommon or rare in BG, PP and MH.

Lodgepole pine has the widest range of environmental tolerance of all North American conifers. Because it grows under a wide variety of climatic conditions, it is present in all of the forested biogeoclimatic zones in B.C. It is most widespread in the cool, dry part of the province's Interior. British Columbia has the majority of North America's lodgepole pine.

Lodgepole pine is a medium-sized conifer with a slender trunk and thin, orangy brown to grey bark. The limbs are generally of small diameter and the open crown is pyramidal. This tree is most easily distinguished by its long needles bundled in groups of two. Lodgepole pine can reach heights of

Sitka spruce

20–40 m (occasionally more), with an average dbh of approximately 30 cm (over 90 cm on exceptional trees).

Note that the closely related but smaller shore pine (*Pinus contorta* var. *contorta*), which is restricted to peat bogs and rock cliffs on the coast, has a twisted or contorted form. Because of its small size, given the better choices available, shore pine seldom serves as a wildlife tree and is not further discussed in this guide.

Fire and mountain pine beetles play major roles in the life cycle of lodgepole pine. Although a forest fire will easily kill even a mature tree because of its thin bark, the intense heat helps to release the seeds from their resin-sealed cones. Between forest fires, large numbers of unopened cones accumulate in stands,

resulting in extremely high densities of reseeding after fire sweeps through an area. As a result, lodgepole pine often grows in extensive pure stands, but it can also occur mixed with other conifers.

Forest fires and mountain pine beetle infestations usually limit the life span of lodgepole pine to 100–140 years. Fire creates optimal conditions for the reestablishment of a new lodgepole stand. Mountain pine beetles can kill all or most of the lodgepole pine in a stand, which may regenerate in lodgepole pine in very dry climate areas or in white spruce, Engelmann spruce, balsam or aspen if these species are already in the understorey or a seed source is available.

Because lodgepole pine commonly forms extensive, even-aged stands, it is the only tree available to wildlife tree–dependent species in some areas. Northern flickers, various other woodpeckers and chickadees occasionally excavate nests in it where more favoured trees are not available. Black-backed, American three-toed, hairy and pileated woodpeckers often forage under the bark for mountain pine beetle larvae. Throughout the Interior, lodgepole pine may be infected by dwarf mistletoe. Large witches' brooms caused by western dwarf mistletoe provide important nesting for flying squirrels and resting features for martens and fishers.

Western White Pine
(Pinus monticola): common in CWH and ICH; uncommon or rare in CDF, ESSF, IDF, MH and MS.

Clockwise from top left: Lodgepole pine male cone, female cone, tree

Western white pine

part of our forests, even if as a minor component.

Western white pine is not used extensively by wildlife tree–dependent species, in part because of its relative scarcity. However, it merits inclusion here because of both its size and its known use by woodpeckers for nesting and foraging and by bats for roosting.

Ponderosa Pine
(Pinus ponderosa): abundant in IDF and PP; uncommon or rare in BG and ICH.

Western white pine is a large conifer with a straight, silvery grey trunk; the bark of mature trees, unlike the bark of any other conifer, is checkered or deeply cut into squares. The needles are bundled in groups of five, the branches are conspicuously whorled, and the symmetrical crown is slender and thin. This attractive pine can live 300–400 years and reach heights of 30–50 m, with a dbh greater than 1 m. The largest western white pines attain heights of more than 60 m and a dbh approaching 2 m.

Typically associated with a wide variety of other conifers, western white pine is seldom more than a minor component in a stand. It is an early-seral species that establishes naturally after disturbances. Western white pine is severely afflicted by white pine blister rust, a pathogen introduced to British Columbia in the early 1900s. As a result, the abundance of this tree species has declined significantly. Crossbreeding programs using the few naturally resistant white pines have had some success in producing resistant seeds. The authors hope that these efforts will help ensure that this majestic pine remains

Ponderosa pine, sometimes called "yellow pine," is an aesthetically pleasing tree with a straight, slightly tapered trunk, orangy brown to cinnamon-coloured bark, stout branches and a broad, open crown. Its needles are bundled in groups of three. Ponderosa pine can live 300–400 years and usually attains heights of 15–30 m and a dbh of 1–1.5 m. Some individuals grow up to 50 m tall or have a dbh of more than 1.7 m. Southern British Columbia is at the northern limit of this species' range, which extends down to southern California.

At low elevations, ponderosa pine is a climax tree species that often grows in pure stands composed of many small, even-aged clusters. At high elevations, it is frequently associated with Douglas-fir, but it is also found in competition with lodgepole pine and western larch.

Fires have a profound effect on the establishment and success of ponderosa pine. Before humans began intervening by introducing coordinated fire suppression activities, understorey fires occurred an estimated 5–20 years in those areas where ponderosa pine grows. The thick bark of large ponderosa pines offers protection from understorey burns, and these trees will survive even if up to half the crown is scorched. Young trees developing in the understorey, including the seedlings of shade-tolerant competitors, do not survive this treatment, so frequent understorey fires that cause some crown damage favour the survival and development of relatively open forests dominated by ponderosa pine. Ponderosa pine will establish after a major natural disturbance, such as wildfire, but because of its need for full sunlight, it cannot establish in the understorey (except where it is very dry). Now, because of successful fire suppression, most ponderosa pine stands have a well-developed understorey, most often of Douglas-fir, rather than the open, park-like conditions that were maintained by frequent understorey burning. In the absence of fire, over time this pine tends to become a minor species as shade-tolerant species take over.

Ponderosa pine

Ponderosa pine produces large cones with heavy seeds, and they do not disperse far from the seed tree. Good cone crops, which depend on the weather and the success of pollination, are sporadic, occurring every 4–5 years, and the best seed production is from large, dominant trees in open situations. Ponderosa pine seeds are a critical part of the white-headed woodpecker's diet and are also eaten by many other birds and mammals.

The bark of a mature ponderosa pine resembles pieces of a jigsaw puzzle layered randomly on top of each other. The intricacy of this "puzzle bark" provides attractive habitat for many insects and thus a rich feeding ground for insectivorous birds.

Woodpeckers commonly forage in and under the bark of ponderosa pine; they greatly prefer this tree for nesting as well. Because of the rapid decay in the thick sapwood layer, they often excavate their nest cavities in it rather than in the heartwood, the usual location in other tree species. The white-headed woodpecker is highly dependent on this species for nesting as well as feeding (seeds plus insects), and the Lewis's woodpecker appears to favour ponderosa pine as well.

Old woodpecker nest holes and natural cavities in ponderosa pines are used by a wide variety of secondary cavity users, including the flammulated owl, whose habitat is restricted to ponderosa pine and Interior Douglas-fir forests. When located close to water, these trees are of very high value to nesting goldeneyes and buffleheads.

Spaces under the thick bark of ponderosa pines are common roosting sites for bats.

Ponderosa pine is an exceptional wildlife tree because of its size, bark characteristics and other features that develop with age, as well as its association with low-elevation grasslands where trees are relatively scarce. However, throughout its range, the number of ponderosa pine stands is declining. Valuable old wildlife trees are being lost and too few young ponderosa pines are being allowed to live long enough to replace the veterans.

Douglas-fir

(Pseudotsuga menziesii var. menziesii): Coastal subspecies—abundant in CDF and CWH; uncommon or rare in MH.

(Pseudotsuga menziesii var. glauca): Interior subspecies—abundant in IDF and MS; common in ICH, PP and SBS; uncommon or rare in BG, ESSF and SBPS.

Douglas-fir is unique to western North America. The northern half of its range extends into British Columbia. Both the coastal subspecies and the Interior subspecies have long, cylindrical trunks with thick, dark brown bark, thick, drooping branches and pyramidal or spire-shaped crowns. The needles of the coastal Douglas-fir are yellowish green, and those of the Interior subspecies are bluish green. The cones of the Interior Douglas-fir are smaller than those of the coastal subspecies.

The coastal subspecies is the larger of the two, reaching heights of 70 m or more (sometimes exceeding 90 m) with a dbh of 1.5–2 m (rarely over 4 m). Coastal Douglas-fir trees usually live for more than 500 years and occasionally exceed 1000 years. The Interior Douglas-fir is a smaller, shorter-lived tree, averaging 25–35 m (rarely 45 m) in height with a dbh of about 1 m (nearly 2 m on exceptional trees) and a maximum age of less than 400 years.

In the Coastal Douglas-fir biogeoclimatic zone, Douglas-fir is the most common tree species in upland forests. Established seedlings prefer direct sunlight for rapid growth, but Douglas-fir is somewhat tolerant of shade and able to regenerate under canopies of open mature and partly open stands. It is commonly associated with western redcedar, grand fir, arbutus, Garry oak and red alder. In the Interior Douglas-fir zone, pure Douglas-fir stands with open canopies are common as a result of historic fires that eliminated competitors without killing the thick-barked mature Douglas-firs.

Douglas-fir

Douglas-fir is an extremely important wildlife tree. Woodpeckers and nuthatches frequently forage on the corky bark, which becomes increasingly thick, rough and furrowed with age, providing good habitat for insects. Woodpeckers also excavate into the inner wood. Many birds and mammals consume the seeds of this species. Dead and dying Douglas-firs provide nesting opportunities for a wide variety of woodpeckers and secondary cavity users, including flammulated owls, American kestrels, goldeneyes, buffle-heads and mergansers. They are also used for roosting by bats and for den-ning by martens and fishers. Witches' brooms in Douglas-firs provide sites for nesting, roosting and resting for great horned, great gray and northern saw-whet owls.

HEMLOCKS

Western Hemlock

(Tsuga heterophylla): abundant in CWH and ICH; common in MH; uncommon or rare in CDF, ESSF, IDF, MS and SBS.

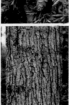

Western hemlock

Mountain Hemlock

(Tsuga mertensiana): abundant in MH; common in ESSF; uncommon or rare in ICH and CWH.

Mountain hemlock

Western hemlock and mountain hemlock are similar in their perform-ance as wildlife trees. Western hemlock is the most widespread tree in British Columbia's humid coastal regions and in the wet mountain regions of the Interior. Mountain hemlock grows in cold, subalpine areas on the coast and in the Interior, at elevations above those where western hemlock is found.

Both species of hemlock have reddish brown to greyish brown bark, slender branches that sweep downward, feathery foliage and narrow crowns. Western hemlock is most commonly distin-guished by its prominent, drooping leader; the leader of mountain hemlock is only slightly drooping. Western hem-lock commonly lives for 400–500 years and can reach heights of up to 60 m (very rarely reaching 75 m) and a dbh of

75–100 cm (nearly 3 m on exceptional trees). Mountain hemlock, which can live up to 800 years, is a slower-growing species. It can grow up to 40 m tall (rarely exceeding 50 m) and 60–100 cm dbh (nearly 2 m on exceptional trees), but in the harshest subalpine climates it assumes a stunted form.

In the Coastal Western Hemlock zone, western hemlock can occur in pure or mixed stands and is commonly associated with western red-cedar, Sitka spruce and yellow-cedar. It is highly tolerant of shade and regenerates freely under the canopy of mature stands. In the Interior Cedar–Hemlock zone, western hemlock forms mature climax forests and also mixes with western red-cedar, white pine, Engelmann spruce and subalpine fir. In the Mountain Hemlock zone, mountain hemlock and amabilis fir commonly regenerate together under the canopy of a mature forest; however, mountain hemlock eventually establishes itself as the climax species.

Shallow roots, with an abundance of fine roots near the soil surface and in the duff layer, make both western hemlock and mountain hemlock susceptible to windthrow. Fires tend to be naturally infrequent or absent in most of the wet regions that support hemlocks. However, because of their shallow roots and thin bark, when fires do occur, both hemlocks are easily damaged.

Both hemlock species are also vulnerable to a number of root rots and stem rots, and they may be killed by defoliating insects or have their growth slowed by mistletoe parasitism. Under humid conditions, hemlock decays rapidly. Once dead, these trees do not persist as long as the cedars or Douglas-fir, usually standing for only 20–30 years after death. Their rate of decay is similar to that of true firs but slower than for the hardwoods.

The abundance of hemlocks makes them important as wildlife trees, but they are generally not the first choice for cavity nesters if large, old trees of other species are available. This disfavour may be because the shelter provided by the thin bark, thin limbs and wispy foliage is not as dry and warm as that provided by other trees, an important consideration in the cold, wet habitats where hemlocks grow. Northern flickers and pileated, American three-toed and hairy woodpeckers regularly use old hemlocks with broken boles and heart rot for nesting and roosting. However, the rapid rate of decay of dead hemlocks means their value to secondary cavity users is relatively limited. Woodpeckers also forage under hemlock bark, and brown creepers, great blue herons and bald eagles sometimes use western hemlock for nesting.

Hardwoods

Eight species provide the majority of the hardwood component of wildlife trees in British Columbia. These broad-leafed trees are all deciduous, with the exception of arbutus, which is an evergreen species. Hardwoods are especially important to many primary cavity excavators.

Bigleaf Maple
(Acer macrophyllum): common in CDF and CWH; uncommon or rare in IDF.

Bigleaf maple grows as far north as the Nimpkish Valley on Vancouver Island and a similar latitude on the adjacent mainland coast, extending up

Bigleaf maple

as four times the mass of the tree's own leaves. Rain-soaked epiphytes increase the risk of windthrow and breakage of major limbs.

Bigleaf maple needs moist conditions to establish and does better under an overstorey than in clear-cuts or large openings. Although it is not a pioneer species, bigleaf maple is present in many stands, and it responds quickly with multiple sprouting if felled.

Their branching habit makes mature bigleaf maples good suppliers of natural cavities. Limb breakage, a common form of damage to these trees, allows fungi to invade, softening the wood and resulting in large natural cavities that are subsequently used by various birds and mammals.

Red Alder
(Alnus rubra): abundant in CDF and CWH.

the Klinaklini Valley. Its range extends as far south as California. It is a relatively large tree, with bark that becomes greyish brown with age. The ridged, five-lobed leaves can grow as big as dinner plates. Bigleaf maple is usually multi-stemmed, and in open areas, the crown spread can equal the height. It can live up to 200 years and reach heights of 35 m (very rarely over 45 m), with a dbh that commonly exceeds 50 cm (reaching 3 m or more on exceptional trees).

In British Columbia, bigleaf maple is found at elevations below 1000 m and is usually associated with Douglas-fir, arbutus, black cottonwood and red alder.

In wet climates, bigleaf maples support an abundance of epiphytes—mosses and lichens that grow on a tree's trunk and branches. The total mass of these epiphytes can be as much

Red alder is the most common hardwood on the B.C. coast. Its thin, grey bark is often covered with white patches of lichen, and it has dull green, deciduous leaves. Clusters of small, brown cones remain on the tree over winter. At maturity it reaches a height of 25–35 m (over 40 m in rare cases) and attains a dbh of up to 75 cm (with exceptional trees exceeding 2 m). This relatively short-lived species matures at 60–70 years, with a maximum age of approximately 100 years.

Red alder occurs in both pure and mixed stands. It is widely distributed as

Red alder

Red alder is not a preferred wildlife tree species, because the trees are large enough and in suitable condition for most wildlife tree–dependent species only for a relatively short period of time. For the most part, alders are used as wildlife trees only when there are no other alternatives, but they do receive some use. Great blue herons often nest in alder stands. Downy, hairy and pileated woodpeckers have been observed nesting in red alders, and wood ducks and western screech-owls do make use of their abandoned cavities when they are available.

Red alder provides good firewood and, except when being used for heron rookeries, it should be cut in preference to trees that are more critical to wildlife, such as Douglas-fir veterans. From a habitat conservation perspective, red alder is one of the safest choices for the firewood buyer.

Arbutus
(Arbutus menziesii): common in CDF; uncommon or rare in CWH.

Arbutus is British Columbia's only native broad-leafed evergreen tree.

a minor species in stands dominated by western hemlock, Sitka spruce, western red-cedar, Douglas-fir or black cottonwood. Pure stands of alder are typically confined to streambanks, floodplains, recently cleared land and old logging roads. Alder is an aggressive, fast-growing tree that thrives on disturbed soils, which it improves by "fixing" atmospheric nitrogen (bacteria in root nodules convert this gas into an essential plant nutrient).

Young seedlings can withstand partial shade, but saplings die without direct sunlight. Among B.C.'s trees, red alder is rivalled in its rapid juvenile growth only by black cottonwood. Only those alders that maintain their height advantage and remain dominant or codominant in the forest canopy will survive. Old trees are susceptible to heart rot and are rapidly decayed by fungi once dead.

Restricted to areas where year-round temperatures remain mild, in British Columbia it grows along the southern tip and east coast of Vancouver Island, on the Gulf Islands and on the facing mainland coast, generally within 8 km of the seashore. Its range extends south along the coast to California.

This highly attractive tree is easily recognized by the thin, reddish brown outer bark that peels off to reveal the

Arbutus

the root crown yet rarely kills the tree. By sending up new sprouts, arbutus is able to retain site dominance after neighbouring conifers are killed by fire.

As a wildlife tree, the main contribution of arbutus is the natural cavities created when large branches die and break off at the main trunk, allowing rot to enter and decay the heartwood. These cavities are primarily used by small secondary cavity users such as swallows.

Paper Birch (White Birch)
(Betula papyrifera): common in BWBS, ICH, IDF and SBS; uncommon or rare in BG, CDF, CWH, MS and PP.

beautiful shiny younger bark beneath and also by its heavy branches, leathery leaves, white spring flowers and orangy red autumn berries. An arbutus tree can uncommonly exceed 25 m in height (rarely surpassing 30 m) and attain a dbh of 80 cm or more (record trees can approach 2.5 m). Some arbutus trees have been aged at 250 years, and it is estimated that certain trees may live for 400–500 years. When crowded, arbutus tends to grow straight, but its most common form is a crooked or leaning trunk with multiple stems and irregular branches.

Arbutus is typically associated with Garry oak and Douglas-fir. It is most common on south- and west-facing sites, where it gains an advantage because it is drought-tolerant and able to extract moisture from soil more effectively than most other trees. Arbutus is easily damaged by frost, a factor that limits its distribution.

The thin bark makes arbutus susceptible to fire, which causes die-back to

Paper birch

Paper birch, also called "white birch" or "canoe birch," is widely distributed within B.C., but it is most common in the southern Interior and northern Interior. This birch is best known for its white to coppery brown bark that peels in papery strips. It has upward-angled branches and is often multi-stemmed with an open crown. Exceptional specimens of this fast-growing hardwood, which rarely lives more than 140 years, can grow up to nearly 30 m in height or have a dbh exceeding 1.5m, but trees 15–25m in height with a dbh of 0.5–1m are more typical.

Paper birch is well adapted to cold climates and prefers well-drained, moist sites. Its seeds are readily dispersed by the wind and establish best in partial shade. If paper birch is disturbed or cut, especially when young, it can also reproduce from suckers, but the survival potential of the suckers decreases with tree age.

Paper birch usually occurs as a minor species in mixed conifer–hardwood forests, but it can form pure, even-aged stands after logging or fire. These even-aged stands usually last only one generation before being replaced by shade-tolerant conifers. Paper birches hold a minor position in spruce-dominated conifer stands, but they provide valuable wildlife tree habitat, particularly in even-aged stands that develop following a disturbance, because they mature and die before the conifers in that stand. Paper birch is easily damaged, and decay is rapid once fungi enter and become established.

Paper birch is commonly used for nesting by northern flickers, sapsuckers and downy, hairy and pileated woodpeckers. It is a favourite of weak excavators such as chickadees and nuthatches, because the bark can provide structural strength while the heartwood is already soft and easy to excavate. The rupturing of the bark as sapsuckers drill their characteristic rows of sap wells in a birch can help bring about decay.

POPLARS
Trembling Aspen
(Populus tremuloides): abundant in BWBS, IDF and SBS; common in ICH, MS and PP; uncommon or rare in BG, CDF, CWH, ESSF, SBPS and SWB.

The most widely distributed tree in North America, trembling aspen is found in all of the biogeoclimatic zones in the Interior of British Columbia. It has greenish grey to blackish bark and a short, rounded crown. This fast-growing, short-lived tree can reach heights of 30 m

Trembling aspen

Trembling aspen

generation or as long as 1000 years in the absence of conifer seed sources. Extensive stands of aspen in an area are usually attributed to repeated wildfires.

With age, trembling aspen becomes increasingly susceptible to stem and root infections. As on all trees, fungal fruiting bodies (conks) on the trunk are reliable indicators of decaying heartwood. Relative to its abundance, trembling aspen receives a disproportionately high level of use by primary cavity excavators and secondary cavity users. It is common for mature aspen to have soft, decayed inner wood suitable for nest hole excavation while the outer sapwood is still alive and sound, thus providing a protective and thermal buffer for cavities.

Trembling aspen is host to more than 300 species of insects that cause damage by boring into the wood, defoliating the branches or sucking the sap. These abundant insects provide a source of food for insectivorous birds.

Although trembling aspen lacks the longevity of most conifers, it is a favoured wildlife tree. Even in conifer forests, where it is often only a minor component, it nevertheless provides excellent potential nest sites during seral stages when the conifers have yet to develop decay.

Trembling aspen is the nest tree of choice for yellow-bellied sapsuckers, and it is also frequently used by red-naped, red-breasted and Williamson's sapsuckers, pileated woodpeckers, hairy woodpeckers and northern flickers. Boreal chickadees, pygmy nuthatches and red-breasted nuthatches also nest and roost in aspen. With all these primary cavity excavators at work, it is no surprise that northern saw-whet owls, Vaux's swifts, tree swallows, American kestrels, flying squirrels and fishers all use aspen cavities. Cavities in aspens located near water are often occupied by nesting wood ducks, buffleheads, goldeneyes or mergansers.

or more and a dbh of 50–75 cm (rarely over 1 m) in its life span of usually less than 200 years.

Trembling aspen can grow singly or in groves of multi-stemmed, genetically identical clones that sprout as root suckers from the extensive shallow root system—an action promoted by harvesting or wildfire. Each group of clones constitutes a multi-stemmed individual that may be thousands of years old and up to 40 ha in size. In spring, all the stems in a clone will leaf together and in autumn, the leaves turn colour as a group. Suckers from existing clones are quick to reestablish site dominance after a disturbance, making successful reproduction from seed rare. Also, the short period of seed viability seldom coincides with environmental conditions suitable for germination.

This species frequently occurs as a minor hardwood component of boreal and sub-boreal conifer forests. In other areas, it forms pure stands or is a significant component in mixedwood forests. Trembling aspen is an aggressive early successional species and is very intolerant of shade, so even-aged stands are common. In the absence of disturbance, most stands are eventually replaced by shade-tolerant conifers. This succession to conifers may take only a single aspen

Black Cottonwood
(Populus balsamifera ssp. *trichocarpa):* common in CDF, CWH, ICH and SBS; uncommon or rare in BG, BWBS, ESSF, IDF, MS, PP and SBPS.

Balsam Poplar
(Populus balsamifera ssp. *balsamifera):* common in BWBS; uncommon or rare in SBS and SWB.

Black cottonwood and balsam poplar are discussed together because their physiology is very similar—they grow and decay in a similar manner—though they play different roles as wildlife trees. Black cottonwood has an extensive range across the province; it is associated with riparian areas and is used by a much larger number of wildlife species than balsam poplar. Balsam poplar is restricted to northeastern British Columbia.

Black cottonwood is the largest North American poplar and the largest, and possibly fastest growing, hardwood in British Columbia. It has deeply furrowed, dark grey bark, resinous, reddish brown buds and a heavy, open, irregular crown with large branches. Black cottonwood commonly grows to about 40 m in height and 100 cm dbh, and it rarely exceeds 200 years of age. Exceptional specimens around 3 m dbh and about 400 years old have recently been discovered in southeastern B.C., and a few individuals in the Fraser Valley are 40–60 m in height and have a dbh of 3–4 m. Balsam poplar is almost indistinguishable from black cottonwood, albeit somewhat smaller in stature, typically reaching 10–15 m in height and occasionally 25 m.

On alluvial sites at low elevations along the coast, black cottonwood forms

Black cottonwood

pure stands, and it is also found in mixed stands with most other conifers and hardwoods, such as red alder, Douglas-fir, western hemlock, western red-cedar, Sitka spruce, grand fir and bigleaf maple. In riparian areas in dry climates, black cottonwood is one of the dominant hardwoods. The wildlife tree habitat it provides in the dry valleys of the southern Interior, where large rotten trunks are scarce, is critically important.

Black cottonwood grows best in full sunlight, and its initial rapid growth allows it to outcompete other tree species to achieve site dominance. Black cottonwood is often damaged by ice, snow, wind and also easily damaged or killed by fire. Once dead, it succumbs quickly to decay by nearly 70 species of fungi.

Balsam poplar grows best in areas where the water table is high. On floodplains, balsam poplar occurs in pure stands. It is also commonly associated with trembling aspen, paper birch, subalpine fir and white spruce. This species produces large seed crops almost every year

'sam poplar

and also reproduces vigorously through root suckers, though not as prolifically as trembling aspen. Balsam poplar is an early-seral species with low shade tolerance, but it grows fast and often becomes the largest tree in the stand. In the absence of a major disturbance, it is often replaced over time by shade-tolerant conifers, usually white spruce.

As balsam poplar and black cottonwood age, they develop thick, deeply furrowed bark, which offers good foraging habitat for insectivorous birds. They also develop a crown of large limbs suitable for use by large open nesters. When the thick bark pulls away from the trunk of a dead tree, the space behind it may be occupied by roosting bats or nesting brown creepers.

In riparian ecosystems in the dry areas of the province, such as the Bunchgrass, Ponderosa Pine and Interior Douglas-fir zones, black cottonwoods are often the only large trees for several kilometers in any direction, and the presence of old cottonwoods can be the limiting factor in the distribution of some wildlife tree–dependent species. Ospreys, bald eagles and great blue herons are highly dependent on cottonwoods for nest sites. Lewis's woodpeckers, pileated woodpeckers, northern flickers and other woodpeckers commonly use cottonwoods for nesting and roosting. Many secondary cavity users, such as western screech-owls, northern saw-whet owls, western bluebirds, bats and black bears, use old woodpecker holes and natural cavities in the trunks and branches of black cottonwoods. Because of the proximity of these trees to water, goldeneyes, buffleheads and wood ducks commonly nest in cavities in black cottonwoods.

The varied habitat features of black cottonwood and balsam poplar and their location near water in riparian ecosystems make them extremely important wildlife trees. Their value is significantly out of proportion to their abundance.

Garry Oak
(Quercus garryana): common in CDF; uncommon or rare in CWH.

Garry oak is the only oak tree native to British Columbia. It is common within the Coastal Douglas-fir zone on the eastern margin of southern Vancouver Island and on the Gulf Islands, and it is also found in the Coastal Western Hemlock zone near Yale and on Sumas Mountain. These B.C. occurrences represent the northern limit of the Garry oak's range, which extends south to California. It is also known as "Oregon white oak" because of its abundance in that state.

This beautiful tree has a short, thick trunk with deeply furrowed and ridged, light grey bark that supports a spreading crown composed of long, heavy, gnarled branches. Garry oak can grow up to 25 m tall and 60–100 cm dbh in good, deep soils (exceptional trees can exceed 30 m in height or have a dbh over 1.6 m), but it is often short and crooked in rocky habitats. The crown width of Garry oak often exceeds the tree's height.

Garry oak frequently grows on rock outcrops, where it forms mixed stands with arbutus. It can tolerate some shading, but it will die if over-topped by conifers. Prior to European settlement, fire played an important role in preventing conifers from dominating open parkland Garry oak stands. The suppression of fire has significantly reduced the extent of historical Garry oak parklands, which are now being overgrown by Douglas-firs.

There are 110 pathogens associated with Garry oak, as well as hundreds of insect species, some of which can defoliate this tree for a season. Garry oak has very dense wood, so it begins to yield cavities only as rot takes hold where branches have broken or where there is damage to the trunk. Most of the old oaks that provide cavities for wildlife today date back to pre-settlement times. In addition to providing nesting and roosting habitat for some primary cavity excavators and secondary cavity users, Garry oaks are also sometimes used by great blue herons for nesting.

Garry oak

PART 5

KNOWING THE WILDLIFE

UNDERSTANDING THE SPECIES ACCOUNTS

The 66 species accounts in this guide are divided into three "guilds" based on similarities in their breeding habitat requirements:

- **Primary cavity excavators:** birds that excavate their own holes in standing dead or live trees for their nesting and roosting needs.
- **Secondary cavity users:** birds and mammals that require either abandoned cavities that were created by primary cavity excavators or natural cavities (formed when trees break, lose large branches or have sufficient internal decay to allow species to enter the tree) to nest, den or roost. Some species in this guild depend on features such as spaces behind bark or witches' brooms for these purposes.
- **Open nesters:** birds that either build a large, open, cup-shaped or platform-like nest supported by large branches or a forked tree trunk or that nest directly on a wildlife tree feature.

Sources used to compile the information on range and distribution, identifying characteristics, habitat requirements and management considerations for each species account are listed in the References section at the end of this guide.

Ecoregion and Biogeoclimatic Ecosystem Classification

Indicator bars in each account show the ecoprovinces and biogeoclimatic zones where that wildlife species regularly occurs. A solid colour indicates that the species is common in all or some part of the ecoprovince or biogeoclimatic zone, and a lighter tint means that it is uncommon or rare in the zone. Possible occurrence is indicated by a question mark.

The ecoregion and biogeoclimatic classification systems complement each other, making it possible to describe the range of a wildlife species using the broad physiography of the ecoregion along with the general climate and the major vegetative features of the biogeoclimatic zone. These classification systems also provide a framework for extending knowledge and research from one ecosystem to similar ecosystems, thus allowing us to predict with greater confidence, using experience from other localities, the effects of planned management activities on the behaviour and response of wildlife species.

ECOPROVINCES

Ecoprovinces are part of a hierarchical ecological classification system based on differences in interactions between macroclimatic processes and physiography. At the broadest geographic scale, three globally recognized terrestrial zones (ecodomains) pertain to British Columbia and adjacent jurisdictions: humid-temperate, dry and polar. These ecodomains are divided into ecoprovinces that reflect differences in macroclimate and regional landscape physiography. These ecoprovinces are further divided into ecoregions and, finally, ecosections. However, the wildlife species distributions in this guide refer only to B.C.'s nine terrestrial ecoprovinces, omitting any that might be found entirely in other nearby jurisdictions (see map, p. 113).

BIOGEOCLIMATIC ZONES

The biogeoclimatic ecosystem classification (BEC) system divides land into areas that are influenced by the same regional climate and characterized by specific climax vegetative associations (plant communities at the final or climax stage of succession). A biogeoclimatic zone is defined as an area with a certain typical combination of major species of trees, shrubs, herbs and mosses (the "bio" part of the term), characteristic soil-forming processes ("geo") and a broadly homogenous macroclimate ("climatic").

British Columbia has 14 biogeoclimatic zones (see map, p. 114). Most of them are named after the dominant climax tree species in the ecosystem. Appendix 3 provides a list of the wildlife tree–dependent animals that inhabit each of the 13 treed biogeoclimatic zones. Biogeoclimatic zones are also used in the descriptions of tree distributions in Part 4 of this guide.

Status

The status section gives the provincial and local (if known) abundance, residency and, if applicable, risk category (or categories) for each species as of this writing. (In some cases, this information is broken down by subspecies or population.) The term "risk" refers to the potential of extinction, meaning the complete elimination of the species (or subspecies or population), or to extirpation, meaning its elimination from a defined area, in this case British Columbia.

Birds and bats may be described as either residents or migrants. Residents remain in British Columbia throughout the year. Migrants spend only part of the year in British Columbia, typically arriving in late winter or spring and leaving in late summer or autumn, though some species overwinter here but breed farther north. A species that is present in an area only at a certain time of year may also be referred to as a visitor.

Species abundance is described using a subjective ranking of abundant, common, uncommon and rare. For birds, the abundance designations are modified from the ones used in *The Birds of British Columbia, Vol. I* (p. 148).

Species Abundance Chart

TERM	FREQUENCY OF OCCURRENCE PER LOCALITY [1,2]
abundant	200–1000 individuals per day
common	20–200 individuals per day
uncommon	1–6 individuals per day
rare	1–6 individuals per season

1. A locality is an area that can be surveyed during one visit—as far as you can see with binoculars—and not a defined area.

2. In this system, frequencies that fall outside the listed terms are handled by prefixing words such as "very" or "somewhat."

British Columbia's Terrestrial Ecoprovinces

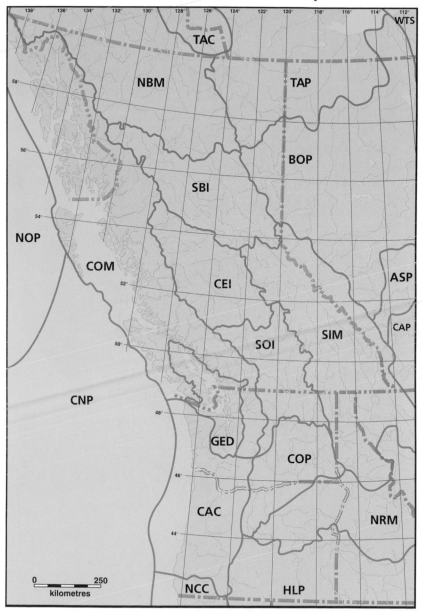

ASP	Aspen Parkland	**NBM**	Northern Boreal Moutains
BOP	Boreal Plains	**NCC**	Northern California Coast Ranges
CAC	Cascades and Coast	**NOP**	Northeast Pacific
COM	Coast and Mountains	**NRM**	Northern Rocky Mountain Forest
CAP	Canadian Prairie	**SBi**	Sub-Boreal Interior
CEI	Central Interior	**SIM**	Southern Interior Mountains
CNP	Central Northeast Pacific	**SOI**	Southern Interior
COP	Columbia Plateau	**TAC**	Taiga Cordillera
GED	Georgia Depression	**TAP**	Taiga Plains
HLP	High Lava Plains	**WTS**	Western Taiga Shield

113

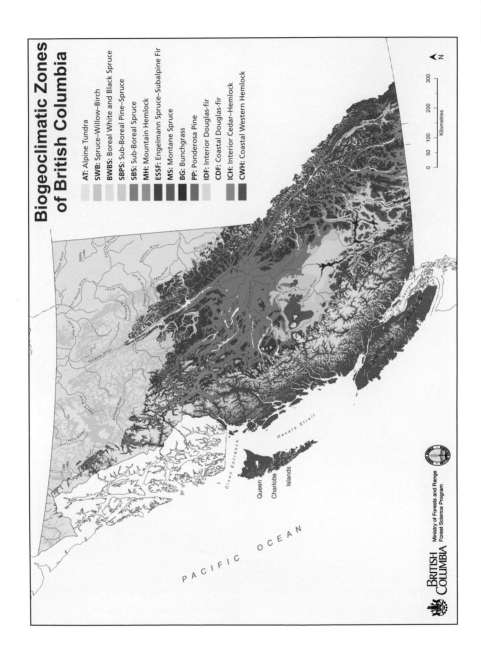

Biogeoclimatic Zones of British Columbia

AT: Alpine Tundra
SWB: Spruce–Willow–Birch
BWBS: Boreal White and Black Spruce
SBPS: Sub-Boreal Pine–Spruce
SBS: Sub-Boreal Spruce
MH: Mountain Hemlock
ESSF: Engelmann Spruce–Subalpine Fir
MS: Montane Spruce
BG: Bunchgrass
PP: Ponderosa Pine
IDF: Interior Douglas-fir
CDF: Coastal Douglas-fir
ICH: Interior Cedar–Hemlock
CWH: Coastal Western Hemlock

BRITISH COLUMBIA   Ministry of Forests and Range
Forest Science Program

When abundance terms are applied to the mammals in the guide, they take their dictionary meanings; they are not quantified as in the system developed for birds.

Risk Designations
Provincial Risk Categories

Conservation priorities are assigned to indigenous species (or subspecies or populations) that provincially are considered to be *at risk* in either of two categories. "Red-listed" refers to species that are extirpated (no longer present in an area historically occupied), endangered (facing imminent extinction or extirpation) or threatened (likely to be endangered if the limiting factors affecting their vulnerability are not reversed). "Blue-listed" refers to species that are considered to be vulnerable (of special concern because of characteristics that make them particularly sensitive to human activities or natural events), but not extirpated, endangered or threatened.

The criteria used to place an animal on either list include population size, population trend, distribution, levels of threats and reproductive potential. Some species are *at risk* because of habitat loss (leading to scarcity of resources or vulnerability as a result of being concentrated into a small area) or because of the presence of introduced non-native species (which compete aggressively for resources or introduce new predation pressures). Species may also be listed if the scientific knowledge regarding their habitat requirements is insufficient or if sightings are infrequent, as is the case for some bats.

As this guide is nearing publication, British Columbia has 68 Red-listed and 68 Blue-listed breeding birds and terrestrial mammals, bringing the *at risk* total to 136. Together, the 12 Red-listed and 11 Blue-listed birds and mammals known to be dependent on wildlife trees and described in this guide account for 17 percent of this total. (These tallies count each *at risk* subspecies or population within a species separately; the total number of wildlife tree–dependent species *at risk* is 19.)

A third category of species is "of management concern" and these species are assigned to the Yellow List. Because of their dependence on wildlife trees, all of the species in this guide are of management concern. Habitat loss is often a critical factor leading to the listing of species, so it is important to focus management efforts on maintaining a good supply of habitat before a species reaches vulnerable or threatened status. Waiting until the wildlife species, subspecies or population is *at risk* reduces its chances of survival and means that the remedial measures will be more difficult. This emphasis on habitat management is the focus of Part 2 of this guide, which deals with wildlife trees and ecosystem management. Yellow-listed species usually have more options for their protection than the Red- or Blue-listed ones.

National Risk Categories

The Committee on the Status of Endangered Wildlife in Canada (COSEWIC) determines the risk status of species at the national level. COSEWIC consists of representatives from four federal government agencies and three private conservation agencies. It meets annually to review the status of species under investigation and to assign appropriate designations. COSEWIC status designations divide species in need of a change in our approach to their management into "special concern," "threatened" and "endangered," with definitions similar to the provincial ones listed above. Species about which little is known may be termed "data deficient." This guide includes 10 species or subspecies that have been placed in these categories by COSEWIC.

Range

The written description of the known range of each species can have several components. Some species have a fairly consistent year-round range. Others are migratory and have a significantly different breeding range (breeding individuals during the breeding season, typically spring and summer) and nonbreeding range (all individuals during the rest of the year). Where the range has changed significantly over the last century or so, the historical range is also given.

Other kinds of information in this section typically include the elevational range and general habitat or topographic features and seasonal occurrences pertaining to each range, migration schedules and major migration routes, as well as the locations of significant breeding concentrations, colonies and roosting areas.

Whereas the text generally refers to B.C. only, the accompanying map, which also covers Washington and Oregon and parts of other areas, puts the information into a regional context.

Species Description and Other Characteristics

The identifying characteristics of most species are divided into two categories (for the bats, because less information is generally available, all the information is in one category):

Description: A brief summary of the most conspicuous and distinctive physical features that are helpful in visually identifying a species, such as:
- relative size (e.g., large, medium or small), comparative size (e.g., sparrow-sized, crow-sized) or actual body length and mass
- plumage or fur colour
- sizes and other particulars of selected features (e.g., wings, tail, ears, bill, etc.).

KEY TO BIOGEOCLIMATIC ZONES, ECOPROVINCES & BREEDING PERIOD

Biogeoclimatic Zones

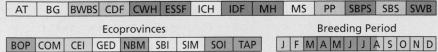

AT	BG	BWBS	CDF	CWH	ESSF	ICH	IDF	MH	MS	PP	SBPS	SBS	SWB

| Ecoprovinces | | | | | | | | | Breeding Period | | | | | | | | | | | |

BOP	COM	CEI	GED	NBM	SBI	SIM	SOI	TAP	J	F	M	A	M	J	J	A	S	O	N	D

- white indicates absent from zone
- light orange indicates former range or very low presence
- dark orange indicates strong presence
- light green indicates former range or very low presence

- dark green indicates strong presence
- light pink indicates non-breeding period
- dark pink indicates breeding period

KEY TO THE DISTRIBUTION MAPS

 current breeding range

 current range outside breeding season

 overlap of breeding and nonbreeding ranges or year-round range.

 All at-risk species show this Fine Filter icon

Other Characteristics: Where applicable, conspicuous and distinctive traits associated with a species' behaviour or ecology that can help in field detection and identification are included, such as foraging behaviour or sign, vocalizations, displays and flight or movement patterns.

Habitat

The habitat requirements of a species have been divided into four categories:

Birds
- feeding
- breeding
- roosting
- territory size/home range

Bats
- feeding
- breeding
- roosting and hibernation
- territory size/home range

Other Mammals
- feeding
- breeding
- denning and resting
- territory size/home range

Because habitat requirements can vary across the range of a species, and not all species have been sufficiently studied within British Columbia, specific provincial information may be lacking for some species or some categories. Any numerical data that has been taken from other provinces or states is qualified by the term "approximately" or similar wording. The sources for such data are listed in the References section in the back of the guide.

Feeding: Describes primary foraging habitat, foraging techniques and major components of the diet. Comments regarding the division of foraging duties in breeding pairs and whether species forage singly or in groups are given where relevant.

Breeding: Describes the primary breeding habitat and essential habitat attributes of each species, along with other information regarding reproduction:
- characteristics of nest sites, denning sites or maternity roosts
- species and any other special features of wildlife trees used (e.g., dbh, decay class, etc.)
- duration of the breeding season, which is generally the time when wildlife is most sensitive to disturbance, is given on a bar graph
- average clutch or litter size and, especially if significantly smaller, the number of young normally fledged or weaned; unless stated otherwise, the number of broods or litters is one per year

Roosting and Hibernation or Denning and Resting: Describes, as applicable, the characteristics and locations of trees typically used for roosting, hibernation, denning or resting, including any gender-specific behaviour and habitat requirements.

Territory Size/Home Range: Describes territory and home range dimensions, the types of territories (e.g., nesting or feeding territory) and typical territorial behaviour, including any notable gender-specific differences. A territory is a regularly patrolled or defended area that is often seasonal, particularly during breeding. A home range, which is defined as the total area that an individual or pair normally occupies, can also vary seasonally and is not necessarily patrolled or defended.

Additional Stewardship Provisions

The majority of species in this guide can have their wildlife tree habitat requirements met by the general landscape- and stand-level ecosystem management provisions described in Part 2. The generic coarse filter approach outlined in Part 2 should always be the starting point in planning for ecosystem management. The details given in the additional stewardship provisions section of each account (or in the introduction to a group of related species) give specific requirements for improving upon the efficiency of this generic approach, indicating how to tailor it to the species found in each area.

The fine filter icon (left) identifies species that require management practices beyond those outlined in Part 2, without which there is a low probability that their needs will be met. For these species, following the generic ecosystem management approach is not enough—according to the best available information, the given stewardship provisions must be applied to enhance their chances of being able to persist in the area.

The additional stewardship provisions were developed on the basis of available research and habitat management information for each species—information derived from work carried out by biologists and foresters in British Columbia, the U.S. Pacific Northwest and other jurisdictions. In many cases, little is known about the distribution and habitat requirements of the species in question, especially the tree-dwelling bats.

The additional stewardship provisions give the following types of information:
- preferences for hardwoods or conifers, feature types, sizes and particular species of trees
- preferences for the locations of trees to retain (e.g., proximity to water or grasslands)
- requirements for essential habitats in addition to wildlife trees (e.g., shrubby understorey, coarse woody debris, patches of old forest or riparian areas)
- sizes of areas to retain
- dates when the species is particularly sensitive to disturbance, so that poten-

tially disruptive activities can be scheduled outside these times, as well as buffer zone specifications
- potential for restoration of wildlife tree features that have been negatively altered by human impacts (for example, enhancement measures such as artificial cavity and snag creation).

The numbers used in this section provide a relative guide and should not be used as a rigid prescription for management. Species respond to a host of factors. There are certain thresholds and combinations of factors that need to be maintained and below which species will not be able to persist.

The recommendations provided in this guide are based on the best information available to the authors at the time of writing. However, research is continually uncovering new information, so this guide cannot claim with absolute certainty that species will be maintained if these management recommendations are followed, so the use of habitat and species success need to be monitored in order to determine and refine the effectiveness of our recommendations. Furthermore, government regulations change from time to time. Therefore, it is the ultimate responsibility of the reader to become aware of and act in accordance with any new inventory and research findings and the current legislation that may apply to his or her local area.

Of Interest

This section focuses on additional important or interesting facts about each species.

The Primary Cavity Excavators

LIST OF PRIMARY CAVITY EXCAVATORS

- Lewis's woodpecker (coastal population is Red-listed; Interior population is Blue-listed; COSEWIC Special Concern)
- Williamson's sapsucker (*nataliae* subspecies is Red-listed; *thyroideus* subspecies is Blue-listed; COSEWIC Endangered)
- yellow-bellied sapsucker
- red-naped sapsucker
- red-breasted sapsucker
- downy woodpecker
- hairy woodpecker (*picoides* subspecies is Blue-listed)
- white-headed woodpecker (Red-listed; COSEWIC Endangered)
- American three-toed woodpecker
- black-backed woodpecker
- northern flicker
- pileated woodpecker
- black-capped chickadee
- mountain chickadee
- chestnut-backed chickadee
- boreal chickadee
- red-breasted nuthatch
- white-breasted nuthatch
- pygmy nuthatch

Overview of the Primary Cavity Excavators

In British Columbia, the primary cavity excavator guild comprises 12 members of the woodpecker family, four chickadee species and three nuthatch species. All of these birds use their bills to excavate nesting and roosting cavities in the trunks or large limbs of wildlife trees.

Members of this guild are categorized as either weak or strong excavators. The weak excavators—chickadees, nuthatches and some woodpeckers, particularly Lewis's woodpecker—need decay-softened wood for successful excavation. The weakest ones make their nest and roost holes in long-dead trees with extensive rotten wood. Strong excavators, such as the pileated, American three-toed and hairy woodpeckers, can hammer their way into more sound wood. The strongest ones favour live trees with some heart rot; the internal softening allows for easy cavity excavation, and the hard outer shell provides thermal insulation and protection from predators.

Each primary cavity excavator species generally has a distinct preference for certain tree species but will use others if necessary. Among conifers, nest observations showed that the greatest diversity of primary excavators use Douglas-fir, followed by ponderosa pine, lodgepole pine, white and Engelmann spruce, western hemlock, western larch and

Male pileated woodpecker at nest cavity in class 2 hardwood

119

western red-cedar. For hardwoods, trembling aspen showed the greatest diversity of nesters, then black cottonwood, paper birch, balsam poplar, red alder and bigleaf maple. However, this summary does not account for actual use and so cannot be taken to reflect the relative importance of these tree species. For instance, 1000 nest records for the red-naped sapsucker from 1000 different Douglas-fir trees would be given equal weight to a single record for the northern flicker nest in a single western red-cedar (a tree it seldom uses).

Cavity excavation is part of the courtship ritual of most woodpeckers, which is why the strong cavity excavators in this guild will rarely reuse nest holes from previous years or use nest boxes. A pair may initiate several new cavities each breeding season, with the male doing most of the work. Completed nest cavities have a round or oblong entrance that opens to a vertical tunnel. At the bottom of the tunnel is an enlarged nest chamber. The weaker cavity excavators— Lewis's woodpecker, the nuthatches and the chickadees—will use existing cavities on many occasions but are capable of making their own cavities when the need arises and decay conditions are favourable. The strong cavity excavators also make roost cavities, which are used mainly at night and in winter and are usually located close to the nest tree or even in the same tree. Roost cavities are similar to those used for nesting but may not be as deep. They provide critical thermal protection and keep the occupants out of sight of predators.

Besides providing secure nests and roosts for woodpeckers, wildlife trees also play an essential role in woodpecker communications, especially during breeding season. The resonating qualities of recently dead trees ("hard" snags) or the dead tops of live trees make them important as drumming stations. From these sites, both male and female woodpeckers broadcast messages related to courtship, pair-bonding and establishment of territorial boundaries.

Primary Cavity Excavators as Keystone Species

Animals that are vital to the integrity of their ecological community are known as "keystone" species. Woodpeckers, especially the strong excavators, earn this designation by providing essential habitat for the group of birds and mammals known as secondary cavity users, which become tenants after the woodpeckers vacate their nest holes. As was shown in Figure 14 (p. 32), the secondary cavity users include waterfowl, falcons, owls, swifts, swallows, bluebirds, bats and squirrels. Incidentally, among the invertebrates, bees are also common users of old woodpecker cavities.

Although chickadees and nuthatches (and to a lesser extent, the Lewis's woodpecker) can excavate their own nest and roost holes if the right type of wildlife tree is available, they often use existing cavities, so they are not considered keystone species like the strong cavity excavators. The contributions of these weak cavity excavators also benefit secondary cavity users, but on a lesser scale.

One of the reasons that woodpeckers are such significant keystone species in British Columbia is that they inhabit all biogeoclimatic zones except the treeless Alpine Tundra zone. Up to eight woodpecker species, one of the highest levels of woodpecker species diversity reported for any area of northern temperate forest, have been found in some forest stands in the Interior.

Large cavities have the most potential to provide for many of the largest secondary cavity users in this guide, so the largest woodpecker in British Columbia, the pileated (which excavates oval entrances ranging in size from 8–10 cm to 10–15 cm), is a very important keystone species. Its abandoned cavities are used by two species *at risk*—the Blue-listed western screech-owl and the flammulated owl—as well as the northern saw-whet owl, boreal owl, northern hawk owl, Vaux's swift, Barrow's goldeneye, common goldeneye, wood duck, hoary bat, silver-haired bat and northern flying squirrel, though many of these species do not depend exclusively on pileated woodpecker cavities.

The northern flicker, although smaller than the pileated woodpecker, is even more important as a keystone species in British Columbia, because it is much more abundant and widely distributed. Its holes become nest cavities and roosts for many secondary cavity users, such as the bufflehead, hooded merganser, northern pygmy-owl, western screech-owl, flammulated owl, northern saw-whet owl, northern hawk owl, mountain bluebird, western bluebird, American kestrel and northern flying squirrel.

Another large woodpecker, Lewis's woodpecker, is associated with the dry forests of the Interior. Its cavities are used by bluebirds and American kestrels, among others. However, this weak excavator will use existing cavities if they are available.

The medium-sized woodpeckers include the four sapsucker species and the white-headed, hairy, American three-toed and black-backed woodpeckers. These woodpeckers provide cavities for such species as the mountain bluebird, western bluebird, tree swallow, flammulated owl, northern pygmy-owl, northern saw-whet owl and northern flying squirrel. Even British Columbia's smallest woodpecker, the diminutive downy, plays a habitat creation role, providing homes for tree swallows and house wrens.

The sapsuckers, of which there are four species in British Columbia, have been called "double keystone" species, because they influence the structure of their ecological communities in two

Northern flicker, female feeding young

ways: they provide nesting and roosting habitat for small secondary cavity users (such as chickadees, wrens and swallows), and they make available a food source for a variety of species. The food comes from "sap wells"—small holes that sapsuckers excavate in live trees. Both the sugar-rich sap that collects in the wells and the insects that are attracted to it are consumed by sapsuckers and other species. For the calliope hummingbird and the rufous hummingbird, sapsucker wells are a vital source of food in early spring before flowering plants can provide sufficient nectar. Some of the other birds and small mammals known to feed from sapsucker wells are the downy woodpecker, warblers, kinglets, red squirrel and chipmunks. The American three-toed woodpecker and the black-backed woodpecker are adapted to foraging on insects that

121

flourish in trees killed by forest fires, and the Lewis's woodpecker often colonizes low-elevation burned areas for nesting. Fire suppression has affected the abundance and distribution of habitat for these species, especially for the Lewis's woodpecker, because fire suppression has been concentrated at low elevations and in valley bottoms.

Collectively, the large, medium and small primary cavity excavators provide an essential function in the forest by creating a supply of cavities for a host of secondary cavity users. The availability of these nest sites strongly affects the breeding success and distribution of many secondary cavity users, as well as the overall diversity of species in the forest. When primary cavity excavators cannot find suitable trees, secondary cavity users are also denied suitable nest sites, and the result is a shift in the food web in the forest: because many of these species are insectivores, their absence allows beetle

Primary cavity excavator. *Black-backed woodpecker*

and other insect populations to expand more rapidly.

Primary Cavity Excavators and Forest Insect Populations

Insects—as eggs, larvae, pupae and adults—are a major component of the diet of all of the primary cavity excavators, and as a result, these birds make a major contribution to maintaining the health and function of forest ecosystems. They help maintain insect populations at endemic (i.e., normal low) levels, delay the onset of insect epidemics and accelerate the decline of outbreaks after the insect population has peaked, which lengthens the time between epidemics. Birds that are present year-round—as woodpeckers, chickadees and nuthatches are through much of British Columbia—are particularly effective biological control agents.

Using a variety of feeding techniques, primary cavity excavators target a wide range of insect prey. Among them are bark beetles and other wood-boring insects (which can cause direct tree mortality); engraver and ambrosia beetles (which attack dead trees); moths, loopers and other defoliators; aphids and other sucking insects; and woody tissue feeders or excavators such as weevils and ants (ant galleries weaken trees and increase their susceptibility to windthrow).

Chickadees and nuthatches are gleaners. They pick their prey from the foliage and bark of trees. Old trees with more textured bark provide better foraging habitat than young, smooth-barked trees.

Most species of woodpeckers tend to use primarily one of two approaches to feeding. The first is surface foraging by pecking, flaking and scaling to remove bark and expose prey. The second is subsurface foraging, which involves drilling and excavating to penetrate into the subcambium layer, from which the birds extract insect larvae, adult ants,

Red-breasted nuthatch

other prey and sap. Strong, chisel-like bills help to get at less accessible prey, and lifelong beak growth compensates for the wear caused by all that excavating. However, the Lewis's woodpecker commonly captures flying insects in midair in a third foraging technique known as "hawking," and the red-breasted sapsucker and the red-breasted nuthatch are also known to catch some of their insect prey on the wing.

Within British Columbia's managed forests, bark beetles (e.g., mountain pine beetle, spruce beetle, Douglas-fir beetle) are the insects of greatest concern to timber production managers. At epidemic levels, they cause rapid, widespread tree mortality, killing vast numbers of trees across large expanses of forest. At lower levels, they impose stress on trees and make them more susceptible to other insects and diseases.

Because they have the ability to respond to insect outbreaks in two complementary ways, woodpeckers are especially important as biological control agents of bark beetles and wood-boring beetles. One type of response is to change their feeding behaviour when an outbreak occurs by increasing the proportion of that insect species in their diet. For example, during mountain pine beetle infestations, both American three-toed and black-backed woodpeckers have been observed to feed exclusively on beetle larvae.

The other way that woodpeckers respond to insect epidemics is by modifying their social organization and congregating in the infestation area. During winter beetle outbreaks, woodpecker densities regularly increase to as much as 85 times their usual level, and on some occasions, up to a dozen birds have been seen feeding on the same tree. Even during summer, when woodpeckers are more territorial, an insect epidemic can result in a local woodpecker population that is seven times larger than usual.

Stewardship

All primary cavity excavators will benefit from the general habitat management measures outlined in Part 2. The coarse filter approach will improve the probability of these keystone species remaining widely distributed across British Columbia's forests, performing their vital role within these ecosystems as providers of nests for secondary cavity users and as highly effective insect predators.

Successful habitat management for primary cavity excavators begins with a knowledge of which species inhabit your local area. To find which of the primary cavity excavators (or any of the other species in the guide) inhabit your area, first consult the biogeoclimatic zone map (p. 114) to find the zone you live in. Then look up the zone in Appendix 3 to find the wildlife tree species that live in it. Reading the accounts for the area's keystone species will assist you to better retain or provide habitat that matches their preferences, and it will help you to recognize their nest and roost cavities, which have well-delineated round or oval entrance holes (reviewing "Finding Wildlife Trees with Existing Use," p. 34, can also be helpful). It is important to retain all trees with nest or roost cavities even if they do not appear to be currently occupied, because these cavities are the future homes of secondary cavity users. As well, a tree that has proven suitable for cavity excavation on one occasion is likely to be used for additional cavities in subsequent years.

Scaling indicates that woodpeckers have been present and removing bark to get at insects.

Male downy woodpecker on deciduous tree

Old-growth ponderosa pine. *Note the fire scars on the surviving old growth. Also note the dense forest indicating the absence of fire and regrowth since the last fire.*

DRY SOUTHERN INTERIOR FORESTS: UNIQUE PRESSURES ON A HIGH-VALUE HABITAT

Historically, the Interior Douglas-fir zone, the Ponderosa Pine zone and some of the southern slopes in the Interior Cedar–Hemlock zone had frequent understorey fires. Since the mid-20th century, however, land-use patterns together with forest practices have significantly altered primary cavity excavator habitat in the dry forests of British Columbia's southern Interior. Agricultural and urban development, combined with fire suppression and the harvesting of old growth, have greatly reduced the number of suitable wildlife trees over vast areas.

The white-headed woodpecker, black-backed woodpecker, Williamson's sapsucker and Lewis's woodpecker are all adapted to living in the dry, open-canopy forests of ponderosa pine, Douglas-fir and western larch. These forests were historically subject to frequent low-intensity burns that maintained a grass-shrub understorey and kept the understorey tree density low. After more than 50 years of fire suppression, clearing of riparian forests, harvesting of large-diameter trees and selective cutting of large snags for firewood, dense Douglas-fir stands are replacing much of the structurally more open natural forest, and these primary cavity excavators have experienced a decreasing supply of habitat, with little original forest remaining.

If these woodpeckers and the species that use their vacated cavities are to persist within these dry Interior forests, a major effort will be needed to decrease understorey tree density, increase the regeneration of ponderosa pine, reestablish a grass-shrub understorey and retain large riparian trees. In the short term, it will be necessary to both maintain the remaining suitable habitats and reintroduce understorey fires to provide these primary cavity excavators with sufficient habitat for the long term.

LEWIS'S WOODPECKER

Melanerpes lewis • LEWO

STATUS

Interior B.C.: Red List
Coastal B.C.: Red List
COSEWIC: Special concern

Within Canada, the Lewis's woodpecker occurs regularly only in British Columbia, where it is an uncommon, locally distributed resident or summer visitor in the southern Interior. It has been extirpated from much of its former range in the Interior and as a breeding species from southeastern Vancouver Island's Garry oak woodlands and the lower Fraser Valley. It is considered vulnerable because of declining numbers (particularly since the 1940s) linked to loss of habitat: the removal of suitable nesting and food-storage trees (large ponderosa pines and riparian black cottonwoods) in combination with forest ingrowth and the conversion of open-canopied forests to closed-canopied as a result of fire suppression.

Lewis's woodpecker near nest cavity in a black cottonwood. Note the multiple cavities. More than one pair is using this wildlife tree.

RANGE

The Lewis's woodpecker is found from near sea level to 1150 m. It breeds locally in lowland areas and valleys of the southern Interior, centred around the Okanagan Valley, north to Williams Lake, Revelstoke and Invermere. Some nonbreeding wanderers reach the coast, lower Fraser Valley and central Interior. A few birds are resident in the Okanagan Valley, overwintering at low elevations around residential areas and orchards, but most are migratory, overwintering anywhere from southern B.C. to northern Mexico. Autumn migration is from late August to early October; spring migration is from early April to mid-May.

Biogeoclimatic Zones

AT	BG	BWBS	CDF	CWH	ESSF	ICH	IDF	MH	MS	PP	SBPS	SBS	SWB

Ecoprovinces

BOP	COM	CEI	GED	NBM	SBI	SIM	SOI	TAP

Breeding Period

J	F	M	A	M	J	J	A	S	O	N	D

DESCRIPTION

This large, chunky woodpecker is slightly smaller than a crow (26–29 cm in length). It has shiny, greenish black upperparts, a grey collar and breast, a dark red facial patch and a pinkish belly. It appears dark overall in flight.

OTHER CHARACTERISTICS

Unlike other woodpeckers, the Lewis's feeds primarily by hawking for flying insects. Relatively quiet compared to other woodpeckers, it is very vocal but not loud during courtship and when disturbed at the nest. Local breeding populations can be concentrated in areas of good habitat. Groups of 6–20 may be seen during migration.

HABITAT

Feeding: Lewis's woodpecker forages in open conifer woodlands, open grasslands adjacent to sparsely treed areas and riparian areas, usually with <30 percent canopy cover. It needs sufficient visibility and space, as well as snags or large trees to supply perches, for effective hawking. In addition to hawking, it also catches insects on the ground and in low brush and occasionally gleans them from tree surfaces. Known as a "burned forest specialist," it does best

Class 3 ponderosa pine—Lewis's woodpecker nest tree. This tree has been used regularly by Lewis's woodpeckers for many years. Inset: Lewis's woodpecker at nest cavity in a decay class 8 Douglas-fir.

shortly after burning, when insects are most abundant. Berries and other fruits are an important part of the diet from midsummer to early autumn. In winter, it mainly eats seeds and fruit. Some food is stored in the bark crevices of mature trees for later use.

Breeding: In the Interior, the preferred breeding habitat, at 275–1000 m elevation, is open ponderosa pine forest, burned low-elevation Douglas-fir forest or grasslands with scattered trees. At low elevations within this range, riparian habitat with black cottonwoods is preferred. Selectively logged or burned forests of other kinds are also desirable habitats, and orchards, pasture and urban areas also used. Important characteristics of breeding habitat are an open canopy, abundant snags and a shrub understorey that harbours abundant insects.

This woodpecker favours ponderosa pine and black cottonwood for excavating its nest cavities but will also use other large (>50 cm dbh) hardwoods (decay classes 4–5) and conifers (preferring decay classes 4–8). Both dead and live trees with decaying centres are used, but snags, often partially stripped of bark, are preferred. Live trees used usually have stem defects caused by limb breakage or lightning scars. Lewis's woodpecker sometimes uses abandoned northern flicker cavities and occasionally uses natural cavities. Most nests are 3.5–9 m above the ground but can be as high as 30 m. Pairs often return to the same cavity year after year.

The former breeding population in the lower Fraser Valley nested in the tops of tall stumps and snags left after land clearing and forest fires, but this habitat is now gone.

The breeding period is early May to late July. The clutch size is 4–7, and 3–6 young successfully fledge.

Roosting: Overwintering birds roost in cavities in snags and live trees similar to those used for nesting.

Territory Size/Home Range: The breeding home range size is approximately 6 ha, and only the immediate nest site is protected. In winter, each bird may defend a small feeding area.

ADDITIONAL STEWARDSHIP PROVISIONS (see also Part 2)
- Use thinning and prescribed understorey burning to restore ponderosa pine forests to a lower stem density to restore open woodlands.
- Where operationally possible, use partial harvesting rather than clear-cutting in ponderosa pine forests, retaining all pine and other conifer snags in decay classes 4–8, >50 cm dbh and >5 m tall.
- Retain all large black cottonwoods in riparian areas, and as many black cottonwood snags (particularly classes 4–5) as practical in other areas.
- When salvage harvesting after a fire or insect kill, conserve habitat diversity by leaving 5–10 percent of the area in scattered wildlife tree patches >5 ha in size that contain standing dead trees.
- Limit cattle grazing and other activities that reduce long-term shrub and berry production.
- Establish a 100-m activity-free buffer zone around known nest sites during the breeding season.

OF INTEREST

Lewis's woodpeckers are most active on hot, sunny days, when they can be readily seen hawking insects. On cold, cloudy days, they remain perched and are seldom observed. Lewis's woodpecker is a weak cavity excavator and needs long-dead trees with extensive rotten wood for successful excavation.

Overview of the Sapsuckers

DESCRIPTION

There are four sapsucker species in B.C. Three—the yellow-bellied, red-naped and red-breasted—are closely related and similar in appearance; their common and distinguishing characteristics are discussed below. The fourth—the Williamson's sapsucker—has a distinctly different appearance and is discussed separately.

Red-breasted sapsucker at sap wells

The breeding range of the red-naped sapsucker overlaps with that of the red-breasted sapsucker in the northern Cariboo-Chilcotin and with the yellow-bellied sapsucker's in the central Interior around Prince George. The breeding range of the red-naped sapsucker also overlaps with that of the Williamson's sapsucker.

The yellow-bellied, red-naped and red-breasted sapsuckers are all about 20–23 cm long. They have black backs, lightly flecked with yellow or white, and pale yellow bellies. Their dark wings are marked by long, white shoulder patches, visible when perched and in flight. Other markings:

- Red-breasted: entirely red head and breast, unlike any other woodpecker west of the Rockies
- Yellow-bellied: red forehead and bold facial stripes in black and white; the male's throat and chin are red, and the female's are white; a black chest band separates the throat from the yellow belly
- Red-naped: distinguished from the yellow-bellied by a small red patch on the nape; the male has a red throat and chin, and the female has a white chin with a variable amount of red on the throat

Williamson's sapsucker is about 24 cm long and similar in size to a robin. The male and female have strikingly different plumages. The male has a black head with narrow white stripes, bright red chin and throat, black back and breast, yellow belly, white rump and large, white wing patches. The female has a brown head, white-barred, dark brown back, wings and sides, a large, dark breast patch, yellowish belly and white rump.

BEHAVIOURAL CHARACTERISTICS

All sapsuckers drill small holes in live trees and feed on the sap that collects in them, as well as on any insects that get trapped in the sap. These sap wells have a characteristic pattern: neatly spaced holes are drilled in horizontal lines, with rows repeated one below the next down the trunk. Sapsucker wells scar the tree and remain visible for many years.

Sapsuckers communicate by drumming in a distinctive rhythm of several rapid taps followed by three or four slow, accented ones: *ta-ta-ta-ta-ta..ta.ta..ta.ta*. They complete two or three series of taps per minute.

Among the variable calls of the yellow-bellied and red-naped sapsuckers are a whining *whaee* that is emitted under many circumstances, a *yewick, yewick* near the nest tree or when two or more birds interact and a plaintive *mew*. The red-breasted sapsucker's calls include a nasal mewing note or squeal and a slurring downward *cheerrr* or *chee-aa*. Williamson's sapsucker makes a variety of sounds similar to some of those made by other sapsuckers.

129

WILLIAMSON'S SAPSUCKER

Sphyrapicus thyroideus • WISA

STATUS

Rocky Mountain subspecies,
S. t. nataliae—B.C.: Red List
Western subspecies, *S. t. thyroideus*—
B.C.: Red List
COSEWIC: Endangered

In Canada, the Williamson's sapsucker occurs only in southern Interior British Columbia and extreme south-western Alberta. Of the two sub-species in B.C., the Rocky Mountain subspecies (in the southern East Kootenay) is considered threatened because of few sightings during the past 50 years, and the Western sub-species is considered vulnerable because of small populations and habitat loss resulting from fire sup-pression and forest ingrowth.

Female Williamson's sapsucker. Inset: Male at nest cavity in class 2 trembling aspen

RANGE

The Williamson's sapsucker breeds at 850–1300 m on the Thompson-Okanagan Plateau, east to Greenwood and west to Manning Provincial Park and Lytton. Small numbers may breed in the East Kootenay anywhere from the Flathead River north to Cranbrook. Williamson's sapsucker overwinters anywhere from Arizona to central Mexico, arriving in B.C. by mid-April and leaving by mid-September.

DESCRIPTION

See "Overview of the Sapsuckers," p. 129.

HABITAT

Feeding: Williamson's sapsucker forages in live trees, in open to semi-open (<75 percent canopy cover) mixed or conifer forests that contain western larch, grand fir or trembling aspen. Ants are the main food, especially in spring and summer, supplemented by sap, cambi-um and insects (e.g., bark beetles and

Biogeoclimatic Zones

AT	BG	BWBS	CDF	CWH	ESSF	ICH	IDF	MH	MS	PP	SBPS	SBS	SWB

Ecoprovinces									Breeding Period											
BOP	COM	CEI	GED	NBM	SBI	SIM	SOI	TAP		J	F	M	A	M	J	J	A	S	O	N	D

spruce budworm) gleaned from sap wells or extracted by surface foraging. Young stands can be used for foraging.

Breeding: Conifer forests, particularly with western larch, Interior Douglas-fir and ponderosa pine, are generally preferred for nesting, but nests in groves of trembling aspen have been found south of Merritt. Williamson's sapsucker requires live or recently dead trees with advanced stages of wood decay for nesting—hardwoods >30 cm dbh and conifers >50 cm dbh in this condition, are preferred. Large-diameter western larch (usually live trees with extensive internal decay) are especially important as nest trees; they will often have other visible defects such as a broken top, stem scars or fungal conks. The cavity is located 2–18 m above the ground. A new nest is usually excavated each year.

The breeding period is May to late July. The clutch size is 4–6.

Roosting: Roost cavities are excavated in trees similar to those used for nesting.

Territory Size/Home Range: Males defend the breeding territory (likely >20 ha) early in the nesting season. Later they defend the nest tree only.

ADDITIONAL STEWARDSHIP PROVISIONS (see also Part 2)
- Focus retention areas around large-diameter trees (>60 cm dbh), especially western larches, that are suitable for nesting: live trees that show evidence of internal decay (fungal conks) or woodpecker activity (e.g., nest holes)

or have broken tops, stem scars or large broken-limb scars.
- Also, where present, retain some large-diameter trembling aspens (>30 cm dbh or the largest for the site) and ponderosa pines and Douglas-firs (>60 cm dbh or the largest for the site), including some trees of this size with heart rot.
- Retain all veteran conifers.
- Use partial harvesting to increase understorey shrubs and decrease stand density to pre–fire suppression conditions; a shrubby understorey provides habitat for insects that are attracted to sap wells.

Semi-open stands of older western larch are preferred habitat for Williamson's sapsucker. Fire scar indicates that understorey burning has helped to maintain this stand in semi-open conditions.

OF INTEREST
Williamson's sapsucker is associated with western larch, a seral species that commonly grows after stand-replacing fires, and with open ponderosa pine and Douglas-fir forests. Fire suppression limits long-term habitat availability.

YELLOW-BELLIED SAPSUCKER
Sphyrapicus varius • YBSA

STATUS
The yellow-bellied sapsucker is an uncommon to fairly common but widespread migrant and summer visitor to the northern Interior. It is not at risk in B.C.

RANGE
This sapsucker breeds from the Liard River and Fort Nelson area south to the Peace, Parsnip and Stikine rivers at elevations of 380–750 m. It generally overwinters from the southern United States to Central America, but a few individuals occasionally overwinter on B.C.'s southwest coast. Migrants arrive in late April and early May and leave by late August.

DESCRIPTION
See "Overview of the Sapsuckers," p. 129.

HABITAT
Feeding: The yellow-bellied sapsucker forages in mixed forests and hardwood groves, mainly on live trees, particularly spruces, lodgepole pine, trembling aspen, willows, paper birch and black cottonwood. It eats insects (e.g., spruce budworm, tent caterpillar, sawfly, scale insects), tree sap, cambium and berries and other fruit.

Breeding: The preferred habitat is riparian forest or other hardwood or mixed forest with trembling aspen, balsam poplar, paper birch and white spruce. Nests are located in hardwoods >25 cm dbh, most commonly trembling aspen and balsam poplar, typically on forest edges adjacent to lakes, ponds, marshes and backwater river channels. Live trees with fungal heart rot are preferred. Pairs often excavate nest cavities in the same tree in successive years, and they occasionally reuse the same hole. Cavities are 2–12 m above the ground, with most at 3–6 m.

Yellow-bellied sapsucker female at cavity in class 2

Biogeoclimatic Zones

AT	BG	**BWBS**	CDF	CWH	ESSF	ICH	IDF	MH	MS	PP	SBPS	**SBS**	SWB

Ecoprovinces								Breeding Period												
BOP	COM	CEI	GED	**NBM**	**SBI**	SIM	SOI	**TAP**		J	F	M	A	M	J	J	A	S	O	N	D

The breeding period is late May to early August. The clutch size is 4–6. Family groups disperse rapidly after the young leave the nest.

Roosting: Night roosts are excavated in trees similar to those used for nesting.

Territory Size/Home Range: The home range is believed to be >20 ha in size. A small area around the nest tree is defended from other sapsuckers. Sap wells are often guarded against other sapsuckers and other species.

ADDITIONAL STEWARDSHIP PROVISIONS (see also Part 2)
- Focus retention on large trembling aspens, paper birch and black cottonwoods (>30 cm dbh or the largest for the site), particularly trees with heart rot.

OF INTEREST
Formerly, the red-naped sapsucker and the red-breasted sapsucker were considered to be subspecies of the yellow-bellied sapsucker.

Yellow-bellied sapsuckers commonly excavate nest cavities in class 2 trembling aspens.
Inset: Yellow-bellied sapsucker male

RED-NAPED SAPSUCKER

Sphyrapicus nuchalis • RNSA

STATUS

The red-naped sapsucker is a fairly common and widespread migrant and summer visitor to the southern Interior. It is not at risk in B.C.

RANGE

This sapsucker breeds throughout the southern Interior, from the U.S. border north to Yoho National Park, Quesnel and the Fraser Plateau, at elevations up to 1300 m. It very rarely breeds on the south coast, and nonbreeding birds occasionally wander to the lower Fraser Valley and southeastern Vancouver Island. It largely overwinters anywhere from the southern U.S. to Mexico. There are no winter records from the B.C. Interior, but a few birds have wintered on the coast. The main spring migration is in April. Autumn

Left: Class 4 paper birch with red-naped sapsucker pair at nest cavity. Right: Male at class 4 trembling aspen

Biogeoclimatic Zones

AT	BG	BWBS	CDF	CWH	ESSF	ICH	IDF	MH	MS	PP	SBPS	SBS	SWB

Ecoprovinces

BOP	COM	CEI	GED	NBM	SBI	SIM	SOI	TAP

Breeding Period

J	F	M	A	M	J	J	A	S	O	N	D

migration is from late August through mid-September.

DESCRIPTION
See "Overview of the Sapsuckers," p. 129.

HABITAT
Feeding: The red-naped sapsucker forages in hardwood and mixed woodlands, usually in live trees. It eats insects, tree sap, cambium and berries and other fruits. Sometimes it consumes pitch from pines, Douglas-fir, spruce and juniper instead of hardwood sap. Sap wells are often established in clumps of willows or paper birch. In spring and summer, about 50 percent of the diet consists of insects such as beetles and ants.

Breeding: This bird breeds widely in a variety of hardwood and mixed woodlands. Nest trees are often on the edges of riparian areas or other open areas (e.g., road edges, cut-blocks, transmission line rights-of-way and mountain meadows). Live hardwoods (trembling aspen, paper birch, balsam poplar, black cottonwood, red alder and willows) with heartwood decay are preferred for nesting, but the red-naped may use dead conifers (ponderosa pine, Douglas-fir, western larch and western hemlock). Nest trees are 15–65 cm dbh, with most 23–30 cm; the cavity is 0.5–23 m above the ground. A new nest cavity is usually excavated each year, often in the same tree.

The breeding period is late May to early August. The clutch size 4–7.

Roosting: The red-naped prefers hardwoods >25 cm dbh for excavating its roost cavities.

Territory Size/Home Range: The breeding home range size is believed to be >20 ha. The nest tree and a small area around it are defended from other sapsuckers. Sap wells are sometimes guarded.

ADDITIONAL STEWARDSHIP PROVISIONS (see also Part 2)
• Focus retention on large trembling aspens, paper birch and black cottonwoods (>30 cm dbh or the largest for the site), particularly trees with heart rot.

OF INTEREST
Although the red-naped sapsucker will defend its nest tree against other sapsuckers, it will share it with other primary cavity excavators or secondary cavity users.

Red-naped sapsucker cavities in class 2 trembling aspen. Wear marks from tail feathers below the entrances indicate that two nest sites are active. Inset: Red-naped sapsucker female

RED-BREASTED SAPSUCKER
Sphyrapicus ruber • RBSA

STATUS
In Canada, the red-breasted sapsucker occurs only in British Columbia. A fairly widespread and common resident along the coast, it is an uncommon summer visitor to low elevations in the central and northwestern Interior. It is not at risk in B.C.

RANGE
This sapsucker breeds anywhere from sea level to 1200 m along the entire coast (including Vancouver Island and the Queen Charlotte Islands), on the eastern slopes of the Pacific Ranges and the Cascade Mountains near Manning Provincial Park and Tulameen and across the central Interior. The nonbreeding range extends to 2000 m.

On the south coast, the red-breasted sapsucker overwinters mainly at the lower elevations of its breeding range. Interior populations probably move to the coast or southward for the winter, returning in April and May. The red-breasted is rarely found in the Interior after August.

DESCRIPTION
See "Overview of the Sapsuckers," p. 129.

HABITAT
Feeding: The red-breasted sapsucker forages in a variety of forested habitats, from mature conifer forest to riparian woodlands. Sap wells, drilled in both hardwoods (alders, maples, willows and trembling aspen) and conifers (western hemlock, Douglas-fir and spruces) are a critical food source early in spring. Insects (especially ants but also weevils and adults and larvae of wood-boring beetles) comprise the majority of the diet during the nesting season, especially the nestling stage. Cambium, berries and seeds are also eaten.

Red-breasted sapsucker at cavity in class 5 red alder

Biogeoclimatic Zones

AT	BG	BWBS	CDF	CWH	ESSF	ICH	IDF	MH	MS	PP	SBPS	SBS	SWB

Ecoprovinces									Breeding Period											
BOP	COM	CEI	GED	NBM	SBI	SIM	SOI	TAP		J	F	M	A	M	J	J	A	S	O	N	D

Breeding: A variety of wooded habitats are used for nesting, including conifer forests (old-growth and mature second-growth Douglas-fir, western red-cedar, western hemlock and spruce forests on the coast; lodgepole pine, Douglas-fir and spruce forests in the Interior), as well as hardwood forests (such as riparian cottonwood forests). The red-breasted sapsucker will also use modified habitats, such as orchards, power line rights-of-way and old burns. Nests are often located in edge habitat adjacent to an estuary, marsh, lake or clearing. Nest trees are more often dead than live, >25 cm dbh and usually hardwoods (e.g., red alder, trembling aspen, bigleaf maple, balsam poplar, black cottonwood and paper birch), especially at lower elevations. However, spruce is preferred on the northwest coast and western hemlock is frequently chosen on the south coast. Cavities are located 2–24 m above the ground.

The breeding period is early May to late July. The clutch size is 4–7, and 3–6 young normally fledge.

Roosting: The red-breasted sapsucker excavates its roost cavities in decaying trees >25 cm dbh near the nest tree. The species may be a winter resident on the coast and at low elevations in the Interior. When present in winter, it remains sedentary or restricted to a very limited area.

Territory Size/Home Range: The breeding home range size is normally >20 ha. Sap wells are often guarded. When the sap stops running in autumn, resident red-breasted sapsuckers may move to warmer areas at lower elevations.

ADDITIONAL STEWARDSHIP PROVISIONS (see also Part 2)
• Retain some stands of densely foliated conifers in upland and riparian areas for protection from the cold in winter.

OF INTEREST
Fledglings are taught how to feed from sap wells while clinging to the nest tree.

Red-breasted sapsucker in aspen habitat

DOWNY WOODPECKER
Picoides pubescens • DOWO

STATUS
Throughout southern and central British Columbia, the downy woodpecker is a widespread resident. It is less common farther north and on the outer coast. It is not at risk in B.C.

RANGE
The downy woodpecker breeds throughout central and southern B.C., including Vancouver Island, from near sea level to 1100 m. There are few winter records north of the Shuswap region; northern Interior populations may overwinter in southern valleys and coastal areas.

DESCRIPTION
B.C.'s smallest woodpecker, the downy closely resembles the hairy woodpecker but is smaller (about 18 cm in length), with a thinner bill and black spots on the white outer tail feathers. It has a white back and underside, black wings barred with white and a black-and-white head; the "white" parts are bright white on Interior birds and grey on coastal birds. The male has a red patch on the back of the head.

OTHER CHARACTERISTICS
Vocalizations include a flat *pik* call and a 1–2-second series of descending notes, like a horse's whinny. During the breeding season, the male drums on trees in 1–2-second bursts.

HABITAT
Feeding: The downy woodpecker forages in hardwood and mixed forests, riparian forests, burns, parklands and urban areas, feeding on both conifers and hardwoods. Mainly insectivorous, it forages at and below the bark surface. Beetles—two-thirds of them wood-boring species—

Female downy woodpecker

Biogeoclimatic Zones

AT	BG	BWBS	CDF	CWH	ESSF	ICH	IDF	MH	MS	PP	SBPS	SBS	SWB

Ecoprovinces

BOP	COM	CEI	GED	NBM	SBI	SIM	SOI	TAP

Breeding Period

J	F	M	A	M	J	J	A	S	O	N	D

comprise >40 percent of the diet volume. Larch and pine sawflies, coddling moth and caterpillars are also eaten. The downy woodpecker also consumes sap from sapsucker wells, fruit and seeds.

Breeding: Nesting in hardwood forests, aspen copses, mixed woods, riparian thickets, old burns, logged areas, gardens and orchards, the downy prefers dead or dying hardwoods (trembling aspen, red alder, black cottonwood, Garry oak, paper birch, willows and Pacific crabapple), generally >25 cm dbh, often choosing trees infected with heart rot. Nests are 1–30 m above the ground. A new cavity is excavated annually, occasionally in the same tree.

The breeding period is mid-April to early August. The clutch size is 4–7.

Roosting: The downy woodpecker roosts in cavities in dead or decaying trees. Each individual excavates a new roosting cavity each winter.

TERRITORY SIZE/HOME RANGE: The breeding territory size is approximately 4 ha or greater. Pairs initially hold a larger territory, which shrinks after the nest site is selected and a cavity is excavated.

ADDITIONAL STEWARDSHIP PROVISIONS (see also Part 2)
- Focus areas for retention around trees >25 cm dbh (or the largest for the site) and of an appropriate species mix (black cottonwood and red alder on the coast; black cottonwood, trembling aspen and paper birch in the Interior), particularly trees with heart rot.

OF INTEREST
In winter, downy woodpeckers are easily attracted to bird feeders stocked with suet.

Left: Class 5 Garry oak with downy woodpecker nest cavity, (note external fungal fruiting). Right: Male downy woodpecker at nest cavity in class 4 red alder

HAIRY WOODPECKER
Picoides villosus • HAWO

STATUS
Queen Charlotte subspecies, *P. v. picoides*—B.C.: Blue List

The hairy woodpecker is an uncommon but widespread resident throughout most of B.C., including the coastal islands. The Queen Charlotte Islands subspecies is considered vulnerable because it is a small population and is more vulnerable to threats to its habitat.

RANGE
The hairy woodpecker breeds throughout the province, anywhere from near sea level to at least 1850 m. It may disperse to higher elevations after breeding.

Migration is mainly altitudinal, taking it from high elevations in summer to valley bottoms during winter, but it may also partially withdraw from northern areas during winter. The Queen Charlotte subspecies is restricted to the Queen Charlotte Islands.

DESCRIPTION
The robin-sized hairy woodpecker (about 24 cm in length) is similar in appearance to the downy woodpecker, but is larger and has a stouter bill. The outer tail feathers are entirely white.

OTHER CHARACTERISTICS
The call is a loud, high-pitched *peek* or slurred whinny. The drumming consists of a loud, rapid burst of rhythmic taps, slowing toward the end.

HABITAT
Feeding: The mainly insectivorous hairy woodpecker subsurface forages in mature forests and along the edges of meadows, marshes, ponds, logged areas and old burns. It eats beetles (mostly wood-boring), which comprise >60 percent of its diet volume, along with larch sawfly, coddling moth and other insects, plus occasional fruits and seeds

Male hairy woodpecker on trembling aspen

Biogeoclimatic Zones

AT	BG	BWBS	CDF	CWH	ESSF	ICH	IDF	MH	MS	PP	SBPS	SBS	SWF

Ecoprovinces									Breeding Period									
BOP	COM	CEI	GED	NBM	SBI	SIM	SOI	TAP		J	F	M	A	M	J	J	A	S	O

extracted from conifer cones. This woodpecker often visits gardens and feeders in winter.

Breeding: The hairy woodpecker prefers semi-open mixed forests or forest edges for breeding. Most nest cavities are excavated in live or dead hardwoods (trembling aspen, red alder, paper birch, black cottonwood, bigleaf maple and arbutus). In mixed forests, it nests mostly in trembling aspen, where available. Conifers (Douglas-fir, lodgepole pine, western hemlock, spruce, western larch, western red-cedar and ponderosa pine) may also be used. Nest trees normally have decayed heartwood, and the minimum dbh is approximately 25 cm; nest cavities are 1–38 m above the ground, with most at 2–6 m. A new cavity is usually excavated each year.

Breeding is from early April to late July. The hairy breeds earlier than other woodpeckers; south coast populations breed up to a month ahead of Interior populations. The clutch size is 3–5.

Roosting: Roosts are in tree cavities, but the requirements are not well known.

Territory Size/Home Range: The breeding territory size is approximately 10 ha.

ADDITIONAL STEWARDSHIP PROVISIONS (see also Part 2)

- Within conifer forests, retain hardwoods >25 cm dbh (or the largest ones for the site), particularly aspens and any trees with heart rot.
- Retain some riparian hardwood forest.

- For the Queen Charlotte Islands subspecies, maintain >4 ha of suitable windfirm habitat around known nest sites and minimize disturbance from early April to late July near nests.

Above: Female hairy woodpecker. Below: Class 2 trembling aspen with hairy woodpecker nest cavity

OF INTEREST

Hairy woodpeckers can in theory consume as many as 21,000 mountain pine beetle larvae per hectare per season. As the number of mountain pine beetles in an area increases, the number of hairy woodpeckers typically increases as well.

WHITE-HEADED WOODPECKER

Picoides albolarvatus • WHWO

STATUS

B.C.: Red List
COSEWIC: Endangered

In Canada, the white-headed woodpecker occurs only in B.C.'s south Okanagan, where it is a very rare resident with an estimated population of <100 pairs and possibly as few as five pairs.

RANGE

The white-headed woodpecker breeds in the Okanagan Valley between Osoyoos and Naramata, at elevations of 450–600 m, and its year-round distribution is similar. Some birds have been found north to Stump Lake and Falkland, east to Creston and west to the Similkameen Valley.

DESCRIPTION

The robin-sized (21–23 cm long) white-headed woodpecker has an unmistakable plumage: a black body with a white head and throat. In flight, a white patch is visible on each wing. The male has a small red patch on the back of the head.

OTHER CHARACTERISTICS

Among the calls are a grating, two-note *peek-it*, a sharp *chick* and sometimes a rapidly repeated *chick-ik-ik-ik*. The male's drumming is in a short, even series.

HABITAT

Feeding: The white-headed woodpecker forages in open, mature to old-growth ponderosa pine and mixed ponderosa pine–Douglas-fir forests up to at least 700 m. Although it depends less on insects than other woodpeckers, in early summer it eats mainly insects (ants, wood-boring beetles and fly larvae), as well as spiders, surface-foraged from the lower portions of large, live ponderosa pines (>60 cm dbh). For the rest of the

White-headed woodpecker, adult male

Biogeoclimatic Zones

AT	BG	BWBS	CDF	CWH	ESSF	ICH	IDF	MH	MS	PP	SBPS	SBS	SWB

Ecoprovinces

BOP	COM	CEI	GED	NBM	SBI	SIM	SOI	TAP

Breeding Period

J	F	M	A	M	J	J	A	S	O	N

year, the most important food is ponderosa pine seeds, and their supply may be a limiting factor in controlling the size of this bird's populations, because good cone crops are produced only every 4–5 years, with the greatest number of seeds being produced by large, dominant trees in open situations. Other, less-favoured seeds (e.g., great mullein) are also eaten.

Breeding: This woodpecker nests only in open stands (<70 percent canopy cover) of mature to old-growth ponderosa pine and Douglas-fir, often on the edges of clearings. It uses dead or dying trees, often with heart rot, and shows a strong preference for large ponderosa pines (>50 cm dbh). Leaning or broken-topped snags or stumps are commonly used. The cavity height is 2.5–9 m.

The breeding period is mid-May to late July. The clutch size is 3–5.

Roosting: This bird roosts in a different cavity each year, but will sometimes use an old cavity or roost under the sloughing bark of a large, usually dead ponderosa pine.

Territory Size/Home Range: The home range of approximately 100–400 ha is larger where the forest is heavily fragmented or where it is too dense or otherwise less suitable.

ADDITIONAL STEWARDSHIP PROVISIONS (see also Part 2)
- Maintain all existing late-seral ponderosa pine forest.
- Do not harvest or salvage in areas of suitable habitat (continuous ponderosa pine forest over areas of 20–500 ha) where white-heads have been detected during recent breeding seasons.
- In other ponderosa pine and ponderosa pine–Douglas-fir forests, use partial harvesting to retain all live and dead ponderosa pines >50 cm dbh or the largest ponderosa pine for the site. Retain significant numbers of cone-producing ponderosa pines (aged 60–100 years or more).
- Manage ponderosa pine–dominated stands on long, 250-year rotations, with reduced stocking densities to allow young ponderosa pines to develop.
- Use understorey burning (or piling and burning) and thinning of Douglas-fir to reduce Douglas-fir density and competition with young ponderosa pines.
- Plant more areas in ponderosa pine and manage them into multi-storey, multi-aged ponderosa pine forest.

OF INTEREST
Because of its rarity and its striking plumage, the white-headed woodpecker is one of the most sought-after species for birders in British Columbia.

White-headed woodpecker nest tree.
Inset: White-headed adult female

AMERICAN THREE-TOED WOODPECKER
Picoides dorsalis • TTWO

STATUS
The American three-toed woodpecker is an uncommon to rare resident at high elevations throughout most of British Columbia. It is very rare west of the Coast Mountains and absent from the Queen Charlotte Islands. It is not at risk in B.C.

RANGE
This species breeds throughout the Interior east of the Coast Mountains, mainly at the upper elevations of its 520–1740 m breeding range. Nesting has also been recorded on east-central Vancouver Island and on the southern mainland coast from the North Shore to Powell River. Nonbreeding birds have been found to 2100 m. Throughout its geographic distribution in B.C., this species winters at the lower end of its elevation range.

DESCRIPTION
Slightly smaller than a robin (20–24 cm in length), this woodpecker has a white breast, throat and belly, black-and-white barring on the flanks and variable barring down the back. The head is black with a white stripe, and the male has a yellow crown. Each foot has three toes (most woodpeckers have four per foot).

OTHER CHARACTERISTICS
The call is a single soft, high-pitched *pik* or a fast, short rattle. The drumming is in short sequences that accelerate toward the end.

HABITAT
Feeding: This woodpecker forages in spruce, true fir, lodgepole pine and mixed forests, mainly on older, burned or diseased trees that provide abundant prey; Engelmann spruce and lodgepole pine may be preferred. Young, even-aged stands do not provide sufficient habitat diversity to maintain this

Male at nest cavity in class 5 trembling aspen

Biogeoclimatic Zones

AT	BG	BWBS	CDF	CWH	ESSF	ICH	IDF	MH	MS	PP	SBPS	SBS	SWB

Ecoprovinces									Breeding Period											
BOP	COM	CEI	GED	NBM	SBI	SIM	SOI	TAP	J	F	M	A	M	J	J	A	S	O	N	

Female at nest cavity in class 3 lodgepole pine.

The breeding period is late April to late July. The clutch size is 3–5, and 2–4 young normally fledge.

Roosting: Roost cavities are excavated in trees similar to those used for nesting.

Territory Size/Home Range: The home range is approximately 50–300 ha.

ADDITIONAL STEWARDSHIP PROVISIONS (see also Part 2)

- Understorey burning and allowing some escape burns will benefit this species.
- When salvage harvesting after a fire or an insect kill, conserve habitat diversity by leaving wildlife tree patches >5 ha in size, totalling 5–10 percent of the area.

species. This woodpecker feeds almost exclusively on insect larvae and pupae, mainly by surface foraging. Wood-boring beetles comprise >75 percent of the diet volume, but this bird also eats larch sawfly, caterpillars and ants. Winter foraging is concentrated in old burns and insect-infested areas.

Breeding: Nests are located in mature and older conifer stands, especially in spruce, true fir or mixed forests with a lodgepole pine component, near openings created by burns, clear-cuts, ponds, lakes and bogs. Preferred nest trees are large (>30 cm dbh), live conifers (e.g., Engelmann spruce, white or black spruce or lodgepole pine) with heart rot or dead ones. This bird uses live conifers much more often than other woodpeckers, but hardwood species (especially trembling aspen) also used. The cavity, which can be 1–24 m above the ground, is usually 1–5 m.

Nest cavity in lodgepole pine

OF INTEREST

During a spruce beetle outbreak, an American three-toed woodpecker will consume thousands of larvae every day.

BLACK-BACKED WOODPECKER
Picoides arcticus • BBWO

STATUS
The black-backed woodpecker is a rare but widely distributed resident throughout the Interior. It is not at risk in B.C.

RANGE
The black-backed woodpecker breeds within an elevation range of 330–1400 m, from the eastern slope of the Coast Mountains to Alberta, and from the southern Interior to the Yukon border. After breeding, it moves locally to recent burns or forests with high insect densities. It overwinters at the lower elevations of the breeding range.

DESCRIPTION
Very similar in appearance to the American three-toed woodpecker, the slightly larger (23 cm long) black-backed woodpecker is distinguished by its solid black back. Males of these two species are the only B.C. woodpeckers with yellow caps.

OTHER CHARACTERISTICS
The call note is a single, sharp metallic *kik* or a rattle (slower than the American three-toed woodpecker's). The black-back drums frequently, with longer sequences and more beats than the American three-toed woodpecker; the beats accelerate near the end of the sequence.

HABITAT
Feeding: The nearly wholly insectivorous black-backed woodpecker surface-forages almost exclusively on old, burned or diseased trees in mature and older stands of lodgepole pine or mixed conifers dominated by lodgepole pine. It congregates in recently burned or insect-infested areas, especially during winter, and it is often the most abundant woodpecker for the first few years after

Male at nest cavity in hardwood

Biogeoclimatic Zones

AT	BG	BWBS	CDF	CWH	ESSF	ICH	IDF	MH	MS	PP	SBPS	SBS	SWB

Ecoprovinces									Breeding Period												
BOP	COM	CEI	GED	NBM	SBI	SIM	SOI	TAP	J	F	M	A	M	J	J	A	S	O	N	D

a fire. Young, even-aged conifer stands do not provide sufficient habitat diversity to maintain this species. Larvae and adults of wood-boring metallic and long-horned beetles, bark beetles and ambrosia beetles are particularly important (bark beetles supply >75 percent of the diet volume).

Breeding: This woodpecker nests in subalpine, sub-boreal and boreal conifer forests and in high-elevation Interior Douglas-fir and western hemlock forests, often in or near openings (e.g., burns, clear-cuts, riparian areas, swamps and bogs). Live or dead conifers (e.g., pine, spruce, Douglas-fir, western larch, western hemlock and western red-cedar), 35–50 cm dbh, are used as nest trees, and this bird uses live conifers much more often than other woodpeckers. Cavities are 1–24 m above the ground.

The breeding period is early May to late July. The clutch size is 3–5, and 2–4 young normally fledge.

Roosting: This bird roosts in cavities or deformities (e.g., scars, western gall rust cankers, mistletoe clumps) in mature and old-growth trees; lodgepole pine may be preferred.

Territory Size/Home Range: The home range is approximately 70–300 ha.

ADDITIONAL STEWARDSHIP PROVISIONS (see also Part 2)
- Understorey burning and allowing some escape burns will benefit this species.
- When salvage harvesting after fire or insect kill, conserve habitat diversity by leaving wildlife tree patches >5 ha over 5–10 percent of the area.

Left: Douglas-fir forest with nest cavities in a class 6 western larch. Right: Female at nest cavity in a conifer with typical scaled bark near entrance

OF INTEREST
A single black-backed woodpecker typically consumes more than 13,000 wood-boring beetle larvae annually.

NORTHERN FLICKER
Colaptes auratus • NOFL

STATUS
The northern flicker is a fairly common resident throughout the province. It is not at risk in B.C.

RANGE
This species breeds throughout the province at anywhere from near sea level to 2100 m. In autumn, northern populations move to southern Interior valleys or to the coast, often congregating in favourable feeding areas, sometimes at urban or agricultural sites. Autumn migration is from late August through October; spring migration is in early March in the south and late May in the north.

DESCRIPTION
A jay-sized woodpecker, 30–35 cm in length, the northern flicker is olive brown with a barred back, crescent-shaped black chest band, spotted belly and conspicuous white rump patch. The colour of the underwings and tail feather shafts (seen in flight) varies: salmon-red is typical west of Rocky Mountains, and yellow is most likely to the east. The male's "moustache" is red for the "red-shafted" subspecies and black for the "yellow-shafted" one.

OTHER CHARACTERISTICS
The flight pattern is an undulating flap-flap-flap–glide. This bird is noisy and highly visible during spring and summer. Calls include a *wick-er, wick-er* (usually repeated >10 times), a rapid *wik-wik-wik-wik* and a loud, sharp *klee-yer* that descends in pitch.

HABITAT
Feeding: The northern flicker forages in open or semi-open forest and in grasslands with scattered trees. It eats

Female feeding young at nest cavity in class 8 paper birch

Biogeoclimatic Zones													
AT	BG	BWBS	CDF	CWH	ESSF	ICH	IDF	MH	MS	PP	SBPS	SBS	SWB

Ecoprovinces										Breeding Period												
BOP	COM	CEI	GED	NBM	SBI	SIM	SOI	TAP		J	F	M	A	M	J	J	A	S	O	N	D

mainly ants and other insects (beetles, caterpillars, wood lice, aphids) but also nuts, grains and fruits. It often forages on the ground, and it occasionally gleans insects from bark surfaces or hawks for flying insects. The northern flicker frequents bird feeders and orchards in winter.

Breeding: The preferred habitat is open forest (e.g., trembling aspen–lodgepole pine, ponderosa pine, Douglas-fir–ponderosa pine and Garry oak–arbutus) or forest edges, but the wide range encompasses riparian woodland, burns, gardens, rangeland, pasture, orchards and alpine meadow edges. This species usually excavates its nest cavities in the dead tops of live trees or in snags or stumps (it requires weakened sapwood and extensive heartwood decay). On occasion it will use wooden poles or buildings, reuse old cavities or occupy nest boxes. The most common nest tree species is trembling aspen, but lodgepole pine, ponderosa pine, black cottonwood, Douglas-fir, paper birch and arbutus are also used. The average tree dbh is 48 cm (coast) or 38 cm (Interior). Cavities are located from near the ground to 27 m above it, but usually <3 m.

Roosting: At night and during inclement weather, the northern flicker roosts in cavities similar to those used for nesting. It sometimes excavates winter roosts in wooden buildings.

The breeding period is April to late July. The clutch size is 5–7.

Territory Size/Home Range: Breeding season home range is approximately 20 ha.

ADDITIONAL STEWARDSHIP PROVISIONS (see also Part 2)
- Manage by using general wildlife tree guidelines, but with an emphasis on retaining the soft class 6–8 conifer and class 4–5 hardwood wildlife trees that the northern flicker prefers.

Class 8 ponderosa pine with nest cavity. Inset: Male at nest cavity in hardwood

OF INTEREST
Where the red-shafted and yellow-shafted forms of the northern flicker meet in central B.C., interbreeding produces hybrids with plumages that have characteristics of both.

PILEATED WOODPECKER

Dryocopus pileatus • PIWO

STATUS

An uncommon but widespread resident throughout southern British Columbia, including Vancouver Island, the pileated woodpecker is very rare elsewhere in the province and absent from the Queen Charlotte Islands and the extreme north-west Interior. It is not at risk in B.C.

RANGE

The pileated wood-pecker breeds any-where from near sea level to about 1200 m throughout southern B.C. and north to the Skeena River, Vanderhoof and the Peace River. In winter, northern populations apparently move to southern valleys and the coast or shift to valley bottoms.

DESCRIPTION

At about 45 cm in length, this crow-sized bird is North America's largest woodpecker. It has a black body, white underwings, a white stripe on the neck and face and a conspicuous red crest. The male has a red "moustache" patch.

OTHER CHARACTERISTICS

The conspicuous large, rectangular feeding notches are diagnostic. Rising and falling in pitch, the fast *kik kik kik* call is repeated up to 12 times in a row. Very loud and rel-atively slow, the drumming lasts 2–3 seconds, softening toward the end, and is repeated every 40–60 seconds. The pileat-ed flies with slow, jerky wing beats.

HABITAT

Feeding: This woodpecker forages in old-growth and mature forests, in younger forests with mature and old-growth rem-nants and in hardwood riparian areas. Using deep excavations or surface-foraging tech-niques, it feeds on snags and living, insect-inhabited trees >20 cm dbh; it uses logs (>30 cm dbh) and stumps more than any other woodpecker. Nest trees are rarely used for foraging. Diet is primarily carpenter

Female feeding young in class 2 hardwood.
Inset: Male feeding

Biogeoclimatic Zones

AT	BG	BWBS	CDF	CWH	ESSF	ICH	IDF	MH	MS	PP	SBPS	SBS	SWB

Ecoprovinces								Breeding Period												
BOP	COM	CEI	GED	NBM	SBI	SIM	SOI	TAP		J	F	M	A	M	J	J	A	S	O	N	D

ants and, to a lesser extent, wood-boring beetle larvae and caterpillars, supplemented by berries and seeds. It also takes ants from ground nests.

Breeding: The pileated woodpecker breeds in a variety of habitats, from open hardwood to mature conifer forests. In B.C., it prefers live hardwoods for nesting, especially trembling aspen and black cottonwood, but paper birch, alder and maple are also used. Although conifers are used less frequently, large-diameter conifers with heart rot—especially grand fir, Douglas-fir and western larch—are suitable nest trees. Nest trees must be large (>45 cm dbh) to accommodate the sizeable (8–10 x 10–15 cm) rectangular-oval entrance hole and a nest depth of 41–66 cm. Nests are 4–30 m above the ground. Pairs excavate a new nest cavity each year.

Large class 5 hardwood with pileated woodpecker nest cavity

The breeding period is early April to late July. The clutch size is 2–4, and 2–3 young successfully fledge.

Roosting: Roost cavities (usually several for each male and female) are excavated in live or dead trees >45 cm dbh.

Territory Size/Home Range: The large home range is estimated to be 120–1400 ha. Home ranges of different pairs do not usually overlap; the male's home range differs slightly from that of the female.

ADDITIONAL STEWARDSHIP PROVISIONS (see also Part 2)
- Since salvage operations decrease availability of habitat for carpenter ants and other prey species, retain large coarse woody debris (>50 cm dbh and >5 m length) and stumps in second-growth stands for foraging substrate.
- Provide at least one large-diameter conifer/ha (>70 cm dbh for coastal forests and Interior wet belt and >50 cm dbh for other Interior forests; decay classes 2–5 recommended) and an abundance of other large trees (>50 cm dbh or the largest for the site, preferably with stem scarring or heart rot) distributed across the landscape for roosting, nesting and feeding habitat.
- Where grand fir occurs (CDF, CWH and ICH zones), provide reserves of mature or old grand fir with >60 percent canopy closure and >10 grand fir/ha (>50 cm dbh) for nesting and roosting habitat. These can be wildlife tree patches or suitable areas already being managed to conserve old-growth or for wintering ungulates in need of snow interception.
- In coastal forests and the Interior wet belt, retain where possible large-diameter hollow red-cedars within wildlife tree patches or other reserve areas. Hollow trees provide important roost sites in these types of forests.
- In the Interior, stands of large trembling aspen are important for nesting habitat. Within each harvest block, retain large-diameter aspen (>40 cm dbh) both singly and in patches.

OF INTEREST

Pileated woodpeckers select trees in the early stages of decay and are able to penetrate relatively sound wood, affording cavities that provide greater protection from predators and that have a longer useful life for secondary cavity users compared to those of other woodpeckers.

151

Overview of the Chickadees

It may come as a surprise to find the diminutive, small-billed chickadees in the same grouping as eminent wood hewers such as the pileated woodpecker, but they are also capable of creating their own nesting and roosting cavities. Chickadees are weak excavators, however, and will use existing cavities when the opportunity arises.

The four species of chickadees resident in British Columbia are the black-capped, the mountain, the boreal and the chestnut-backed. All are nonmigratory, but they may make seasonal shifts in elevation, going to higher elevations in late summer and lower ones in winter, especially during severe weather.

Chickadees are mainly insectivorous gleaners, eating all life stages of a wide range of small insect species, many of which damage trees in forests and orchards (e.g., coddling moth, gypsy moth, Douglas-fir tussock moth, spruce budworm, pine budworm, pine sawfly, larch sawfly, forest loopers, bark beetles, tent caterpillars, needle miners and weevils). They also eat small seeds, berries, spiders and carrion. In winter, they often form feeding flocks with other chickadees, nuthatches, kinglets and brown creepers. They are frequent visitors to backyard feeders.

DESCRIPTION

Chickadees are small, rotund birds, about 13 cm in length, with short wings and long tails. The male and female are nearly identical. The black-capped chickadee has a black "cap" and throat "bib" that contrast with a white cheek patch and breast; the back is grey, and the flank is buffy. The similar mountain chickadee can be distinguished by its distinct white "eyebrow" streak. The boreal chickadee is mainly brown and grey; its brown "cap," grey cheek, brown back and rusty flank differentiate it

from the other chickadees. The chestnut-backed chickadee has a dark brown "cap" and black throat "bib" that contrast with a white cheek patch and a chestnut back and flank.

OTHER CHARACTERISTICS

All chickadees have a distinctive *chicka-dee-dee* type of call. The black-capped's call is purer in tone than those of the others. The mountain chickadee's call is a hoarser *chicka-deer-deer* that is reminiscent of a black-capped with nasal congestion. Another distinctive call of the black-capped chickadee and mountain chickadee is a whistled *fee-bee;* a precursor to breeding activity, it is usually heard in late winter and spring. The boreal is the quietest chickadee; its call is more like *sicka-DAY* and is slower and more highly pitched than the black-capped's. The chestnut-backed's call is a lispy *sicka-dee-dee*, faster and harsher than the calls of other chickadees. Chestnut-backed chickadees forage high in the canopy and are more often heard than seen.

Chickadees often hang upside down from the ends of branches while foraging. They are weak fliers that move from tree to tree with rapid bursts of wing beats interspersed with short pauses, resulting in a slow and shallow, undulating flight pattern.

NESTING AND ROOSTING TREE REQUIREMENTS

Because chickadees are weak cavity excavators, they require trees in advanced stages of decay (classes 4–8 for conifers and 3–5 for hardwoods) for nesting and roosting. Large dead branches (>10 cm dbh) or relatively small snags (>10 cm dbh) will meet their needs. A wide range of tree species are used. They also nest and roost in old woodpecker cavities, natural cavities and nest boxes. Nests are usually 2–7 m above the ground. Nest cavity entrances are inconspicuous (about 4 cm in diameter), and it is difficult to know whether a cavity is being used unless birds are observed coming and going.

ADDITIONAL STEWARDSHIP PROVISIONS (see also Part 2)

- Retain wildlife trees in a state of advanced decay (classes 4–8 for conifers and classes 3–5 for hardwoods) for nesting and roosting.
- Because territories may be as small as 5 ha, wildlife tree patches of this size within clear-cuts can generally provide sufficient habitat for isolated chickadee pairs.
- High-cut stumps can provide future nest sites as second-growth stands mature and these stumps move to suitable decay stages.
- Black-capped chickadees require riparian forest or disturbed, open hardwood or mixed forests with a selection of potential nest trees. Forest edges along wetlands and streams are particularly valuable habitat, as are copses of trembling aspens.
- Mountain chickadees appear to use old sapsucker cavities more often than do other chickadees. The provision of breeding habitat for this species is thus strongly linked with the presence of good sapsucker breeding habitat.
- Local populations of chickadees can be enhanced through the placement of suitable nest boxes.

OF INTEREST

In winter, all four species of chickadees (less so for the black-capped) form mixed-species feeding flocks with birds such as other chickadee species, kinglets, nuthatches, bushtits and small woodpeckers. These assemblages may increase feeding efficiency and predator detection. Experiments have shown that downy woodpeckers foraging in mixed-species flocks use chickadees as sentinels.

Engelmann spruce forest—typical boreal chickadee habitat

BLACK-CAPPED CHICKADEE
Poecile atricapillus • BCCH

STATUS
The black-capped chickadee is widely and commonly distributed throughout most of the Interior and on the southern mainland coast. It is not at risk in B.C.

RANGE
Found anywhere from near sea level to 1400 m, the black-capped chickadee breeds throughout the Interior (more commonly in the south than the north), in the lower Fraser Valley and along some major river valleys in the north and central coastal ranges.

HABITAT
Feeding: The black-capped chickadee forages mainly in riparian areas, in the lower forest canopy and along the edges of openings.

Breeding: Nesting is mainly in riparian habitat or along forest edges (e.g., meadows, clearings and old burns), in species such as paper birch, poplars, willows, pines and Douglas-fir. (See "Overview of the Chickadees," p. 152, for nest tree details.)

Black-capped chickadee, adult

Biogeoclimatic Zones

AT	BG	BWBS	CDF	CWH	ESSF	ICH	IDF	MH	MS	PP	SBPS	SBS	SWB

Ecoprovinces

BOP	COM	CEI	GED	NBM	SBI	SIM	SOI	TAP

Breeding Period

J	F	M	A	M	J	J	A	S	O	N	D

The breeding season is early March to mid-August. The clutch size is 5–7. Some pairs in southern areas produce two broods annually.

Roosting: This bird roosts in tree cavities and dense conifers, plus possibly holes excavated in snow. Cavities and dense conifers provide critical thermal protection in winter and at night. During nesting, the female roosts in the nest cavity and the male roosts in a nearby cavity. Several roosting cavities are required on each home range. Flocks roost communally in winter.

Left: Nest cavity in class 5 paper birch (note conk)
Above: Black-capped chickadee, adult

Territory Size/Home Range: Breeding territories are about 5–10 ha. The home range outside of the breeding season can be 2–3 times larger.

ADDITIONAL STEWARDSHIP PROVISIONS: See "Overview of the Chickadees," p. 152.

MOUNTAIN CHICKADEE
Poecile gambeli • MOCH

STATUS
Widely distributed throughout the southern and central Interior, the mountain chickadee is the most abundant chickadee in these areas, but it is much less common in the northern Interior and on the coast. It is not at risk in B.C.

RANGE
The mountain chickadee breeds mainly throughout the southern and central Interior from the eastern slope of the Coast Mountains to the Alberta border, mostly at 500–1600 m, sometimes up to near treeline. It does not breed in coastal regions.

HABITAT
Feeding: This chickadee forages in all forest types and at all levels in the forest canopy, but it generally feeds higher into the canopy than the black-capped chickadee.

Breeding: Nests are in open conifer forests. In the southern Interior, they are mostly in forests dominated by ponderosa pine, Interior Douglas-fir and montane spruce. Common nest trees are trembling aspen, willows, ponderosa

Mountain chickadee

Biogeoclimatic Zones

AT	BG	BWBS	CDF	CWH	ESSF	ICH	IDF	MH	MS	PP	SBPS	SBS	SWB

Ecoprovinces

BOP	COM	CEI	GED	NBM	SBI	SIM	SOI	TAP

Breeding Period

J	F	M	A	M	J	J	A	S	O	N	D

pine, lodgepole pine and Douglas-fir. (See "Overview of the Chickadees," p. 152, for nest tree details.) This species reuses nest cavities and uses preexisting cavities more frequently than the other chickadee species. Abandoned sapsucker cavities in aspen stands are frequently used. The mountain chickadee's breeding habitat overlaps with the black-capped's at lower elevations and the boreal's at higher elevations.

The breeding season is mid-April to mid-August. The usual clutch size is 5–7. Some pairs in southern areas produce two broods annually.

Roosting: This bird roosts in tree cavities and dense conifers, plus possibly holes excavated in snow. Cavities and dense conifers provide critical thermal protection in winter and at night. During nesting, the female roosts in the nest cavity and the male roosts in a nearby cavity. Several roosting cavities are required on each home range. Flocks roost communally in winter.

Territory Size/Home Range: Breeding territories are about 5–10 ha. The home range outside of the breeding season can be 2–3 times larger.

Territory Size/Home Range: Breeding territories are about 5–10 ha. The home range outside of the breeding season can be 2–3 times larger.

ADDITIONAL STEWARDSHIP PROVISIONS: See "Overview of the Chickadees," p. 152.

Above: Mountain chickadee at nest cavity in class 8 ponderosa pine. Below: Nest cavities in class 5 hardwood

CHESTNUT-BACKED CHICKADEE

Poecile rufescens • CBCH

STATUS

Widely and commonly distributed in coastal British Columbia, the chestnut-backed chickadee is less common and more locally distributed in southern Interior and northwestern mountains. It is not at risk in B.C.

RANGE

The chestnut-backed chickadee breeds anywhere from near sea level to about 1800 m, along the entire coast (including Vancouver Island and Queen Charlotte Islands), inland along the major river valleys in the northwest (Skeena, Stikine, Nass, Taku and Tatshenshini) and locally in the wettest ecosystems of the southern Interior where western red-cedar is present (e.g., Manning Provincial Park, the Kootenays and the upper Shuswap region).

HABITAT

Feeding: The chestnut-backed chickadee forages mainly in the mid- to upper forest canopy of conifers, but, on coastal islands where there is no competition with the black-capped chickadee, it also uses hardwoods.

Adding nest material to natural Garry oak cavity

Biogeoclimatic Zones														
AT	BG	BWBS	CDF	CWH	ESSF	ICH	IDF	MH	MS	PP	SBPS	SBS	SWB

Ecoprovinces									Breeding Period													
BOP	COM	CEI	GED	NBM	SBI	SIM	SOI	TAP	J	F	M	A	M	J	J	A	S	O	N	D

Left: Class 8 coastal Douglas-fir with nest cavity
Above: Excavating nest cavity in class 8 conifer

Breeding: Nests are mainly in conifer forests, both within continuous, dense forest and along openings. Douglas-fir, cedars, hemlocks and spruces are among the nest tree species. (See "Overview of the Chickadees," p. 152, for nest tree details.) On the south coast, the crumbling stumps of Douglas-firs harvested a century ago are often used for nesting.

The breeding season is early April to mid-August. The usual clutch size is 5–7.

Roosting: This bird roosts in tree cavities and dense conifers, plus possibly holes excavated in snow. Cavities and dense conifers provide critical thermal protection in winter and at night. During nesting, the female roosts in the nest cavity and the male roosts in a nearby cavity. Several roosting cavities are required on each home range. Flocks roost communally in winter.

Territory Size/Home Range: Breeding territories are about 5–10 ha. The home range outside of the breeding season can be 2–3 times larger.

ADDITIONAL STEWARDSHIP PROVISIONS: See "Overview of the Chickadees," p. 152.

BOREAL CHICKADEE
Poecile hudsonica • BOCH

STATUS

Widely distributed at higher elevations throughout most of the Interior, the boreal chickadee occasionally appears west of the Coast Mountains and in the lower Fraser Valley. It is not at risk in B.C.

Boreal chickadee, adult

RANGE

The boreal chickadee breeds throughout most of the Interior, but it is not known to breed in coastal regions.

HABITAT

Feeding: Foraging is mainly in the upper and middle canopy of conifer and mixed forests and in subalpine parkland and alpine meadows.

Breeding: The boreal chickadee nests in open conifer forests, often using edge habitat. In northern regions, it nests anywhere from valley bottoms up to near treeline; in southern regions, it breeds mainly in Engelmann spruce–subalpine fir forests above 1200 m. Spruces, poplars, paper birch and willows are among the species used. (See "Overview of the Chickadees," p. 152, for nest tree details.) This chickadee also uses old woodpecker cavities and natural cavities.

The breeding season is May to July. The clutch size is 2–8.

Roosting: This bird roosts in tree cavities and dense conifers, plus possibly holes excavated in snow. Cavities and dense conifers provide critical thermal protection in winter and at night. During nesting, the female roosts in the nest cavity and the male roosts in a nearby cavity. Several roosting cavities are required on each home range. Flocks roost communally in winter.

Territory Size/Home Range: Breeding territories are about 5–10 ha. The home range outside of the breeding season can be 2–3 times larger.

ADDITIONAL STEWARDSHIP PROVISIONS: See "Overview of the Chickadees," p. 152.

Biogeoclimatic Zones

AT	BG	BWBS	CDF	CWH	ESSF	ICH	IDF	MH	MS	PP	SBPS	SBS	SWB

Ecoprovinces									Breeding Period											
BOP	COM	CEI	GED	NBM	SBI	SIM	SOI	TAP	J	F	M	A	M	J	J	A	S	O	N	D

Overview of the Nuthatches

Nuthatches are not as well designed as woodpeckers for cavity excavation, but they can use their woodpecker-like bills to chisel out their own holes for nesting and roosting in sufficiently decayed trees. Like chickadees, nuthatches will use preexisting cavities when they are readily available instead of creating new ones.

British Columbia has three nuthatch species: the red-breasted (one of B.C.'s most widespread birds), the white-breasted (the least abundant of the three) and the pygmy. The breeding habitats of the pygmy and white-breasted nuthatches overlap.

Nuthatches are mainly insectivorous gleaners, eating all life stages of a variety of small insects and spiders. All three nuthatch species eat bark beetles, weevils, spruce budworm and wood-boring beetles. Among the species-specific prey are leaf beetles (pygmy and red-breasted nuthatches), pine budworm and Douglas-fir tussock moth (red-breasted) and gypsy moth and tent caterpillars (white-breasted).

Nuthatches often form winter feeding flocks with other nuthatch species, chickadees, kinglets and brown creepers. Pygmies are the most gregarious, with several family groups commonly uniting in winter. Red-breasted nuthatches join feeding flocks in twos or threes, with other species making up the majority of the flock. White-breasted nuthatches are not as gregarious, but breeding pairs remain together throughout winter.

DESCRIPTION

Their chisel-like bills and very short tails give the nuthatches a distinctive profile. In flight, they can be recognized as small, pointy-headed birds that appear tail-less. The slightly upturned bills of the red-breasted and white-breasted are noticeable at close range.

Barely longer than a typical hummingbird, the pygmy nuthatch is about 10 cm in length. It has a blue-grey back, pale buff underparts, a subtle black eye line and a distinctive greyish brown crown.

The red-breasted nuthatch is 11–12 cm in length. Its blue-grey back contrasts with distinctive rusty-orange underparts, a white face and throat and a black eye stripe and "cap." The male's colours are brighter than the female's. Juveniles have very pale underparts.

At about 14 cm in length, the white-breasted is the largest nuthatch. Its bright white underparts and face contrast with a dark bluish grey back and a black nape; the male's "cap" is black and the female's is grey.

OTHER CHARACTERISTICS

The pygmy's call is a highly pitched *te-dee, te-dee* or *pit-pi-dit-pi-dit*. It calls frequently when in flocks. The call of the red-breasted is a loud, nasal *yank-yank* or *nyak-nyak*. When foraging, it may make rapid, nasal *hit-hit* calls. The white-breasted nuthatch has a single or repeated nasal *yank* call, slightly lower pitched than the red-breasted's. Foraging white-breasted pairs often repeatedly make thin, variably pitched *hi-tuck* calls back and forth.

Pygmy and red-breasted nuthatches are very weak fliers. They fly from tree to tree with short bursts of wing flaps that produce an undulating flight. The white-breasted nuthatch is a stronger flier, but it exhibits the same short bursts of wing flaps and undulating flight pattern. All three nuthatches fly faster than chickadees.

Nuthatches typically move headfirst down tree trunks while searching for prey, rather than moving from the base upward. They are highly acrobatic, often hanging upside down when foraging.

ADDITIONAL STEWARDSHIP PROVISIONS (see also Part 2)

- Retain wildlife trees in advanced stages of decay for nesting and roosting: conifers in classes 4–8 and hardwoods in classes 3–5 and >20 cm dbh for the pygmy and the red-breasted; conifers in classes 2–8 and hardwoods in classes 3–5 and >30 cm dbh for the white-breasted. These trees should be retained in small, scattered groups, 0.25 ha or more in size.

- To maintain populations of pygmy nuthatches, provide for a long-term supply of ponderosa pine snags in logged areas.
- High-cut stumps can provide future nest sites as second-growth stands mature and these stumps reach suitable decay stages.
- Nest boxes may enhance local populations in areas that have good foraging habitat but few suitable nest trees.

Open ponderosa pine forests are typical habitat of the white-breasted nuthatch.

RED-BREASTED NUTHATCH
Sitta canadensis • RBNU

STATUS
A fairly common resident throughout much of British Columbia, the red-breasted nuthatch is most abundant in the south and central Interior, becoming less abundant in the north and on the coast. It is not at risk in B.C.

RANGE
The red-breasted nuthatch breeds from near sea level to 800 m throughout the province, including coastal islands. On the coast and in the southern Interior, it generally winters near its breeding areas, but at lower elevations. During most winters, the northern portion of the population migrates southward.

HABITAT
Feeding: The red-breasted nuthatch prefers to forage in conifer stands with diverse structure and species composition, but will also use a wide variety of other conifer or hardwood forest habitats, pure or mixed, open or closed. It gleans prey from foliage, branches and trunks throughout the canopy, mostly in conifers and occasionally on shrubs and logs, and hawks for flying insects. It will feed heavily on conifer and understorey plant seeds and comes readily to bird feeders.

Breeding: Nests can be anywhere from lowland valleys up to treeline in a wide range of forest habitats, but they are

Red-breasted nuthatch, adult

mostly in mature conifer or mixed forest. In the extreme southern Interior, this species rarely nests in the dry valley bottoms where pygmy and white-breasted nuthatches are common, preferring instead the moister riparian areas and shady, north-facing slopes. A nest tree, >20 cm dbh preferred, must have soft heartwood. The main nest tree species are trembling aspen, cottonwood, Douglas-fir, lodgepole pine and spruces. The nest is usually 2–8 m above the ground, sometimes as much as 20 m. This nuthatch often coats the sides of

Biogeoclimatic Zones
AT	BG	BWBS	CDF	CWH	ESSF	ICH	IDF	MH	MS	PP	SBPS	SBS	SWB

Ecoprovinces
BOP	COM	CEI	GED	NBM	SBI	SIM	SOI	TAP

Breeding Period
J	F	M	A	M	J	J	A	S	O	N	D

the nest cavity entrance with pitch to deter predators and competitors. Cavities may be used year after year, and old woodpecker cavities and nest boxes are also used.

The breeding season is early April to late July. The clutch size is 5–8.

Roosting: This bird roosts in a nest cavity or other tree cavity. Roost sites provide essential thermal cover during winter and at night. Several cavities are needed for roosting in winter. No communal roosting occurs.

Territory Size/Home Range: The breeding territory size is estimated at 1–2 ha.

ADDITIONAL STEWARDSHIP PROVISIONS: See "Overview of the Nuthatches," p. 161.

*Above: At nest cavity in class 4 trembling aspen
Below: Decay class 7 interior Douglas-fir with red-breasted nuthatch cavity*

WHITE-BREASTED NUTHATCH
Sitta carolinensis • WBNU

STATUS
The white-breasted nuthatch is an uncommon resident at low elevations in the southernmost Interior and locally in the Peace River region. It is not at risk in B.C.

At nest cavity in class 8 western larch

RANGE
The white-breasted nuthatch breeds mainly in the southern Interior, west to Lillooet, east through the southern Kootenays and north to Golden. A small population has recently established itself in the Peace River region and appears to be expanding southwestward toward Prince George. Breeding occurs mainly at 335–1000 m. The range in the non-breeding season is similar to the breeding range. A general movement to lower elevations may occur in autumn and winter. Juveniles disperse after fledging.

HABITAT
Feeding: The white-breasted nuthatch prefers open forest. In the south, it forages mainly in mature ponderosa pine, Douglas-fir or western larch forests. Generally foraging lower in the canopy

Biogeoclimatic Zones

AT	BG	BWBS	CDF	CWH	ESSF	ICH	IDF	MH	MS	PP	SBPS	SBS	SWB

Ecoprovinces										Breeding Period												
BOP	COM	CEI	GED	NBM	SBI	SIM	SOI	TAP		J	F	M	A	M	J	J	A	S	O	N	D

cavities may be reused year after year. Nests are usually 3–8 m above the ground but may be as high as 21 m.

The breeding season is early April to mid-July. The clutch size is 6–7.

Roosting: Roosts are mainly in natural cavities or old woodpecker cavities and occasionally behind loose bark. Nest cavities are sometimes used for roosting, but the male and female roost separately year-round. Several roost cavities are needed on each territory.

Territory Size/Home Range: Breeding pairs vigorously defend their large breeding and winter foraging territories (estimated at 25 ha) from other white-breasted nuthatches year-round.

ADDITIONAL STEWARDSHIP PROVISIONS: See "Overview of the Nuthatches," p. 161.

Above: Class 8 western larch with white-breasted nuthatch nest cavity. Right: Departing from cavity in burned class 7 ponderosa pine

(3–10 m) than the pygmy nuthatch, it gleans prey from the bark of trunks and major limbs, with very little foraging in the foliage. It also extracts seeds from cones (e.g., ponderosa pine and Douglas-fir).

Breeding: Nests are in open (<70 percent canopy closure) old-growth ponderosa pine, pine–Douglas-fir–trembling aspen or Douglas-fir–western larch forests. Nests are mostly in natural cavities— although these birds will excavate their own nests if necessary—in living or dead conifers (mainly ponderosa pine in the south, with decay classes 2–8 and >30 cm dbh preferred), and they also take over old woodpecker cavities. Nest

PYGMY NUTHATCH
Sitta pygmaea • PYNU

STATUS

A fairly common resident at lower elevations in the southern Interior, the pygmy nuthatch becomes less abundant and more locally distributed through the southern Kootenays. It is not at risk in B.C.

RANGE

This species breeds mainly at 335–700 m throughout the Okanagan Valley and the Thompson River Valley, west to Lytton and Lillooet, north to Cache Creek and Kamloops and east through Grand Forks, and in the East Kootenay. The range in the nonbreeding season is similar to the breeding range, although some birds move to slightly higher elevations, mainly into Douglas-fir forests, or wander as far as Manning Provincial Park, Canim Lake and Shuswap Lake.

HABITAT

Feeding: This nuthatch forages is mainly in old-growth ponderosa pine forest or mixed pine–Douglas-fir forest, especially open and burned stands and along the edges of dense forests. The pygmy nuthatch gleans prey from terminal needle clusters, new shoots, cones and bark at a height of 8–12 m, which is higher in the canopy than the white-breasted nuthatch forages. Pine seeds are also a year-round staple food.

Breeding: Nests are in open (<70 percent canopy closure) old-growth

At nest cavity in class 6 ponderosa pine

ponderosa pine or mixed pine–Douglas-fir–trembling aspen forests. This nuthatch excavates nest cavities in dead or decayed conifers (>20 cm dbh) with soft heartwood (decay classes 4–8, especially classes 6–8) or hardwoods (decay classes 4–5) and sometimes in rotten fence posts. It prefers ponderosa pine but also uses Douglas-fir, trembling

Biogeoclimatic Zones												
AT	**BG**	BWBS	CDF	CWH	ESSF	ICH	**IDF**	MH	MS	**PP**	SBPS	SBS	SWB

Ecoprovinces										Breeding Period													
BOP	**COM**	CEI	GED	NBM	SBI	**SIM**	SOI	TAP		J	F	**M**	**A**	**M**	J	J	**A**	S	**O**	N	D

young remain with the parents until spring and then disperse to nesting areas. Nonbreeders often help tend the young of breeding pairs.

Roosting: This bird roosts in a nest cavity or another tree cavity, which provides essential thermal cover during winter and at night. One or more family groups (up to 150 birds) may roost communally outside the breeding season. A winter flock needs several cavities for roosting in the home range.

Territory Size/Home Range: Breeding territory size is estimated at 1–2 ha, although only the immediate area around the nest is defended. The home range is likely several times larger.

Additional Stewardship Provisions: See "Overview of the Nuthatches," p. 161.

Above: Class 8 ponderosa pine with nest cavity
Right: Class 4 ponderosa pine with nest cavity

aspen and paper birch. Nest hole entrances can be as small as 3 cm in diameter. Cracks around the nest hole entrance are often stuffed with hair or moss. Nests are usually 2–8 m above the ground and sometimes as high as 21 m. Cavities may be reused year after year, and this species will nest in old woodpecker cavities and nest boxes.

The breeding season is early April to late July. The clutch size is 6–8, and 1–2 broods are produced annually. The

The Secondary Cavity Users

LIST OF SECONDARY CAVITY USERS

BIRDS
- wood duck
- bufflehead
- common goldeneye
- Barrow's goldeneye
- hooded merganser
- common merganser
- American kestrel
- flammulated owl (Blue-listed)
- western screech-owl (*macfarlanei* subspecies is Red-listed; *kennicottii* subspecies is Blue-listed)
- northern hawk owl
- northern pygmy-owl (*swarthi* subspecies is Blue-listed)
- barred owl
- boreal owl
- northern saw-whet owl (*brooksi* subspecies is Blue-listed)
- Vaux's swift
- tree swallow
- brown creeper
- house wren
- western bluebird (western population is Red-listed)
- mountain bluebird

BATS
- California myotis
- western long-eared myotis
- Keen's long-eared myotis (Red-listed)
- little brown myotis
- northern long-eared myotis (Blue-listed)
- long-legged myotis
- Yuma myotis
- western red bat (Red-listed)
- hoary bat
- silver-haired bat
- big brown bat

OTHER MAMMALS
- bushy-tailed woodrat
- Keen's mouse
- northern flying squirrel
- red-tailed chipmunk (*ruficaudus* subspecies is Red-listed; *simulans* subspecies is Blue-listed)
- marten
- fisher (Blue-listed)
- black bear (*emmonsii* subspecies is Blue-listed)

Overview of the Secondary Cavity Users

Secondary cavity users are animals that use tree cavities for nesting, roosting, denning or food storage but are physically unable to excavate holes for themselves. In British Columbia, this guild contains 20 species of birds and 18 species of bats and other mammals that require cavities in part or all of their range. (Additional species, such as starlings, will use cavities opportunistically but are not dependent on them.) These cavity-dependent species rely either on abandoned cavities that were made by primary cavity excavators or on natural cavities that result from internal or external tree decay. Treetop breakage, branch loss and lightning strikes are among the events that accelerate decay. Natural entrance holes can develop when a branch breaks close to the trunk and decay proceeds into the trunk.

Male wood duck in cavity

Spaces behind loose, sloughing bark provide suitable habitat for some species of bats and for the brown creeper, species that are also considered to be part of this guild.

In addition to nesting and roosting in cavities, some secondary cavity users also depend on other wildlife tree features, such as witches' brooms. As well, wildlife trees serve as foraging sites or hunting perches for certain secondary cavity users.

Maintaining habitat for primary cavity excavators (particularly woodpeckers) greatly benefits populations of secondary cavity users. Because most woodpeckers excavate new nesting and roosting cavities for themselves every year, they constantly provide new habitat for secondary cavity users. This ongoing resupply of cavities is essential, because existing cavities are regularly lost as old wildlife trees decay and fall and as nests become unusable as a result of the excess accumulation of nest material.

Unlike most woodpeckers, many secondary cavity users will accept artificial cavities for nesting or roosting. The species that are most receptive to using boxes are ducks, bluebirds, wrens, tree swallows, bats and northern flying squirrels. Success is most likely when the boxes are constructed and placed with the needs of the intended user in mind. Local ecology centres and naturalist or birding clubs may be able to supply construction plans and siting information. Building, erecting and maintaining nest boxes or bat boxes are excellent activities for conservation organizations and youth groups.

However, nest and roost boxes are not a panacea. They require a long-term commitment to annual maintenance and may favour one species over another, as discussed in some of the species accounts. Understand the potential for inter-species interactions before embarking on a nest-box program. Furthermore, as noted earlier, boxes for nesting and roosting should be used only as an interim measure until new wildlife trees develop, not as a permanent replacement for natural or primary cavity excavator cavities.

ABOUT THE BIRDS

The secondary cavity–using birds come from a diverse array of avian families— owls (seven species), ducks (six species), bluebirds (two species) and five families represented by one species each (American kestrel, Vaux's swift, tree swallow, brown creeper and house wren). Some of the primary cavity excavators may also choose to nest in an existing cavity, when available, rather than excavating a new cavity; these birds are the Lewis's woodpecker, the northern flicker and all of the nuthatches and chickadees.

Like the primary cavity excavators, all of the secondary cavity–using birds make an important contribution to maintaining the ecological balance of the ecosystems in which they live. The bluebirds, tree swallow and Vaux's swift consume large numbers of flying insects. The brown creeper specializes in gleaning insects (adults, eggs, larvae and pupae) from crevices in tree bark. The house wren is also an insectivorous gleaner. Raptors, although usually thought of as eating small mammals and birds, may also eat insects. For example, the American kestrel preys partly on grasshoppers, and the flammulated owl is almost exclusively insectivorous. Any spraying of insecticides in forests, grasslands and orchards upsets the ecological balance of these ecosystems by reducing prey availability for all of these species.

The secondary cavity–nesting owls— the western screech-owl, northern hawk owl, northern pygmy-owl, barred owl, boreal owl and northern saw-whet owl—are significant predators of small forest rodents and shrews. Owls are at the top of the food chain, and their presence is an indicator of the overall integrity and health of a forest.

WOOD DUCK
Aix sponsa • WODU

STATUS

The wood duck is a common resident in the lower Fraser Valley and scattered locations on the Sunshine Coast and southern Vancouver Island. The diets of overwintering populations on the south coast are supplemented by feed provided in parks and reserves. Across the southern Interior, it is a rare to uncommon summer visitor and very rare in winter. It is not at risk in B.C.

Male wood duck

RANGE

The wood duck is found locally from near sea level to 1200 m across southern British Columbia and rarely north to the Peace River region, Mount Robson area and the Queen Charlotte Islands. It breeds on Vancouver Island from the south end to Tofino on the west coast and Cortes Island on the east, through-out the lower Fraser Valley and in the Interior north to Prince George. Centres of abundance are the lower Fraser Valley on the coast and the Creston Valley in the Interior. This duck overwinters any-where from southern British Columbia

Biogeoclimatic Zones

AT	BG	BWBS	CDF	CWH	ESSF	ICH	IDF	MH	MS	PP	SBPS	SBS	SWB

Ecoprovinces										Breeding Period												
BOP	COM	CEI	GED	NBM	SBI	SIM	SOI	TAP		J	F	M	A	M	J	J	A	S	O	N	D

Female wood duck

to central Mexico, with very few birds remaining in the Okanagan. Autumn migrants depart in September and October. Spring migrants return to the south coast in mid-March and to the southern Interior in April.

DESCRIPTION

The wood duck is about the size of a crow (about 50 cm in length). The colourful, exotic-looking male has an iridescent, green, crested head with white markings, red eyes and a distinctive red bill; his breast is chestnut, the shoulders have a vertical white bar bordered by black, and the sides are buff-coloured. The mainly brownish grey female can be distinguished from other species by her head crest and the white teardrop shape surrounding the eye. The distinctive flight profile shows the large head with the bill angled downward and a relatively long, squared-off tail.

OTHER CHARACTERISTICS

The wood duck does not dive as it forages secretively in small groups. As it swims, its head bobs with each stroke. Using the sharp claws on its toes to help grip branches, it is the only B.C. duck that routinely perches in trees. The squealing flight call is a loud, rising *oo-eek*.

HABITAT

Feeding: This duck forages in wetlands (e.g., sloughs, swamps, flooded fields, sewage lagoons, oxbows, ponds and slow-moving rivers) with heavy shoreline cover of forest, cattails or overhanging brush. Adults feed mainly on aquatic and emergent plants, invertebrates and seeds, including grains from agricultural sources. Young ducks depend more on aquatic invertebrates, often consuming them along with duckweed.

Breeding: These ducks breed in mature hardwood woodlands near quiet, fresh or brackish waterways. Good brood habitat features shallow wetlands with overhanging woody shoreline vegetation, emergent vegetation for escape cover and abundant downed logs or low islands. Nests are usually located in open forest near water or in snags in flooded areas. Abandoned pileated woodpecker holes or cavities created by broken limbs are preferred for nesting, but the species readily uses nest boxes. Nest cavity entrances are >12 cm in diameter and 5–25 m above the ground in large, mature hardwoods (e.g., black cottonwood, trembling aspen, red alder and bigleaf maple). Females show strong nest-site tenacity, returning to the same nest year after year. About 24 hours after hatching, the young exit the nest and tumble to the ground. They are very vulnerable to predation and need cover as they move to water.

The breeding period extends from the end of March through early September, although most birds leave their nests by the end of July. The clutch size is 6–16.

Roosting: The wood duck roosts on logs, the shore and large branches of hardwoods; it also rests on the water.

Territory Size/Home Range: Breeding territories and nest sites are not defended, and sometimes 2–3 females will lay in the same box. The home range size is not known, but a pair will remain in the vicinity of its nest site during the breeding season. Good wetland habitat with abundant suitable wildlife trees can support one nesting pair per hectare.

ADDITIONAL STEWARDSHIP
PROVISIONS (see also Part 2)
- Manage as for pileated woodpeckers.
- Retain all existing nest trees and an adequate supply of large (>50 cm dbh) hardwoods within 50 m of

suitable wetland habitats throughout southern B.C.
- Maintain understorey shrubs along shorelines of known and potential nesting areas.
- Retain live and dead trees (standing or fallen) in flooded areas created by beaver activity.
- Consider nest-box programs in areas of high habitat value where wildlife trees are scarce.

OF INTEREST
The sharp claws of day-old wood ducks enable them to scramble up the inside walls of the nest cavity, ascending as much as 2–3 m to reach the exit. These claws, which remain on the toe tips of the webbed feet of the adult, allow wood ducks to perch on tree branches.

BUFFLEHEAD
Bucephala albeola • BUFF

STATUS

In the Interior, the bufflehead is a common migrant and breeding species except in the extreme north, where it is rare to uncommon. It is a common to locally abundant migrant and winter visitor along the coast. It is not at risk in B.C.

RANGE

Found anywhere from sea level to at least 1900 m, the bufflehead breeds at 300–1450 m throughout most of the Interior, though only rarely in the low-elevation valleys of the southern Interior. Breeding populations are highest in the Cariboo-Chilcotin region. It seldom breeds near the coast—the only records are for Sumas and Pitt Meadows—but a few nonbreeding birds occur along the coast in summer. The bufflehead overwinters anywhere from Alaska southward to the southern U.S. and Mexico. In B.C., it overwinters mainly along the coast, including the Queen Charlotte Islands, and its centre of abundance is southern Vancouver Island and the Gulf Islands, where it concentrates in late winter and early spring to feed on Pacific herring spawn. The bufflehead also overwinters in the Interior, from the Okanagan to the West Kootenay and north to the South Thompson River. The main spring movement to the Interior occurs in April; initial concentrations on large, ice-free lakes are followed by dispersal to breeding lakes by May. Most birds return to the coast between late October and November.

DESCRIPTION

This small duck (smaller than a crow; about 35 cm in length) has a large, puffy head, steep forehead and short bill. The male's strongly contrasting plumage shows black above, black wings, white sides and belly and a large, white patch on the back and sides of the head. The female is dark brown with white on the sides of the head.

OTHER CHARACTERISTICS

The wing beats of the bufflehead are very fast, and it often flies very close to the water. It dives when foraging. Flocks

Male and female buffleheads

Biogeoclimatic Zones

AT	BG	BWBS	CDF	CWH	ESSF	ICH	IDF	MH	MS	PP	SBPS	SBS	SWB

Ecoprovinces										Breeding Period												
BOP	COM	CEI	GED	NBM	SBI	SIM	SOI	TAP		J	F	M	A	M	J	J	A	S	O	N	D

are compact in flight and on the water. The female's call is a hoarse croak similar to the goldeneye's, but weaker. The male emits a squeaky whistle.

HABITAT

Feeding: Foraging occurs in shallow water along the seashore and lake shores. In fresh and brackish waters, the bufflehead feeds on aquatic insects, crustaceans and the seeds of aquatic vegetation. In marine habitats, it feeds on crustaceans, molluscs, herring spawn and some aquatic vegetation. Small fish are an important component of its winter diet.

Breeding: Nests are primarily within 50 m of lakes, rivers, sloughs and ponds in Interior Douglas-fir forests, ponderosa pine forests, aspen parklands and grasslands, but some can be 200 m away. Live or dead trees are used, especially trembling aspen and Douglas-fir, but also lodgepole pine, ponderosa pine, black cottonwood, spruce and balsam poplar. Nests are 2–14 m above the ground. Cavities excavated by northern flickers and enlarged through decay are the main natural sites, and nest boxes are also readily used. A female may return to the same nest site year after year.

The breeding period extends from mid-April to the end of August. The clutch size is 6–12.

Roosting: The bufflehead rests mainly on the water and rarely roosts on the shore.

Territory Size/Home Range: Little is known, but a small area on the water near the nest site is defended from other buffleheads.

Class 7 conifer, cavity occupied by bufflehead

ADDITIONAL STEWARDSHIP PROVISIONS (see also Part 2)

- Manage as for northern flickers.
- Retain some stands of mature aspen (>40 cm dbh, decay classes 2–5) within 200 m of wetlands.
- Retain all existing nest trees and leave some woody vegetation along the shorelines of nesting areas for protective cover.
- Retain live and dead trees in flooded areas created by beaver activity.
- Consider nest-box programs in areas of high habitat value with few nest sites in places where there is no overlap with the breeding range of the common goldeneye or the Barrow's goldeneye. In areas of overlap, note that an entrance hole with a diameter of 6.5 cm will admit the bufflehead but not the other two species.

OF INTEREST

Transfers of young from one bufflehead brood to another are fairly common, often resulting in numbers in excess of the clutch size. Sometimes two broods combine and are attended by both mothers.

The Common Goldeneye and Barrow's Goldeneye: Similarities and Differences

DESCRIPTION

Both the common goldeneye and the Barrow's goldeneye are medium-sized (about 50 cm in length), heavy-bodied ducks. The male common goldeneye has a greenish black head and a round, white spot on each side of the face. The male Barrow's is distinguished by a purplish black head and a white crescent-shaped patch on the face. Males of both species have a black back and white breast, but the common goldeneye has more white on his sides. The females of both species have a dark brown head and greyish brown body. They are difficult to differentiate, but the female Barrow's has a steeper forehead and a shorter bill that may become entirely yellow in breeding season. Both species and genders have white wing patches visible in flight.

OTHER CHARACTERISTICS

Courting male goldeneyes make a harsh, vibrating, double-noted *zee-att*. Females produce a variety of harsh, low-pitched *grrk* calls. In flight, which is fast and level, flocks form tight "V"s or half-"V"s, and they produce a louder musical whistle with their wings during takeoff and in flight than other ducks do. Goldeneyes dive repeatedly when foraging.

RELATIONSHIP TO PRIMARY CAVITY EXCAVATORS

The large cavities (entrances >15 cm in diameter) required by goldeneyes for nesting are relatively rare. The pileated woodpecker is the only woodpecker that creates cavities large enough for goldeneyes but are rarely found near suitable goldeneye brood-rearing habitat. The process of decay can make abandoned northern flicker cavities large enough for goldeneyes, but trees at this decay stage are susceptible to blowdown, so nesting opportunities may be short-lived. Females that are unable to find a suitable nest cavity in time for breeding spend the summer looking for a nest site for the following year.

ADDITIONAL STEWARDSHIP PROVISIONS (see also Part 2)

- Retain numerous large, soft snags (decay classes 5–8 for conifers and 3–5 for hardwoods) within 500 m of wetlands.
- Retain patches (>0.5 ha) of large hardwoods and a selection of conifers (>50 cm dbh) in riparian areas and in uplands within 500 m of wetlands.
- Consider nest-box programs to increase populations in areas of high habitat value with few suitable wildlife trees. If nest-box programs are initiated, keep in mind that increasing the density of goldeneyes (common or Barrow's) may result in a decline in the density of buffleheads, because the former usually dominate in aggressive encounters. Additional nest boxes with 6.5-cm-diameter entrances, which will suit the smaller bufflehead but keep the two goldeneye species out, will help alleviate this problem.

COMMON GOLDENEYE
Bucephala clangula • COGO

STATUS
Uncommon but widespread throughout the Interior in summer, the common goldeneye is common on the coast in winter and uncommon in the southern Interior. It is not at risk in B.C.

Male common goldeneye

RANGE
This species breed at elevations of 180–1550 m and occurs widely throughout the southern third of the province east of the Coast Mountains, more sparsely farther north and very rarely on eastern Vancouver Island and in the lower Fraser Valley. It overwinters mainly on the coast from Alaska to California, with birds in B.C. largely around Vancouver Island and the Queen Charlotte Islands and in mainland fjords. Autumn migration takes place from October to late November, but during mild winters, some birds remain in the Interior, congregating in major southern valleys and as far north as Prince George. Spring migration is from late March to mid-April in the south and late April to early May in the north.

HABITAT
Feeding: The freshwater diet consists of aquatic insects, crustaceans and some aquatic vegetation; the marine diet is mostly molluscs, crustaceans and herring eggs. Favoured coastal habitats include the shallow waters of estuaries, bays, lakes and lagoons, as well as along spits, beaches and, occasionally, rivers and creeks. In late winter and early spring, concentrations occur where Pacific herring are spawning. In the Interior, the common goldeneye frequents lakes, woodland ponds and slow-moving rivers; it also uses sloughs, creeks and marshes.

Breeding: Nests are near standing or slow-moving water, primarily in mature

Biogeoclimatic Zones

AT	BG	BWBS	CDF	CWH	ESSF	ICH	IDF	MH	MS	PP	SBPS	SBS	SWB

Ecoprovinces									Breeding Period									
BOP	COM	CEI	GED	NBM	SBI	SIM	SOI	TAP	J	F	M	A	M	J	J	A	S	O	N	D

Female bufflehead with young

and old-growth forests. Lakes, ponds and river backwaters with some overhanging brush and logs are good brood habitat. Nest sites within 100 m of water are preferred, but in rangeland habitats with few suitable nest trees, goldeneyes may nest up to 500 m from water. Nest trees are usually dead and must be large enough to accommodate a cavity entrance >15 cm diameter. Nests, at a height of 2–15 m, have been found in natural cavities in black cottonwood, ponderosa pine and Douglas-fir and in sufficiently large abandoned woodpecker cavities. This duck also takes readily to nest boxes and occasionally nests in witches' brooms.

The breeding period extends from the beginning of April to the end of August. The clutch size is 5–9.

Roosting: The common goldeneye roosts on logs and the shore; it also rests on the water.

Territory Size/Home Range: This duck defends small areas on the water around or near the nest from other goldeneyes. Breeding ponds can be as small as 0.5 ha. Pairs show strong year-to-year fidelity to nest sites, breeding territories and wintering sites.

ADDITIONAL STEWARDSHIP PROVISIONS: See "The Common Goldeneye and Barrow's Goldeneye: Similarities and Differences," p.176.

Natural cavity in a class 3 trembling aspen occupied by common goldeneye

OF INTEREST

Common goldeneye courtship is among the most complex of any North American duck; male postures include head-throwing and backward kicking that sprays water behind the displaying bird.

BARROW'S GOLDENEYE
Bucephala islandica • BAGO

STATUS

Fairly common and widely distributed in British Columbia, the Barrow's goldeneye is abundant in the Interior and uncommon on the coast during breeding; the reverse occurs in winter. It is not at risk in B.C.

Male and female Barrow's goldeneyes

RANGE

The Barrow's goldeneye breeds throughout the Interior, with its abundance peaking among the wetlands of the Chilcotin–Cariboo region. West of the Coast Mountains, it breeds only very rarely and locally. It has been recorded from sea level to as high as 2400 m in summer. From late August to November, its distribution is centred on large lakes in the Interior. The Barrow's overwinters along the Pacific Coast from Alaska to California and locally inland from southern B.C. to the southern U.S. In B.C., winter concentrations occur along the mainland coast, and small numbers overwinter in major southern Interior valleys. Late winter and early spring concentrations occur in coastal areas where Pacific herring are spawning. Spring migrants arrive in the Interior from early March to mid-April and return to the coast from late October through November.

Biogeoclimatic Zones

AT	BG	BWBS	CDF	CWH	ESSF	ICH	IDF	MH	MS	PP	SBPS	SBS	SWB

Ecoprovinces									Breeding Period											
BOP	COM	CEI	GED	NBM	SBI	SIM	SOI	TAP	J	F	M	A	M	J	J	A	S	O	N	D

Natural cavity in a class 8 conifer, occupied by Barrow's goldeneye.

HABITAT
Feeding: In the Interior, the Barrow's goldeneye forages in ponds, lakes and slow-moving rivers for aquatic insects, crustaceans and some aquatic vegetation. In marine environments, it forages in shallow, protected shoreline waters, feeding mainly on molluscs and crustaceans.

Breeding: Nests are in open, late-seral forest edges along slow-moving rivers, sloughs, lakes and ponds. Nest trees may be hardwoods (trembling aspen or black cottonwood) or conifers (Douglas-fir, ponderosa pine, spruce or lodgepole pine) that are almost always dead and must be large. Abandoned woodpecker cavities are used if they are large enough; otherwise natural cavities (such as ones formed by branch breakage) are used. Nests are normally 2–18 m above the ground. Sometimes they are in rock crevices or on the ground under shrubs and other such places, but these nests have a higher risk of brood failure. This duck also takes readily to nest boxes.

The breeding period extends from mid-March through mid-August. The clutch size is 5–9.

Roosting: The Barrow's goldeneye roosts on logs and on the shore; it also rests on the water.

Territory Size/Home Range: A pair will defend a small area on the water around or near the nest from other goldeneyes. Females strongly defend their brood territories and attack young of the same and other species. Breeding ponds can be as small as 0.5 ha. Pairs show strong year-to-year fidelity to nest sites, breeding territories and overwintering sites.

ADDITIONAL STEWARDSHIP PROVISIONS: See "The Common Goldeneye and Barrow's Goldeneye: Similarities and Differences," p.176.

OF INTEREST
An estimated 60–90 percent of the world's Barrow's goldeneye population breeds in B.C., giving the province a global responsibility for the future of this species.

HOODED MERGANSER
Lophodytes cucullatus • HOME

STATUS
A fairly common and widely distributed resident in the south, the hooded merganser is becoming less common in the north. It is not at risk in B.C.

Female and male hooded mergansers

RANGE
The hooded merganser breeds anywhere from the northern Queen Charlotte Islands, Kitsault, Fort St. James and Prince George south throughout much of the rest of the province, from near sea level to 1200 m. It is widely distributed along the coast (although breeding has not been documented in all areas) and throughout the southern two-thirds of the Interior, but it is sparser in northern areas. This duck overwinters anywhere from southern British Columbia to Mexico. On the coast, its B.C. winter distribution is centred on the Strait of Georgia, particularly around Victoria; in the Interior, it is centred on the south Okanagan. Autumn migration occurs from late October to early December in coastal areas and from early October to November in the Interior. Wintering birds disperse to breed by mid- to late May in the southern Interior and by the end of April on the south coast.

DESCRIPTION
This small duck (smaller than a crow, with a length of 43–49 cm) has a crested head and a thin, serrated bill. The male has a black body, rusty sides and a black head and bill. He can raise or lower his fan-shaped head crest, which is white with a black border. The female is mostly brown and has a rust-coloured crest.

OTHER CHARACTERISTICS
The hooded merganser is commonly seen in flocks of 4–6 in quiet backwaters. It needs a long takeoff run, and its wings slap at the water as it runs. In flight, it can be recognized by its rapid

Biogeoclimatic Zones

AT	BG	BWBS	CDF	CWH	ESSF	ICH	IDF	MH	MS	PP	SBPS	SBS	SWB

Ecoprovinces									Breeding Period												
BOP	COM	CEI	GED	NBM	SBI	SIM	SOI	TAP	J	F	M	A	M	J	J	A	S	O	N	D

Wetland habitat class 5 hardwood woodpecker cavity typically used by hooded merganser

wingbeats, pointed wings and distinctive profile with the bill, head, body and wings on the same horizontal plane; the head crest flattens in flight.

HABITAT

Feeding: This duck eats mostly salmon and trout fry and fingerlings and small nongame fish but also takes crustaceans, insects and some amphibians and molluscs. On the coast, it is most often found in estuaries and protected harbours, bays and inlets. It also frequents coastal lakes, marshes, sloughs and, in autumn, salmon-spawning streams. In the Interior, it is found on lakes, slow-moving rivers, beaver ponds, sewage lagoons and marshes.

Breeding: Preferred breeding sites are near fresh or, occasionally, brackish water (e.g., rivers, lakes, marshes, streams, beaver ponds and sloughs), usually with forested shorelines, overhanging woody vegetation and logs or low islands. Sensitive to disturbance by humans, the hooded merganser often uses small, secluded wetlands. Broods are sometimes seen in irrigation ditches and sewage lagoons. Nests are found in trees such as black cottonwood, western red-cedar or Douglas-fir, alive or dead, with a 30–90 cm dbh. Abandoned woodpecker cavities or natural cavities with an entrance diameter >9 cm at a height of 4–15 m are normally selected, and nest boxes are frequently used as well.

The breeding period extends from late March through September. The clutch size is 6–15.

Roosting: The hooded merganser rests mainly on the water.

Territory Size/Home Range: Territories are not defended. Females may use the same nest site year after year.

ADDITIONAL STEWARDSHIP PROVISIONS (see also Part 2)

- Manage as for northern flickers and pileated woodpeckers.
- Retain a suitable number of large (>40 cm dbh) black cottonwoods, red-cedars and Douglas-firs and a shrubby understorey within 50 m of shallow wetlands.
- Retain live and dead trees (standing or fallen) in flooded areas created by beaver activity.
- Consider nest-box programs in areas of high habitat value with few nest sites.

OF INTEREST

Once incubation begins, male hooded mergansers leave their mates and disperse to moulting areas. They are rejoined in autumn, mainly in coastal areas, by the females and juveniles.

COMMON MERGANSER
Mergus merganser • COME

STATUS
A common and widely distributed resident along the coast and in the southern Interior, the common merganser is much less plentiful in the northern Interior. It is not at risk in B.C.

RANGE
The common merganser breeds throughout most of B.C., anywhere from sea level to about 1000 m. On the Pacific Coast, it overwinters from Alaska to southern California. In British Columbia, it overwinters along the coast in protected marine waters and on freshwater lakes. Some flocks overwinter locally in the southern Interior, and a very few birds overwinter at the edge of the ice on rivers and lake outlets in the northern Interior, but most Interior birds are forced out by the freezing of lakes and rivers; they migrate from early October (in the north) to early December (in the south). Spring migration is from mid-March in the south to early May in the north. After incubation begins, the males disperse to moulting areas, and then most of them move to the coast in autumn, where they are joined by females and juveniles.

DESCRIPTION
This large duck (much larger than a mallard, at about 65 cm in length) has a slender head and neck and a long, serrated, red bill. The male's dark back and

Female common merganser with young, inside cavity

green head contrast sharply with his white breast and flank. The female, with her chestnut-coloured crested head, white chin and breast and grey back, is easily mistaken for a female red-breasted merganser.

OTHER CHARACTERISTICS
The common merganser needs a long takeoff run, its wings slapping at the water as it runs. In flight, it shows pointed wings and a distinctive profile in which the bill, head, body and wings are all on the same horizontal plane. This duck is typically seen flying along rivers at 1–10 m above the water. Small flocks often swim in formation and search for prey by ducking their heads underwater.

Biogeoclimatic Zones

AT	BG	BWBS	CDF	CWH	ESSF	ICH	IDF	MH	MS	PP	SBPS	SBS	SWB

Ecoprovinces									Breeding Period											
BOP	COM	CEI	GED	NBM	SBI	SIM	SOI	TAP	J	F	M	A	M	J	J	A	S	O	N	D

183

Class 7 conifer with natural cavity occupied by a common merganser

spawning sites in spring and salmon-spawning rivers and streams in autumn.

Breeding: Nests are built along the forested shores of clear lakes, streams (except steeply descending ones), rivers and beaver ponds and also along marine shorelines. The common merganser mostly uses cavities in live or dead trees or depressions in the tops of broken snags. Trees must be >50 cm dbh to accommodate the >18-cm-diameter nest-cavity entrance. The nest height is typically 1–24 m, but this duck will also nest on the ground (especially on small islands in lakes) or in rock crevices in cliffs, and it sometimes uses nest boxes.

The breeding period extends from the beginning of March to early September. The clutch size is 5–15.

Roosting: Midstream rocks, river bars, cobble beaches, shoals, island shorelines, riverbanks, protruding logs and log booms are used for roosting.

Territory Size/Home Range: Females exhibit strong nest site fidelity from year to year.

ADDITIONAL STEWARDSHIP PROVISIONS (see also Part 2)

- Retain some large (>50 cm dbh) dead and living wildlife trees with large broken branches or natural cavities within 50 m of lakes, streams and beaver ponds.
- Retain some mature riparian forest along waterways for a future supply of nest trees.
- Nest-box programs may not be practical because of the low density of breeding pairs.

HABITAT
Feeding: Primarily a fish-eater, the common merganser consumes large numbers of salmon and trout fry and fingerlings as well as nongame fish. In spring, when fish may be scarce, it will feed on aquatic invertebrates. Clear waters free of aquatic vegetation are preferred (and probably necessary) for feeding. On the coast, it frequents fresh and brackish waters, especially in estuaries, protected bays and inlets. Inland from the coast it uses the lower reaches of wide rivers and sloughs that have roost sites. In the Interior, this duck prefers medium to large lakes, rivers and streams. It frequents Pacific herring

OF INTEREST
Large broods of 20–30 young are sometimes encountered on Interior lakes. They result when two broods meet and some of the young accidentally depart with the other female rather than with their mother.

AMERICAN KESTREL
Falco sparverius • AMKE

STATUS
A fairly common summer visitor throughout the Interior, the American kestrel is much less common in southern coastal areas and rare on the north coast. It is not at risk in B.C.

RANGE
Widely distributed throughout the province from sea level to 2500 m, the American kestrel is most abundant in the central and southern Interior. It breeds anywhere from near sea level to at least 1800 m, widely through most of the Interior and also on southeastern Vancouver Island, locally in the lower Fraser Valley and at the heads of some fjords along the Central Coast and north coast. In the nonbreeding period, it migrates southwards, perhaps as far as Central America; the kestrel will rarely overwinter in southern B.C. Spring migration is from early March to early May. Autumn migration is from mid-August to October.

DESCRIPTION
A colourful, jay-sized falcon (25–30 cm in length), the American kestrel has a rufous back and tail, paler underparts and two vertical black stripes on its pale face. The male has bluish grey wings and is brighter than the female, which has brownish wings. The juveniles resemble the adults but have more streaking on their underparts.

Male American kestrel at cavity in class 8 conifer
Inset: Female

Biogeoclimatic Zones

AT	BG	BWBS	CDF	CWH	ESSF	ICH	IDF	MH	MS	PP	SBPS	SBS	SWB

Ecoprovinces

BOP	COM	CEI	GED	NBM	SBI	SIM	SOI	TAP

Breeding Period

J	F	M	A	M	J	J	A	S	O	N	D

American kestrel at old woodpecker cavity in a class 2 ponderosa pine

and chipmunks) and small songbirds (e.g., sparrows and warblers). Often capturing flying prey in midair or hovering and dropping to seize prey on the ground, it sometimes hunts directly from a perch. The male feeds his mate and young during incubation and the early nestling period.

Breeding: Trembling aspen and ponderosa pine parklands are favoured for breeding, but natural grasslands, river bottomlands, meadows, bogs and agricultural areas are also used, particularly near forest edges. The nest is usually in a woodpecker hole or natural cavity, 4.5–9 m above the ground, in a live or dead tree. The preferred nest trees are ponderosa pine, Douglas-fir, black cottonwood and trembling aspen >30 cm dbh. Nest boxes and cavities in power poles, fence posts and cliffs are occasionally used.

The breeding period extends from early April to late August. The clutch size is 4–5, and an average of 3–4 young successfully fledge.

Roosting: This species is thought to roost in tree cavities.

Territory Size/Home Range: The breeding territory can be 100–150 ha in size. Breeding and nonbreeding season territories are defended from other kestrels.

ADDITIONAL STEWARDSHIP PROVISIONS (see also Part 2)
- Manage as for the northern flickers, pileated woodpecker and Lewis's woodpecker.
- Consider nest-box programs in areas with good foraging habitat but few suitable wildlife trees.

OTHER CHARACTERISTICS
The call is a shrill, loud *killy-killy-killy.* This species is often seen perched on fence posts or utility wires near roads. It hovers with rapidly beating wings when hunting.

HABITAT
Feeding: The American kestrel hunts in open, nonforested uplands, agricultural areas, grasslands, rangelands, meadows and marshes and along forest edges and roadsides with trees or other perches. It eats mainly large insects (e.g., grasshoppers), small mammals (e.g., voles, mice

OF INTEREST
This species was formerly known as "sparrow hawk," even though rodents and grasshoppers are its main prey.

FLAMMULATED OWL
Otus flammeolus • FLOW

STATUS
B.C.: Blue List
COSEWIC: Special Concern

An uncommon to locally fairly common summer visitor in the southern Interior, the flammulated owl is a rare summer visitor north to Williams Lake and in the East Kootenay. In Canada, this species occurs only in B.C. It is at risk because of its small population (estimated at 500–2000 breeding pairs in B.C.) and threats to its habitat.

Flammulated owl in an abandonded woodpecker cavity in a ponderosa pine

RANGE
The flammulated owl has one of the most restricted breeding distributions of all B.C. owls. At elevations of 400–1400 m, it breeds locally in the Thompson-Okanagan Plateau region, throughout most of the Okanagan Valley and west to Pavilion Lake, as well as in the East Kootenay, where it is likely more widely distributed than is currently known. It overwinters in Mexico and Guatemala, with most birds arriving in B.C. by mid-May and leaving by early September.

DESCRIPTION
The small (16–19 cm in length), compact flammulated owl has a variegated red-and-grey plumage that resembles tree bark. It has dark brown eyes. Its small ear tufts are often indistinct.

Biogeoclimatic Zones

AT	BG	BWBS	CDF	CWH	ESSF	ICH	IDF	MH	MS	PP	SBPS	SBS	SWB

Ecoprovinces

BOP	COM	CEI	GED	NBM	SBI	SIM	SOI	TAP

Breeding Period

J	F	M	A	M	J	J	A	S	O	N	D

Flammulated owl, adult

OTHER CHARACTERISTICS
Strictly nocturnal and seldom seen, the flammulated owl utters a series of low-pitched, single (or rarely paired) hollow hoots, repeated steadily at 2–3-second intervals.

HABITAT
Feeding: Foraging is mainly <200–300 m from the nest site, in open, mature or old-growth, conifer-dominated forests or along the edges of clearings in early-seral forest. Grassy openings in and adjacent to forest stands are important foraging sites, but to avoid predation by larger owls, this bird rarely ventures more than a few metres from the forest edge. Unlike British Columbia's other owls, the flammulated owl is insectivorous—taking its prey on the ground, in the air and from foliage—and only rarely eats small vertebrates. The breeding season diet comprises mainly crickets, beetles, grasshoppers, moths, centipedes and spruce budworm larvae.

Breeding: Breeding is largely in mature, open ponderosa pine–Douglas-fir forest with trees of varying ages, including some dense clumps of young trees, an open understorey of pinegrass, bluebunch wheatgrass, birch-leaved spirea and a few larger shrubs (e.g., Saskatoon). Trembling aspen copses within conifer forests also provide nest trees. Thickets of regenerating Douglas-fir 5–8 m in height, 80–120 years old and within about 50 m of the nest tree provide critical escape cover. Breeding territories are typically found in core areas of mature timber (>200 years old) with a multi-level canopy and often near, or adjacent to, clearings with 10–80 percent brush cover. Populations are sparser in the ponderosa pine zone than in the Interior Douglas-fir zone. In the hottest parts of the breeding range, nesting is restricted to areas with large Douglas-firs and heavy grass cover on north-facing slopes. In cooler parts of the breeding range, the nests are on steep slopes at higher elevations than elsewhere. The nests are situated in abandoned woodpecker (usually northern flicker) cavities, 1.5–14 m above the ground, usually in a ponderosa pine (preferred) or Douglas-fir snag >30 cm dbh. The flammulated owl rarely uses nest boxes.

The breeding period is from the beginning of June to the end of August. The clutch size is 2–4.

Roosting: Dense, multilayered stands (often Douglas-fir) that provide thermal cover and protection from predators are used for day roosts. This owl typically perches on a horizontal limb next to the trunk. Fledglings use nearby day roosts for about 2 weeks after leaving the nest.

Territory Size/Home Range: The home range averages an estimated 14–16 ha in size and encompasses foraging, nesting and roosting habitats. It usually does not overlap other home ranges and is defended while the fledglings are present. Densities as low as 1 male per 100 ha have been recorded in B.C. during the breeding season.

ADDITIONAL STEWARDSHIP PROVISIONS (see also Part 2)

- Manage as for the northern flicker, medium-sized woodpeckers and the pileated woodpecker.
- Retain a supply of coniferous wildlife trees, especially ponderosa pine, of decay classes 4–8, >50 cm dbh and >6 m in height.
- Maintain patches of mature forest >10 ha in size and some densely stocked, regenerating Douglas-fir near grassy openings.
- Do not disturb (no harvesting or road construction) the vicinity of known nest sites during the breeding season (beginning of June to the end of August).
- For each known nest site, retain a foraging and security habitat area 7–22 ha in size (depends on the suitability and productivity of the habitat).

Class 7 ponderosa pine

- Consider habitat enhancement near known nest sites. Deactivate roads and use partial harvesting to develop a multilayered forest with a healthy upper canopy provided by >50 percent mature and older trees—do not cut any mature (> 35 cm dbh), veteran or wildlife trees and retain all ponderosa pine and trembling aspen to develop as future wildlife trees, or establish these species if they are lacking. Retain thickets for security cover.

OF INTEREST

Because they reach the breeding areas later in spring than other secondary cavity users, flammulated owls may face a shortage of suitable nest sites.

WESTERN SCREECH-OWL

Megascops kennicottii • WSOW

STATUS

Interior: MacFarlane's subspecies, *M. k. macfarlanei*—B.C.: Red List; COSEWIC: Endangered
Coastal: Kennicott's subspecies, *M. k. kennicottii*—B.C.: Blue List; COSEWIC: Special Concern

In Canada, the western screech-owl occurs only in British Columbia, where it appears as two subspecies. MacFarlane's western screech-owl (*M. k. macfarlanei*) is a rare resident in the southern Interior, where it is at the northern limit of its range; its numbers are quite low and declining because of loss and fragmentation of breeding and foraging habitat. The coastal Kennecott's subspecies (*M. k. kennicottii*) extends from Washington and Oregon into British Columbia. It is an uncommon but widespread resident on the east coast of Vancouver Island and the Gulf Islands and an uncommon to fairly common resident on the mainland coast from the Fraser Valley north to Terrace and further north to Alaska. Direct predation by expanding barred owl populations may be a threat to it, especially on Vancouver Island and the Gulf Islands.

RANGE

The nonmigratory western screech-owl is one of the province's most sedentary owl species. It occurs year-round through-out its breeding range. The coastal subspecies breeds at relatively low elevations (<600 m) on Vancouver Island, the Gulf Islands, the mainland coast from Delta and Chilliwack north to Kitimat, and on most large coastal islands except the Queen Charlotte Islands. The only known breeding areas for the MacFarlane's sub-species are in the Okanagan, Thompson, Nicola and Shuswap valleys and in the Creston Valley, but it likely also breeds in major river valleys in the East Kootenay.

Old pileated woodpecker cavities in red alder are excellent nest cavities for western screech-owl.

Biogeoclimatic Zones

AT	BG	BWBS	CDF	CWH	ESSF	ICH	IDF	MH	MS	PP	SBPS	SBS	SWB

Ecoprovinces

BOP	COM	CEI	GED	NBM	SBI	SIM	SOI	TAP

Breeding Period

J	F	M	A	M	J	J	A	S	O	N	D

Western screech-owl, adult

DESCRIPTION

The heavyset western screech-owl (19–25 cm long) is slightly larger than a robin. It has yellow eyes and a dark beak. Its ear tufts are prominent when raised, but when they are flattened, the head appears round. MacFarlane's subspecies is grey overall; Kennicotts' is browner or has a slight rusty tinge.

OTHER CHARACTERISTICS

This nocturnal owl is most easily located and identified by voice. Two common calls are a series of short whistles on the same pitch, accelerating in tempo, and a short trill followed immediately by a longer trill. Most vocal in early spring, this owl also does some calling in autumn, when the juveniles disperse. The wing-beats are rapid on its short, fluttering flights beneath the forest canopy.

HABITAT

Feeding: The western screech-owl's regionally variable diet consists of a variety of prey: arthropods, voles, mice, shrews, small birds, amphibians, earthworms, reptiles and fish. Kennicotts' screech-owl is found in most low-elevation woodland habitats, but it prefers to forage in mixed hardwood–conifer forests, usually near water. MacFarlane's subspecies is found in hardwood (e.g., cottonwood–waterbirch and aspen stands) and mixed woodlands at low elevations along streams and lake shores. Both subspecies hunt in edge habitat and are generally associated with riparian habitats. Poorly drained moist areas that support an abundance of amphibians (as prey) appear to provide good habitat for the coastal subspecies.

191

Day roost and nest site in class 2 bigleaf maple

Breeding: Breeding occurs in open hardwood and conifer forests associated with the riparian areas of rivers, creeks, marshes, bogs, lakes and large ponds. Near urban and residential areas, this owl frequents orchards, parks and gardens. The nests, 1.5–12 m above the ground, are in abandoned northern flicker and pileated woodpecker holes or natural cavities in hardwoods or conifers >30 cm dbh. Black cottonwood, red alder, Douglas-fir, western red-cedar, western hemlock and arbutus are among the nest tree species. This owl readily uses nest boxes.

The breeding period extends from mid-March through mid-August. The clutch size is 2–5. The number of young fledged depends mainly on the food supply.

Roosting: During daytime, the western screech-owl usually roosts in the foliage of large trees or in the dense crowns of young trees. It is also known to roost in tree cavities, nest boxes, vines, dense undergrowth and cliff crevices.

Territory Size/Home Range: The defended home range is 10–60 ha, depending on habitat.

ADDITIONAL STEWARDSHIP PROVISIONS (see also Part 2)
- Manage as for primary cavity nesters such as the pileated woodpecker and the northern flicker.
- In the Interior, retain sufficient mature riparian forest in valley bottoms (the highest quality habitat is found on floodplains and in areas with black cottonwood and trembling aspen having suitable cavities). Also, in areas with known nest sites, do not harvest or salvage in the 5–12 ha of suitable habitat surrounding forested riparian stands.
- For both coastal and Interior subspecies, minimize disturbance from mid-March until mid-August.
- On the coast, retain sufficient riparian forest and low-elevation mixed hardwood–conifer forest.
- Consider nest-box programs in areas with good foraging habitat but few suitable wildlife trees.

OF INTEREST

The western screech-owl is highly susceptible to being killed in collisions with vehicles, especially in the Interior, as it forages along roadways (and even on roads for worms during rainfall). In the southern Interior in particular, roads that parallel water bodies in the valley bottoms are the sites of many such incidents.

NORTHERN HAWK OWL
Surnia ulula • NHOW

STATUS

The northern hawk owl is an uncommon resident in the northern Interior and a rare resident at high elevations in the southern Interior, but it is only an irregular winter visitor to the south coast. It is not at risk in B.C.

RANGE

The northern hawk owl breeds throughout the Interior, from Manning Provincial Park east to the Moyie River and north to the Yukon border, but it is most abundant in the northern third of the province. Found at elevations up to 2700 m, it breeds at 550–1830 m. It overwinters throughout its breeding range, with most individuals moving locally to lower elevations in the Interior; the Peace River Valley likely supports a substantial wintering population. Some birds wander irregularly from their breeding areas, appearing occasionally on the south coast in winter, and some migrate as far as the northern U.S.

DESCRIPTION

This crow-sized owl (about 40 cm total length) has a distinctive long (16 cm), tapered tail banded with white, a white-spotted, brown back and pale under-parts completely barred with fine brown lines. It has yellow eyes and white facial discs bordered with black.

OTHER CHARACTERISTICS

Most active at dawn and dusk, the northern hawk owl may hunt at any

Northern hawk owl, adult

time of the day or night. Its flight is low and swift, and it often perches in treetops, usually adjacent to clearings. It does not sit as erectly as other owls, and its tail makes jerky movements. Among this owl's calls are a series of whistled *ulululu* notes, a rapid, sharp *ki-ki-ki-ki* that is

Biogeoclimatic Zones

AT	BG	BWBS	CDF	CWH	ESSF	ICH	IDF	MH	MS	PP	SBPS	SBS	SWB

Ecoprovinces									Breeding Period												
BOP	COM	CEI	GED	NBM	SBI	SIM	SOI	TAP	J	F	M	A	M	J	J	A	S	O	N	D

Class 4 perch tree in northern hawk owl habitat

breeding season, this owl eats mainly small mammals, but the diet during the rest of the year includes more small and medium-sized birds.

Breeding: Breeding information for B.C. is sparse. The habitats around known nests have been open conifer and mixed forests of white spruce, Engelmann spruce, subalpine fir, trembling aspen, birches and mountain hemlock. The northern hawk owl mainly uses natural cavities, the concave tops of broken trunks or decayed northern flicker and pileated woodpecker cavities. In Alaska, it prefers to nest along the edge of open forest (20–60 percent canopy cover) or near treeline. In Alberta, it favours spruce muskeg forest habitat, with a nest height of 5–18 m.

The breeding period extends from March through mid-August. The clutch size is 5–7.

Roosting: This owl is believed to roost in tree cavities or dense tree foliage.

Territory Size/Home Range: The home range, estimated at 140–180 ha, is believed to be established anew each breeding season, with little reuse of previous areas.

ADDITIONAL STEWARDSHIP PROVISIONS (see also Part 2)
- Manage as for the northern flicker and the pileated woodpecker.
- Retain some conifer and hardwood snags (>40 cm dbh, especially those with suitable large cavities) within harvested areas and natural burns.

reminiscent of a falcon, a kestrel-like *illy-illy-illy-illy* and a harsh screech.

HABITAT
Feeding: Perches in open areas of many kinds are used for hunting. During the

OF INTEREST
Northern hawk owl families usually remain together throughout winter.

NORTHERN PYGMY-OWL
Glaucidium gnoma • NPOW

STATUS
Vancouver Island subspecies, *G. g. swarthi*—B.C.: Blue List
An uncommon but widespread resident across southern British Columbia, the northern pygmy-owl is a less abundant resident along the north coast and in the central and northwestern Interior. The Vancouver Island subspecies (*G. g. swarthi*) is considered vulnerable because of a lack of population data in areas of intensive forest management.

RANGE
The northern pygmy-owl breeds at elevations of 490–1220 m along eastern Vancouver Island and the adjacent mainland coast and in the Interior from near Williams Lake through the Okanagan Valley, and probably in the Kootenays. The range outside of the breeding season encompasses central and northwestern B.C. and extends from sea level to 1700 m. Southern populations are relatively sedentary, but northern populations disperse to lower elevations or southward in October and November, returning to their breeding areas in February and March.

At cavity in class 2 Interior Douglas-fir

DESCRIPTION
This small owl (about 17 cm in length) has a small head without ear tufts. Its upperparts are either rusty brown (red phase) or greyish brown (grey phase) and are finely spotted with white, especially on the top of the head. The underparts are pale with dark streaks, and the long, dark brown tail has 6–7 pale bars across it.

The eyes are yellow. Black spots on the nape look like a second pair of eyes.

OTHER CHARACTERISTICS
The northern pygmy-owl hunts by day and is most active at dawn and dusk. Its wingbeats are audible, unlike those of nocturnal owls. It often holds its tail slightly elevated when perching.

Biogeoclimatic Zones

AT	BG	BWBS	CDF	CWH	ESSF	ICH	IDF	MH	MS	PP	SBPS	SBS	SWB

Ecoprovinces									Breeding Period												
BOP	COM	CEI	GED	NBM	SBI	SIM	SOI	TAP	J	F	M	A	M	J	J	A	S	O	N	D	

Class 2 Interior Douglas-fir with northern pygmy-owl at cavity.

nest sites are abandoned woodpecker holes in dead conifers, 3–20 m above the ground.

The breeding period is from the beginning of March to the end of June. The clutch size is 4–7.

Roosting: Old woodpecker nests and natural tree cavities are used for roosting.

Territory Size/Home Range: The home range, which is thought to be defended from other pygmy-owls, is estimated at 50–200 ha.

ADDITIONAL STEWARDSHIP PROVISIONS (see also Part 2)
- Manage as for the medium-sized and large woodpeckers.
- During the breeding season, minimize disturbance within 300–400 m of known nest sites, especially for the Vancouver Island subspecies.
- For the Vancouver Island subspecies, do not, at any time, harvest or construct roads within a 12-ha core area encompassing the nest site and a windfirm area chosen to retain all nearby trees with visible cavities and those with the most cavity potential (> 70 cm dbh amabilis fir, Douglas-fir and western hemlock).
- For the Vancouver Island subspecies, designate an 80–100 ha area surrounding the core area and retain all amabilis fir, Douglas-fir and western hemlock >40 cm dbh—if these species are insufficient, choose grand fir, red alder, bigleaf maple, western white pine and western red-cedar or the largest trees available for the site. Leave the stand windfirm, with the upper canopy closure reduced by no more than 50 percent. Do not harvest or construct roads in this area from early March to late June.

The most common call is a series of whistled hoots that is repeated every 1–25 seconds, and it also gives a repeated *too-too-too-too-too, toot, toot, toot* call.

HABITAT
Feeding: Foraging in a wide variety of forest habitats with low to moderate canopy cover, the northern pygmy-owl hunts mainly along the edges of openings. It eats mostly voles, mice and shrews, sometimes small birds and large insects and occasionally reptiles and amphibians.

Breeding: This owl breeds in mixed conifer forest (e.g., Douglas-fir–western red-cedar–western hemlock or ponderosa pine–lodgepole pine–western larch), often on steep hillsides, talus slopes or ravines, near openings and water. The preferred

OF INTEREST
Northern pygmy-owls are frequently "mobbed" by small birds that are potential prey. Their actions may serve to drive the owl away or thwart a surprise attack.

BARRED OWL
Strix varia • BAOW

STATUS
An uncommon but widespread resident of the central Interior plateau around Prince George and the Peace River Valley, though becoming very sparsely distributed north to the Liard River, the barred owl is also widespread and common on eastern Vancouver Island, the Gulf Islands and the mainland coast. Since it was first recorded in British Columbia in 1943, it has dramatically expanded its range and increased in number. It is not at risk in B.C.

RANGE
This owl breeds from sea level to at least 1250 m, from southern Vancouver Island and the lower Fraser Valley north to the Skeena River and throughout the southern and central Interior, and its breeding range continues to expand westward and northward. The barred owl is a year-round resident in southern areas, but most individuals in northern areas move southward in late autumn.

DESCRIPTION
This medium-large owl (larger than a crow; 46–58 cm in length) has a "puffy" head and no ear tufts; its eyes are dark. The upper breast has dark horizontal barring, and the belly has dark vertical streaking, which most easily distinguishes this species from the spotted owl.

OTHER CHARACTERISTICS
Chiefly nocturnal but often seen during the day, the barred owl calls more by day than other owls. It gives a rhythmic series of loud hoots, *hoo, hoo, hoo-hoo;*

Barred owl, adult

Biogeoclimatic Zones

AT	BG	BWBS	CDF	CWH	ESSF	ICH	IDF	MH	MS	PP	SBPS	SBS	SWB

Ecoprovinces

BOP	COM	CEI	GED	NBM	SBI	SIM	SOI	TAP

Breeding Period

J	F	M	A	M	J	J	A	S	O	N	D

197

Class 2 black cottonwood natural cavity large enough for a barred owl

Breeding: Often near water (e.g., lakes, swamps, creek valleys and river bottomlands), the nests are found in a wide variety of conifer forests (Douglas-fir–lodgepole pine, Douglas-fir–western red-cedar, spruce–lodgepole pine and western larch) and mixed woodlands (western red-cedar, Douglas-fir, western hemlock and black cottonwood). Readily able to use disturbed habitats, the barred owl has likely been helped in its range expansion by the fragmentation of dense coastal forest by logging. Located in natural cavities or rotted depressions in the broken tops of trees, the nests are 6–30 m above the ground. Nest trees are generally large (>50 cm dbh), mature conifers or hardwoods (e.g., Douglas-fir or black cottonwood), often with the tops or large limbs broken off or with extensive internal decay or both. Nests are reused year after year.

The breeding period extends from late March through mid-August. The clutch size is 2–4. The parents care for the young for up to four months.

hoo, hoo, hoo-hoo, hoo, or a drawn-out *hoo-ah,* sometimes preceded by an ascending agitated barking. It also audibly snaps its beak. This easily flushed owl does not generally tolerate close approach. Slow flapping and much gliding characterize its flight.

Roosting: Roosting is in dense conifers or hardwoods within forests.

HABITAT

Feeding: The barred owl is an opportunistic forager that hunts in forests that have stands of varying ages and openings. In winter, it occasionally hunts in grasslands with scattered trees. Its diet is mainly small mammals and small to medium-sized birds. It also eats some reptiles and amphibians.

Territory Size/Home Range: The home range, which is defended from other barred owls and remains relatively consistent between years, measures approximately 250–300 ha. In southern areas, the home range is probably occupied year-round.

ADDITIONAL STEWARDSHIP PROVISIONS (see also Part 2)

- Retain some large black cottonwoods and conifers (>50 cm dbh), particularly in riparian areas.

OF INTEREST

Recent barred owl population expansions in southwestern B.C. have created range overlap with the spotted owl. The implications of competition between these species are not yet fully understood. There is evidence both of hybridization between the two species and of predation on the spotted owl by the barred owl.

BOREAL OWL
Aegolius funereus • BOOW

STATUS
The boreal owl is a rare but widespread resident in the northern Interior and a rare resident at high elevations in the southern Interior. It is an irregular winter visitor to low elevations in the southern Interior. Occurring at very low densities throughout its range, it is one of the province's least-known owls. It is not at risk in B.C.

RANGE
The boreal owl breeds throughout the Interior, from the eastern slope of the Coast Mountains to Alberta and north to the Yukon. Occasional vagrants are found on the coast. It is usually a year-round resident, with some autumn movement to lower elevations; during periods of low winter food supplies, birds will move southward. Significant dispersal of breeding adults occurs between years.

DESCRIPTION
Slightly larger than a robin (about 25 cm in length), the boreal owl has a large head with no ear tufts. A brownish back and head complement brown-streaked, white underparts. This owl has black-bordered, whitish facial discs, a thickly white-spotted dark forehead, yellow eyes and a pale beak.

OTHER CHARACTERISTICS
Mainly nocturnal, the boreal owl occasionally hunts by day. Its most common call, heard mainly at night in the breeding season, is a short, rapid series of

Boreal owl, adult

hollow *hoo* notes, similar to the "winnowing" of the Wilson's snipe.

HABITAT
Feeding: In northern areas, the preferred foraging habitat is mature to

Biogeoclimatic Zones

AT	BG	BWBS	CDF	CWH	ESSF	ICH	IDF	MH	MS	PP	SBPS	SBS	SWB

Ecoprovinces									Breeding Period											
BOP	COM	CEI	GED	NBM	SBI	SIM	SOI	TAP	J	F	M	A	M	J	J	A	S	O	N	D

Class 5 black cottonwood with a pileated woodpecker cavity suitable for a boreal owl

Breeding: Little breeding information exists for B.C. Among the potential breeding habitats are closed hardwood and mixed forests stands (60–100 percent canopy cover) and high-elevation subalpine forests. Nest trees used in B.C. probably include alder, birch, trembling aspen, Engelmann spruce and lodgepole pine. The boreal owl uses abandoned woodpecker nests (often northern flicker) and natural cavities in trees >35 cm dbh. Nest boxes are used occasionally. Nest sites are usually used only once.

The full extent of the breeding period in British Columbia is unknown, but eggs may be found in April and young from May to about mid-July. The clutch size is 4–7. The parents feed the young for 3–6 weeks after they leave the nest.

Roosting: During the day, the boreal owl roosts in dense cover, usually close to the trunk of a conifer. Because they offer more cover, spruce trees are preferred over firs and pines. Different roost trees used each day, so many are needed. A male's roost may be 2–3 km from the nest site.

Territory Size/Home Range: The estimated home range is 1500 ha, and the home ranges of neighbouring pairs often overlap by 50 percent. The estimated summer territory is 350–850 ha. Smaller core areas are used intensively.

old-growth stands of white spruce and trembling aspen. In southern areas, the boreal owl forages in Engelmann spruce, Douglas-fir–lodgepole pine, subalpine fir–lodgepole pine and Douglas-fir–western red-cedar forests. It eats primarily voles, mice, shrews, birds and also, rarely, frogs and insects. Excess food is cached in tree forks and crevices. This owl commonly travels several kilometres during each nocturnal foraging bout.

ADDITIONAL STEWARDSHIP PROVISIONS (see also Part 2)
- Manage as for the northern flicker and pileated woodpecker.
- Retain a selection of roosting trees with dense foliage (preferably spruces) within each cut-block.

OF INTEREST
The boreal owl also inhabits the boreal forest of Europe, where it is known as "Tengmalm's owl."

NORTHERN SAW-WHET OWL
Aegolius acadicus • NSWO

STATUS
Queen Charlotte subspecies, *A. a. brooksi*—B.C.: Blue List
An uncommon but widespread resident across southern British Columbia, the northern saw-whet owl decreases in abundance northward to the Skeena River and the Peace River and toward the outer coasts. It is rare in the extreme north-west. The subspecies found outside the Queen Charlotte Islands (*A. a. acadicus*) is not considered to be at risk, but the one restricted to the Queen Charlottes (*A. a. brooksi*) is considered vulnerable because of its limited distribution and threats to its habitat.

RANGE
Found anywhere from sea level to at least 2200 m throughout much of southern B.C., with scattered records from the north coast and the northern Interior, the northern saw-whet owl probably breeds throughout its provincial range. Nesting has been confirmed, at anywhere from sea level to 1400 m, on the Queen Charlotte Islands, southeastern Vancouver Island, the southern mainland coast, across the southern Interior, north to Prince George and locally in the Peace River Valley. Coastal populations are thought to be resident, but Interior populations generally move southward during the last half of October or early November and return in February.

DESCRIPTION
A compact owl (about 20 cm in length) with yellow eyes and no ear tufts, the

Northern saw-whet owl, adult

Biogeoclimatic Zones

AT	BG	BWBS	CDF	CWH	ESSF	ICH	IDF	MH	MS	PP	SBPS	SBS	SWB

Ecoprovinces									Breeding Period												

BOP	COM	CEI	GED	NBM	SBI	SIM	SOI	TAP	J	F	M	A	M	J	J	A	S	O	N	D

Old woodpecker cavity in class 6 ponderosa pine occupied by a northern saw-whet owl

northern saw-whet owl is reddish-brown above and white with reddish-brown vertical streaks below. It has prominent, pale reddish brown facial discs and white streaks on its head (the similar boreal owl has white spots on its head and dark-bordered facial discs).

OTHER CHARACTERISTICS

This nocturnal owl is most active for several hours after dusk and just before dawn. As suggested by its name, it has a raspy call that sounds like a saw being sharpened. A single-whistle note, repeated monotonously 100–130 times per minute, *too too too too*, is heard mainly in the breeding season.

HABITAT

Feeding: Foraging in early-seral stages and in mature and old-growth forest provides prey diversity for a diet that consists mainly of voles, mice and shrews but also songbirds and insects. Coastal saw-whets typically forage in intertidal areas and feed on amphipods (sandhoppers), but the Queen Charlotte subspecies primarily uses the edges of meadows, streams, estuaries and bogs.

Breeding: The northern saw-whet owl breeds in a variety of habitats (e.g., open forest, sparsely treed rangeland, wooded valleys and canyons, marshes and bogs with clumps of trees and thickets). Typical forest types include Douglas-fir–ponderosa pine, Engelmann spruce–trembling aspen–lodgepole pine, black cotton-wood–willow, trembling aspen, western larch and Garry oak–Douglas-fir. Riparian forest is particularly valuable. Nests are in living or dead conifers or hardwoods (e.g., western red-cedar, Douglas-fir, ponderosa pine, western larch, black cottonwood, poplar, trembling aspen or birch), mainly in abandoned northern flicker and pileated woodpecker cavities 3–14 m above the ground. This owl is known to use young trembling aspen forest (30–40 years old) where older nest trees (40–60 cm dbh) are present, and it will use nest boxes.

The breeding period extends from late February through mid-August. The clutch size is 4–7.

Roosting: Daytime roosts are in dense tangles of branches (e.g., witches' brooms). The preferred winter roosts are in small, dense conifers or near the ends of large conifer branches where forks provide concealed niches. Regurgitated pellets and "whitewash" accumulate below favoured winter roosts. The average dbh of roost trees is 35 cm. This owl also uses buildings (e.g., garages, barns and greenhouses). During the breeding season, the male changes roost sites daily.

Territory Size/Home Range: The estimated defended home range for breeding males is 140–160 ha (smaller in high-quality habitats).

ADDITIONAL STEWARDSHIP
PROVISIONS (see also Part 2)
- Manage as for the large and medium-sized woodpeckers.
- Consider nest-box programs in areas of high habitat value where wildlife trees are scarce.
- For the Queen Charlotte Islands subspecies, do not, at any time, harvest or construct roads within a 12-ha (larger for poor habitat) core area surrounding each known nest site or its estimated location. This area should encompass all nearby trees with visible cavities and those with the most cavity potential as well as large Sitka spruce and western hemlocks (>85 cm dbh or the largest for the site). This area needs to be windfirm.
- For the Queen Charlotte Islands subspecies, designate a 140–160 ha home range area surrounding the core area. Retain all large-diameter wildlife trees and optimize for woodpeckers (to

Northern saw-whet owl in an old woodpecker cavity in class 6 conifer

create additional nest cavities). Do not salvage within this area. Avoid disturbance (road building and harvesting) from the beginning of March to mid-July within 300 m of a known nest.

OF INTEREST
Northern saw-whet owls leave a hard mat of dried prey in their nest cavities, so a thorough annual cleaning of nest boxes is essential.

VAUX'S SWIFT
Chaetura vauxi • VASW

STATUS
The Vaux's swift is a fairly common summer visitor to southern and central British Columbia, and it can be very common during migration. It is most abundant in the south but more scattered in the northern mountains. It is not at risk in B.C., but it is very dependent on habitat elements characteristic of old-growth forests.

RANGE
Breeding, at anywhere from near sea level to about 2000 m, occurs in the southern and central Interior as far north as Prince George and along the coast from Vancouver Island to Stewart or farther north (probably to the Tatshenshini River). Breeding has recently been recorded on the southern Queen Charlotte Islands. After overwintering anywhere from Mexico to South America, this species returns to B.C. in flocks of 20–75 between mid-April and May. Autumn migrants depart in flocks of 25–200 in late August and September. Migrants follow major river valleys and coastlines, their movements coinciding with storm fronts.

DESCRIPTION
A swallow-like bird (about 11 cm in length, smaller than a barn swallow) with no apparent tail, the Vaux's swift has very slender wings; in flight they appear to be straight and stiff. Dark brown above and smoky grey on the throat and breast, this swift has a tiny beak that is visible only at close range.

OTHER CHARACTERISTICS
Smaller and darker than other B.C. swallows, the Vaux's swift is most easily identified by its size and flight characteristics. It flies quickly and erratically, with extremely rapid, shallow wingbeats, often in sweeping arcs with frequent direction changes as it chases flying insects. Along rivers or riparian forest, it flies in straighter lines, following the river or forest contour. Migrant

Vaux's swift. Inset: Class 4 black cottonwood with chimney-like cavity

Biogeoclimatic Zones

AT	BG	BWBS	CDF	CWH	ESSF	ICH	IDF	MH	MS	PP	SBPS	SBS	SWB

Ecoprovinces

BOP	COM	CEI	GED	NBM	SBI	SIM	SOI	TAP

Breeding Period

J	F	M	A	M	J	J	A	S	O	N	D

flocks fly swiftly and directly in compact groups. Flocks of 20 or more swallow-like birds that swoop into chimneys or hollow trees at dusk are undoubtedly swifts. The call is a weak, high-pitched twittering.

HABITAT

Feeding: Exclusively an aerial feeder, the Vaux's swift forages relatively high over forest canopies, rivers, lakes, marshes and other open areas. Most foraging by breeding birds is above the forest canopy near their nest tree. In summer, this swift sometimes forages with mixed swallow, swift and common nighthawk flocks over Interior lakes. It eats a diverse array and great quantity of small flying insects (e.g., flies, mayflies, click beetles, leaf rollers, bark beetles, leaf hoppers, aphids, whiteflies, parasitic wasps and ants). One breeding pair may feed over 150,000 insects to their young during the nestling period.

Breeding: The Vaux's swift is apparently mainly dependent on old-growth forest for breeding, especially old-growth Douglas-fir forests and burned-over areas with large snags, but it may nest in heavily wooded suburban areas. Nesting occurs in cavities or hollow trunks in large live or dead wildlife trees or in unused chimneys. Hollow trees were long thought to provide most of the nesting habitat, but recent research indicates that pileated woodpecker roost cavities are frequently used. Most of these cavities are found in mature conifers, but they may also occur in large black cottonwoods, trembling aspens and bigleaf maples. The nest tree's dbh is usually >50 cm and often >100 cm. The same nest sites are reused year after year, usually with a single pair per cavity, but several pairs may nest near each other. Made of twigs and conifer needles, the nest is glued together and to the cavity wall with saliva.

The breeding season extends from early June to mid-August. The young remain with their parents for a short time after fledging and are fed on the wing. The clutch size is 4–6.

Roosting: Hollows and cavities used for night roosts are similar to those used for nesting. During migration, flocks swarm into large communal roosts at dusk and leave at dawn.

Territory Size/Home Range: Territory sizes are unknown. Most foraging is done near the nest, but the home range may extend more than 5 km from the nest site.

ADDITIONAL STEWARDSHIP PROVISIONS (see also Part 2)

- Manage as for the pileated woodpecker, especially riparian areas that contain mature cottonwood, bigleaf maple, and western red-cedar >50 cm dbh.
- Retain large wildlife trees that have natural cavities, especially ones with chimney-like hollow centres.

OF INTEREST

Vaux's swifts are highly aerial, landing only at the nest or roost, and their tiny feet are sufficient only for clinging to the surfaces of these sites.

Vaux's swifts investigate a chimney-like tree during the breeding season.

TREE SWALLOW
Tachycineta bicolor • TRSW

STATUS

A common summer visitor to most of B.C., the tree swallow may be abundant during migration. It is not at risk in B.C.

RANGE

Found throughout most of British Columbia, including the Queen Charlotte Islands and other coastal islands, this swallow is most abundant in southern B.C. and more scattered in the northern mountains. It breeds throughout its provincial range, from near sea level to 1450 m. It overwinters mainly from California to Central America, with migrants departing in August and September in mixed flocks with other swallows. Returning flocks of 20–100 arrive in B.C. in March and April.

DESCRIPTION

This small (about 14 cm in length), streamlined bird has long wings. The male sports a sharply contrasting plumage, with bright white underparts and a steely, iridescent, bluish black back. At a distance, the upperparts look very dark. The female appears much duller than the male, with little iridescence. The juvenile is white below and dusky brown above.

OTHER CHARACTERISTICS

Gliding, circular flight alternates with quick flaps. The tree swallow changes direction rapidly when pursuing flying insects. Over water, it often skims along close to the surface. Like all swallows, it often perches in rows on wires, fences and bridge railings. Around wetlands, it perches on the branches of dead trees. It can be seen in large flocks during migration.

HABITAT

Feeding: The tree swallow eats mainly small flying insects (e.g., midges, mayflies, ants, mosquitoes, gnats, larch

Female at nest cavity in class 4 trembling aspen

Biogeoclimatic Zones

AT	BG	BWBS	CDF	CWH	ESSF	ICH	IDF	MH	MS	PP	SBPS	SBS	SWB

Ecoprovinces

BOP	COM	CEI	GED	NBM	SBI	SIM	SOI	TAP

Breeding Period

J	F	M	A	M	J	J	A	S	O	N	D

sawflies, bark beetles and grasshoppers), as well as spiders, seeds and berries. It forages where flying insects are abundant, anywhere from just above the surface of the ground or water to heights of about 100 m, mainly over lakes, ponds, large rivers, marshes, estuaries and wet meadows, but also over grasslands and forest canopy. It forages in mixed flocks with other swallows.

Breeding: Breeding occurs mostly near water (e.g., along the edges of small lakes, beaver ponds, rivers and wet meadows) but sometimes in grasslands, burns, agricultural areas and open aspen forests. The habitats for nesting and foraging must be close together. Almost entirely dependent on old woodpecker cavities for natural nest sites, this swallow also readily uses nest boxes or crevices in buildings. The nest height is normally 2–7 m. In open grasslands, it will use nest boxes placed on fence posts. House wrens, bluebirds, mountain chickadees and violet-green swallows compete for the same nest sites. Nest sites are reused year after year.

The breeding season extends from mid-April to mid-August. The clutch size is 4–6. The young remain with the parents for a short time after fledging and are fed on the wing.

Roosting: During the breeding season, night roosting is in abandoned woodpecker holes or natural cavities. Migrant flocks roost in thick cattail or bulrush marshes or in dense, scrubby trees.

Territory Size/Home Range: No information is available on home ranges, but

Class 6 conifer with tree swallow perching near nest cavity. Inset. Male tree swallow

foraging during the nesting season is mainly in the vicinity of the nest. Nests are often in loose colonies, with a preferred distance of >20 m from other tree swallow nests. A pair will vigorously defend its own nest cavity from other secondary cavity nesters but will accept the presence of other species nearby, such as woodpeckers, bluebirds and nuthatches that nest in the same tree.

ADDITIONAL STEWARDSHIP PROVISIONS (see also Part 2)

- Manage as for sapsuckers and medium-sized woodpeckers.
- Maintain riparian forest along the edges of beaver ponds, small lakes, marshes and sloughs.
- Retain living and dead trees in flooded areas created by beaver activity.
- Consider nest-box programs in areas of high habitat value where wildlife trees are scarce.

OF INTEREST

A 1994 study found that tree swallows nesting in orchards had eight times more DDT (dichlorodiphenyltrichloroethene) and three times more DDE (dichlorodiphenyldichloroethane) in their eggs than tree swallows nesting elsewhere, even though these chemicals had not been used since the 1970s.

BROWN CREEPER
Certhia americana • BRCR

STATUS

An uncommon but widespread resident throughout B.C., the brown creeper is not considered to be at risk in the province, but it is sensitive to fragmentation of old-growth forests.

RANGE

The brown creeper breeds on the coast, including Vancouver Island and the Queen Charlotte Islands, and throughout the Interior northward to Stewart, Babine and Williston lakes and the Peace River. Most of the breeding habitat is in forests at low to moderate elevations, but some is in subalpine forests. Outside the breeding season, the range likely extends northward. Some downward movement from high elevations occurs in winter, and far northern populations may move southward during severe winters.

Brown creeper, adult

DESCRIPTION

A sparrow-sized bird (about 13 cm in length), the brown creeper has a long, thin, downcurved bill and a long tail of stiff, sharply pointed feathers. The brown back and head, lightly streaked with pale buff, contrast with the white underparts.

OTHER CHARACTERISTICS

In its distinctive foraging pattern, this bird creeps up a tree trunk in a straight line or spiral, bracing itself with its stiff tail, then flies down to the base of another tree and creeps upward again. The thin, high-pitched call is a single *seet*, and the high-pitched song is sometimes described as *trees, trees, trees, see the trees*. In winter, the brown creeper is most often found singly or in pairs at the end of mixed-species foraging flocks of chickadees, kinglets and nuthatches.

Biogeoclimatic Zones

AT	BG	BWBS	CDF	CWH	ESSF	ICH	IDF	MH	MS	PP	SBPS	SBS	SWB

Ecoprovinces

BOP	COM	CEI	GED	NBM	SBI	SIM	SOI	TAP

Breeding Period

J	F	M	A	M	J	J	A	S	O	N	D

Left: Class 1 western red-cedar with brown creeper nest in a natural cavity where bark separates from trunk
Right: Immature brown creepers at nest

HABITAT

Feeding: The brown creeper forages in old-growth forest habitats, including pure and mixed conifer and hardwood stands that are closed to semi-open, but it prefers conifer stands with a diverse physical structure and species composition. Most abundant in stands with a high proportion of conifers >100 cm dbh, it forages almost entirely on the trunks and main limbs of large conifers, probing bark crevices for prey. Mainly insectivorous, it eats all life stages of small insects (e.g., bark beetles, leaf beetles, spruce budworm, larch sawfly, moths and scale insects) and spiders and occasionally tree seeds.

Breeding: Breeding in a variety of mature coniferous or mixed forest habitats, this bird prefers extensive old-growth conifer forest with a closed canopy. It nests mainly in large (>25 cm dbh), living or dead conifers (e.g., Douglas-fir, western red-cedar, western hemlock, Sitka spruce, ponderosa pine and lodgepole pine). The distinctive hammock-like nest, typically 2–15 m above the ground, is well concealed and very difficult to find, usually behind loose bark but occasionally in a cavity. Specially designed nest boxes are sometimes used.

The breeding season extends from mid-April to late July. The clutch size is 5–7.

Roosting: Roosting, in natural cavities, behind loose bark or in old woodpecker nests, is occasionally communal. Roosting habitat must provide critical thermal cover during winter and at night. Several cavities or large trees with sloughing bark are likely required in the home range of a winter flock.

Territory Size/Home Range: The marked, defended breeding territory is estimated at approximately 4 ha, and the home range is larger.

ADDITIONAL STEWARDSHIP PROVISIONS (see also Part 2)

- Retain groups of mature conifers, some with large (>30 cm dbh) dead or dying trees with loose or peeling bark.

OF INTEREST

The brown creeper's cryptic coloration is an important defence. When pursued, it lands on a tree trunk, flattens its body, spreads its wings and remains motionless until the danger has passed.

HOUSE WREN
Troglodytes aedon • HOWR

STATUS

The house wren is a fairly common and widespread summer visitor in the south-ern and central-eastern Interior and on southeastern Vancouver Island. It is not at risk in B.C.

Above: House wren. Right: Class 5 paper birch with cavity used by a house wren

RANGE

In the Interior, this wren breeds at 270–1200 m, most abundantly in the south and the Peace River Valley, and also in the central Interior south of Prince George and at Fort Nelson. On the coast, it breeds anywhere from near sea level to 400 m, regularly on southeastern Vancouver Island and the Gulf Islands but rarely in the lower Fraser Valley. Nonbreeders range northward to Fort Nelson and westward along the Nechako Valley and the Bulkley Valley to Hazelton. Departing from mid-August through September, this species over-winters anywhere from the southern

Biogeoclimatic Zones

AT	BG	BWBS	CDF	CWH	ESSF	ICH	IDF	MH	MS	PP	SBPS	SBS	SWB

Ecoprovinces									Breeding Period												
BOP	COM	CEI	GED	NBM	SBI	SIM	SOI	TAP		J	F	M	A	M	J	J	A	S	O	N	D

U.S. to southern Mexico. It arrives back in B.C. between late April and mid-May.

DESCRIPTION

This chickadee-sized bird (about 12 cm in length) has a thin, slightly down-curved bill and a short, stubby tail, usually upraised. It is brownish overall, with lighter underparts and narrow, black tail bars.

OTHER CHARACTERISTICS

Loud for its size, the house wren gives a raspy scolding call when agitated. The male's song is a long, melodious warble, sung repeatedly with short pauses, from singing posts on the breeding territory. This bird flies short distances low to the ground, usually from one shrubby tangle to another. Twigs typically protrude from the nest entrance.

HABITAT

Feeding: The house wren forages mostly near the ground in thickets, on logs and in the lower tree canopy, mainly near the nest site, in open conifer and hardwood forest with a well-developed shrub layer or in agricultural habitats and gardens. Mainly insectivorous, this wren eats all life stages of small insects (e.g., bark beetles, leaf beetles, spruce budworm and pine budworm) plus millipedes, spiders and snails and occasionally seeds.

Breeding: The house wren breeds in aspen copses, old burns and clearings, open forests with an extensive hardwood shrub understorey, hedgerows, gardens and riparian habitat. In the Interior, it is most abundant in ponderosa pine–Douglas-fir forests with abundant aspen and shrubby undergrowth. On the south coast, it prefers Garry oak forest with shrubs and rocky outcroppings. At a height of 1–15 m, the nests are usually in old cavities made by woodpeckers, nuthatches or chickadees or in natural cavities, mostly in hardwoods, but this species also readily uses nest boxes.

The breeding season extends from early May to early August. The clutch size is 5–7, with up to two broods per year. A male usually mates with several females.

Roosting: This bird roosts in cavities similar to those used for nesting and in dense shrubbery.

Territory Size/Home Range. The breeding territory averages 0.5–1.5 ha, and the home range is slightly larger. Breeding birds rarely leave their territories. Defending males try to evict other males and females try to evict other females.

ADDITIONAL STEWARDSHIP PROVISIONS (see also Part 2)

- Manage as for the small woodpeckers.
- Maintain a shrubby understorey as well as suitable wildlife trees.

OF INTEREST

House wren breeding populations are limited mainly by the availability of nest sites and will increase if nest boxes are provided. However, artificially increased house wren populations may negatively affect other species, so nest-box programs are not recommended. House wrens routinely destroy the nests, eggs and nestlings of competing secondary cavity users such as chickadees, swallows and bluebirds. Competition for nest sites is intensified by the tendency of male house wrens to build one or more "dummy" nests in addition to the active nest.

Overview of the Bluebirds

DESCRIPTION

The western bluebird and mountain bluebird are both about two-thirds the size of a robin (17–19 cm in length). The male western bluebird has a deep blue head, neck, tail and wings, with reddish brown on the upper back and flanks, fading to white on the lower belly. The female is similar but duller.

The male mountain bluebird has a bright sky blue back, "cap" and tail, with the face, throat and flanks a duller blue, fading to white on the belly; there is no reddish brown coloration. The female has blue wings, rump and tail, a grey back and "cap" and buffy grey underparts.

OTHER CHARACTERISTICS

Bluebirds are typically seen in small flocks or, during the breeding season, in pairs. They are usually found perched on snags, fences, posts or wires along the edge of open country.

DIET AND FORAGING BEHAVIOUR

Primarily insectivorous, bluebirds eat a wide range of flying and crawling insects (e.g., grasshoppers, moths, wasps, flies, bark beetles and other beetles) and also spiders, seeds and berries. While foraging, they often hover 3–6 m above the ground. They capture prey mostly on the ground but sometimes in midair, and they may glean insects from vegetation while hovering.

RELATIONSHIP TO PRIMARY CAVITY EXCAVATORS AND OTHER SECONDARY CAVITY USERS

The primary natural nest site for bluebirds is an abandoned woodpecker cavity with an entrance hole approximately 4 cm in diameter. When bluebirds compete for nest cavities with European starlings, house sparrows, tree swallows or house wrens, the bluebirds are usually displaced. Breeding failure results unless another, uncontested nest site can be found in time for a second breeding attempt.

ADDITIONAL STEWARDSHIP PROVISIONS (see also Part 2)

- Manage as for the small to medium-sized woodpeckers.
- Well-managed nest-box programs may dramatically increase local populations, particularly in areas with few natural nest sites. Competition with other secondary cavity users must be reduced for nest-box programs to be successful. Nest-box programs on southeastern Vancouver Island and in the lower Fraser Valley have not been successful, possibly because of the large and increasing population of introduced European starlings. In the Interior, installing pairs of nest boxes close together, with about 100 m between pairs, has proven effective in providing nest sites for both tree swallows and bluebirds without having the swallows evict the bluebirds.

Class 6–8 conifers in burned area provide nest sites.

WESTERN BLUEBIRD
Sialia mexicana • WEBL

STATUS
Coastal population—B.C.: Red list
The western bluebird is an uncommon summer visitor to the southern Interior and a rare visitor to the south coast. The Interior population is not at risk, but the coastal breeding population is Red-listed because of a dramatic decrease from historical numbers.

Female western bluebird

RANGE
In the southern Interior, this bluebird breeds anywhere from Princeton and Lillooet eastward through the Okanagan Valley to the Rocky Mountain Trench and northward to Lac la Hache. On the coast, it breeds locally on the Gulf Islands and near Victoria, Duncan and Nanaimo. Breeding abundance peaks in the Okanagan Valley and the southern East Kootenay. Nesting occurs anywhere from near sea level to about 1200 m. Outside the breeding season, the range is marginally larger. Most birds depart for the western U.S. and

Biogeoclimatic Zones

AT	BG	BWBS	CDF	CWH	ESSF	ICH	IDF	MH	MS	PP	SBPS	SBS	SWB

Ecoprovinces	Breeding Period

BOP	COM	CEI	GED	NBM	SBI	SIM	SOI	TAP		J	F	M	A	M	J	J	A	S	O	N	D

Left: Male at cavity in class 2 ponderosa pine. Right: Class 4 trembling aspen with western bluebird emerging from nest cavity.

Mexico in October and November, but a few flocks overwinter in B.C.'s southernmost Interior. Spring migrants arrive in small flocks in March and April.

HABITAT

Feeding: This bird forages in semi-open and open habitats (e.g., grasslands, meadows, shrublands, open conifer forests, burns and clear-cuts).

Breeding: The western bluebird breeds in semi-open coniferous or mixed conifer-hardwood forests adjacent to open areas and also in farmlands, orchards and rural gardens. In the Interior, it nests primarily in open forests of ponderosa pine or Douglas-fir, often with copses of trembling aspen or black cottonwood. On the coast, it favours open, rocky hills that rise above the surrounding forest and open Garry oak woodlands. Primarily dependent on abandoned woodpecker cavities, it occasionally uses

natural cavities and readily uses nest boxes. Nests are usually 2–6 m above the ground, but can be up to 12 m, and typical nest trees are decaying, mature aspens and dead pines or firs >25 cm dbh.

The breeding season extends from late April to early August. The clutch size is 4–6. Two broods are usually produced annually.

Roosting: Night roosting is in old woodpecker nests, natural cavities or nest boxes.

Territory Size/Home Range: The male attempts to defend the breeding home range of several hectares, and the female attempts to defend the nest site against other bluebirds and other secondary cavity users.

ADDITIONAL STEWARDSHIP PROVISIONS (see "Overview of the Bluebirds," p. 212)

MOUNTAIN BLUEBIRD

Sialia currucoides • MOBL

STATUS

The mountain bluebird is a fairly common and widespread summer visitor to the Interior and a rare migrant on the coast. It is not at risk in B.C.

Left: Female at nest cavity in class 8 Interior Douglas-fir. Right: Male at cavity in class 5 black cottonwood

RANGE

Found throughout the province, though rarely on coastal islands or the central mainland coast, the mountain bluebird is most abundant in the valleys and parklands of southern and central British Columbia, becoming more scattered in northern areas. It breeds throughout the Interior east of the Coast Mountains, except in the northeastern corner, and not on the coast. Most birds depart in September and October, often moving along alpine areas, to overwinter in the southwestern U.S. and Mexico, but occasional individuals overwinter in

Biogeoclimatic Zones

AT	BG	BWBS	CDF	CWH	ESSF	ICH	IDF	MH	MS	PP	SBPS	SBS	SWB

Ecoprovinces

BOP	COM	CEI	GED	NBM	SBI	SIM	SOI	TAP

Breeding Period

J	F	M	A	M	J	J	A	S	O	N	D

Male at nest cavity in class 2 trembling aspen

is mainly dependent on abandoned woodpecker nests, usually in decaying mature trembling aspens >25 cm dbh, with a nest height of typically 2–7 m and sometimes up to 16 m. However, it occasionally nests in crevices in cliffs, old machinery, pipes or buildings and readily uses nest boxes.

The breeding season extends from late April to early August. The clutch size is 4–6. One brood annually is normal in northern regions and at high altitudes, but two broods are common in southern regions at lower altitudes.

Roosting: Night roosting is in old woodpecker nests, natural cavities or nest boxes.

Territory Size/Home Range: The male attempts to defend the breeding home range of several hectares, and the female attempts to defend the nest site against other bluebirds and other secondary cavity users.

ADDITIONAL STEWARDSHIP PROVISIONS (see "Overview of the Bluebirds," p. 212)

B.C. in the southern Interior or on the south coast. Spring migration is very early compared to other songbirds, with most migrants arriving in March and April and some in late February.

HABITAT
Feeding: This bird forages in open habitats (e.g., grasslands, meadows, shrublands, alpine tundra, burns and clear-cuts).

Breeding: This bluebird breeds in semi-open to open habitats such as grasslands, ponderosa pine parklands, trembling aspen forest, burns, clear-cuts, subalpine meadows, forest edges, lake shores, farmlands and orchards. Having open foraging habitat adjacent to nest sites is essential. The mountain bluebird

Class 8 conifer with a woodpecker cavity now occupied by a mountain bluebird

Overview of the Bats

British Columbia has Canada's greatest diversity of bats. Information about their biology, habitat needs and distribution is relatively limited, in part because they are nocturnal mammals and therefore difficult to observe. Because bats are not well understood by many people, they are feared, disliked and unappreciated. A basic bat biology overview is provided here to help explain this unique and important group of mammals. This type of overview has not been provided for the other mammals or birds because their basic biology is considered to be more common knowledge.

Of the 16 species of bats inhabiting B.C., at least 11 use wildlife trees for daytime, nighttime and maternity roosts and hibernacula (hibernation roosts). Bats depend on these trees for shelter, thermal insulation, concealment from predators and protection from disturbance. Roost sites include hollows, cavities or cracks in trunks, spaces under loose bark, and branches concealed by foliage. Roost preference varies according to species, gender and stage in the reproductive cycle.

The roosts occupied by females and their young (pups) are called "maternity roosts" or "nurseries." Because newborn pups are poorly developed and without fur, nurseries must be located in sites with sufficiently high temperatures to promote maternal lactation and the rapid growth of the young. Building attics have often been chosen as an alternative to trees to provide the appropriate thermal conditions for maternity roosts.

The separate day roosts occupied by adult males are typically cooler, allowing them to become torpid, meaning that they lower their body temperature and metabolic rate for a short period of time to conserve energy. Most tree-roosting bats, except those in hibernacula or maternity roosts, change roosts regularly. They often move short distances of up to several hundred metres, but moves of two or more kilometres have been recorded. Bats switch roosts to avoid predators, to reduce high parasite loads or to find sites with more suitable thermal characteristics.

Night roosts are where foraging bats rest and digest their food between feeding bouts. Wildlife trees close to foraging areas are very important as night roosts,

Loose bark, known bat roost

217

because they allow bats to conserve energy by minimizing travel.

In winter, bats hibernate, lowering their body temperature and metabolic rate to conserve energy through the months when insects are scarce. Hibernation roosts are occupied by both males and females, and sometimes by more than one bat species. Temperatures of 0–5°C and relatively high humidity are important criteria for the selection of suitable hibernacula. Caves, mine entrances, buildings and thick-walled, hollow trees are the most likely sites to provide these cool, stable temperatures and buffered humidity conditions.

Little is known about the overwintering behaviour of British Columbia's bats. Individuals of some species have been found hibernating within the province, but most of the hibernacula that have been discovered in B.C. contain only a small number of bats, so the location of the rest of the population remains a mystery. Other species are believed to all migrate to warmer climates south of the border to overwinter.

All bats found in British Columbia are insectivorous. As the primary predators of night-flying insects, they play a significant role in local ecosystems. Bats have enormous appetites, consuming half or more of their body weight in insects every night. Nursing females have extremely high energy demands and may eat more than their own weight in insects nightly. Flying insects are generally caught in the membrane that extends between the hind legs and the tail; the bat then grasps the prey with its mouth while continuing to fly.

The only provincial information on the diet of bats comes from studies of a few species in the Okanagan Valley. Food preferences are very dependent on prey availability, so they vary regionally. Dietary data from the Okanagan cannot necessarily be extrapolated to other areas, but it provides some insight into the types of insects a species might eat.

STEWARDSHIP PROVISIONS FOR BATS (see also Part 2)

- Because many bat species take advantage of forest edges as movement corridors between roosting and foraging habitat, treed corridors should be established and maintained to ensure connectivity.
- In grassland areas, retain or allow the development of some late-seral habitat in forests or riparian areas as well as some adjacent patches of mature grassland in order to maintain insect populations. Some management of cattle grazing may be required.
- Because wetland and riparian habitats are important for foraging activity and production, establish riparian reserves with an adequate retention zone of mature or older trees.
- Retain large (>40 cm dbh), living and dead wildlife trees, both conifers and hardwoods, in a range of decay classes, especially near riparian areas. Thick bark with cracks and crevices and bark that is pulling away from the trunk or peeling are desirable features for current use; healthier trees are for future use.
- Establish a 100-m buffer zone and prohibit any activity around known hibernacula and maternity roosts; their protection is especially important. Mark these trees with wildlife tree signs (see p. 77). To minimize disturbance to breeding females and juveniles, permit harvesting adjacent to maternity roost buffer areas only between September and April.

CALIFORNIA MYOTIS

Myotis californicus • MYCA

STATUS

The California myotis is relatively common throughout its range in B.C. It is not considered to be at risk.

RANGE

The British Columbia range of the California myotis includes Vancouver Island, the Queen Charlotte Islands and other major coastal islands and the adjacent coastline as far north as Bella Coola, and extends into the Interior northward to Wells Gray Provincial Park and eastward to the Rockies. This bat has also been sighted in the Liard River area. Found anywhere from sea level to 1300 m, it is thought to breed throughout its provincial range. The few winter records for B.C. suggest that the nonbreeding range extends

Biogeoclimatic Zones

AT	BG	BWBS	CDF	CWH	ESSF	ICH	IDF	MH	MS	PP	SBPS	SBS	SWB

Ecoprovinces

BOP	COM	CEI	GED	NBM	SBI	SIM	SOI	TAP

Breeding Period

J	F	M	A	M	J	J	A	S	O	N	D

across the southern portion of the province. Individuals in coastal areas occasionally emerge from winter hibernation to feed.

DESCRIPTION
The California myotis is one of the two smallest bats (3–5 g; 65–95 mm in length) found in B.C. Its fur varies in colour from tan to rusty to nearly black; the wing and tail membranes and ears are black. The ears extend past the nostrils when laid forward. Where its range overlaps, the western small-footed myotis can be distinguished by its paler fur and black eye mask.

HABITAT
The habitat of the California myotis ranges from coastal conifer forests and montane forests to arid semi-desert and grasslands.

Feeding: This bat forages mostly over lakes near the water's surface, but it may also hunt in the tree canopy, especially

in poplar groves. In the Okanagan, it has been found to eat caddisflies, flies, moths and small beetles.

Breeding: Small maternity colonies (up to 60 individuals) have been found in tree cavities (such as abandoned woodpecker holes), spaces under loose bark, rock crevices, mine tunnels, bridges and buildings. Mating takes place at swarming sites or within hibernacula in early autumn. Females probably give birth to their single young in late June or early July. Beyond this general knowledge, little is known about this bat's behaviour or reproduction in B.C., because it has been studied only in the Okanagan.

Roosting and Hibernation: Locations for day roosting are similar to those used for maternity colonies. The males, who live separately in summer, have been observed to change their roosting locations daily. Wildlife trees are likely important as night roosts. Little is known about hibernation habits.

STEWARDSHIP PROVISIONS
(see p. 218)

OF INTEREST
In the Okanagan in summer, the California myotis emerges shortly after dusk, and its hunting activity peaks twice during the night, at 10–11 PM and 1–2 AM.

WESTERN LONG-EARED MYOTIS
Myotis evotis • MYEV

STATUS
This bat's abundance within B.C. is unknown, but this widely distributed species is not considered to be at risk.

RANGE
The western long-eared myotis is found throughout southern B.C., including Vancouver Island, and as far north as Smithers, anywhere from sea level to 1220 m, but it is apparently absent from the Queen Charlotte Islands. It breeds throughout its range and can breed at higher, cooler elevations than most other bat species. It probably hibernates in B.C., but no winter records exist.

DESCRIPTION
This medium-sized bat (4–9 g; 74–103 mm in length) has long ears that extend

Biogeoclimatic Zones

AT	BG	BWBS	CDF	CWH	ESSF	ICH	IDF	MH	MS	PP	SBPS	SBS	SWB

Ecoprovinces

BOP	COM	CEI	GED	NBM	SBI	SIM	SOI	TAP

Breeding Period

J	F	M	A	M	J	J	A	S	O	N	D

past the nostrils when laid forward. The fur ranges from light brown to nearly black, with blackish brown shoulder patches. The wing and tail membranes and the ears are black. Where ranges overlap, careful inspection can reveal features such as tiny hairs on the tail membrane and a longer forearm that distinguish the western long-eared from the similar-looking Keen's long-eared, northern long-eared and fringed myotises.

HABITAT

The western long-eared myotis uses a wide variety of habitats, from arid grasslands and ponderosa pine forests to coastal and montane forests.

Feeding: This bat hunts in forested areas, anywhere from ground level to the tree canopy. Its slow, manoeuvrable flight allows it to hunt in heavy vegetation. Prey—mainly moths, but also flies, beetles and spiders—is caught in flight or gleaned from vegetation or off the ground.

Breeding: Maternity colonies (1–30 individuals, including young) are mostly found in buildings but may be located under tree bark, in tree cavities or in rock crevices. Mating, thought to occur in autumn or early winter, results in a single pup. Reproductive data for B.C., limited to a few capture records of pregnant or lactating females and flying juveniles, indicates that the young are probably born in late June or early July in the Interior; no information is available for the coast.

Roosting and Hibernation: Very flexible in its choice of roost sites, this bat is most often associated with forests. In coastal regions, it prefers wooded areas where rock outcroppings predominate. In the Interior, riparian forests near small lakes and marshes have been found to be typical locations. Spaces under bark, tree cavities, stumps, fallen logs, buildings and rock crevices are used for day roosts. Caves and mines may provide temporary summer night roosts and hibernation sites.

STEWARDSHIP PROVISIONS
(see p. 218)

OF INTEREST

This bat is one of the few that can be found regularly at high elevations in western Canada.

KEEN'S LONG-EARED MYOTIS
Myotis keenii • MYKE

STATUS
B.C.: Red List
COSEWIC: Data deficient

The Keen's long-eared myotis is the only North American bat restricted to a strip along the Pacific Coast, and most of the total population resides in B.C. It is considered to be provincially at risk because of its apparent rarity in B.C. and the lack of knowledge about its basic biology, which is also reflected in its COSEWIC status. Additional field studies are required to better understand the biology and habitat requirements of this species.

RANGE
The Keen's long-eared myotis inhabits the Queen Charlotte Islands, Vancouver Island and the coastal mainland northward to the Stikine River. The only known colony is on Hotspring Island in Gwaii Hanaas National Park Reserve (Queen Charlotte Islands), where 70 individuals roost in association with little brown bats in a rock crevice adjacent to a hot spring pool. Breeding likely occurs throughout the species' provincial range. No winter records exist for B.C., nor any information about possible migration.

DESCRIPTION
This medium-sized bat (4–6 g; 63–94 mm in length) has dark, glossy fur, dark patches on the back of the shoulders, a paler underside and dark brown ears and wing membranes. When laid forward, the ears extend beyond the nostrils.

Biogeoclimatic Zones

AT	BG	BWBS	CDF	CWH	ESSF	ICH	IDF	MH	MS	PP	SBPS	SBS	SWB

Ecoprovinces				Breeding Period											
BOP	COM	CEI	GED	NBM	SBI	SIM	SOI	TAP	J	F	M	A	M	J	J	A	S	O	N	D

Where their ranges overlap, this species can be easily confused with the western long-eared myotis.

HABITAT

The Keen's long-eared myotis is associated primarily with dense tracts of coastal forest, particularly low-elevation forest dominated by western hemlock.

Feeding: Members of the Hotspring Island colony have been seen hunting over hot spring pools and clearings above salal; some were seen flying into the tree canopy but could not be observed further. Moths and beetles likely make up most of the diet. Based on wing structure and echolocation calls, this species likely captures flying insects on the wing and gleans insects from leaves or the ground.

Breeding: This bat probably uses tree cavities, rock crevices and small caves for maternity roosts. The limited information available suggests that mating occurs during autumn and that the single young is born in June or early July.

Roosting and Hibernation: The colony on Hotspring Island roosts under rocks warmed by a hot spring, which provides a warm (22–27°C), humid environment. Loose bark, tree cavities and rock crevices are likely also used as colonial summer roost sites. No information is available about hibernation.

ADDITIONAL STEWARDSHIP PROVISIONS (see also p. 218)

- Protect known maternity roosts, hibernacula and day-roosting sites as well as the adjacent core foraging areas within about 100 m of these sites. The minimum distance in each direction in a given situation depends on the locations of riparian zones, available roost trees and movement corridors. Do not harvest or salvage in this area.
- Retain, in windfirm condition, all existing potential roost trees in the area immediately adjacent to known maternity roosts, hibernacula and day-roosting sites and in habitat corridors (not less than 20 m in width) within 500 m of a known site.
- Do not carry out disruptive activities, such as road construction, blasting and harvesting within 300 m of maternity roosts between mid-May and late September or from October through May for other hibernation sites.
- Any harvesting within 300 m of maternity roosts, hibernacula and day-roosting sites needs to retain all potential roost trees (decay classes 2–8) so that there is no loss of habitat offering peeling bark, cracks, cavities or hollow stems. Use a partial harvest system to leave, in windfirm condition, >70 percent of all the trees within this area.

OF INTEREST

Located below the high-tide line, the roost on Hotspring Island is often submerged for several hours. When the tide rises, the bats leave to forage or roost elsewhere.

LITTLE BROWN MYOTIS
Myotis lucifugus • MYLU

STATUS
One of B.C.'s most abundant bats, the little brown myotis is not considered to be at risk.

RANGE
Found throughout B.C. (including coastal islands), anywhere from sea level to about 2300 m, the little brown myotis breeds and likely hibernates throughout its provincial range, but the wintering locations of most of the population are unknown. Some hibernacula in eastern North America contain thousands of individuals, but hibernacula found in B.C. to date are limited to several old mines in the Interior, each with several individuals. In eastern Canada, this bat is known to migrate >200 km between summer and winter hibernacula.

Biogeoclimatic Zones

AT	BG	BWBS	CDF	CWH	ESSF	ICH	IDF	MH	MS	PP	SBPS	SBS	SWB

Ecoprovinces

BOP	COM	CEI	GED	NBM	SBI	SIM	SOI	TAP

Breeding Period

J	F	M	A	M	J	J	A	S	O	N	D

DESCRIPTION

This medium-sized bat (6–10 g; 70–108 mm in length) has glossy back fur that varies in colour from yellow (dry Interior populations) to blackish (coastal populations), with a lighter underside that ranges from light brown to tan. The wing membranes and ears are dark. When laid forward, the ears reach the nostrils. The similar looking Yuma myotis, is smaller, with shorter, duller fur.

HABITAT

The little brown myotis uses a wide variety of habitats, such as arid grasslands and ponderosa pine, boreal and coastal forests. It is closely associated with aquatic habitats.

Feeding: In the Okanagan, this bat forages in forests and openings and over bluffs or calm water (e.g., small lakes, riverine pools, irrigation flumes, marshes and the edges of large water bodies). The prey, which is caught and eaten on the wing and changes with the season and insect abundance, is mainly aquatic insects, but also beetles, craneflies, moths and leafhoppers.

Breeding: Maternity colonies require high, stable temperatures (30–55°C); attics are often used by hundreds or thousands of females. Colonies in natural sites (e.g., tree cavities, rock crevices) are typically smaller (<100 females) and individuals frequently switch roosts; one colony was found in a hot spring–heated cave on the Grayling River in northern B.C. Males and females live separately in summer. Mating occurs in late summer or early autumn. In the south Okanagan, the single young is born between early June and early July, probably later at higher elevations and latitudes.

Roosting and Hibernation: Summer roost sites include spaces under loose bark, tree cavities, rock crevices, caves, mines and buildings. An initial evening feeding period of up to one hour is followed by retirement to temporary night roosts near day roosts; these protected roosts may help the bats remain warm and active, thus speeding digestion. Males roost alone or in small groups, in cooler sites than those used for nurseries. In B.C., this species hibernates alone or in small clusters in caves and old mines where the humidity is high (70–95 percent) and temperatures remain above freezing.

STEWARDSHIP PROVISIONS

(see p. 218)

OF INTEREST

The little brown myotis can often be seen at dusk, skimming the surfaces of water bodies.

NORTHERN LONG-EARED MYOTIS
Myotis septentrionalis • MYSE

STATUS
B.C.: Blue List

Because it is one of the province's rarest bats, the northern long-eared myotis is considered to be at risk in B.C.

RANGE
Records exist for the Hudson's Hope, Mount Revelstoke National Park, Revelstoke Dam and Liard River areas. Although rare, the northern long-eared myotis is believed to be a regular inhabitant of northeastern B.C., but there are no provincial winter records. In eastern Canada, this species migrates up to 56 km from summer roosts to winter hibernacula.

DESCRIPTION
This medium-sized bat (5–10 g; 80–94 mm in length) has dark brown back fur, a paler underside and dark brown ears and flight membranes. When laid forward, the long ears extend beyond the nostrils. The western long-eared myotis, which has an overlapping range, has larger ears and characteristic dark brown shoulder spots and tail membrane hairs.

HABITAT
Very limited information is available for B.C. Elsewhere, this species is generally associated with boreal and high-elevation forests.

Feeding: The northern long-eared myotis hunts over small ponds and forest openings, typically flying 1–3 m above the ground, just above the understorey. It mostly captures flying insects on the wing, but it sometimes gleans prey from twigs or foliage. The diet includes moths, caddisflies, flies, mosquitoes, beetles and leafhoppers.

Biogeoclimatic Zones

AT	BG	**BWBS**	CDF	CWH	ESSF	**ICH**	IDF	MH	MS	PP	SBPS	SBS	SWB

Ecoprovinces									Breeding Period												
BOP	COM	CEI	GED	**NBM**	SBI	**SIM**	SOI	TAP		J	F	M	A	M	J	J	A	S	O	N	D

Breeding: No maternity roosts have been found in the province, but this species is thought to breed within its range in northeastern B.C. Captures of lactating females indicate breeding in Mount Revelstoke National Park, where this bat occurs exclusively in old-growth western red-cedar and western hemlock forests at an elevation of about 700 m. A post-lactating female was also captured in the Liard River area. In eastern North America, relatively small (<30 individuals) nursery colonies have been found under loose bark and in buildings, so trees are probably used as maternity roosts in B.C. Mating likely takes place in September or October, with the single young being born in June or early July.

Roosting and Hibernation: This bat likely uses spaces under loose bark or tree cavities for solitary summer roosts, and it may also use caves for temporary roosts. In the Liard River area, five bats of this species were found roosting in an abandoned cabin, and a bridge was used as a night roost. In eastern North America, the northern long-eared myotis hibernates alone or in small clusters in narrow rock crevices and tight holes in mine shafts; outside B.C., this bat has been found sharing hibernacula with other species.

STEWARDSHIP PROVISIONS
(see p. 218)

OF INTEREST
The Giant Cedars Trail in Mount Revelstoke National Park is B.C.'s most reliable viewing site for the northern long-eared myotis. Lucky observers may see these bats at dusk, hunting or drinking from small pools in forest clearings.

LONG-LEGGED MYOTIS
Myotis volans • MYVO

STATUS
The widely distributed long-legged myotis is locally abundant in some locations in B.C. and is not at risk in the province.

RANGE
On the coast, this bat is found around Vancouver and on Vancouver Island. In the Interior, it occurs northward to Atlin and eastward to the Rocky Mountain Trench, and it is locally abundant in the Williams Lake and Fraser Canyon areas. It ranges from sea level to 1040 m in B.C. No provincial winter records exist.

DESCRIPTION
One of the largest *Myotis* bats in B.C. (6–10 g; 83–105 mm in length), the long-legged myotis has fur that varies

Biogeoclimatic Zones

AT	BG	BWBS	CDF	CWH	ESSF	ICH	IDF	MH	MS	PP	SBPS	SBS	SWB

Ecoprovinces

BOP	COM	CEI	GED	NBM	SBI	SIM	SOI	TAP

Breeding Period

J	F	M	A	M	J	J	A	S	O	N	D

from reddish brown to dark brown. The underside of the wing membrane is often densely furred as far as the elbow and the knee. When laid forward, the rounded, relatively short ears barely extend to the nostrils. Despite its common name, this species does not have noticeably long legs. The western small-footed myotis and California myotis could be confused with this species, but both are smaller. The big brown bat is also similar, but the undersides of its wings are unfurred.

HABITAT
This bat's various habitats range from arid rangelands to montane and coastal forests.

Feeding: An opportunistic hunter, the long-legged myotis captures aerial prey over water, in and above the forest canopy and in clearings. Research in Alberta suggests that it prefers to hunt along the edges of tree groves and cliff faces. It eats primarily moths (about 75 percent of the diet), as well as beetles, termites, spiders, flies, leafhoppers and lacewings.

Breeding: Only two maternity colonies have been discovered in B.C., one in an attic on Vancouver Island and another in an old barn near Williams Lake. In the western U.S., maternity colonies have been found under tree bark, in fissures in the ground and in attics. Mating begins in late August or September, before hibernation. In the dry Interior, the single young is likely born between mid-June and early July.

Roosting and Hibernation: In the western U.S., this bat is known to use spaces behind tree bark, streambanks, rock crevices and buildings as solitary summer day roosts. Little information is available on summer roosts in B.C., though a male was found roosting in a crack in a dead poplar, a juvenile was found roosting in a church attic with a Yuma myotis nursery colony, and near Nelson, one female and one male were found roosting in separate sites under the loose bark of western white pines. Caves and old mines are used for night roosts, and elsewhere, have served as hibernacula for small numbers of individuals.

STEWARDSHIP PROVISIONS
(see p. 218)

OF INTEREST
Recoveries of banded individuals indicate that this species can live up to 21 years in the wild.

YUMA MYOTIS
Myotis yumanensis • MYYU

STATUS

Locally abundant at a few sites in B.C., the Yuma myotis is not considered to be at risk. The largest known colony in B.C. (3000–4000 individuals) was at Squilax, near Shuswap Lake, but the main nursery site was destroyed by fire in March 1994, before the bats returned for the summer.

RANGE

Found on Vancouver Island and other coastal islands, on the mainland coast as far north as Prince Rupert, and in the Okanagan, South Thompson and Fraser valleys north to Williams Lake and the intervening areas east to Nelson, the Yuma myotis is restricted to low elevations (sea level to 730 m). It probably hibernates in B.C., but only one winter record exists, and there are no known hibernation sites.

DESCRIPTION

A medium-sized bat (4–9 g; 60–99 mm in length), the Yuma myotis has light brown to nearly black fur on its back, a pale belly and dark brown ears and wing membranes. When laid forward,

Biogeoclimatic Zones

AT	BG	BWBS	CDF	CWH	ESSF	ICH	IDF	MH	MS	PP	SBPS	SBS	SWB

Ecoprovinces

BOP	COM	CEI	GED	NBM	SBI	SIM	SOI	TAP

Breeding Period

J	F	M	A	M	J	J	A	S	O	N	D

the ears reach the tip of the nose. The Yuma myotis is slightly smaller than the little brown myotis, with duller fur and lighter ears and wing membranes.

HABITAT

The Yuma myotis is found in low-elevation coastal forests, ponderosa pine–Douglas-fir forests and dry grasslands. No other B.C. bat is so closely associated with water.

Feeding: The Yuma is one of few bats of our region that feeds over salt water as well as over lakes, rivers and streams. It may travel long distances (up to 4 km recorded at Squilax) from day roosts to aquatic hunting areas. It uses temporary night roosts near foraging areas between feeding bouts. The diet, which relies heavily on aquatic insects and changes through summer as different insects emerge, includes caddisflies, mayflies, midges, flies, termites, moths and beetles.

Breeding: Maternity roosts are located in buildings, under the bark or in cavi-ties of wildlife trees or rock crevices and may be shared with other *Myotis* species (e.g., little brown, western long-eared and California). Colonies in buildings can contain a few thousand females, but colonies in natural structures are usually smaller (<100). In the Squilax maternity roost, midday summer temperatures often reached 40°C. Mating occurs in autumn, and the single young is born between early June and mid-July.

Roosting and Hibernation: In the Okanagan, this bat roosts in open habitats near water. Wildlife trees, caves, rock crevices and built structures are used for summer day-roost sites. Mainly human-built structures are used at night. Males roost separately, alone or in small groups. Hibernation in caves and mine entrances has been observed in Washington.

STEWARDSHIP PROVISIONS
(see p. 218)

OF INTEREST

After the abandoned church that housed the Squilax maternity colony burned down, volunteers built and erected bat houses. The number of Yuma myotis found roosting in the area that summer was much lower than before the fire but has been climbing steadily ever since.

WESTERN RED BAT
Lasiurus blossevillii • LABL

STATUS
B.C.: Red List

The western red bat is one of the rarest bats in B.C. Its occurrence in the province was originally thought to be accidental, but recent records suggest there is a small, isolated resident summer population. It is considered to be at risk in the province because of its rarity.

RANGE
The only provincial records are from low elevations in forested areas near rivers in the Skagit Valley and the Okanagan Valley. British Columbia is at the extreme northern limit of this bat's summer range. Because no winter records exist for Canada, and because it is migratory in other parts of its range, this species is assumed to overwinter south of the B.C.–U.S. border.

DESCRIPTION
This large bat (10–19 g; 87–120 mm in length) is easily distinguished by its

Biogeoclimatic Zones

AT	BG	BWBS	CDF	CWH	ESSF	ICH	IDF	MH	MS	PP	SBPS	SBS	SWB

Ecoprovinces

BOP	COM	CEI	GED	NBM	SBI	SIM	SOI	TAP

Breeding Period

J	F	M	A	M	J	J	A	S	O	N	D

unique coloration, which varies from pale orange to rusty red. Each long hair has a black base, pale middle and reddish tip. The belly is paler than the back. Patches of yellowish fur are visible on the shoulder, the base of the thumb and the underside of the wing membrane. The hind feet and the upper surface of the tail membrane are covered with thick fur. The ears are short and rounded.

HABITAT

Feeding: This bat likely hunts in small clearings and semi-open areas within forested habitats, usually near water. It is sometimes attracted to lights, where large numbers of insects often concentrate. The diet probably consists mainly of large moths, supplemented by beetles and grasshoppers.

Breeding: The females are solitary and roost with their young in the foliage of hardwoods. Mothers carry their young when changing roost locations. Mating probably occurs during the fall migration period. The little information that exists for this species suggests that most commonly three young are born, probably in June or early July.

Roosting and Hibernation: Well camouflaged by their resemblance to dead leaves, these bats roost in the foliage of large shrubs or hardwoods in habitats bordering forests, rivers and agricultural and urban areas, usually 1–5 m above the ground. Males roost alone. Females with young tend to select higher roosts than do males, probably to minimize disturbance and risk of predation. In the Okanagan, western red bats have been observed flying above stands of black cottonwoods, so they probably use this tree species for roosting.

ADDITIONAL STEWARDSHIP PROVISIONS (see also p. 218)

- Protect known maternity roosts, hibernacula and day-roosting sites as well as the adjacent core foraging areas within about 100 m of these sites. The minimum distance in each direction in a given situation depends on the locations of riparian zones, available roost trees and movement corridors. Do not harvest or salvage in this area.

OF INTEREST

Western red bats use two different types of echolocation: long calls for hunting in open areas and shorter calls in tight situations where the range is 5–10 m or less.

HOARY BAT
Lasiurus cinereus • LACI

STATUS
Very little is known about the provincial abundance of the hoary bat, but it is widely distributed and not considered to be at risk in B.C.

RANGE
This bat can be found anywhere from sea level to 1250 m across southern B.C., including Vancouver Island, the coastal mainland northward into Garibaldi Provincial Park and the Interior northward to Williams Lake. The B.C. population is probably migratory; it is presumed to leave the province between mid-August and early October and may overwinter in southern California and Mexico.

DESCRIPTION
British Columbia's largest bat (20–38 g; 125–144 mm in length) is named for the distinctive coloration of the long

Biogeoclimatic Zones

AT	BG	BWBS	CDF	CWH	ESSF	ICH	IDF	MH	MS	PP	SBPS	SBS	SWB

Ecoprovinces									Breeding Period													
BOP	COM	CEI	GED	NBM	SBI	SIM	SOI	TAP		J	F	M	A	M	J	J	A	S	O	N	D

235

hunt throughout the night, flying up to 20 km from its roost. Its prey, captured on the wing, is mainly large flying insects (moths, beetles and dragonflies), supplemented by some smaller insects.

Breeding: Females do not congregate in maternity colonies but raise their young from a maternity roost instead. Branches (in conifers or hardwoods) are the preferred maternal roosts, and tree cavities are rarely used. A family will occupy the same site for more than a month. Mating likely occurs during autumn migration or in winter. No breeding information exists for B.C., but elsewhere females give birth to 1–4 young (usually two) in early to mid-June.

Roosting and Hibernation: In summer, the males roost alone and the females roost with their young, usually in branches (in conifers or hardwoods, including fruit trees in the Okanagan). Tree cavity roosts have been found in B.C.: one in a hollow in a western redcedar and another in an abandoned woodpecker nest. Roosts are generally near the ends of branches, high up and open from below, so occupants are concealed from predators by foliage, and the flight path to and from the roost is unobstructed. The foliage of old conifers, being higher and farther from the trunk than on younger ones, is more likely to provide appropriate conditions. In eastern Canada, very tall, mature trees are preferred for roosting.

back fur—a mix of brown and grey hairs with white tips—which provides camouflage against lichen-covered bark. A yellow ruff surrounds the wide, brown face, and white or yellow patches mark the shoulders and wrists. The small, rounded ears are close to the head. This bat's flight is fast and direct. The high-pitched chirping calls are audible to humans when a hoary bat is defending a rich feeding area (e.g., around outdoor lights) from other bats.

HABITAT
The hoary bat is associated with a variety of forested and grassland habitats.

Feeding: Foraging at treetop level over fields and forest openings, this bat may

STEWARDSHIP PROVISIONS
(see p. 218)

OF INTEREST
Female hoary bats care for their young longer than is typical for other North American bats. The young are capable of sustained flight at five weeks, but family groups remain together for several more weeks. This longer period of offspring care may be related to a reduced need to accumulate fat reserves for winter; rather than hibernate, this species continues to eat in winter.

SILVER-HAIRED BAT

Lasionycteris noctivagans • LANO

STATUS

The silver-haired bat is difficult to find and study. Although no reliable information exists regarding its abundance, it is not considered to be at risk in B.C.

RANGE

Found anywhere from sea level to 1220 m in elevation, this bat has a range that covers Vancouver Island, the Queen Charlotte Islands and the coastal mainland northward to Rivers Inlet and the Interior at least as far north as the Peace River region, the Spatsizi Plateau and the Liard River area. It is thought to breed throughout its B.C. range. More cold-hardy than most other bats, it can probably overwinter anywhere that the mean daily temperature for January is above –7°C, but it may withdraw from northerly places and high elevations to hibernate in southern areas of the province. Winter records exist for Victoria, Vancouver, the north Okanagan and the Williams Lake area.

DESCRIPTION

This medium-sized bat (8–13 g; 90–117 mm in length) is distinguished by dark brown to black fur and scattered silver-tipped hairs, particularly on the back. The wing membranes and short, round ears are black. The only similar B.C. bat, the hoary, is much larger, with a yellow ruff around the face.

Biogeoclimatic Zones

AT	BG	BWBS	CDF	CWH	ESSF	ICH	IDF	MH	MS	PP	SBPS	SBS	SWB

Ecoprovinces									Breeding Period											
BOP	COM	CEI	GED	NBM	SBI	SIM	SOI	TAP	J	F	M	A	M	J	J	A	S	O	N	D

HABITAT

The silver-haired bat is associated with forests and grassland habitats.

Feeding: This bat hunts over water and at treetop level in small clearings. Its two peak activity periods are the first half-hour after dark and the hour before dawn. It catches prey, such as moths, flies, caddisflies, midges, beetles, ants and termites, on the wing, often exploiting swarms of flying insects.

Breeding: Maternity roosts are located in tree cavities, especially abandoned woodpecker nest holes and cavities formed by limb breakage, and spaces beneath bark. In B.C., maternity colonies have been found in western white pines,

hemlocks and larches (near Nelson); aspens (Pend d'Oreille Valley); and Douglas-firs near Kamloops. Colonies are generally small (<10 females). Mating takes place in September and October. One or two young are born, probably in late June or early July.

Roosting and Hibernation: This bat roosts alone or in small groups (usually 2–6, but up to 21 individuals) in spaces beneath bark, tree hollows, deep furrows in bark, abandoned woodpecker holes, bird nests or rock crevices. In the Okanagan, black cottonwoods are apparently preferred. In Oregon and Alberta, this species is closely associated with old-growth forest, likely because old and dead trees provide abundant roost sites. Similarly, B.C. individuals have been found hibernating under the bark of a western red-cedar and in a Douglas-fir snag; consequently, old-growth structures are considered potentially important winter hibernation sites. Trees appear to be the most important hibernation sites in B.C.

STEWARDSHIP PROVISIONS
(see p. 218)

OF INTEREST

When migrating through urban areas, silver-haired bats are often detected as they roost on the walls of buildings. If found dormant, they should not be considered ill: to conserve energy for their migration, they can lower their body temperature during the day and go into torpor.

BIG BROWN BAT

Eptesicus fuscus • EPFU

STATUS

The big brown bat is relatively common in the dry Interior and the Columbia Valley and possibly in other parts of B.C.

The northern Interior limits are unknown, but because it inhabits inland Alaska, the B.C. range may extend to the Yukon border. In the Interior, this bat hibernates from November to April, but in southern coastal regions it may be active for short periods in winter. Migrations of up to 300 km are known, but winter and summer roosts are usually <80 km apart.

DESCRIPTION

The relatively large (12–22 g; 98–131 mm in length) big brown bat has a broad nose. The fur colour varies from pale to dark brown, and the wing membranes and ears are usually black. When laid forward, the short ears extend just to the nostrils.

HABITAT

Arid grasslands and coastal and interior forests are among the various habitats used by this species.

RANGE

The big brown bat can be found anywhere from sea level to 1070 m throughout southern B.C. and northwards to Bella Coola and the Peace River.

Feeding: The big brown bat forages over forest canopies, waterways and cliffs, along forest edges and clearings and in urban areas, often around streetlights. It makes several 30–60-minute feeding forays each night (sometimes continuing all night) to capture flying insects on the wing—mainly beetles but

Biogeoclimatic Zones

AT	BG	BWBS	CDF	CWH	ESSF	ICH	IDF	MH	MS	PP	SBPS	SBS	SWB

Ecoprovinces									Breeding Period											
BOP	COM	CEI	GED	NBM	SBI	SIM	SOI	TAP		J	F	M	A	M	J	J	A	S	O	N	D

also moths, carpenter ants, termites, lacewings, flies and caddisflies.

Breeding: Proximity to water and feeding sites are important selection criteria for maternity colonies. In the Okanagan, cavities in dead ponderosa pines and rock crevices are used for this purpose, but elsewhere buildings are commonly used. Colony sizes have been recorded at 40–100 bats in B.C. and up to 700 elsewhere. Mating occurs in autumn and winter before hibernation. In B.C., the single young is probably born between mid-June and early July, but variation is possible among the individuals within a colony or as a result of prevailing weather conditions.

Roosting and Hibernation: Summer day roosts are located in spaces under bark, hollows in trees, rock crevices or buildings. In the Okanagan, roosts may be up to 4 km from feeding areas. Temporary night roosts are located close to feeding areas. Site fidelity is high for buildings and rock crevices, but individuals roosting in trees seem to move regularly between several established sites. The winter biology for this bat in B.C. is little known, but elsewhere the species hibernates in dry, cool (–10°C to –5°C) sites in buildings, caves and mines, singly or in clusters of up to 100 individuals. Hibernacula may be shared with other species (e.g., pallid bat and Yuma myotis). This bat may become active for short times during winter, particularly when in buildings.

STEWARDSHIP PROVISIONS
(see p. 218)

OF INTEREST
A big brown bat can find, catch and eat an insect every three seconds.

Other Mammals

In addition to bats, at least seven other species of mammals regularly use wildlife trees. They are a diverse group, ranging in size from the Keen's mouse to the black bear. These mammals depend on wildlife trees for maternal dens, for hibernation dens, for shelter from the elements while resting or for protection from predators. As explained in the individual species accounts, some of them, rather than being completely dependent on wildlife trees, are opportunistic users of this kind of habitat. Sometimes the level of wildlife tree use varies geographically, with members of the species that live in one region being more dependent on wildlife trees than those in another.

The smallest of the cavity-using mammals (bushy-tailed woodrat, Keen's mouse, northern flying squirrel and red-tailed chipmunk) take advantage of abandoned woodpecker nest holes or use natural cavities. For the largest of the tree-using mammals (marten, fisher and black bear), standing or fallen hollow trees in many cases provide vital habitat. Because a fallen tree will not develop the hollow core that these species require, standing hollow trees are an important present and future habitat resource.

These wildlife tree–dependent mammals play a number of important roles within forest ecosystems. The marten, for example, preys on mice, voles, squirrels, snowshoe hares and porcupines, all of which feed on young tree seedlings and undergo rapid population increases when food is abundant and predators are scarce. Similarly, the fisher is a significant predator of porcupines and snowshoe hares. As explained in the introduction to this guide, the Keen's mouse and the northern flying squirrel are effective dispersal agents for beneficial mycorrhizal soil fungi. Through their foraging activities and fecal droppings, they also help distribute seeds, organic nutrients and inorganic nutrients, such as nitrogen.

Dense, moist conifer forests such as this interior cedar hemlock stand are preferred fisher habitat.

241

BUSHY-TAILED WOODRAT
Neotoma cinerea • NECI

STATUS
The bushy-tailed woodrat is widely distributed throughout mainland B.C. Its populations may be limited by nest site availability, but it is not at risk.

Bushy-tailed woodrat emerging from old woodpecker cavity in a true fir

RANGE
Resident from sea level to the alpine in suitable habitat throughout the province, this rodent is active year-round, but it winters below the snowpack.

DESCRIPTION
At about 40 cm in length, including a 9-cm-long bushy tail, the bushy-tailed woodrat is slightly larger than the common rat. It has large ears and very long whiskers. The soft, dense fur is brownish grey, with white on the feet and underparts and the underside of the tail. The young have bluish grey fur.

Biogeoclimatic Zones

AT	BG	BWBS	CDF	CWH	ESSF	ICH	IDF	MH	MS	PP	SBPS	SBS	SWB

Ecoprovinces										Breeding Period												
BOP	COM	CEI	GED	NBM	SBI	SIM	SOI	TAP		J	F	M	A	M	J	J	A	S	O	N	D

OTHER CHARACTERISTICS

This rodent is most active at dusk and dawn. The adult male marks his territory with a strong, musky-smelling oily secretion from the abdominal scent gland.

HABITAT

Habitat usage ranges from coastal rainforest to dry, rocky areas in the Interior, where this woodrat mainly inhabits cliffs, caves, rock outcroppings and talus slopes.

Feeding: The bushy-tailed woodrat forages close to its den. It primarily eats fresh and dried foliage, mushrooms, fruits and seeds but also carrion, insects and small reptiles. Dried vegetation is cached for winter use.

Breeding: In the Coastal Douglas-fir zone and on the driest slopes of the Coastal Western Hemlock zone of southern Vancouver Island and the Lower Mainland, nests are almost exclusively in trees (e.g., Douglas-fir), either in natural cavities or abandoned woodpecker nests or on branches 4–15 m above the ground. In the Interior, rocky habitats are mostly used. In both areas, this species also nests in buildings. The young, rarely >4, are born in spring or summer and disperse at 2–3 months.

Denning: Each adult has at least one den—a cup-shaped or domed mass of soft fibres (e.g., grass or shredded bark) located in a crevice or hollow. The young are born and raised in the mother's den. Once independent, a juvenile's survival depends on finding a suitable winter den site. Good dens are used for years by successive generations.

Territory Size/Home Range: This woodrat is solitary except during the breeding season. A male will defend his territory from other males, but 1–3 females may live within each male's territory.

ADDITIONAL STEWARDSHIP PROVISIONS (see also Part 2)

- In dry coastal Douglas-fir stands, manage as for the medium-sized to large woodpeckers.
- To maintain a supply of natural cavities in coastal areas, retain some large (>50 cm dbh) snags and live trees (decay class 2, with defects such as dead or broken tops and limbs), especially in dry Douglas-fir stands.

OF INTEREST

Woodrats are often called "packrats" because of their habit of collecting bones, sticks and feathers, as well as small articles found in cabins or camps. These items may be used to partially block the den entrance or to build into a feeding platform or food-drying rack.

KEEN'S MOUSE
Peromyscus keenii • PEKE

STATUS
The Keen's mouse populations appear to be stable throughout most of its range. It is not at risk.

Keen's mouse in a woodpecker cavity

RANGE
The Keen's mouse is found in the Coast Mountains (perhaps as far east as the eastern slopes) and the coastal lowlands from Washington State northward on the B.C. mainland, and on Vancouver Island, the Queen Charlotte Islands and some other islands of the central and north coast.

DESCRIPTION
Larger than the more common and wide-ranging deer mouse, the brownish grey Keen's mouse has a body length of 109–117 mm, and the almost equally

Biogeoclimatic Zones

AT	BG	BWBS	CDF	CWH	ESSF	ICH	IDF	MH	MS	PP	SBPS	SBS	SWB

Ecoprovinces									Breeding Period											
BOP	COM	CEI	GED	NBM	SBI	SIM	SOI	TAP		J	F	M	A	M	J	J	A	S	O	N	D

long tail (97–114 mm in length) is uniform in colour. (The deer mouse has a sharply bicoloured tail, white below and dark above.) The feet are usually white.

OTHER CHARACTERISTICS
Active nocturnally and year-round, the Keen's mouse often travels on top of the snow rather than in tunnels.

HABITAT
The Keen's mouse primarily inhabits coastal conifer and mixedwood forests, often choosing stands dominated by Sitka spruce.

Feeding: Feeding largely on conifer seeds (often spruce), this rodent also eats berries, nuts, fungi and insects and other arthropods.

Breeding: This species' nests are in hollow logs, hollow trees or tree cavities, under rocks or in shallow burrows. The exact breeding period, which is usually between February and November, varies with latitude. A pair usually produces 2–4 litters of 1–8 young (usually 3–5) per year. This species can breed at 5–6 weeks of age.

Denning and Resting: The Keen's mouse will den in abandoned woodpecker cavities and natural cavities (e.g., broken branch stubs) in trees if available. These sites, which are also used for resting, are preferred because of the shelter they provide from wet coastal weather, plus increased protection from predators. Den sites are also found in hollow logs and beneath woody debris.

Territory Size/Home Range: The home range size is 0.2–1.9 ha. Territories are defended only during the breeding season. Depending on the food supply, weather conditions and predation rates, summer population densities can be as high as 37 mice/ha.

ADDITIONAL STEWARDSHIP PROVISIONS (see also Part 2)
- Manage for a supply of wildlife trees with natural cavities or hollows, especially in Sitka spruce forests.

OF INTEREST
Keen's mouse is the most arboreal mouse species found in British Columbia. Its droppings have been found in cavities 20 m above the ground.

NORTHERN FLYING SQUIRREL

Glaucomys sabrinus • GLSA

STATUS

Common throughout its B.C. range, the northern flying squirrel is not considered to be at risk. Because of its strictly nocturnal habits, it is rarely seen, even where it is abundant.

DESCRIPTION

The northern flying squirrel has a body length of 140–170 mm and a tail length of 110–140 mm. Its soft, dense fur ranges from reddish brown to greyish buff, becoming pale on the belly and the underside of the tail. This squirrel can be distinguished from other tree squirrels by its large eyes (adapted for night vision) and a distinctive fold of skin along each flank.

OTHER CHARACTERISTICS

Flying squirrels are active all winter and do not hibernate or enter torpor. They are a favoured prey species for many owls and are extremely important for spotted owls.

HABITAT

The range of forest types and seral stages used by this squirrel encompasses conifer and mixedwood stands and young to old-growth forests.

RANGE

This year-round resident inhabits forested areas throughout B.C., including those on several coastal islands, but not on Vancouver Island or the Queen Charlotte Islands.

Feeding: Foraging mostly on the ground, its diet varying with forest type, the northern flying squirrel eats such things as the fruiting bodies of underground fungi, seeds and lichens—and sometimes bird eggs and nestlings and carrion. It may raid red squirrel food caches in winter and sometimes visits bird feeders in the evening.

Biogeoclimatic Zones

AT	BG	BWBS	CDF	CWH	ESSF	ICH	IDF	MH	MS	PP	SBPS	SBS	SWB

Ecoprovinces										Breeding Period												
BOP	COM	CEI	GED	NBM	SBI	SIM	SOI	TAP		J	F	M	A	M	J	J	A	S	O	N	D

Breeding: Nest and den sites (described below) are used year-round. Mating usually occurs twice a year (March and May), with a gestation period of about 40 days. The litter size is 2–6 (the average is three). Pups are weaned around five weeks and reach sexual maturity at one year.

Denning and Resting: Nests and dens are mainly in cavities with a minimum internal diameter of 11 cm. Cavity trees are typically >25 cm dbh. In coastal forests, this squirrel mostly uses old woodpecker cavities. In the Interior, it commonly uses both tree cavities and nests ("dreys") made of twigs and leaves positioned in branch forks. In boreal and sub-boreal forests, it often nests and dens in large witches' brooms (25–100 cm horizontal diameter); this use of (and perhaps dependence on) brooms may be in lieu of suitably large tree cavities or because of favourable thermal properties. This squirrel is also known to use nest boxes.

The availability of suitable sites for nests or dens may sometimes limit populations. The number of nests or dens needed per squirrel is unknown, but up to 13 per individual have been reported, with some sites being used repeatedly. In winter, particularly in cold climates, communal dens with up to a dozen squirrels are common.

Territory Size/Home Range: Not vigorously territorial, these squirrels can have extensive overlap in their home ranges, which vary from 0.75 ha (coastal Douglas-fir forest) to 30 ha (boreal and sub-boreal Interior forests).

Northern flying squirrel in a woodpecker cavity in class 4 western larch

ADDITIONAL STEWARDSHIP PROVISIONS (see also Part 2)

- Manage as for the medium-sized and large woodpeckers.
- In Interior boreal and sub-boreal forests, maintain trees with large witches' brooms, especially if trees >30 cm dbh with large cavities are lacking.

OF INTEREST

Although it is not capable of true flight, the northern flying squirrel can glide long distances from tree to tree or from a tree to the ground. The folds of skin along each side of its body, extending from "wrist" to "ankle," act like a parachute, and the flattened tail helps it steer while airborne.

RED-TAILED CHIPMUNK
Tamias ruficaudus • TARU

STATUS
Rocky Mountains subspecies, *T. r. ruficaudus*—B.C.: Red List
Selkirk Mountains subspecies, *T. r. simulans*—B.C.: Blue List

Two subspecies of red-tailed chipmunk, geographically isolated from each other, occur in southeastern B.C. Because of limited records, both are considered to be at risk.

Red-tailed chipmunk in cavity

Akamina Pass–Wall Lake and Middle Kootenay Pass, at only three known locations in B.C. The Selkirk Mountains subspecies (*T. r. simulans*) is widespread from 560 to 1830 m in the southern Selkirks between the Kootenay River and the Columbia River.

DESCRIPTION
This large chipmunk, about 22 cm in length, including the 9-cm-long tail, has a back marked with five dark stripes and four light ones, and its face is also striped. The Rocky Mountains subspecies is reddish on the sides and shoulders and the back of the head; the bright rufous colouring on the underside of its tail is responsible for the species name. The Selkirk Mountains population is more tan or yellow.

OTHER CHARACTERISTICS
An excellent climber, this species is more arboreal than other chipmunks. It is active during the day.

RANGE
The Rocky Mountains subspecies (*T. r. ruficaudus*) is restricted to a narrow elevational band (1785–1950 m) in the southern Rockies between

HABITAT
The Rocky Mountains subspecies is found only in subalpine conifer forest and associated openings (e.g., recent burns). The Selkirk Mountains subspecies occupies a variety of conifer forest habitats from early seral to mature, and

Biogeoclimatic Zones

AT	BG	BWBS	CDF	CWH	**ESSF**	**ICH**	IDF	MH	**MS**	**PP**	SBPS	SBS	SWB

Ecoprovinces								Breeding Period												
BOP	COM	CEI	GED	NBM	SBI	**SIM**	SOI	TAP		J	F	M	**A**	M	J	J	A	S	O	N	D

it frequents forest edges and openings with an abundant shrub layer and woody debris.

Feeding: Seeds (e.g., bull thistle, ponderosa pine, snowberry, serviceberry and ninebark) are the most important food. This chipmunk also eats leaves, flowers (e.g. dandelion and arnica), fruit and invertebrates. In spring, it forages mainly on the forest floor. In summer and autumn, it forages extensively in shrubs and trees. Seeds are cached in the burrow for winter feeding.

Breeding: The young are born in tree nests or in underground burrows and later transferred to tree nests. Used in summer and autumn, the tree nests, 5–18 m above the ground, are made of dried plant material (e.g., grass and lichen) and may be built in dense branches near the tree trunk (often in a live Engelmann spruce) or located in a natural tree cavity or abandoned woodpecker nest. Born sometime from late April through June, the young first appear outside the nest in mid-July. The usual litter size is 4–6.

Denning and Resting: This species remains inactive in an underground burrow from late October to early April.

Territory Size/Home Range: Males have larger home ranges than females. No other information is available.

ADDITIONAL STEWARDSHIP PROVISIONS (see also Part 2)

- Manage as for the medium-sized woodpeckers.
- Maintain a shrub layer to provide foraging opportunities.

OF INTEREST
Some evidence suggests that the two types of red-tailed chipmunk found here are two distinct species.

MARTEN
Martes americana • MAAM

STATUS

The marten is common to abundant throughout B.C., with a population estimated at 150,000–200,000.

RANGE

Resident in forested regions of B.C., including the coastal islands, the marten is most common in the southern Interior mountains and west of the Rockies in the northern Interior.

DESCRIPTION

This medium-sized member of the weasel family has a body length of 40–45 cm for the male, with a tail 20–23 cm long, and 35–38 cm for the female, with an 18–20-cm tail. It has short legs and large, furred feet. The soft, dense fur is yellowish brown to brown, darker on the legs and bushy tail, with a pale buff patch on the throat and breast.

Biogeoclimatic Zones

AT	BG	BWBS	CDF	CWH	ESSF	ICH	IDF	MH	MS	PP	SBPS	SBS	SWB

Ecoprovinces

BOP	COM	CEI	GED	NBM	SBI	SIM	SOI	TAP

Breeding Period

J	F	M	A	M	J	J	A	S	O	N	D

OTHER CHARACTERISTICS

Semi-retractable claws assist in tree climbing.

HABITAT

The marten prefers conifer and conifer-hardwood stands that are mature or older, especially in moist sites (e.g., riparian areas), but it can be found in all forest types and seral stages.

Feeding: Active throughout the day, this carnivore hunts in the tree canopy or on the forest floor for mice, voles, shrews, squirrels, chipmunks and snowshoe hares. It supplements its diet with bird eggs, fish, insects, fruits, nuts and carrion. In areas with winter snowpack, it typically forages beneath the snow for small mammals (e.g., mice and voles), using downed and leaning logs, decayed stumps and large-diameter trees for access to prey. In coastal areas, small birds (e.g., winter wren) are the major winter prey.

Breeding: The marten is solitary except during the breeding season (June–September). Maternity dens are located in large-diameter hollow snags, hollow logs, slash piles or underground burrows; dry, secure sites are essential. Usually 2–4 young (kits) are born in late March or April, and they are weaned at 6–7 weeks. They begin breeding in their second year.

Denning and Resting: Nonmaternity dens are often beneath large stumps or the root masses of large trees. Large witches' brooms in live conifers are regularly used as resting platforms.

Territory Size/Home Range: Home ranges are 200–1600 ha for males and 80–800 ha for females.

ADDITIONAL STEWARDSHIP PROVISIONS (see also Part 2)

- Retain large live and dead trees (preferably >50 cm dbh) with natural cavities, especially hollow trunks.

Mature and older forests provide habitat for marten prey species and the coarse woody debris provides access below the snow in areas where there is a snow pack.

- Retain some trees with large witches' brooms.
- Retain areas of mature forest >25 ha to provide sufficient forest interior habitat and reduce the fragmentation of mature and old-forest habitats. Moist sites are particularly important.
- Areas of suitable habitat need to be linked by corridors of mature forest >200 m in width (e.g., along streams or lakeshores, through saddles and gullies or over ridges).
- Retain abundant coarse woody debris (>20 cm diameter) and maintain multi-storey canopies (30–70 percent crown closure) and low to moderate understorey shrub densities. These conditions will encourage prey populations for the marten.

OF INTEREST

Highly curious, the marten is easily attracted to both feeding stations and traps.

FISHER
Martes pennanti • MAPE

STATUS
B.C.: Blue List

Fisher populations are cyclic, varying with prey numbers. The fisher is rare along the coast and generally uncommon in B.C. Populations are suspected to be declining throughout the province because of loss of habitat and continued exploitation for furs.

RANGE
The fisher formerly occurred in all mainland forested regions of B.C, but it is now absent from south-central and southeastern B.C. It is not found on Vancouver Island, the Queen Charlotte Islands or other coastal islands.

DESCRIPTION
The male of this large member of the weasel family has a body length of 50–63 cm and a long (30–38 cm), bushy tail. At about 80 percent the length of the male, the substantially lighter female has an average weight of 2.6 kg, compared to 4.8 kg for the male. The fur is dark brown to nearly black, and the white-tipped hairs give this animal a frosted appearance.

OTHER CHARACTERISTICS
This secretive mammal is seldom observed. The arboreal agility of both the fisher and marten is enhanced by the ability to rotate the hind limbs to permit a squirrel-like, headfirst descent of trees.

HABITAT
Habitat information is limited, but in B.C. the fisher is most often associated with wet riparian areas and dense, moist conifer forests.

Biogeoclimatic Zones

AT	BG	BWBS	CDF	CWH	ESSF	ICH	IDF	MH	MS	PP	SBPS	SBS	SWB

Ecoprovinces

BOP	COM	CEI	GED	NBM	SBI	SIM	SOI	TAP

Breeding Period

J	F	M	A	M	J	J	A	S	O	N	D

Feeding: The fisher hunts at dusk and dawn, both on the ground and in trees, and occasionally moves about by day. Usually varying its diet according to food availability, this generalist predator eats small mammals (e.g., mice, voles, chipmunks and squirrels), small birds, berries and carrion, but in some areas, it may specialize in porcupines and snowshoe hares. Summer foraging is strongly associated with coarse woody debris, areas of higher prey abundance, and areas where there is a well-developed understorey of shrub cover. The fisher moves mostly above the snow in winter, and snow conditions likely influence its foraging and distribution patterns.

Breeding: Females without kits and adult males are solitary except during the mating season (March–April). The typical maternal denning habitat is mature or old-growth forest with large, dead and declining trees (conifers or hardwoods in decay classes 2–4), large-diameter woody debris and a canopy closure of >30 percent. Maternal dens are usually located in large, declining black cottonwoods and trembling aspens with hollow trunks or rotting branch holes, often near standing or running water, but trees such as Douglas-firs, with broken, rotted tops or large branch-hole cavities, are also used. Usually 1–4 young (the average is 3) are born in March or April, and they stay with their mother for one year.

Denning and Resting: Large-diameter spruces with large witches' brooms are often used as resting platforms. Nonmaternal dens in tree cavities generally have the same characteristics as maternal dens.

Territory Size/Home Range: The annual home range size of fishers in B.C. averages 35 km^2 for an adult female and 137 km^2 for an adult male. There is little overlap in home ranges for animals of the same gender, but extensive overlap between the ranges of males and females is common.

ADDITIONAL STEWARDSHIP PROVISIONS (see also Part 2)

- Retain large trees (>50 cm dbh for conifers, >75 cm dbh for black cottonwood) with natural cavities and those made by primary cavity excavators; choose species such as black cottonwood, balsam poplar, white spruce, Englemann spruce and Douglas-fir with broken tops, hollow trunks or branch-hole cavities, especially those in riparian areas. Also retain trees with large witches' brooms.
- Maintain diverse understorey habitats with high levels of coarse woody debris, shrub diversity and productivity to support a variety of small and medium-sized prey species.
- Retain distributed large areas of old-growth and mature forest and the connections between them to accommodate movement and dispersal and the fisher's relatively large home range requirements. Focus the retention of mature and old-seral forest on riparian buffers, with a 100-m management zone on each side of large and small streams in forests with habitat that favours fisher prey.
- Do not salvage in riparian, wildlife tree and old-forest reserves.

OF INTEREST

The gestation period of the fisher is remarkably long for a mammal of its size. Mating occurs in March or April, but implantation of the fertilized egg is delayed until the following year, in late January or early February. The young are born about one year after conception.

BLACK BEAR
Ursus americanus • URAM

STATUS
Glacier subspecies, *U. a. emmonsii*—B.C.: Blue list

The black bear is relatively common throughout B.C., with populations estimated at 120,000 and considered to be stable. However, because of its rarity and limited range, the *emmonsii* subspecies, known as the "glacier bear" or "blue bear," is on the provincial Blue List.

RANGE
The species is a year-round resident in forested regions of B.C. The Kermode subspecies (*U. a. kermodei*) is locally common in the Terrace-Kitimat area (Burke Channel to the Nass River) and on some adjacent islands (e.g., Princess Royal, Pitt and Gribbell). The rarer *U. a. emmonsii* subspecies is restricted to the Tatshenshini-Alsek area of extreme northwestern B.C.

Note: The biogeoclamatic zones and ecoprovinces highlighted below show where black bears use trees for denning.

Biogeoclimatic Zones

AT	BG	BWBS	CDF	CWH	ESSF	ICH	IDF	MH	MS	PP	SBPS	SBS	SWB

Ecoprovinces

BOP	COM	CEI	GED	NBM	SBI	SIM	SOI	TAP

Breeding Period

J	F	M	A	M	J	J	A	S	O	N	D

DESCRIPTION

The most common fur colour is solid black or black with a white chest patch or blaze, but shades of brown (from light cinnamon to dark chocolate) are common in some Interior locations. The primarily black Kermode subspecies has a relatively high incidence of all-white individuals, and glacier bears are bluish grey. Together, the head and body typically measure 150–185 cm in length, with a shoulder height of 60–100 cm. The male is larger than the female; at maturity, an adult male is commonly 85–160 kg (up to 272 kg), and an adult female is usually 50–90 kg. Bears feeding on large quantities of protein-rich fish or carbohydrate-rich berries can gain large amounts of weight very quickly, so coastal bears are often larger than Interior bears.

OTHER CHARACTERISTICS

The curved, relatively short (2–4 cm) claws are well adapted for climbing trees.

HABITAT

Black bears use a variety of habitats and forest types, ranging from early-seral forest to old-growth forest and from valley-bottom meadows to alpine parkland.

Feeding: The diet changes seasonally, and the foraging habitat corresponds to where preferred foods are abundant. Some typical foods: for early spring, sedges, horsetail, grasses and skunk cabbage; for late spring and early summer, clover, miner's lettuce and fireweed; for late summer and autumn, various berries, particularly salmonberry, blueberry and soopolallie (buffalo berry) and, where available, spawning salmon. Depending on availability, the diet also includes ants, insect larvae, honey, bird eggs, small mammals and carrion. Bears also prey opportunistically on medium-sized to large mammals (e.g., beaver, ungulate calves and fawns and old or injured adult ungulates). Bedding sites near feeding areas are important for

protection from summer heat or rain and, for females with cubs, visual security cover; the best sites are under intermediate to closed forest canopies.

Breeding: The breeding habitat is the same as for feeding and hibernation. The mating season is late May to early July. The cubs (usually 2–3 per litter) are born in the hibernation den in late January or early February, and they must remain in a dry, warm and secure structure, safe from predation, if they are to grow and strengthen. The young usually stay with their mother until their second or third year; they reach sexual maturity at 3–4 years.

Denning: Throughout their range, bears hibernate from late fall until early spring, for as long as six months. During hibernation they do not eat, drink, urinate or defecate. The hibernation den protects against inclement weather and, especially for cubs, against predation. Coastal black bears in particular are highly dependent on wildlife trees for shelter from the heavy winter rains. Dens in hollow trees may be from ground level to 15 m above the ground, and the entry is often from the top of the tree. Hollow trees and logs used for denning average >140 cm dbh. In parts of the Interior, bears dig their dens instead, usually under the base and roots of a large tree or stump, beneath a large log, in a hillside or below a rock ledge (typically on a north- or east-facing slope).

Dens are generally not used consecutively year to year, but reuse may occur across generations, with female bears showing their offspring potential den sites. These sites are especially important for sub-adults during their first winter on their own. A den entrance just large enough to allow entry for the occupant is the best for defence against predators. A first-winter bear can fit through a 20–40 cm entry.

Hibernation dens can be identified by the presence of bear hair and claw and bite marks, and the surrounding trees may be marked; bedding sign but no scats will be found inside the den.

Territory Size/Home Range: The female has a well-defined home range of 800–5000 ha. The male, especially as a sub-adult, has a much larger home range and may travel >50 km to a preferred food source or winter den site. The normally solitary male may spend several days with a female during the mating season. Females with cubs avoid other families and independent adults or sub-adults except around high concentrations of food (e.g., spawning salmon or a productive berry patch).

ADDITIONAL STEWARDSHIP PROVISIONS (see also Part 2)

- Assess road locations and proposed harvesting areas for dens, particularly maternal dens. Avoid road construction and harvesting activities near maternal dens, because disturbing a female bear with cubs may cause abandonment and subsequent death of the year's cubs. Revise the plans as required to avoid any dens.
- Establish a wildlife tree–retention patch approximately 0.5 ha in size around each den to provide the cubs with cover to escape from predators. For dens with aboveground entrances, retain a sufficient number of adjacent trees so that the den tree remains windfirm.
- Manage for a supply of large, hollow red-cedars and yellow-cedars.
- Retain some large damaged and irregular live trees for future den sites.

- Manage for a supply of trees with large root masses.
- For large-diameter trees (>1.5 m dbh) that have suitable future den structures but cannot be retained whole, leave high stumps (>2 m). The top of the stump needs to be sound.
- Maintain a diversity of suitable stand characteristics—shaded forested areas for bedding sites and patchy habitats for herbs and berry-producing shrubs for feeding—across the forested landscape.
- Retain berry-producing shrubs (e.g., salmonberry, blueberry and soopolallie); these shrubs require an intermediate canopy closure (20–60 percent) so that light can reach them. Periodic prescribed burning can be used to restore or establish berry production and keep some areas in an early-seral shrub stage.
- Retain wet seepage micro-habitats with food plants such as skunk cabbage and horsetail.

Black bear den

OF INTEREST

Black bears have a widely varied vocal repertoire. For example, very young cubs "cry" when they are afraid and "hum" when they are content.

The Open Nesters

Overview of the Open Nesters

Many bird species build open, cup-shaped or platform nests using materials such as branches, twigs, grass and moss. These nests are supported by tree limbs, forked tree trunks or broken trunks. In British Columbia, nine species of these open nesters depend on wildlife trees: one heron, one seabird, four diurnal raptors (birds of prey active by day) and three owls.

The great blue heron often uses large lateral branches of large trees to support its nests, often several in one tree. The marbled murrelet's specialized nest site is a large, moss-covered horizontal branch high in the canopy of an old-growth coastal conifer, a kind of habitat not typically found in forests where the primary trees are <200 years old. The diurnal raptors generally build large, heavy nests in the sub-canopy of large trees or in the top fork of a snag; younger, smaller trees are not strong enough or do not have large enough limbs to support these nests. The owls in this guild may reuse an old stick nest made by another open nester or build their own nest on top of a broken tree or high stump, where decay has formed a saucer-like depression, or on a large witches' broom.

For some of these species, particularly the marbled murrelet, the northern goshawk and the spotted owl, the condition of both the forest stand and the nest tree are vitally important. These species need large areas of old forest that contain a selection of suitable nest trees.

Large stick nests are relatively easy to spot, especially when they are built in snags or in the dead tops of live trees, and stick nests of almost any size in deciduous trees are easily visible in winter or prior to spring leaf-out. Conversely, stick nests built within the upper tree canopy of conifers or tucked in just below it are difficult to locate. Examples of these types of less conspicuous nests are those of the spotted owl and the great grey owl. The secretive behaviour of the nocturnal great grey, particularly during the nesting season, makes its nests especially hard to find.

The nests of the marbled murrelet are also difficult to find, because they are small and located high in the canopy. However, it is possible to locate stands used for nesting by looking for breeding birds flying to and from their nests at first light.

ECOLOGICAL RELATIONSHIPS

Several of the species in the open nesting guild interact indirectly by providing prefabricated nests for other birds or by taking advantage of the nest-building skills of others. The great horned owl is known to use the abandoned nests of the red-tailed hawk, the great blue heron, the bald eagle and the northern goshawk. This owl will also, if there is sufficient surrounding security cover, use the nests of several more adaptable species (e.g, the Cooper's hawk, crows and the common raven) that build open stick nests but are not, (because they will use younger or second-growth trees) considered dependent on wildlife trees. Similarly, the great grey owl also uses the abandoned nests of species such as the red-tailed hawk and the northern goshawk. On occasion, bald eagles and great blue herons will take over abandoned osprey nests.

Great blue herons, hawks and owls face a common threat because of their position at the top of the food chain. They are highly susceptible to the effects of toxic contaminants found in the environment, especially persistent organochlorines, such as DDT (dichlorodiphenyltrichloroethane), PCBs (polychlorinated biphenyls), dioxins and furans. These chemicals have a high fat solubility and accumulate in the tissues of several prey eaten by these species. When contaminated prey is consumed by predators, contaminant levels increase with each step up the food chain. High concentrations of organochlorines cause birds to lay thin-shelled eggs, which break before hatching, or produce malformed chicks with low survivorship.

The hawks and owls that depend on wildlife trees perform a critical balancing function in forest ecosystems by preying on small mammals that strip bark and eat conifer seedlings and seeds. From a commercial forestry point of view, the most notable of these prey species are snowshoe hares, red squirrels and voles—all of which can do considerable damage to regenerating forests.

STEWARDSHIP

The general conservation measures that will benefit all open-nesting bird species are presented in the stand and landscape management section of this guide (Part 2). Table 1 summarizes the wildlife tree characteristics and adjacent habitat requirements for the province's nine wildlife tree–dependent open nesters. It is important to protect both nest and roost trees by leaving uncut buffers of standing trees around these features. Post-fledging areas are also believed to be vital to the survival of the young of certain species. Suggested sizes for these buffers are also given in Table 1.

The availability of trees for nesting and roosting is essential, but a shortage of other habitat requirements can also severely limit population sizes. The marbled murrelet, northern goshawk and spotted owl are open-nesting species that will not persist if stewardship efforts are limited to the retention of suitable nest trees only. These species require habitat retention over large forest areas, within which there need to be suitable nest trees. The species accounts detail the importance of nest tree options, buffers and post-fledging areas.

Some species, such as ospreys, great horned owls, great grey owls and red-tailed hawks, have been known to use artificial nest structures, including nest platforms and nest baskets. Ospreys often build their nests on structures such as pilings and power poles. In areas where human activities have resulted in a shortage of natural foraging perches, the provision of posts or poles as substitutes can be beneficial to great grey owls and red-tailed hawks.

Open nesters are sensitive to disturbance from the beginning of the courtship period at least until the young leave the nest. In some cases, the sensitive dependent period extends until the young disperse from their natal areas, because disturbances can interfere with the adults' prey deliveries to them during the post-fledging period (PFP), especially for species with a long PFP. Scheduling any necessary nearby development activities outside these critical times will avoid causing the birds to abandon a nest area or nest site because of excessive stress.

In the stewardship section in the individual species accounts, the term "disruptive activities" refers to operations such as logging, blasting, the building of roads and landings, mechanized agriculture and the construction of houses, wharves or other structures. These activities should not be carried out in the vicinity of active nests during the breeding season or near roost sites used by bald eagles or great blue herons in winter and spring. Prescribed burning in areas adjacent to nest sites can also be disruptive to breeding birds.

Summary of General Wildlife Tree Characteristics and Habitat Needs for Open Nesters

(further details are given in the additional stewardship provisions for each species)

BIRD SPECIES	BREEDING PERIOD	NEST BUFFER OR HABITAT AREA	NEST & ROOST TREE REQUIREMENTS
great blue heron (nests singly or in colonies of up to 200 pairs)	*coast:* February to August *Interior:* March to August	• 300-m buffer around active nests; avoid disturbing winter colony sites • retain suitable nest trees in a 4-ha buffer around colonies, as well as understorey trees that provide visual cover to reduce disturbance • living trees usually >20 m in height	• branch structure to support stick nests is vital • usually <3 km (must be <6 km) of foraging areas (tidal flats for coastal herons; lakes and sloughs for Interior birds)
osprey (active and alternative nests within territory)	mid-April to late August	• 100-m buffer early in the breeding season and throughout for birds not habituated to humans	• living and dead trees >50 cm dbh and near water (will often use artificial structures)
bald eagle (active and alternative nests within territory)	February through August	• 150-m buffer for nests • 75–100-m buffer for roost trees (November to April)	• large, strong-limbed trees near water for nesting • roost trees must protect from wind, rain and snow

BIRD SPECIES	BREEDING PERIOD	NEST BUFFER OR HABITAT AREA	NEST & ROOST TREE REQUIREMENTS
northern goshawk (nest area [NA] encompasses both active and alternative nest trees; post-fledging area [PFA])	*coast:* mid-March to late June *Interior:* mid-March to late October	• NA: approx. 12 ha around nest tree • PFA: approx. 200 ha around the NA (includes the area around active and alternative nest trees); a much larger foraging area (usually >2000 ha) surrounds the PFA	• *Interior:* living (occasionally dead) Douglas-fir, white spruce, and Englemannn spruce, as well as trembling aspen and black cotton-wood • *coast:* Douglas-fir, western hemlock witches' broom platforms and red alder
red-tailed hawk (nests are well concealed)	March to late July	• 50–75-m buffer	• living and dead conifers and hard-woods
marbled murrelet (secretive; nests singly, but a stand may have multiple pairs)	late April through September	• ideally >100-ha area of old growth with suitable wildlife trees, within 30 km of tidewater at about 600 m in elevation	• ideally living trees >40 m in height with large horizontal branches • Sitka spruce, amabilis fir, western hem lock and other suitable large conifers
great horned owl	early February to mid- September	• 50–75-m buffer	• often uses witches' brooms or old stick nests of other large birds
spotted owl	April to July	• manage spotted owl conservation areas of about 3600 ha, of which approximately two-thirds should be suitable old- growth	• typically nests in a depression in a broken top of a large tree • nests and roosts are in dense conif-erous old-growth
great grey owl	late March to mid-August	• 50–75-m buffer	• often uses witches' brooms or old stick nests of other large birds

GREAT BLUE HERON

Ardea herodias • GBHE

STATUS

B.C.: Blue List
COSEWIC: *A. h. fannini* is of Special Concern

A common resident on the south coast of British Columbia, the great blue heron is an uncommon resident on the north coast and a fairly common resident in southern Interior areas that have open water during winter. Two subspecies are recognized in B.C.: *A. h. fannini* on the coast and *A. h. herodias* in the Interior. Both are considered *vulnerable* because of their sensitivity to disturbance when nesting, the effects of chemical pollution on reproduction, habitat loss and growing predation from increasing bald eagle populations. The coastal population numbers about 2000 pairs but is declining.

RANGE

Breeding is centred on the lower Fraser Valley, southeastern Vancouver Island and the southern Gulf Islands, with a few scattered colonies on the west coast of Vancouver Island, the northern mainland coast and the Queen Charlotte Islands, at elevations below 200 m. In the Interior, this heron breeds as far north as Clearwater, New Denver and Golden, at elevations up to 1100 m.

The range from late summer to early spring encompasses the entire coast and low elevations throughout the southern Interior. Post-breeding wanderers stray

Biogeoclimatic Zones

AT	BG	BWBS	CDF	CWH	ESSF	ICH	IDF	MH	MS	PP	SBPS	SBS	SWB

Ecoprovinces									Breeding Period												
BOP	COM	CEI	GED	NBM	SBI	SIM	SOI	TAP		J	F	M	A	M	J	J	A	S	O	N	D

261

Approaching nest in class 1 black cottonwood

Distinctive in flight, it has slow, deep wingbeats, its long legs trail behind its body, and its long neck is normally held in an S-shape; the sandhill crane, in contrast, flies with its neck outstretched.

HABITAT

Feeding: The great blue heron feeds primarily on aquatic animals (e.g., fish, frogs and crabs) in shallow marine, brackish and freshwater environments. In winter, it feeds heavily on voles in farm fields.

Breeding: Nesting colonies are located in mature or older second-growth forests (hardwood, conifer or mixedwood), usually within 3 km of feeding areas. Breeding herons vary in their levels of tolerance to human activities: some colonies are situated near roads, in well-used parks or near settlements, but extremely sensitive colonies will abandon their nests if disturbed. Coastal colonies are usually located near tidal mudflats, and Interior colonies are usually on the banks of slow-moving rivers, sloughs or marshy lakes. Colony sites are often used for many years, but not always consecutively—an abandoned site may later be reused. Pairs nest singly or in colonies that occupy up to 2 ha of forest and consist of up to 200 breeding pairs.

Great blues build large, shallow stick nests in the largest available trees (mainly at heights of 20–70 m). The nests are defended from other herons, but a nest tree may have more than one nest. Live trees with several large horizontal branches are usually chosen. On the coast, red alder is the most common choice, but bigleaf maple, arbutus, Douglas-fir, western hemlock, western red-cedar and Sitka spruce are also utilized. In the Interior, the most common nest-tree species is black cottonwood, with poplar, western white pine and ponderosa pine also being used. Alternative nest trees are important, because, over time, heron excrement can

as far north as the Peace River Valley. This heron overwinters anywhere from coastal B.C. and southern Interior B.C. (as long as the lakes remain unfrozen) to northern South America, with migrants heading south in September and October. B.C.'s highest winter numbers are found in the Fraser River delta and the Okanagan Valley.

DESCRIPTION

With a length of 1.1–1.3 m and a 1.7-m wingspan, the great blue is B.C.'s largest heron. It has a mostly white head with a black stripe above the eye, a greyish blue back and wings and dark underparts. The breeding adult has long plumes on the head, neck and back. The juvenile has a black or grey crown.

OTHER CHARACTERISTICS

This heron is frequently seen standing in fields, on mudflats and along ditches. Its calls are a squawk and a croak, with a guttural *frahak* when stressed.

Great blue heron nests in class 1 coastal Douglas-fir

kill a nest tree, causing the colony to move around within the general area.

Birds move to breeding colonies in February (coast) or March (Interior) and begin nesting one month later. The breeding season continues through August. The clutch size is 3–8.

Roosting: Night roosting, either singly or in small groups, is mainly in conifers.

Territory/Home Range: The size and location of foraging territories can change from year to year; along shorelines, they are typically 200–400 m long. Members of a breeding colony usually forage in the same general area, but foraging birds will defend a small individual space from other herons. Coastal birds forage an average of 2.3 km (up to 6 km) from the colony; similar data for the Interior is not available.

ADDITIONAL STEWARDSHIP PROVISIONS (see also Part 2)
- Avoid disturbances near the nest site, especially during courtship and egg-laying—and at all times in remote areas. Maintain a 300-m buffer zone throughout the breeding season; for colony sites with winter roosting, restrict disturbing activities from November through August. Even disturbances that cause herons to temporarily abandon the nest will permit predators to take eggs. Motorized, loud or continuous activities are the most disturbing.
- In the vicinity of colony sites and feeding areas, maintain a selection of large trees (>20 m tall) over a 4-ha area. Protect alternative nesting and feeding habitat to ensure the long-term stability of colonies.
- Establish a 200-m no-harvest buffer zone around nesting colonies.
- At colony sites, retain or provide hardwoods and conifers to offer a visual screen and, over time, develop into nest and perch trees.
- Retain perch trees next to major summer and winter feeding areas.
- Protect forage areas, especially those within 4 km of colonies, from increases in activities disruptive to feeding and from pollution.

OF INTEREST
Levels of DDE (a breakdown product of DDT) and PCBs in great blue heron eggs are monitored as a primary environmental indicator in B.C.

OSPREY
Pandion haliaetus • OSPR

STATUS
An uncommon to fairly common migrant and summer visitor across southern B.C., the osprey is uncommon in northern areas and very rare on the Queen Charlotte Islands. With its stable population, the osprey is not considered at risk in B.C. Protection of nest sites and hunting perches along lakeshores and rivers becomes more important as foreshore development increases.

RANGE
Breeding is widespread throughout much of southern British Columbia, along major valleys, watersheds and protected marine shorelines from near sea level to about 1100 m. Breeding concentrations are in the Creston Valley, on the west arm of Kootenay Lake and along the Kootenay River and the Columbia River, but are more sparsely distributed in northern B.C. and along the coast (none on the Queen Charlotte Islands). Nonbreeders range across most of the province, usually at low elevations. Most birds migrate southward from their breeding areas in late September to overwinter from the southern U.S. to South America. The first spring migrants return to the B.C. coast in mid- to late February and to the Interior in mid-April.

DESCRIPTION
About three-quarters the size of a bald eagle, with a wingspan of 1.4–1.8 m, the osprey is dark brown above and white below, with variable brown streaking on the female's breast. The white head has a prominent dark eye-stripe. In flight, the dark "wrist" patches are conspicuous, and the long, narrow wings bend back at the "wrist," like a gull's wings.

OTHER CHARACTERISTICS
The call is a loud, whistled *kyew, kyew, kyew, kyew.* In its highly specialized and distinctive hunting behaviour, the osprey hovers over water, dives vertically, plunges in feet-first to capture fish in its talons, then emerges and flies to its nest or a feeding perch. During courtship, the male makes semicircular aerial dives

Osprey pair at nest in a class 6 conifer

Biogeoclimatic Zones

AT	BG	BWBS	CDF	CWH	ESSF	ICH	IDF	MH	MS	PP	SBPS	SBS	SWB

Ecoprovinces									Breeding Period												
BOP	COM	CEI	GED	NBM	SBI	SIM	SOI	TAP		J	F	M	A	M	J	J	A	S	O	N	D

and presents fish to the female in mid-air while uttering repetitive, high-pitched screams. The species can be gregarious or solitary, depending on the availability of nest sites and fish.

HABITAT

Feeding: The osprey feeds almost exclusively on fish caught in open water bodies (e.g., large rivers, lakes, sloughs, marshes, protected bays and lagoons). Slow-moving fish near the surface (e.g., suckers and northern pike minnow) are common prey, as are trout and salmon smaller than 2 kg. During the breeding season, the male is the sole provider of fish. He generally eats at a perch in a large tree, whereas the female stays on the nest to feed and protect the chicks. The parents continue to feed the fledged young at or near the nest site for 2–3 weeks after fledging.

Breeding: The nest is usually built near a permanent water body, but it may be several hundred metres from water. Made of sticks, it may be small and compact or large and conspicuous. It is constructed on top of a broken-topped live or dead tree, most often a black cottonwood, or on an artificial structure (e.g., power pole, piling, bridge, navigation beacon or nest platform), typically 9–20 m above the ground. A breeding pair will reuse its nest for many years.

The breeding season is mid-April to late August. The usual clutch size is 3, and on average, two young successfully fledge.

Roosting: The male roosts in a large, living or dead tree in a riparian zone near the nest. The female roosts on the nest.

Territory Size/Home Range: The feeding territory size, which depends on the location and quality of the nesting territory, can cover several square kilometres. How intensely this territory is defended varies with the season and the local abundance of fish. The nesting territory can be up to several hundred hectares and often contains alternative nests, which may be used if the primary nest is disturbed or destroyed. The breeding home range is larger than the defended territory and can overlap with those of other ospreys.

ADDITIONAL STEWARDSHIP PROVISIONS (see also Part 2)

- Early in the breeding season or, where ospreys are not habituated to humans, throughout the breeding season, disruptive activities should not be carried out within 100 m of active nests.
- Near each nest tree, retain some large (>50 cm dbh) living or dead trees for hunting perches (with water views), roost trees and alternative nest sites. Retain some healthy younger trees for future roosting and nesting habitat.

Class 5 conifer supporting osprey nest

OF INTEREST

Ospreys reach their highest numbers within B.C. on a number of reservoirs, such as Kootenay Lake, Lake Koocanusa and the Arrow Lakes, where residual standing snags and an abundance of fish provide excellent conditions for this opportunistic species.

BALD EAGLE
Haliaeetus leucocephalus • BAEA

STATUS
The bald eagle is a fairly common and widespread resident throughout most of B.C. During late autumn and winter, it is scarce in the Interior but locally very common in coastal areas. About 7500 pairs nest in British Columbia—about 50 percent of the Canadian population. In winter, about 30,000 bald eagles—40 percent of the world population—reside in B.C. Since the 1960s, breeding populations have increased fivefold and wintering populations on the coast have increased tenfold. This species is not at risk in B.C.

RANGE
This eagle breeds widely throughout B.C., from sea level to about 1400 m, with breeding centred along the coast, especially on the Queen Charlotte Islands and the Gulf Islands. Interior breeding populations are much sparser in the north than in the south. Nonbreeding birds are found at elevations up to 2400 m, especially in late summer and during autumn migration.

The bald eagle overwinters along the coast and on major Interior river systems. Preferred winter habitats are south coastal rivers and estuaries where salmon spawn. Winter concentrations are at Rivers Inlet, on the Squamish, Cheakamus and lower Harrison rivers and along southeastern Vancouver Island. Interior wintering populations and locations depend on the availability of open water and waterfowl populations. The Adams River is a major Interior wintering site. The highest spring densities (>1000 eagles) occur on the lower Nass River and at Cape St. James. The Klinaklini River, Gabriola Island and the lower parts of the Skeena River and the Kitimat River are other notable spring concentration sites.

DESCRIPTION
With a wingspan of 1.8–2.3 m and a weight of 7 kg or more, the adult bald eagle is B.C.'s largest raptor. It has a

Biogeoclimatic Zones

AT	BG	BWBS	CDF	CWH	ESSF	ICH	IDF	MH	MS	PP	SBPS	SBS	SWB

Ecoprovinces										Breeding Period													
BOP	COM	CEI	GED	NBM	SBI	SIM	SOI	TAP		J	F	M	A	M	J	J	A	S	O	N	D

Nest in a class 3 ponderosa pine

dark brown body, white head, white tail and large, yellow bill. The immature is an irregularly white-mottled brown until age four.

OTHER CHARACTERISTICS
The flight is flat-winged and soaring. In the spectacular aerial courtship display, pairs interlock talons in flight and somersault through the sky. The call is a harsh, high-pitched *kleek-kik-ik-ik-ik* or lower *kak-kak-kak.*

HABITAT
Feeding: Feeding is primarily associated with aquatic habitats (e.g., seashores, lakes, rivers, sloughs and marshes). Foraging and perch trees, typically snags or dead-topped black cottonwoods, maples and conifers with unobstructed views of foraging areas, are usually the tallest trees along shorelines and near feeding areas. The diet of mainly fish (especially salmon) is supplemented by waterfowl, seabirds, small mammals and carrion.

Breeding: This bird nests in conifer, hardwood or mixed forest, typically within 100 m of a sizeable water body (e.g., ocean, lake, large river or large marsh). The nest is a massive (0.8–1.4 m diameter, 0.4–0.9 m deep), cup-shaped platform built in a crotch or crown or on lateral branches, usually 12–20 m above the ground. A pair will use the same nest year after year, adding new material annually. Nest trees must be large, with strong limbs; typically they are live and have an open structure that provides good water views and easy access to the nest. Dead trees are occasionally used. Conifers (e.g., Sitka spruce, western red-cedar, western hemlock and Douglas-fir) are preferred for nesting on a marine coast; live hardwoods, primarily black cottonwood, are favoured in the Interior. Black cottonwood is also used along coastal river valleys.

The breeding period is early February through August. The clutch size is 1–3, and usually 1–2 young are fledged.

Roosting: In winter and spring, large groups congregate in sheltered upland forests of mature to old-growth conifers and cottonwoods and spend up to two-thirds of their time roosting together. Protection from wind, rain and snow afforded by suitable conifers reduces the daily energy budget by up to five percent. Although food scarcity is the main cause of winter mortality, good roosting sites enhance winter survival. Stands of

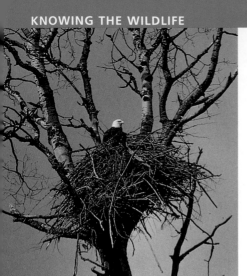

Nest in class 1 hardwood in early spring before leaves have developed

tall trees along salmon rivers are especially important roosting habitat and are heavily used during fall and winter. Summer daytime roosting is in large, tall trees, or on stumps and logs in estuaries and on marine beaches. Summer aggregations occur only on the coast where surface-feeding fish and herring are concentrated.

Nest in class 2 coastal Douglas-fir

Territory Size/Home Range: Breeding bald eagles defend 1–2 square km within the larger breeding home range (usually several square kilometres in size, larger in less productive areas), which often contains one or more additional nests that are used in alternating years or when the primary nest is disturbed or destroyed. Preferred perch trees within breeding territories are defended from other bald eagles. The nonbreeding home range can be thousands of square kilometres.

ADDITIONAL STEWARDSHIP PROVISIONS (see also Part 2)

- At nest sites, leave windfirm patches that protect the nest tree, a selection of alternative nest, perch and roost trees (>50 cm dbh) and trees that screen the nest from human activity.
- Observe a no-entry zone that extends out 150 m or more from active nest sites and schedule nearby disruptive activities for the nonbreeding season.
- Protect suitable roosting trees at winter (November to March) and spring (March to April) roosting sites and retain a sufficient supply of mature and old-growth trees in riparian forests along rivers, lakes and marine shorelines to provide future roost and nest trees.
- Leave a 75–100-m buffer zone around significant roosting sites if road construction, falling, etc. is necessary nearby, or schedule such disruptive activities for when the sites are not in use. Do not harvest the roost site.

OF INTEREST

Pairs reuse old nests, adding up to 20 kg of new material annually. Bald eagle nests often weigh >1 tonne, and the largest ones have been estimated at 6.1 m tall and 2.9 m in diameter, with a weight of 2 tonnes. Some nests become so heavy that the supporting branches collapse under their weight.

NORTHERN GOSHAWK
Accipiter gentilis • NOGO

STATUS
Coastal subspecies, *A. g. laingi*—B.C.: Red List; COSEWIC: Threatened

The northern goshawk is an uncommon but widespread resident and migrant throughout B.C. The coastal subspecies (Queen Charlotte goshawk, *A. g. laingi*) occurs on Vancouver Island, the Queen Charlotte Islands and probably on the coastal mainland; it is at risk because of its small population (a few hundred pairs in B.C.) and its dependence on large, contiguous areas of mature and old-growth coastal forest. The Interior subspecies (*A. g. atricapillus*) is sensitive to habitat reduction and fragmentation as a result of forest harvesting activities, but it is not considered to be at risk in B.C.

RANGE
The northern goshawk breeds anywhere from near sea level to approximately 900 m (the typical upper limit of breeding habitat) on Vancouver Island and most other large coastal islands, including the Queen Charlottes, as well as the mainland coast. It is found throughout mainland British Columbia (generally to around 1400 m in eleva-tion), reaching its highest abundance in the northern Interior. Goshawks in the northern Interior disperse southward during winters when prey is scarce. The coastal subspecies is largely a year-round resident.

DESCRIPTION
This raven-sized (55–61 cm in length) hawk has a large, robust body, long tail and short, rounded wings. The back is bluish grey and the finely barred underparts are pale grey. A conspicuous white eye-stripe separates the blackish crown and the "cheeks." The immature is brown, with a buff-coloured breast and brown streaking.

OTHER CHARACTERISTICS
The call is a long series of short, high notes: *kak-kak-kak* or *kuk-kuk-kuk.*

Biogeoclimatic Zones

AT	BG	BWBS	CDF	CWH	ESSF	ICH	IDF	MH	MS	PP	SBPS	SBS	SWB

Ecoprovinces

BOP	COM	CEI	GED	NBM	SBI	SIM	SOI	TAP

Breeding Period

J	F	M	A	M	J	J	A	S	O	N	D

Class 1 older coastal Douglas-fir with coastal sub-species on nest

Northern goshawk courtship displays consist of dawn vocalizing near nests and circular aerial flights above nest sites. Prey remains, "whitewash," moulted feathers and regurgitated pellets provide clues to the location of plucking perches, roost trees and nest trees.

HABITAT

Feeding: Foraging is below the canopy in mature or old-growth forest and in forest-edge habitats associated with riparian zones, meadows, burns or water bodies. This species makes little use of dense, young (<40 years old) second-growth forest. Concealed hunting perches are important. Prey is captured in the air or on the ground: mainly medium-sized birds (e.g., grouse, ptarmigan, jays, woodpeckers and thrushes) and small mammals (e.g., snowshoe hares, tree squirrels, ground squirrels and chipmunks). The male does most of the hunting during the incubation and early nestling phases. Stumps, logs and large horizontal limbs below the canopy are used extensively as plucking perches.

Breeding: The northern goshawk usually nests in mature or old-growth conifer or mixed forest with generally >60 percent canopy closure (which provides young fledglings with both protection from predators and thermal cover) and a relatively open understorey (which allows clear flight paths for hunting). In some cases, younger stands are used, provided they have the necessary crown-canopy structure and understorey characteristics. Nest sites are usually on slopes with a grade of <30 percent. Both hardwoods and conifers (e.g., trembling aspen, Douglas-fir, black cottonwood, red alder, western hemlock and spruces) are used for nesting. Often the largest trees available are used; living ones are preferred. The stick nest, on average 100 cm in diameter and 36 cm in depth, is constructed in the main crotch or a branch fork, against the trunk or on a broken tree top, usually 6–30 m above the ground. Pairs frequently nest in alternative nest trees or nest stands within their home range in successive years, or they may occupy the same nest for >5 years.

The breeding season is from mid-March to early September. Nesting and fledging occur from early April to late July, and the young remain in the vicinity of the nest territory until early September. The clutch size is 2–4, and an average of two young successfully fledge.

Roosting: A closed-canopy forest area is important for providing thermal protection for roosting sites in winter.

Territory/Home Range: Three successively larger areas are needed during the breeding period:

- The nest area (NA), the centre of breeding activity, contains the alternative nest trees (commonly 2–5), roost trees and plucking posts. The size, approximately 12 ha, can be determined relative to a known nest tree through observations of the adults, the movements of the young during the early post-fledgling period and the locations of suitable nearby alternative nest trees, roost sites and plucking posts.
- The post-fledging area (PFA), which typically surrounds the NA, is used by fledglings to develop hunting skills

before they disperse from their natal area. Approximately 200 ha in size, the PFA is characterized by an abundance of habitat attributes that provide hiding cover for vulnerable fledglings (i.e., extensive canopy cover) as well as snags and coarse woody debris that can support an abundant prey source. The adults actively defend it from other goshawks.

- The foraging area (FA), which usually surrounds the PFA, makes up the majority of a pair's breeding home range. Used opportunistically, depending on prey availability, brood size, foraging experience and inter-territorial spacing between goshawk pairs, it can vary widely in size (2000–5000 ha).

ADDITIONAL STEWARDSHIP PROVISIONS (see also Part 2)

- Avoid disturbing goshawks, particularly during their extremely sensitive breeding period (March 1 to August 15). During this time, allow no road construction, blasting, heli-logging or fly-overs within a 200-m radius of any active nest trees, and minimize the use of existing roads within NAs and PFAs. Activity restrictions can be lifted after June 30 if a standardized raptor inventory indicates that the NA is inactive or that breeding has been unsuccessful.
- Do not harvest, salvage or construct roads in the 12-ha NA surrounding a nest. However, outside of the breeding season, habitat suitability can be improved in some areas by understorey thinning of small-diameter trees to promote single-storied, multilayered canopies to provide for a wider diversity of prey. The thinning of some small trees to provide access to prey and promote canopy growth is also

recommended in old growth with >60 percent crown closure and trees >60 cm dbh, but maintain some below-canopy hiding cover (e.g., some tall shrubs and saplings).

- Locate any new roads >300 m from any active nest trees.

The status of the Queen Charlotte goshawk, A. g. laingi, requires that the following additional provisions apply:

- In each known and occupied home range, retain at least three suitable nest areas (based on actual observations of nest or roost trees or on habitat characteristics) plus their associated PFAs (the average distance between NAs is about 250 m), for a total of about 200 ha. (Note that the PFA cannot be biologically distinguished from the NA, because both are required to successfully fledge the young.)
- Do not harvest or salvage within the 200-ha PFA.
- Any harvest activities within an FA should retain some mature and old-growth, open-understorey, closed-canopy forest that is contiguous with the PFA and NA. Plan for retention (or recruitment, if necessary) of some mature and old-growth stands within a 2400-ha area surrounding each known nest site (a target seral stage distribution of >50 percent mature and older forest within this area is recommended). Where operationally possible during harvest activities, retain several snags and sufficient downed woody debris. Foraging opportunities close to the nest site result in less work for the parents and hence a higher probability of successfully fledging young.

OF INTEREST

Extremely defensive at their nests, adult northern goshawks will dive at and strike intruders—including humans.

RED-TAILED HAWK
Buteo jamaicensis • RTHA

STATUS

A widespread but uncommon breeder throughout British Columbia, including Vancouver Island and the Queen Charlotte Islands, the red-tailed hawk is resident on the coast and in the southern Interior but mostly migratory elsewhere. It does well in rural, agricultural and logged (fragmented or harvested) areas, but it requires some large trees for nesting. It is not at risk in B.C.

Left: Red-tailed hawk. Right: Class 5 conifer supporting hawk nest with young

RANGE

This hawk breeds throughout the province, anywhere from sea level to about 2300 m. Breeding densities are highest in the Fraser Valley, the south and central Interior and the Peace River Valley. It overwinters from southern B.C. to Central America. The main B.C. overwintering area is the lower Fraser Valley.

DESCRIPTION

About half the size of a bald eagle (at 45–65 cm long and weighing 690–1460 g, with females larger than males) the red-tailed hawk has broad, rounded wings

Biogeoclimatic Zones

AT	BG	BWBS	CDF	CWH	ESSF	ICH	IDF	MH	MS	PP	SBPS	SBS	SWB

Ecoprovinces									Breeding Period											
BOP	COM	CEI	GED	NBM	SBI	SIM	SOI	TAP		J	F	M	A	M	J	J	A	S	O	N	D

and a wide tail. The extremely variable plumage ranges from mottled light buff and brown to very dark brown. The upper side of the tail is rufous, and a red tinge may show when seen from below. The immature has a greyish brown tail banded with black.

OTHER CHARACTERISTICS
This hawk is often seen perching on poles or treetops. The wings are held level in soaring flight. The call is a harsh, descending *keeeeer*.

HABITAT
Feeding: Hunting in open or semi-open upland forest, agricultural fields, orchards, rangeland and wetlands, this raptor searches for prey while soaring or while perched on a tall tree or pole with an unobstructed view. The diet is mainly small to medium-sized mammals (e.g., pocket gophers, ground squirrels, weasels and rabbits), birds and snakes.

Breeding: The preferred habitat includes the edges of hardwood, conifer and mixed woodlands, agricultural areas with scattered trees and riparian areas. Forests with a sparse to medium canopy cover are favoured. The most frequent nest trees are black cottonwood, Douglas-fir, ponderosa pine and spruces. A stick nest (37–107 cm in diameter and 23–122 cm deep) is usually built in a large, live tree, but a dead tree or high stump is occasionally used. The nest is typically 12–18 m above the ground and well concealed in a crotch or on a branch by the trunk. Old nests are frequently reused.

The breeding period is March to late July. The clutch size is 2–4, and usually two young are fledged.

Class 1 ponderosa pine with red-tailed hawk nest with young

Roosting: Roosting is generally in a large tree near a clearing edge.

Territory/Home Range: The minimum home range size is estimated at 300 ha (breeding season) and 500 ha (rest of year), larger in areas with low food availability. A pair will actively defend its nesting territory during the breeding season and less aggressively during the rest of the year (if used year-round).

ADDITIONAL STEWARDSHIP PROVISIONS (see also Part 2)
- Keep disruptive activities at least 50–75 m from an active nest or schedule them between August and February.

OF INTEREST
The red-tailed hawk is the most abundant raptor in the Fraser Delta and lower Fraser Valley during winter. Its numbers peak between December and February.

MARBLED MURRELET

Brachyramphus marmoratus • MAMU

STATUS
B.C.: Red List
COSEWIC: Threatened

Within Canada, the marbled murrelet occurs only in British Columbia, where it is a fairly common and widespread resident along most of the coast. About 66,000 marbled murrelets, 20–30 percent of the world population, live in B.C. The loss of old-growth nesting habitat, leading to reduced breeding and probable population declines, is placing the species at risk. Oil spills and gill nets pose additional threats. The potential for population recovery is limited by the one-egg clutch size and relatively low breeding success. Research is needed on many aspects of marbled murrelet biology, especially their breeding biology.

RANGE
The marbled murrelet is seen most often on inshore marine waters and occasionally on coastal lakes. Breeding probably occurs along the entire B.C. coast, but active nests are difficult to find. Known breeding areas include large, forested coastal islands, exposed and protected inlets and mainland forests up to 50 km inland. Most populations nest in the Coastal Western Hemlock zone, with smaller numbers in the Coastal Douglas-fir and Mountain Hemlock zones. Large concentrations of breeding birds occur on the west coast of Vancouver Island and in some parts of the south coast and central mainland coast and the Queen Charlotte Islands. Most nests are found below 900 m, and a few are at 900–1500 m, but nesting is unlikely above 1500 m. The known provincial range in the nonbreeding season centres on the Strait of Georgia, Howe Sound and Juan de Fuca Strait. The largest winter concentrations have been found near Cortes Island, off Sechelt and at Skookumchuck Narrows. Local migration has been recorded, but the distance limits have not been established.

DESCRIPTION
This small (24 cm in length), chunky seabird has a pointed bill, large head, compact body and short neck, tail and wings. The breeding plumage is dark brown above and heavily mottled brown below. The nonbreeding plumage is blackish above and white below.

Biogeoclimatic Zones

AT	BG	BWBS	CDF	CWH	ESSF	ICH	IDF	MH	MS	PP	SBPS	SBS	SWB

Ecoprovinces

BOP	COM	CEI	GED	NBM	SBI	SIM	SOI	TAP

Breeding Period

J	F	M	A	M	J	J	A	S	O	N	D

OTHER CHARACTERISTICS

At sea, this murrelet flies rapidly just above the water, tilting jerkily from side to side. Inland, it is more often heard than seen, usually while flying to or from nesting areas at daybreak and dusk. The most common call is a series of high-pitched, sharp *keer* notes.

HABITAT

Feeding: This bird feeds mainly in relatively protected marine waters, usually within 2 km of shore. Its primary prey is small fish (e.g., sand lance and immature herring) and shrimplike crustaceans. Tidal rips through narrow passages, shelves at the mouths of inlets and shallow banks are important foraging sites.

Breeding: A single egg is laid in a shallow depression on a large horizontal branch that provides a platform at least 15 cm wide, usually thickly covered with moss and protected against rain, wind and predators by other branches. Mistletoe, limb deformities and tree damage all contribute to creating nest platforms. Nesting habitat must be within flying range of marine foraging habitats, preferably within 30 km of marine waters. In British Columbia, nearly all located nests have been in old-growth stands or in residual old-growth trees, with a few on mossy cliff-ledges on mountain ridges. Nests have been found in forest patches that range widely in size. In areas of fragmented forest near human activities, breeding success may be reduced by edge-dwelling nest-predators, such as jays and crows. The marbled murrelet is a solitary nester, but several pairs may nest in one stand. Most nest sites are not reused in subsequent years, although the pair might use another nearby site.

The preferred nest trees are tall (>40 m), old (>200 years) conifers (especially Sitka spruce, Douglas-fir, western hemlock, western red-cedar and

Marbled murrelet in class 1 old-growth conifer with well-developed moss layer

yellow-cedar) with large limbs >15 m above ground. The nest height is important, because murrelets can become airborne only when they run across water or take off from a high branch. A fledgling's first flight must take it to salt water. A variable forest structure, small canopy gaps and sloping terrain have been identified as enhancing access to nest sites in old-growth forest.

Monitoring data consistently shows that the number of murrelets commuting between marine foraging areas and nesting habitat is related to the amount of old forest. The configuration of the old forests also appears to be important, because murrelet numbers are lower for areas of fragmented old forest than for areas with a similar amount of intact forest.

The breeding period is late April through September. The reproductive rate is extremely low (one egg per pair each year), but replacement laying after early failure has been documented. Nest predation contributes to the low breeding success (generally <30 percent).

Roosting: Marbled murrelets roost at sea.

Territory Size/Home Range: Most recorded nests in B.C. have been within 30–50 km of marine capture sites (for radio-telemetry studies) and foraging aggregations. In some situations, such as nest sites inland from long, deep fjords, murrelets commute large distances (occasionally >100 km) to feed at prey concentrations. Murrelets often aggregate predictably at favoured sites. Some individuals breeding on Vancouver Island were seen to forage in both Clayoquot Sound and the Strait of Georgia within the same season.

ADDITIONAL STEWARDSHIP PROVISIONS (see also Part 2)

- Large, contiguous areas of suitable old forest (nest reserves) need to be retained over the entire range of the species. Coordinate the conservation of representative old forests needed for old-forest biodiversity with the conservation of suitable marbled murrelet habitat so that sufficient areas of suitable old-forest stands where harvesting will not occur are identified within coastal forest drainages. Forest patches to be retained for murrelet habitat should contain several large stands (>200 ha).
- To reduce nest predation, maximize Interior forest conditions (i.e., areas of old growth >50 m from clear-cuts, roads or regenerating forest <40 years

old). Advanced second growth (>40 years old) that has developed after clearcutting or other disturbances provides a useful buffer around old-growth patches but cannot provide nesting habitat.

- In general, nest reserves should contain a suitable number of trees >40 m tall at low elevations or >30 m tall at higher elevations. Stands with a complex vertical structure located <30 km from salt water, at <600 m in elevation and aged >250 years are most likely to support successful nesting, whereas stands that are less complex, >50 km from salt water, at >900 m elevation, or with trees <20 m in height are the least likely. Confirmed evidence of nesting is required before designating nest reserves.
- Where old growth is insufficient, blocks of maturing second growth with good future nest-site potential should be designated as long-term reserves.
- No timber harvesting or road building should be done in reserve areas.
- Recreation sites should not be located in reserves, because they tend to attract corvids (crows, jays and ravens), which are common nest predators of murrelets.
- Fire prevention should be a priority in reserves.
- Any disruptive activities and prescribed burning in areas adjacent to reserves should be scheduled between September 15 and April 15.
- For all small reserves (<100 ha), long-term planning is required to ensure that no more than one-half of the adjacent forest is early seral.
- Windthrow reduction is important in areas adjacent to reserves.

Old-growth western red-cedar with well-developed lateral branches and moss community

OF INTEREST
The marbled murrelet is the only member of the alcid family that nests in trees; the others nest in burrows or on cliffs on offshore islands.

GREAT HORNED OWL
Bubo virginianus • GHOW

STATUS
An uncommon resident throughout most of British Columbia, the great horned owl is an occasional visitor to the Queen Charlotte Islands. It is not at risk in B.C.

RANGE
This owl breeds throughout British Columbia (except the Queen Charlotte Islands) at anywhere from sea level to 1250 m, and it has been sighted at elevations up to 2100 m. Breeding is less common in the north and at high elevations. The species is usually nonmigratory in B.C., but some birds from northern populations move southward during severe winters and periods of food shortage.

DESCRIPTION
This large (50–63 cm in length), heavy-bodied owl has a large head, yellow eyes, prominent ear tufts (no other large owl has noticeable ear tufts), a white throat "bib" and heavy barring below. Interior birds tend to have lighter-coloured plumage than coastal birds.

OTHER CHARACTERISTICS
Chiefly nocturnal, this owl also hunts at dawn and dusk. The male's *hoo!, hu-hu-hu, hoo! hoo!* hoots are loud and deep; the female's are higher pitched and shorter in sequence.

HABITAT
Feeding: This owl forages in forests, agricultural and residential areas, open grasslands with scattered trees, swamps, estuaries and marshes, but edge habitats and open woodlands are favoured. The diet is mainly medium-sized mammals (especially rabbits, hares and rodents) and birds.

Breeding: Habitats such as dense forests, open woodlands, riparian forest,

Biogeoclimatic Zones

AT	BG	BWBS	CDF	CWH	ESSF	ICH	IDF	MH	MS	PP	SBPS	SBS	SWB

Ecoprovinces									Breeding Period												
BOP	COM	CEI	GED	NBM	SBI	SIM	SOI	TAP	J	F	M	A	M	J	J	A	S	O	N	D

277

more than black cottonwood, trembling aspen and birches. A pair will often reuse the same nest in successive years.

The breeding period is early February to mid-August. On the coast, the young often leave the nest by early May. The average clutch size is 1–4.

Roosting: Daytime roosting is near the trunk in a dense conifer.

Territory Size/Home Range: A resident pair defends and occupies its home range (approximately 100–300 ha) year-round, usually excluding other large owls.

ADDITIONAL STEWARDSHIP PROVISIONS (see also Part 2)

- Manage for a supply of large conifers and hardwoods for nesting and roosting.
- Keep disruptive activities at least 50–75 m from an active nest or schedule them between September and February.
- Protect the abandoned stick nests of other large open nesters where possible.

Class 7 coastal Douglas-fir supporting great horned owl with young

hedgerows and woodlots are used for breeding. Not dependent on mature or old forests, this species often selects nest trees in younger stands with nearby feeding habitat. Open nests at a height of 1.5–34 m—generally old stick nests of other large birds or witches' brooms—are most common. Most nests are positioned in crotches or on branches next to the trunk. This owl also nests on top of broken snags or in large tree cavities. Douglas-fir, white spruce, ponderosa pine and western red-cedar are used

Class 1 hardwood with great horned owl occupying an existing stick nest (likely built by red-tailed hawk)

OF INTEREST

Great horned owls will cache excess prey. In winter, they thaw frozen meals by incubating them like eggs.

SPOTTED OWL
Strix occidentalis • SPOW

STATUS

Northern spotted owl, *S. o. caurina*—B.C.: Red List
COSEWIC: Endangered

A rare, local resident on the extreme southern mainland coast, which is at the northwestern tip of its range, the northern spotted owl had an estimated historic B.C. breeding population of 500 pairs. Current estimates are 4–25 pairs. The historic range likely included much of the old-growth conifer forest on slopes throughout the Fraser Valley. The significant population decline has been attributed to the fragmentation and loss of habitat, predation, low recruitment to adulthood and competition from the barred owl. Projections based on the current population trend show the spotted owl disappearing from the province before 2013. Retaining the extant habitat will help to stabilize the remaining population. A species recovery team is recommending appropriate remedial action to government at the time of this writing.

RANGE

Resident from Anderson Lake south to the North Shore Mountains and east to Lytton and Manning Provincial Park, the spotted owl does not occur on the coastal islands, but its full range remains to be determined. It has been recorded at elevations of 250–1400 m. The species is nonmigratory in British Columbia. When left with suitable habitat, paired adults rarely disperse, but juveniles disperse widely each autumn.

DESCRIPTION

This medium-sized owl (about 45 cm long) has dark eyes and a large head without ear tufts. The head and back are

a medium brown, heavily spotted with white. The pale belly is spotted.

OTHER CHARACTERISTICS

The secretive spotted owl is strictly nocturnal. Its territorial call is a series of high-pitched hoots: *hoo, hoo-hoo, hoo* or *who-who-who-whooo* or *hoo-hoo, who, hoo, hoo-hoo, who*, like the barking of a

Biogeoclimatic Zones

AT	BG	BWBS	CDF	**CWH**	**ESSF**	ICH	**IDF**	**MH**	MS	PP	SBPS	SBS	SWB

Ecoprovinces									Breeding Period												
BOP	**COM**	CEI	**GED**	NBM	SBI	SIM	**SOI**	TAP	J	F	M	A	M	J	J	A	S	O	N	D

Remnant hemlock-cedar old-growth forest

small dog. This owl also gives a longer series of rapid hoots in crescendo, as well as other varied vocalizations (e.g., high-pitched screams, cooing and bill-clicking) The female vocalizes at a higher pitch and less often than the male.

HABITAT
Feeding: This owl forages in old-growth or mature forests with a multilevel canopy and occasionally in old second-growth forests with similar structural characteristics. The northern flying squirrel and bushy-tailed woodrat are the primary prey, followed by several species of voles, the deer mouse and a variety of small forest birds. Excess prey is often cached on tree limbs or on the ground beside logs, trees or large rocks.

Breeding: The spotted owl prefers old-growth conifer forests (>200 years old with an open, multilayered canopy), particularly Douglas-fir or Douglas-fir–western hemlock forests with variable amounts of western red-cedar and amabilis fir. Breeding sites usually contain a higher proportion, relative to the general availability in the stand, of trees with deformities (e.g., broken-topped large-diameter trees). Within its range, the

spotted owl may be found in large remaining tracts of old-growth forest dominated by Douglas-fir, which are situated mainly in steep or rocky areas, because similar stands on gentle gradients and in less rocky places have already been logged. Nests are typically built in rotted depressions in the broken tops and broken trunks of large-diameter trees, especially where these sites are located below the surrounding canopy, thereby providing better shelter and security cover. This owl is also known to use the old nests of eagles, hawks, ravens and squirrels, as well as witches' brooms and platforms of natural accumulations of debris entrapped by tree limbs. Proximity to water may be important. A pair tends to occupy the same area year after year and reuse the same nest or nest stand.

The breeding period extends from April to late June. The clutch size is 1–4 (typically 1–2). Juveniles usually remain with their parents in the nest stand until late July or as late as September before dispersing. Dispersal is approximately 25 km in suitable habitat, but longer distances, up to 200 km through less suitable (i.e., young forests) or fragmented habitats, increase exposure to predation. High predation rates and energetic stresses during dispersal and overwintering restrict first-year survival to <25 percent. Survival to breeding age is estimated at <10 percent (thought to be largely dependent on habitat quality). Breeding normally begins during the third or fourth year, provided a mate and suitable habitat are available, and every second or third year thereafter, if prey is sufficiently abundant.

Roosting: Daytime roosts are in dense conifers that provide a cool microclimate, almost always in an old-growth forest.

Territory Size/Home Range: The home range is estimated at 3400 ha or greater, depending on the site conditions and prey productivity. During the breeding season, activities are mostly confined to within 2 km of the nest. After breeding, the movements of the adults gradually expand to use the whole home range. Home ranges are not exclusive, and the ranges of neighbouring pairs may overlap.

ADDITIONAL STEWARDSHIP PROVISIONS (see also Part 2)

- Because much of the low-elevation old-growth forest within the range of this species has already been logged, long-term landscape-level planning and monitoring of the remaining owls is required within the remaining suitable habitat.
- Maintain areas of approximately 3600 ha (of which at least two-thirds should be suitable old growth) for nesting, roosting and post-fledging habitat. To facilitate successful dispersal and population connectivity, these areas should be <20 km apart.
- Provide avenues for dispersal from nest sites to other suitable habitats through the maintenance of linked or closely linked areas of mature- and old-forest with suitable feeding and security cover characteristics.
- Any forest harvesting in suitable spotted owl habitat needs to focus on the retention of old-growth forest that contains the following components: large, dominant, living wildlife trees (especially trees with large cavities, broken tops or dwarf mistletoe infections); large, dead wildlife trees (>75 cm dbh); coarse woody debris; and open, multilayered, multispecies canopies with no fewer than 240 stems/ha.

Class 7 conifer supporting northern spotted owl and young

- Harvesting and thinning of small-diameter trees (<40 cm dbh) within mature forests can speed the development of suitable old-growth forest structures (and begin to restore owl habitat) provided that a density of 240 stems/ha or more is maintained.
- Salvage logging is not appropriate in areas being managed for spotted owl habitat.
- Road construction and thinning to restore habitat in spotted owl areas should not take place in the breeding season.

OF INTEREST

The spotted owl is adept at both climbing trees and walking on the ground or along branches. When mammalian prey on the forest floor escape the first strike, a spotted owl will often pursue on foot, running on fully extended legs with widespread wings.

GREAT GREY OWL
Strix nebulosa • GGOW

STATUS

An uncommon resident in the northern British Columbia Interior and a rare resident in the southern Interior, the great grey owl is an irregular winter visitor to the south coast. It is not at risk in B.C.

RANGE

The provincial distribution of this owl is poorly known. Most observations—largely nonbreeding birds—have been in the southern and central Interior and the northeastern corner of the province. The few nests found in B.C. have been at elevations of 900–1250 m. This semi-nomadic bird settles in areas with high food supplies.

DESCRIPTION

Generally considered North America's largest owl, the great grey can reach 83 cm in length and has relatively long wings and tail. It has a round head without ear tufts, yellow eyes set in large, strongly lined facial discs and a black "chin" spot bordered by white "moustache" patches. The body plumage is brownish grey, heavily striped lengthwise on the underparts.

OTHER CHARACTERISTICS

The great grey owl hunts mainly at night and occasionally by day. The call is a series of deep *whoo-hoo-hoo*s or a single, deep *whoo*.

HABITAT

Feeding: This owl hunts in and over forest clearings and open country with little shrub understorey. Perch sites (e.g., small trees, snags and poles) are used to survey for prey—mainly voles, northern flying squirrels and medium-sized birds (e.g., small hawks, falcons, spruce grouse and ducks).

Breeding: Nesting occurs within or under the forest canopy in conifer, hardwood

Biogeoclimatic Zones

AT	BG	BWBS	CDF	CWH	ESSF	ICH	IDF	MH	MS	PP	SBPS	SBS	SWB

Ecoprovinces

BOP	COM	CEI	GED	NBM	SBI	SIM	SOI	TAP

Breeding Period

J	F	M	A	M	J	J	A	S	O	N	D

Class 7 conifer supporting great grey owl on nest with young

or mixed woodlands (such as Douglas-fir–trembling aspen, lodgepole pine–Engelmann spruce or Douglas-fir–lodgepole pine, pure black spruce or Engelmann spruce) and in old burns. This species is thought to prefer nest sites near clearings in mature and old-growth forests. It uses abandoned nests of other large birds or situates its nests in witches' brooms or on broken tree tops or high stumps. The average dbh of trees containing stick nests is approximately 60 cm; for broken-topped trees, it is 80 cm. Nests found in B.C. are typically 3–15 m above the ground. The fidelity to the nest site and mate are irregular and depend on the food supply.

The breeding period is late March through mid-August. The clutch size is 2–5.

Roosting: Adults roost in dense conifers. Recently fledged young roost in the nest.

Territory Size/Home Range: The average home range size is approximately 5000 ha for adults and 10,000 ha for first-year juveniles.

ADDITIONAL STEWARDSHIP PROVISIONS (see also Part 2)

- Manage for a supply of large conifers and hardwoods for nesting and roosting.
- Keep disruptive activities at least 50–75 m from an active nest or schedule them between September and February.
- Protect the abandoned stick nests of other large open nesters where possible.

OF INTEREST

Great grey owls hunting in winter can hear prey moving beneath the snow. Diving from the air, they can break through a crust hard enough to support an 80-kg person and capture prey 45 cm below the snow's surface, leaving an impression of themselves in the snow.

Class 1 conifer with great grey owl occupying an existing stick nest (likely built by a hawk species)

283

Glossary

biomass: the total mass of all living organisms in an ecosystem at any given time; a measure of net primary productivity of an ecosystem or total mass of all species, large or small; an ecosystem will consistently produce a higher biomass when healthy than when unhealthy.

bole: a tree trunk with substantial thickness and generally capable of yielding forest products such as timber, pulp logs and poles; in contrast, seedlings, saplings and small trees have stems rather than boles (see "stem").

butt: the base of a tree or the lower part of a tree trunk.

cambium: a cylindrical layer of cells responsible for lateral growth in vascular plants, situated between the xylem (woody, water-bearing) and phloem (food-bearing) layers; as they divide, these cells add a new layer of woody material to the inner side of the root or stem and a new layer to the outside or bark.

climax: the culminating stage in plant succession, which is relatively stable, self-perpetuating and in equilibrium with existing environmental conditions; in forest ecosystems, climax tree species are shade tolerant, and, when old trees die, shade-tolerant species fill the gaps; old-forest wildlife species associated with climax forests are also considered climax species; climax may also be defined as the stage at which the greatest biomass or biodiversity is achieved.

coarse woody debris: sound or rotting logs, stumps or large branches found on the forest floor; they are usually larger than 10 cm in diameter and 3 m in length.

conk: a firm, protruding, spore-producing structure of a wood-decaying fungus, typically found on the external surfaces of a tree trunk, fallen tree, stump or branch ; often referred to as "bracket fungus."

crown: the upper part of a tree or shrub that carries the main foliage.

cut-block: an area defined on the ground in which a timber harvest is planned, usually within one season.

diameter at breast height (dbh): on a tree, measured at 1.3 m above the estimated germination point of the seed (usually approximately 1.3 m above ground level).

disruptive activities: operations such as logging, blasting, the building of roads and landings, mechanized agriculture and the construction of houses, wharves or other structures, which should be avoided near active wildlife breeding areas or roost sites.

duff: a layer of loosely compacted, decaying debris underlying the litter layer on the forest floor.

ecosystem: a community of interacting organisms (plants, animals, fungi and microorganisms) together with their environment (soil, water, air and nutrients).

endangered: refers to any species facing imminent extinction or extirpation.

epiphyte: a nonparasitic plant, such as a moss or fern, that grows on a tree and gets its water and nutrients from the air and rain.

extinction: the termination of a species caused by failure to reproduce and the death of all the remaining members of that species; can be natural or human-induced.

extirpation: the elimination of a species or sub-species from a particular area but not from its entire range; local extinction.

fragmentation: the change in forest landscape from continuous forest cover to a mosaic of smaller patches of very young forests or non-forested open areas; this process of reducing the size and degree of connectivity of pieces of habitat, as well as their separation (such as by road construction, urban developments or logging), often leads to the remaining forested patches becoming too small and isolated to support the species indigenous to the area.

hardwood: typically refers to the broad-leaved trees (or their wood), most of which are both angiosperms (plants with seeds that develop inside flowers) and deciduous (drop their leaves annually).

hawking: the act of catching insects while in flight.

heartwood: the inner layers of wood situated in the centre of the tree away from the cambium; this central portion of a tree trunk is no longer active in transporting or storing water or nutrients.

leader: the terminal or topmost shoot of a tree's main stem

microsite: a small area that has localized climatic, soil or other characteristics not found in the surrounding area.

migrant: a species that has a regular seasonal movement, often of considerable distance, between different areas, so that only a part of the year is spent in a specified area.

mistletoe: a parasitic plant that absorb nutrients, water and carbohydrates from a host tree.

mixedwood: conifers and hardwoods occurring together

mycorrhizae: root-inhabiting fungi that have a symbiotic relationship with the root system of a host plant in which energy, water and nutrients flow from the mycorrhizae to the root of the host plant.

non-native species: species that have been introduced to an area; also referred to as exotic or invasive species.

open nester: a species that nests on or among the branches or in the broken bole of a tree rather than in the shelter of a cavity within a tree bole.

overstory: the foliage of the upper canopy of a forest.

pathogen: any organism that can cause disease or a toxic response in another organism.

pioneer species: a species that is capable of colonizing disturbed areas, often in large numbers and over considerable areas, and persisting until displaced by other species as succession proceeds.

plucking perch: a place where a bird of prey consumes its catches.

primary cavity excavator: any bird species capable of making its own roost or nest cavities in trees by using its beak to hammer or otherwise excavate the nesting chamber.

raptor: any bird of prey, such as an eagle, hawk or owl, that has feet with sharp talons for seizing prey and a hooked beak for tearing flesh.

resident: a species that remains in a specified area throughout the year.

sapwood: the living portion of a growing tree, it encircles the heartwood and carries water and nutrients from the roots to the leaves.

secondary cavity user: a wildlife species dependent (for nesting, denning or roosting) on a sheltered chamber within the bole of tree or beneath loose bark; the cavity can have been made either by a primary cavity excavator or by natural processes, such as limb breakage and decay fungi.

sedentary: refers to a species that normally confines its activities to a limited area and is generally fairly stationary.

seed tree: a tree reserved to provide a seed source for natural regeneration; seed trees are left after the initial harvest, typically to be harvested once the new forest is established.

seral species: the dominant vegetation associated with a given seral stage; in a forest management context, this term refers specifically to trees.

seral stage: (also called successional stage) a phase in the ecological progression of a plant community; typically, forests progress from early seral (on recently disturbed soils) to mid-seral to late seral (mature) to old-growth (climax).

shelterwood: a method of forest harvesting designed to establish new trees under the protection of selected trees from the existing stand.

snag: a standing dead, defective, deformed, damaged or broken tree.

special concern: refers to a species that has characteristics that make it particularly sensitive to human activities or natural events.

stand: a group of trees of one or more species that can be distinguished from its surroundings by its composition or structural differences.

stand structure: relates to the variation in height, diameter and distribution of the trees in a forest stand.

stem: the principle axis of a plant from which buds and shoots develop, giving the plant its characteristic form; this term can apply to all ages and thicknesses, unlike "trunk" and "bole," which refer to tree stems of substantial thickness.

stub: a high-cut stump that reaches a few to several metres above the ground.

succession: a series of dynamic changes in ecosystem structure, function and species composition over time, as a result of which one group of organisms succeeds another during the progression of seral stages.

threatened: refers to a species that is likely to be endangered if the factors affecting its vulnerability are not reversed.

torpor: a state in which an animal's body temperature, heartbeat and body activities slow down; animals in torpor are sluggish and take a while to awaken; this state is not as deep as hibernation and can last a short period (for example, bats often go into torpor for only part of a day).

understorey: the plants below the main canopy of a forest.

ungulate: any member of the group of hoofed, grazing mammals that have antlers or horns (e.g., deer, sheep, moose, mountain goats and elk).

veteran (vet): refers to a mature tree that is considerably older than the rest of the stand—it may have survived one or more fires—and has a new forest growing up around it.

visitor: a species that is present in an area only during a certain part of the year.

vulnerable: refers to a species of special concern in B.C. because of characteristics that make it particularly sensitive to human activities or natural events.

whitewash: patches of white fecal matter on surfaces below a nest or perch of certain bird species.

wildlife tree: any standing dead or live tree with special characteristics that provide vitally important habitat for the conservation or enhancement of wildlife.

witches' broom: a characteristic tree growth caused by abnormal shortening to the internodes and a proliferation of weak shoots, to create a dense, brush-like mass of twigs; it is typically caused by rust fungi or dwarf mistletoe.

Appendix 1:
Human Safety and Liability

SAFETY ISSUES

A dangerous tree is defined by Workers' Compensation Board Occupational Health and Safety Regulations as "any tree that is hazardous to people or facilities because of location or lean, physical damage, overhead hazards, deterioration of the limbs, stem or root system, or a combination of these." Because the best wildlife trees are often dead, dying or damaged, they can be potentially dangerous.

For many years, safety regulations classified all dead trees as dangerous. Thus, all dead trees in forestry operations had to be removed progressively with the felling of timber. Cumulatively, this practice markedly decreased the number of dead trees in second-growth forests. The current regulation is a significant improvement that focuses on tree hazard and permits dead trees to be safely retained. It is now acceptable for fallers and others to leave dead trees that are assessed as safe; it is also acceptable to retain dangerous trees with high wildlife value if they are properly buffered with a no-work zone.

Integral to the understanding of tree danger is an understanding of the concept of "risk," which can be expressed as a simple equation:

$$\text{Risk} = \text{Hazard} \times \text{Exposure}.$$

"Hazard," which entails the likelihood of a tree or part thereof failing (and potentially causing damage or injury), is a function of the amount and location of any decay or damage the tree has as well as the condition of its roots and branches and its vulnerability to stress forces caused by wind and snow. "Exposure" exists when "targets" (such as buildings, equipment, power lines or people) are or are likely to be within striking range of a dangerous tree. If a tree has no hazardous defects, there is little or no risk or danger, regardless of the type of activity or target exposure around the tree. Likewise, a tree that has numerous defects or hazards will not pose a significant risk if there is no exposure to persons or facilities near the tree; for example, trees in backcountry areas rarely visited by people pose little risk or danger.

If a tree is determined to be dangerous for a particular type of work activity or other situation, then the appropriate safety procedures must be implemented. These measures can include

- establishing an appropriately sized buffer area (called a "hazard zone" or "no-work zone") around the tree to eliminate exposure to the hazard
- modifying the target location or facility (e.g., rerouting the hiking trail or moving the outhouse)
- using cables or other devices to support hazardous parts or the whole tree (normally done only in populated settings)
- removing any hazardous parts (e.g., top or limbs) or, if necessary, the whole tree

LIABILITY AND TRAINING

Determining risk requires an assessment of the likelihood of tree failure and the consequences of that failure. Resource managers and landowners must therefore take steps to minimize risk and concurrently establish the acceptable levels of risk for a given situation. This obligation on the part of the landowner or resource manager is called "duty of care," and it is their legal responsibility to reasonably ensure the safety of persons working on or using that property. Duty of care is often established by various acts or policies, such as British Columbia's Occupiers Liability Act.

Duty of care invokes a certain level of conduct, called the "standard of care," which involves using the best available guidelines, techniques and practices to carry out established procedures and meet accepted standards. In British Columbia, the Wildlife/Danger Tree Assessor's Course is recognized as the current standard of care for determining tree danger and hazards. This provincially sponsored course provides technical information and practical field skills to persons who wish to assess trees for hazards and wildlife habitat value and then make appropriate safety decisions under various situations. Currently, such courses exist for forestry, parks and municipal applications.

Generally, liability hinges on whether or not there was a legal duty of care to be exercised, and, if so, whether or not it was appropriately implemented—that is, was the accepted standard of care adhered to? Liability has to be proven, usually by showing that some sort of negligence or lack of due diligence has occurred. The best way to alleviate concerns about liability surrounding a potentially dangerous tree is to demonstrate that owner responsibility, the timing of assessments and the appropriate training and skills of the person or people involved in the tree assessment all adhered to the accepted standard of care.

Because of our growing understanding of what makes trees dangerous in various situations, plus our increasing awareness of the ecological value of dead or partially dead trees, changed policies now recognize that not all dead trees (snags) are a safety risk and a potential liability. Staying current with ongoing refinements of what makes a tree dangerous will allow you to make decisions that are more ecologically sound and safe.

Appendix 2:
Summary of Wildlife Tree–Dependent Species:
Provincial Status, Use of Wildlife Trees and Occurrence by Biogeoclimatic Zone

PROVINCIAL STATUS
Red—Extirpated, Endangered or Threatened

Blue—Special Concern

COSEWIC
E—Endangered

T—Threatened

SC—Special Concern

DD—Data Deficient

CODES FOR USES (see species accounts for details)
HB—Highly dependent on wildlife tree features for breeding sites (i.e., cavity nests, open nests, maternal roosts and natal dens).

HBa—Highly dependent on wildlife tree features for breeding sites, but may use artificial structures (e.g., nest boxes or platforms and abandoned buildings) when available.

MB—Moderately dependent and commonly uses wildlife tree features for breeding sites; also uses other natural sites or artificial structures.

HF—Highly dependent on food sources associated with wildlife trees (i.e., insects in or on trees and seed crops produced by mature trees).

MF—Moderately dependent on food sources associated with wildlife trees.

HO—Highly dependent on wildlife tree features for other needs (e.g., roosts, dens and hunting perches).

MO—Moderately dependent and commonly uses wildlife tree features for other needs; also uses other natural sites or artificial structures.

?—indicates a degree of uncertainty with the classification; the extent of the species-habitat relationships is not well understood.

OCCURRENCE IN ZONES
x—occurs in this zone

r—rarely reported or rarely occurs in this zone

?—possibly occurs in this zone

•—occurs, but does not use wildlife trees in this zone

BIOGEOCLIMATIC ZONES
AT—Alpine Tundra

BG—Bunchgrass

BWBS—Boreal White and Black Spruce

CDF—Coastal Douglas-fir

CWH—Coastal Western Hemlock

ESSF—Engelmann Spruce–Subalpine Fir

ICH—Interior Cedar–Hemlock

IDF—Interior Douglas-fir

MH—Mountain Hemlock

MS—Montane Spruce

PP—Ponderosa Pine

SBPS—Sub-Boreal Pine–Spruce

SBS—Sub-Boreal Spruce

SWB—Spruce–Willow–Birch

Wildlife Tree–Dependent Species

	COSEWIC	Provincial Status	Use	SWB	SBS	SBPS	PP	MS	MH	IDF	ICH	ESSF	CWH	CDF	BWBS	BG	AT
AQUATIC BIRDS																	
Great Blue Heron *Ardea herodias*	SC (*fannini* ssp)	Blue	MB		×	×	×	×		×	×		×	×	×	×	
Wood Duck *Aix sponsa*			HBa		×		×	×		×	×		×	×	×	×	
Common Goldeneye *Bucephala clangula*			HBa	×	×	×	×	×	×	×	×	×	×	×	×	×	•
Barrow's Goldeneye *Bucephala islandica*			HBa	×	×	×	×	×	×	×	×	×	×	×	×	×	•
Bufflehead *Bucephala albeola*			HBa	×	×	×	×	×	×	×	×	×	×	×	×	×	•
Common Merganser *Mergus merganser*			MB		×	×	×	×	×	×	×	×	×	×	×	×	
Hooded Merganser *Lophodytes cucullatus*			HBa		×	×	×	×		×	×	×	×	×	×	×	•
Marbled Murrelet *Brachyramphus marmoratus*	T	Red	MB						×				×	×			
BIRDS OF PREY																	
Osprey *Pandion haliaetus*			HBa, MO	r	×	×	×	×	×		×		×		×	×	
Bald Eagle *Haliaeetus leucocephalus*			MB, MO	×	×	×	×	×	×	×	×		×	×	×	×	•
Northern Goshawk *Accipiter gentilis*	T (*laingi* ssp)	Red (*laingi* ssp)	MB	×	×	×	×	×	×	×	×	×	×	×	×	×	
Red-tailed Hawk *Buteo jamaicensis*			MB	×	×	×	×	×	×	×	×	×	×	×	×	×	•

	COSEWIC	Provincial Status	Use	AT	BG	BWBS	CDF	CWH	ESSF	ICH	IDF	MH	MS	PP	SBPS	SBS	SWB
BIRDS OF PREY																	
American Kestrel *Falco sparverius*			HBa, MO	•	x	x	x	x	x	x	x	x	x	x	x	x	x
Flammulated Owl *Otus flammeolus*	SC	Blue	HB		x						x			x			
Western Screech-Owl *Megascops kennicottii*	E (*macfarlanei* ssp) SC (*kennicottii* ssp)	Red (*macfarlanei* ssp) Blue (*kennicottii* ssp)	HBa, MO		x		x	x		x	x		x	x	x		
Great Horned Owl *Bubo virginianus*			MB		x	x	x	x	x	x	x	x	x	x	x	x	x
Northern Hawk Owl *Surnia ulula*			MB, MO		r	x		r	x	x	r	r	r	r	x	x	x
Northern Pygmy-Owl *Glaucidium gnoma*		Blue (*swarthi* ssp)	HB, HO				x	x	x	x	x	x	x	x	x	x	
Spotted Owl *Strix occidentalis*	E (*caurina* ssp)	Red	MB				x	r	r	x	r	r					
Barred Owl *Strix varia*			HB		x	x	x	r	r	x	x	x	x	x			
Great Grey Owl *Strix nebulosa*			MB, MO		r	x			r	x	r	r	x	r	x	x	x
Boreal Owl *Aegolius funereus*			HBa			r		r	x	r	r	r	x		x	x	r
Northern Saw-whet Owl *Aegolius acadicus*		Blue (*brooksi* ssp)	HBa		x	r	x	r	x	x	x	x		x	r	r	
WOODPECKERS																	
Lewis's Woodpecker *Melanerpes lewis*	SC	Red (coastal population) Red (Interior population)	HB, HO		x		r	r		x	x			x	r	r	

	COSEWIC	Provincial Status	Use	AT	BG	BWBS	CDF	CWH	ESSF	ICH	IDF	MH	MS	PP	SBPS	SBS	SWB
WOODPECKERS																	
Yellow-bellied Sapsucker *Sphyrapicus varius*			HB, HO		×	×										×	
Red-naped Sapsucker *Sphyrapicus nuchalis*			HB, HO					r	×	×	×		×	×	×	×	
Red-breasted Sapsucker *Sphyrapicus ruber*			HB, HC				×	×			r	×		r		×	
Williamson's Sapsucker *Sphyrapicus thyroideus*	E	Red (*thyroideus* ssp) Red (*nataliae* ssp)	HB, HO						×	×			×				
Downy Woodpecker *Picoides pubescens*			HE, IN, CH		×	×	×	×	×	×	×	×	×	×	×	×	×
Hairy Woodpecker *Picoides villosus*		Blue (*picoides* ssp)	HB, MF, HO		×	×	×	×	×	×	×	×	×	×	×	×	×
White-headed Woodpecker *Picoides albolarvatus*	E	Red	HB, HF, HO		×									×			
American Three-toed Woodpecker *Picoides dorsalis*			HB, HF, HC			×		×	×	×	×	×	r	r	×	×	×
Black-backed Woodpecker *Picoides arcticus*			HE, HF, HO			r			r	r	r	×	r	r	r	r	r
Northern Flicker *Colaptes auratus*			HB, HO		×	×	×	×	×	×	×	×	×	×	×	×	×
Pileated Woodpecker *Dryocopus pileatus*			HB, MF, HO			×	×	×	×	×	×	×	×	×	×	×	
OTHER BIRDS																	
Vaux's Swift *Chaetura vauxi*			HE, CH	•	×	×	×	×	×	×	×	×	×	×	×	×	×

291

	COSEWIC	Provincial Status	Use	AT	BG	BWBS	CDF	CWH	ESSF	ICH	IDF	MH	MS	PP	SBPS	SBS	SWB
OTHER BIRDS																	
Tree Swallow *Tachycineta bicolor*			HBa, HO		x	x	x	x	x	x	x	x	x	x	x	x	x
Black-capped Chickadee *Poecile atricapillus*			HBa, HO		x	x		x	x	x	x	x	x	x	x	x	
Mountain Chickadee *Poecile gambeli*			HBa, HO		r	x	x	r	x	x	x		x	x	x	x	x
Boreal Chickadee *Poecile hudsonica*			HBa, HO			x			x	x	x	x	x		x	x	x
Chestnut-backed Chickadee *Poecile rufescens*			HBa, HO				x	x		x	x	r	x		x	x	
Pygmy Nuthatch *Sitta pygmaea*			HBa, MF, HO		x						x			x			
Red-breasted Nuthatch *Sitta canadensis*			HBa, HO		x	x	x	x	x	x	x	x	x	x	x	x	
White-breasted Nuthatch *Sitta carolinensis*			HBa, MF, HO		x	x	x	x	x	x	x	x	r	x	r	x	
Brown Creeper *Certhia americana*			HBa, MF, HO			r	x	x	x	x	x	x	x	x	x	x	r
House Wren *Troglodytes aedon*			HBa, MO		x	x	x	x		x	x	x	x	x		x	
Western Bluebird *Sialia mexicana*		Red (western population)	HBa, HO		x		r	x	x	x	x			x			
Mountain Bluebird *Sialia currucoides*			HBa, MO		x	r	x	x	x	x	x	x	x	x	x	x	r
BATS																	
California Myotis *Myotis californicus*			MB, MO		x	x	x	x	x	x	x	x	x	x	x	x	

292

	COSEWIC	Provincial Status	Use	AT	BG	BWBS	CDF	CWH	ESSF	ICH	IDF	MH	MS	PP	SBPS	SBS	SWB
BATS																	
Western Long-eared Myotis *Myotis evotis*			MB, MO		x	x	x	x	x	x	x	?	?	?	?	?	
Keen's Long-eared Myotis *Myotis keenii*	DD	Red	MB?, MO?				?	x									
Little Brown Myotis *Myotis lucifugus*			MB, MC		x	x	x	x	x	x	x	?	?	?	?	?	?
Northern Long-eared Myotis *Myotis septentrionalis*		Blue	MB?, MO?			x				x		?					
Long-legged Myotis *Myotis volans*			MB?, MC		x		x	x	x	x	x		x	x	x	x	
Yuma Myotis *Myotis yumanensis*			MB, MO		x		x	x		x	x			x			
Western Red Bat *Lasiurus blossevillii*		Red	MB, MO					x									
Hoary Bat *Lasiurus cinereus*			MO		x	x	x	x	x	x	x		x	x	x	x	x
Silver-haired Bat *Lasionycteris noctivagans*			HB, HO		x	x	x	x	x	x	x	x	x	x	x	x	x
Big Brown Bat *Eptesicus fuscus*			MB, MO		x	x	x	x	x	x	x	x	x	x	x	x	
OTHER MAMMALS																	
Bushy-tailed Woodrat *Neotoma cinerea*			MB, MO	•	•	•		•	•	•	•	•	•	•	•	•	•
Keen's Mouse *Peromyscus keeni*			MB				x	x				x					
Northern Flying Squirrel *Glaucomys sabrinus*			HBa, HO			x	x	x	x	x	x	x	x	x	x	x	x

Occurrence by Biogeoclimatic Zone

	COSEWIC	Provincial Status	Use	AT	BG	BWBS	CDF	CWH	ESSF	ICH	IDF	MH	MS	PP	SBPS	SBS	SWB
OTHER MAMMALS																	
Red-tailed Chipmunk *Tamias ruficaudus*		Red (*ruficaudus* ssp) Blue (*simulans* ssp)	MB, MO						×	×			×	×			
Marten *Martes americana*			MB, MO			×	×	×	×	×	×	×	×	×	×	×	×
Fisher *Martes pennanti*		Red	HB, MO			×		×	×	×	×	×	×		×	×	×
Black Bear *Ursus americanus*		Blue (*emmonsii* ssp)	MB, MO	•	•	•	•	×	•	×	×	×	•	•	•	×	•

Appendix 3:
Wildlife Tree–Dependent Species Lists for Each Forested Biogeoclimatic Zone

BUNCHGRASS (BG)

The dry, hot grasslands that dominate the low elevations of the major valleys of the southern Interior of British Columbia (along with portions of some of the adjacent plateaus) constitute the Bunchgrass zone. This zone occurs at elevations below the Ponderosa Pine zone, but it grades directly into the Interior Douglas-fir zone in several places. The occasional ponderosa pines and Douglas-firs that grow within this normally treeless, dry, open steppe habitat can become important wildlife trees, as can the black cottonwoods and aspens in the riparian woodlands of this zone. In spite of its very small size and scant forest cover, the Bunchgrass zone is inhabited by 46 wildlife tree–dependent species (70 percent of the provincial total).

AQUATIC BIRDS

Great Blue Heron	p. 261
Wood Duck	p. 171
Common Goldeneye	p. 177
Barrow's Goldeneye	p. 179
Bufflehead	p. 174
Common Merganser	p. 183
Hooded Merganser	p. 181

BIRDS OF PREY

Osprey	p. 264
Bald Eagle	p. 266
Northern Goshawk	p. 269
Red-tailed Hawk	p. 272
American Kestrel	p. 185
Flammulated Owl	p. 187
Western Screech-Owl	p. 190
Great Horned Owl	p. 277
Northern Pygmy-Owl (rarely)	p. 195
Barred Owl	p. 197
Great Grey Owl (rarely)	p. 282
Northern Saw-whet Owl	p. 201

WOODPECKERS

Lewis's Woodpecker	p. 126
Red-naped Sapsucker	p. 134
Downy Woodpecker	p. 138
Hairy Woodpecker	p. 140
White-headed Woodpecker	p. 142
Northern Flicker	p. 148
Pileated Woodpecker	p. 150

OTHER BIRDS

Vaux's Swift	p. 204
Tree Swallow	p. 206
Black-capped Chickadee	p. 154
Mountain Chickadee (rarely)	p. 156
Pygmy Nuthatch	p. 167
Red-breasted Nuthatch	p. 163
White-breasted Nuthatch	p. 165
House Wren	p. 210
Western Bluebird	p. 213
Mountain Bluebird	p. 215

BATS

California Myotis	p. 219
Western Long-eared Myotis	p. 221
Little Brown Myotis	p. 225
Long-legged Myotis	p. 229
Yuma Myotis	p. 231
Western Red Bat	p. 233
Hoary Bat	p. 235
Silver-haired Bat	p. 237
Big Brown Bat	p. 239

OTHER MAMMALS

Black Bear (rarely)	p. 254

BOREAL WHITE AND BLACK SPRUCE (BWBS)

The Boreal Black and White Spruce zone occurs mostly on an extension of the Great Plains east of the northern Rocky Mountains, but parts of it are found at low elevations of the main valleys west of the northern Rockies. Most of this zone is at 600–1300 m, but some of it is as low as 230 m. In the north, it is found below the Spruce–Willow–Birch zone, and farther south it is below the Engelmann

Spruce–Subalpine Fir zone. The mix of wildlife species in this zone is less like the province's other zones but more typical of Canada's most widespread forest zone, the much larger boreal forest. The Boreal White and Black Spruce zone is home to 44 wildlife tree–dependent species (67 percent of the provincial total).

<table>
<tr><td colspan="2">AQUATIC BIRDS</td><td>Black-backed Woodpecker (rarely)</td><td>p. 146</td></tr>
<tr><td>Great Blue Heron</td><td>p. 261</td><td>Northern Flicker</td><td>p. 148</td></tr>
<tr><td>Wood Duck</td><td>p. 171</td><td>Pileated Woodpecker (rarely)</td><td>p. 150</td></tr>
<tr><td>Common Goldeneye</td><td>p. 177</td><td colspan="2">OTHER BIRDS</td></tr>
<tr><td>Barrow's Goldeneye</td><td>p. 179</td><td>Vaux's Swift (rarely)</td><td>p. 204</td></tr>
<tr><td>Bufflehead</td><td>p. 174</td><td>Tree Swallow</td><td>p. 206</td></tr>
<tr><td>Common Merganser</td><td>p. 183</td><td>Black-capped Chickadee</td><td>p. 154</td></tr>
<tr><td colspan="2">BIRDS OF PREY</td><td>Mountain Chickadee</td><td>p. 156</td></tr>
<tr><td>Osprey</td><td>p. 264</td><td>Boreal Chickadee</td><td>p. 160</td></tr>
<tr><td>Bald Eagle</td><td>p. 266</td><td>Red-breasted Nuthatch</td><td>p. 163</td></tr>
<tr><td>Northern Goshawk</td><td>p. 269</td><td>White-breasted Nuthatch</td><td>p. 165</td></tr>
<tr><td>Red-tailed Hawk</td><td>p. 272</td><td>Brown Creeper (rarely)</td><td>p. 208</td></tr>
<tr><td>American Kestrel</td><td>p. 185</td><td>House Wren</td><td>p. 210</td></tr>
<tr><td>Great Horned Owl</td><td>p. 277</td><td>Mountain Bluebird (rarely)</td><td>p. 215</td></tr>
<tr><td>Northern Hawk Owl</td><td>p. 193</td><td colspan="2">BATS</td></tr>
<tr><td>Northern Pygmy-Owl</td><td>p. 195</td><td>Western Long-eared Myotis</td><td>p. 221</td></tr>
<tr><td>Barred Owl</td><td>p. 197</td><td>Little Brown Myotis</td><td>p. 225</td></tr>
<tr><td>Great Grey Owl</td><td>p. 282</td><td>Northern Long-eared Myotis</td><td>p. 227</td></tr>
<tr><td>Boreal Owl (rarely)</td><td>p. 199</td><td>Silver-haired Bat</td><td>p. 237</td></tr>
<tr><td>Northern Saw-whet Owl (rarely)</td><td>p. 201</td><td>Big Brown Bat</td><td>p. 239</td></tr>
<tr><td colspan="2">WOODPECKERS</td><td colspan="2">OTHER MAMMALS</td></tr>
<tr><td>Yellow-bellied Sapsucker</td><td>p. 132</td><td>Northern Flying Squirrel</td><td>p. 246</td></tr>
<tr><td>Downy Woodpecker</td><td>p. 138</td><td>Marten</td><td>p. 250</td></tr>
<tr><td>Hairy Woodpecker</td><td>p. 140</td><td>Fisher</td><td>p. 252</td></tr>
<tr><td>American Three-toed Woodpecker</td><td>p. 144</td><td>Black Bear</td><td>p. 254</td></tr>
</table>

COASTAL DOUGLAS-FIR (CDF)

In British Columbia, this zone is limited to elevations below 150 m along a small part of southeastern Vancouver Island, the southern Gulf Islands and a narrow portion of the adjacent mainland coast. The Douglas-fir, for which this zone is named and the most abundant tree in it, is an extremely important wildlife tree. Also common in this zone are western red-cedar, grand fir, lodgepole pine, arbutus, Garry oak, red alder, black cottonwood and bigleaf maple. Although the Coastal Douglas-fir zone is the smallest biogeoclimatic zone in the province, it supports 46 wildlife tree–dependent species (70 percent of the provincial total).

<table>
<tr><td colspan="2">AQUATIC BIRDS</td><td>Hooded Merganser</td><td>p. 181</td></tr>
<tr><td>Great Blue Heron</td><td>p. 261</td><td>Marbled Murrelet</td><td>p. 274</td></tr>
<tr><td>Wood Duck</td><td>p. 171</td><td colspan="2">BIRDS OF PREY</td></tr>
<tr><td>Common Goldeneye</td><td>p. 177</td><td>Osprey</td><td>p. 264</td></tr>
<tr><td>Barrow's Goldeneye</td><td>p. 179</td><td>Bald Eagle</td><td>p. 266</td></tr>
<tr><td>Bufflehead</td><td>p. 174</td><td>Northern Goshawk</td><td>p. 269</td></tr>
<tr><td>Common Merganser</td><td>p. 183</td><td>Red-tailed Hawk</td><td>p. 272</td></tr>
</table>

COASTAL WESTERN HEMLOCK (CWH)

The Coastal Western Hemlock zone extends along B.C.'s entire coast (except for certain southern dry areas), rising from sea level up the west-facing side of the Coast Mountains, which receive the prevailing winds, and inland along the major valleys of the Stikine, Nass and Fraser rivers. It encompasses rocky coastal islands, fiords, estuaries and dense coastal conifer forests. This zone attains an elevation of approximately 1000 m in the south and 300 m in the north. The Mountain Hemlock zone is normally just above it, but up northern B.C.'s large river valleys, it gives way to the Interior Cedar–Hemlock zone. Western hemlock is the most plentiful tree in the Coastal Western Hemlock zone, but western red-cedar, amabilis fir, Sitka spruce, Douglas fir and red alder are also abundant, and yellow-cedar and bigleaf maple are common. The Coastal Western Hemlock zone has the greatest diversity of habitat classes of any biogeoclimatic zone in B.C. The Fraser Lowlands ecosection, which occurs completely within this zone (taking in the entire Fraser Valley west of Hope), has a greater diversity of birds than any other ecosection in British Columbia. The Coastal Western Hemlock zone has 56 wildlife tree–dependent species (85 percent of the provincial total).

ENGELMANN SPRUCE–SUBALPINE FIR (ESSF)

Ranging in elevation from 1200–2300 m, the Engelmann Spruce–Subalpine Fir zone is B.C.'s most widely distributed subalpine zone and the uppermost forested zone in the southern and western three-quarters of the province (except for a coastal band where the Mountain Hemlock zone dominates), with the Alpine Tundra zone directly above it. In the north, it gives way to the Spruce–Willow–Birch zone. Depending on the location, any of five or so zones can be immediately below the Engelmann Spruce–Subalpine Fir zone. Englemann spruce and subalpine fir give this zone its name, but lodgepole pine is also abundant, and alpine larch, white spruce, and mountain hemlock are common. The Engelmann Spruce–Subalpine Fir zone supports 42 wildlife tree–dependent species (64 percent of the provincial total).

INTERIOR CEDAR–HEMLOCK (ICH)

The Interior Cedar–Hemlock zone is found primarily at 400–1500 m in southeastern B.C., but some of it is east of the Coast Mountains in the upper Nass and Skeena valleys and in middle portions of the valleys of the Stikine and Iskut rivers, at 100–1000 m. This zone includes narrow valley bottoms and extensive forested uplands. Depending on the location, it adjoins the Coastal Western Hemlock, Sub-Boreal Spruce or Interior Douglas-fir zones, and the Engelmann Spruce–Subalpine Fir zone is above it. The abundant western red-cedar and western hemlock give this zone its name, and other common trees are grand fir, subalpine fir, western larch, Englemann spruce, lodgepole pine, western white pine, Douglas-fir, paper birch, black cottonwood and trembling aspen. With 57 wildlife tree–dependent species (86 percent of the provincial total), the Interior Cedar–Hemlock zone has the second highest number of such species, after the Interior Douglas-fir zone.

BATS

California Myotis	p. 219	Silver-haired Bat	p. 237
Western Long-eared Myotis	p. 221	Big Brown Bat	p. 239
Little Brown Myotis	p. 225	**OTHER MAMMALS**	
Northern Long-eared Myotis	p. 227	Northern Flying Squirrel	p. 246
Long-legged Myotis	p. 229	Red-tailed Chipmunk	p. 248
Yuma Myotis	p. 231	Marten	p. 250
Hoary Bat	p. 235	Fisher	p. 252
		Black Bear	p. 254

INTERIOR DOUGLAS-FIR (IDF)

The Interior Douglas-fir zone dominates the low to mid-elevations of B.C.'s south-central Interior. Its lower boundary is at 350–600 m in the valleys and the upper boundary is at 900–1450 m. This zone typically occurs above the Bunchgrass zone or Ponderosa Pine zone. It adjoins the Sub-Boreal Spruce zone in the north, the Interior Cedar–Hemlock in the east and, in parts of the west, the Coastal Western Hemlock zone. Much of this zone tends to be below the Montane Spruce zone, except in the north, where the Sub-Boreal Pine–Spruce zone is found instead. Douglas-fir, ponderosa pine, western larch, lodgepole pine and trembling aspen are abundant in this zone, and white spruce, western red-cedar and paper birch are common. Habitat elements in the driest subzones of the IDF are similar to those in the dry Bunchgrass zone, whereas elements of the IDF's wettest subzones are similar to those in the Coastal Western Hemlock zone's relatively dry submaritime subzone. The diversity of wildlife in the IDF reflects this moisture continuum. Mild winters in parts of the IDF also attract wintering birds and mammals. With 58 wildlife tree–dependent species (88 percent of the provincial total), the widespread Interior Douglas-fir zone has the most wildlife tree–dependent species of any zone in B.C.

AQUATIC BIRDS

Great Blue Heron	p. 261	Boreal Owl (rarely)	p. 199
Wood Duck	p. 171	Northern Saw-whet Owl	p. 201
Common Goldeneye	p. 177	**WOODPECKERS**	
Barrow's Goldeneye	p. 179	Lewis's Woodpecker	p. 126
Bufflehead	p. 174	Red-naped Sapsucker	p. 134
Common Merganser	p. 183	Red-breasted Sapsucker (rarely)	p. 136
Hooded Merganser	p. 181	Williamson's Sapsucker	p. 130
BIRDS OF PREY		Downy Woodpecker	p. 138
Osprey	p. 264	Hairy Woodpecker	p. 140
Bald Eagle	p. 266	White-headed Woodpecker	p. 142
Northern Goshawk	p. 269	American Three-toed Woodpecker	p. 144
Red-tailed Hawk	p. 272	Black-backed Woodpecker (rarely)	p. 146
American Kestrel	p. 185	Northern Flicker	p. 148
Flammulated Owl	p. 187	Pileated Woodpecker	p. 150
Western Screech-Owl	p. 190	**OTHER BIRDS**	
Great Horned Owl	p. 277	Vaux's Swift	p. 204
Northern Hawk Owl (rarely)	p. 193	Tree Swallow	p. 206
Northern Pygmy-Owl	p. 195	Black-capped Chickadee	p. 154
Spotted Owl (ssp. *caurina*) (rarely)	p. 279	Mountain Chickadee	p. 156
Barred Owl	p. 197	Boreal Chickadee	p. 160
Great Grey Owl (rarely)	p. 282	Chestnut-backed Chickadee	p. 158

MOUNTAIN HEMLOCK (MH)

This zone occurs along the coast of British Columbia at elevations of 900–1800 m in the south and 400–1000 m in the north. Within these ranges, the zone is lower on the windward side and higher on the leeward slopes of the Coast Mountains and Vancouver Island. It occurs primarily above the Coastal Western Hemlock zone and, in places on the leeward side of the Coast Mountains, above the Englemann Spruce–Sub-alpine Fir zone. Mountain hemlock, yellow-cedar and amabalis fir are abundant, and subalpine fir and western hemlock are common. The wildlife in this zone must contend with steep terrain and long, cold, wet winters with heavy snowfall. The landscape is much interrupted by glaciers, and the habitat here is used in a patchy way, both spatially and temporally. The Mountain Hemlock zone has 36 wildlife tree–dependent species (55 percent of the provincial total).

MONTANE SPRUCE (MS)

The Montane Spruce zone occurs at elevations of 1100–1500 m in the wettest parts of the zone and 1250–1700 m in its driest parts. It is found in the southern Interior, largely above the Interior Douglas-fir zone and below the Englemann Spruce–Subalpine Fir zone, but toward its northern limits, it is above the Sub-Boreal Pine–Spruce zone. This Montane Spruce zone has longer, colder winters and steeper topography than the Bunchgrass, Ponderosa Pine or Interior Douglas-fir zones. Subalpine-fir, western larch, Engelmann spruce, white spruce, lodgepole pine and Douglas-fir are all abundant in this zone, and trembling aspen is common. The Montane Spruce zone has 51 wildlife tree–dependent species (77 percent of the provincial total).

AQUATIC BIRDS
Great Blue Heron	p. 261
Common Goldeneye	p. 177
Barrow's Goldeneye	p. 179
Bufflehead	p. 174
Common Merganser	p. 183
Hooded Merganser	p. 181

BIRDS OF PREY
Osprey	p. 264
Bald Eagle	p. 266
Northern Goshawk	p. 269
Red-tailed Hawk	p. 272
American Kestrel	p. 185
Great Horned Owl	p. 277
Northern Hawk Owl (rarely)	p. 193
Northern Pygmy-Owl	p. 195
Spotted Owl (ssp. *caurina*) (rarely)	p. 279
Barred Owl	p. 197
Great Grey Owl	p. 282
Boreal Owl	p. 199

WOODPECKERS
Red-naped Sapsucker	p. 134
Williamson's Sapsucker	p. 130
Downy Woodpecker	p. 138
Hairy Woodpecker	p. 140
White-headed Woodpecker (rarely)	p. 142
American Three-toed Woodpecker	p. 144
Black-backed Woodpecker (rarely)	p. 154
Northern Flicker	p. 148
Pileated Woodpecker	p. 150

OTHER BIRDS
Vaux's Swift	p. 204
Tree Swallow	p. 206
Black-capped Chickadee	p. 154
Mountain Chickadee	p. 156
Boreal Chickadee	p. 160
Chestnut-backed Chickadee	p. 158
Red-breasted Nuthatch	p. 163
White-breasted Nuthatch (rarely)	p. 165
Brown Creeper	p. 208
House Wren	p. 210
Western Bluebird	p. 213
Mountain Bluebird	p. 215

BATS
California Myotis	p. 219
Western Long-eared Myotis (possible)	p. 221
Little Brown Myotis (possible)	p. 225
Long-legged Myotis	p. 229
Hoary Bat	p. 235
Silver-haired Bat	p. 237
Big Brown Bat	p. 239

OTHER MAMMALS
Northern Flying Squirrel	p. 246
Red-tailed Chipmunk	p. 248
Marten	p. 250
Fisher	p. 252
Black Bear	p. 254

PONDEROSA PINE (PP)

The small Ponderosa Pine zone occurs along the very dry valleys of B.C.'s southern Interior Plateau at elevations of 335–900 m. It is typically above the Bunchgrass zone and below the Interior Douglas-fir zone. Moister than the Bunchgrass zone, the Ponderosa Pine zone supports more forested habitat. The principle tree species, for which the zone is named, is an exceptional wildlife tree. As well, trembling aspen and Douglas-fir are common. The Ponderosa Pine zone is home to 54 wildlife tree–dependent species (82 percent of the provincial total).

AQUATIC BIRDS

Great Blue Heron	p. 261
Wood Duck	p. 171
Common Goldeneye	p. 177
Barrow's Goldeneye	p. 179
Bufflehead	p. 174
Hooded Merganser	p. 181
Common Merganser	p. 183

BIRDS OF PREY

Osprey	p. 264
Bald Eagle	p. 266
Northern Goshawk	p. 269
Red-tailed Hawk	p. 272
American Kestrel	p. 185
Flammulated Owl	p. 187
Western Screech-Owl	p. 190
Great Horned Owl	p. 277
Northern Hawk Owl (rarely)	p. 193
Northern Pygmy-Owl	p. 195
Barred Owl	p. 197
Great Grey Owl (rarely)	p. 282
Northern Saw-whet Owl	p. 201

WOODPECKERS

Lewis's Woodpecker	p. 126
Red-naped Sapsucker	p. 134
Red-breasted Sapsucker (rarely)	p. 136
Downy Woodpecker	p. 138
Hairy Woodpecker	p. 140
White-headed Woodpecker	p. 142
American Three-toed Woodpecker (rarely)	p. 144
Black-backed Woodpecker (rarely)	p. 154
Northern Flicker	p. 148
Pileated Woodpecker	p. 150

OTHER BIRDS

Vaux's Swift	p. 204
Tree Swallow	p. 206
Black-capped Chickadee	p. 154
Mountain Chickadee	p. 156
Pygmy Nuthatch	p. 167
Red-breasted Nuthatch	p. 163
White-breasted Nuthatch	p. 165
Brown Creeper	p. 208
House Wren	p. 210
Western Bluebird	p. 213
Mountain Bluebird	p. 215

BATS

California Myotis	p. 219
Western Long-eared Myotis (possible)	p. 221
Little Brown Myotis (possible)	p. 225
Long-legged Myotis	p. 229
Yuma Myotis	p. 231
Hoary Bat	p. 235
Silver-haired Bat	p. 237
Big Brown Bat	p. 239

OTHER MAMMALS

Northern Flying Squirrel	p. 246
Red-tailed Chipmunk	p. 248
Marten	p. 250
Fisher	p. 252
Black Bear	p. 254

SUB-BOREAL PINE–SPRUCE (SBPS)

The Sub-Boreal Pine–Spruce zone occurs at elevations of 850–1500 m on the gently rolling high Interior plateaus just south of central B.C., largely in the rain-shadow of the Coast Mountains. It generally occurs above the Interior Douglas-Fir zone or the Sub-boreal Spruce zone and below the Montane Spruce zone. White spruce and lodgepole pine are abundant. The Sub-Boreal Pine–Spruce zone is dry in both summer and winter, but it has extensive wetlands. Summers in this zone are cool, and winters are cold. Birds and mammals found here are either specifically adapted to cold winters or tend to be seasonal visitors. The Sub-Boreal Pine–Spruce zone has 46 wildlife tree–dependent species (70 percent of the provincial total).

AQUATIC BIRDS

Great Blue Heron	p. 261
Common Goldeneye	p. 177
Barrow's Goldeneye	p. 179
Bufflehead	p. 174
Common Merganser	p. 183
Hooded Merganser	p. 181

BIRDS OF PREY

Osprey	p. 264
Bald Eagle	p. 266
Northern Goshawk	p. 269
Red-tailed Hawk	p. 272
American Kestrel	p. 185
Great Horned Owl	p. 277

SUB-BOREAL SPRUCE (SBS)

The Sub-Boreal Spruce zone dominates the gently rolling plateaus in the central Interior at elevations of 1100–1300 m. This zone adjoins the Boreal Black and White Spruce zone in the northeast, the Interior Cedar–Hemlock zone in the wetter northwest and southeast, the Sub-Boreal Pine–Spruce zone in the dry southwest and part of the southeast and the Interior Douglas-fir zone in the south. The Engelmann Spruce–Subalpine Fir zone is typically the zone above it. Subalpine fir, white spruce, lodgepole pine and trembling aspen are abundant, and Douglas-fir, paper birch and black cottonwood are common. Wildlife species adapted to long, snowy winters hibernate or remain active in nests and tunnels beneath the snow, whereas other species migrate. Because of the extensive lakes and wetlands, this zone is the world's breeding centre for Barrow's goldeneye. The Sub-Boreal Spruce zone is home to 49 wildlife tree–dependent species (74 percent of the provincial total).

SPRUCE–WILLOW–BIRCH (SWB)

The Spruce–Willow–Birch zone occurs at 1000–1700 m in the south of its extent and 900–1500 m in the north, above the Boreal White and Black Spruce zone and below the untreed Alpine Tundra zone. This most northerly subalpine zone in British Columbia is replaced farther south and west by the Englemann Spruce–Subalpine Fir zone. Subalpine-fir and white spruce are abundant, but the severe climate greatly restricts tree sizes. The Spruce–Willow–Birch zone is home to 28 wildlife tree–dependent species (42 percent of the provincial total).

References

GENERAL REFERENCES

Acorn, J. and I. Sheldon. 2001. *Bugs of British Columbia*. Lone Pine Publishing, Edmonton, AB.

Backhouse, F. 1993. *Wildlife Tree Management in British Columbia*. Government of Canada and Province of British Columbia, Victoria, BC.

Baron, N. and J. Acorn. 1997. *Birds of Coastal British Columbia*. Lone Pine Publishing, Edmonton, AB.

British Columbia Ministry of Environment, Lands and Parks and British Columbia Ministry of Forests. 1995. *Managing Identified Wildlife Guidebook. Forest Practices Code of British Columbia*. Victoria, BC.

_____. 1995. *Biodiversity Guidebook. Forest Practices Code of British Columbia*. Victoria, BC.

British Columbia Ministry of Environment, Lands and Parks and Environment Canada. 1993. *State of the Environment Report for British Columbia*. Victoria, BC.

Bookhout, T.A., ed. 1994. *Research and Management Techniques for Wildlife and Habitats*. Fifth edition. The Wildlife Society, Bethesda, MD.

Campbell, R.W., N.K. Dawe, I. McTaggart-Cowan, J.M. Cooper, G.W. Kaiser and M.C.E. McNall. 1990. *Birds of British Columbia, Vol. 1: Loons through Waterfowl*. Royal British Columbia Museum and Canadian Wildlife Service, Victoria, BC.

_____. 1990. *Birds of British Columbia, Vol. 2: Diurnal Birds of Prey through Woodpeckers*. Royal British Columbia Museum and Canadian Wildlife Service, Victoria, BC.

Campbell, R.W., N.K. Dawe, I. McTaggart-Cowan, J.M. Cooper, G.W. Kaiser, M.C.E. McNall and G.E.J. Smith. 1997. *Birds of British Columbia, Vol. 3: Flycatchers through Vireos*. University of British Columbia Press, Vancouver, BC.

Campbell, R.W., K.H. Morgan and C. Palmateer. 1988. *Wildlife Habitat Handbooks for the Southern Interior Ecoprovince, Vol. 2: Species Notes for Selected Birds*. BC Ministry of Environment, BC Ministry of Forests and Wildlife Habitat Canada, Victoria, BC. Wildlife Report No. R-16.

Cannings, R.A., R.J. Cannings and S.G. Cannings. 1987. *Birds of the Okanagan Valley, British Columbia*. Royal British Columbia Museum, Victoria, BC.

Davis, J.W., G.A. Goodwin and R.A. Ockenfels, tech. eds. 1983. *Snag Management: Proceedings of the Symposium, 7–9 June 1983, Flagstaff, AZ*. USDA Forest Service, Rocky Mountain Forest and Range Experimental Station, Fort Collins, CO. General Technical Report RM-99.

Diaz, N. and D. Apostol. 1992. *Forest Landscape Analysis and Design: A Process for Developing and Implementing Land Management Objectives for Landscape Patterns*. USDA Forest Service, Pacific Northwest Region.

Dunster, K. and L. Dunster. 1996. *Dictionary of Natural Resource Management*. University of British Columbia Press, Vancouver, BC.

Ehrlich, P.R., D.S. Dobkin and D. Wheye. 1988. *The Birder's Handbook: A Field Guide to the Natural History of North American Birds*. Simon and Schuster, New York, NY.

Erskine, A.J. and W.D. McLaren. 1976. Comparative nesting biology of some hole-nesting birds in the Cariboo parklands, British Columbia. *Wilson Bulletin* 88:611–619.

Fenger, M.A., E.H. Miller, J.A. Johnson and E.J.R. Williams, eds. 1993. *Our Living Legacy: Proceedings of a Symposium on Biological Diversity.* Royal British Columbia Museum, Victoria, BC.

Forman, R.T.T. 1995. *Land Mosaics: The Ecology of Landscapes and Regions.* Cambridge University Press.

Guy, S. and T. Manning. 1995. *Wildlife/Danger Tree Assessor's Course Workbook. Fourth edition.* BC Ministry of Environment, BC Ministry of Forests and Worker's Compensation Board of BC, Victoria, BC.

Harding, L.E. and E. McCullum, eds. 1994. *Biodiversity in British Columbia: Our Changing Environment.* Environment Canada and Canadian Wildlife Service, Pacific and Yukon Region, Vancouver, BC.

Harris, L.D. 1984. *The Fragmented Forest: Island Biogeography Theory and the Preservation of Biotic Diversity.* University of Chicago Press, Chicago, IL.

Machmer, M.M. and C. Steeger. 1995. *The Ecological Roles of Wildlife Tree Users in Forest Ecosystems.* BC Ministry of Forests, Research Branch, Victoria, BC. Land Management Handbook 35.

Manning, T. 1995. *Stand Level Biodiversity for Forest Managers.* Course Workbook. BC Ministry of Forests and BC Ministry of Environment, Victoria, BC.

Maser, C. 1994. *Sustainable Forestry: Philosophy, Science and Economics.* St. Lucie Press, Delray Beach, FL.

_____. 1988. *The Redesigned Forest.* R & E Miles, San Pedro, CA.

Meidinger, D. and J. Pojar. 1991. *Ecosystems of British Columbia.* BC Ministry of Forests, Victoria, BC.

Ministry of Environment Lands and Parks, September 14, 1999. *Inventory Methods for Woodpeckers, Version 2.0. Standards for Components of British Columbia's Biodiversity No. 19.* Terrestrial Ecosystem Task Force, Resources Inventory Committee.

_____. February 1998. *Inventory Methods for Bats; Standards for Components of British Columbia's Biodiversity No. 20, Version 2.0.* Resources Inventory Branch for the Terrestrial Ecosystems Task Force Resources Inventory Committee.

_____. May 12, 1998. *Inventory Methods for Bears, Standards for Components of British Columbia's Biodiversity No. 21.* Resources Inventory Branch for the Terrestrial Ecosystems Task Force Resources Inventory Committee.

_____. November 2, 1998. *Inventory Methods for Marten and Weasels. Version 2.0. Standards for Components of British Columbia's Biodiversity No. 24.* Resources Inventory Branch for the Terrestrial Ecosystems Task Force Resources Inventory Committee.

_____. October 6, 1998. *Inventory Methods for Mountain Beaver, Bushy-tailed Woodrat & Porcupine. Version 2.0. Standards for Components of British Columbia's Biodiversity No. 27.* Resources Inventory Branch for the Terrestrial Ecosystems Task Force Resources Inventory Committee.

_____. April, 10, 2001. *Inventory Methods for Marbled Murrelets in Marine and Terrestrial Habitats. Version 2.0. Standards for Components of British Columbia's Biodiversity No. 10.* Resources Inventory Branch for the Terrestrial Ecosystems Task Force Resources Inventory Committee.

_____. October, 2001. *Inventory Methods for Raptors. Version 2.0. Standards for Components of British Columbia's Biodiversity No. 11*. Resources Inventory Branch for the Terrestrial Ecosystems Task Force Resources Inventory Committee.

_____. March 1998. *Inventory Methods for Swallows and Swifts. Version 2.0. Standards for Components of British Columbia's Biodiversity No. 16*. Resources Inventory Branch for the Terrestrial Ecosystems Task Force Resources Inventory Committee.

_____. March 16, 1999. *Inventory Methods for Forest and Grassland Songbirds. Version 2.0. Standards for Components of British Columbia's Biodiversity No. 15*. Resources Inventory Branch for the Terrestrial Ecosystems Task Force Resources Inventory Committee.

_____. June 1999. *Inventory Methods for Medium-sized Territorial Carnivores: Coyote, Red Fox, Lynx, Bobcat, Wolverine, Fisher & Badger. Version 2.0. Standards for Components of British Columbia's Biodiversity No. 25*. Resources Inventory Branch for the Terrestrial Ecosystems Task Force Resources Inventory Committee.

_____. May 11, 1999. *Inventory Methods for Waterfowl and Allied Species: Loons, Grebes, Swans, Geese, Ducks, American Coot and Sandhill Crane. Version 2.0. Standards for Components of British Columbia's Biodiversity No.18*. Resources Inventory Branch for the Terrestrial Ecosystem Task Force Resources Inventory Committee.

Morgan, K.H. and M.A. Lashmer, eds. 1993. *Riparian Habitat Management and Research: Proceedings of a Workshop, 4–5 May 1993, Kamloops, BC*. Environment Canada and BC Forestry Continuing Studies Network.

Nagorsen, D.W. 1990. *Mammals of British Columbia: A Taxonomic Catalogue*. Memoir No. 4, Royal British Columbia Museum and BC Ministry of Environment, Wildlife Branch, Victoria, BC.

_____. 2002. *An Identification Manual to the Small Mammals of British Columbia*. BC Ministry of Sustainable Resource Management, BC Ministry of Water, Land and Air Protection and Royal British Columbia Museum, Victoria, BC.

Neitro, W.A., V.W. Binkley, S.P. Cline, R.W. Mannan, B.G. Marcot, D. Taylor and F.F. Wagner. 1985. Snags (wildlife trees). E.R. Brown, ed. *Management of Wildlife and Fish Habitats in Forests of Western Oregon and Washington, Part 1: Chapter Narratives*, 129-235. USDA Forest Service, Portland, OR.

Patton, D.R. 1992. *Wildlife Habitat Relationships in Forested Ecosystems*. Timber Press, Portland, OR.

Stevens V. and S. Lofts. 1988. *Wildlife Habitat Handbooks for the Southern Interior Ecoprovince, Vol. 1: Species Notes for Mammals*. BC Ministry of Environment, BC Ministry of Forests and Wildlife Habitat Canada, Victoria, BC. Wildlife Report No. R-15.

Thomas, J.W., tech. ed. 1979. *Wildlife Habitats in Managed Forests in the Blue Mountains of Oregon and Washington*. USDA Forest Service Handbook No. 553.

Voller, J. and S. Harrison. 1998. *Conservation Biology Principles for Forested Landscapes*. University of British Columbia Press, Vancouver, BC.

Wildlife Tree Committee of British Columbia. 1991. *A Bibliography of Selected Literature on Wildlife Trees with Annotations and Abstracts*. BC Ministry of Environment, Lands and Parks, Wildlife Branch, Victoria, BC. Wildlife Working Report WR-66.

Wooding, F.H. 1982. *Wild Mammals of Canada*. McGraw-Hill Ryerson, Toronto, ON.

Wright, V. and B. Wales. 1993. *Bibliography of Selected Literature Regarding the Management of Cavity Excavators in Eastside Habitats: Oregon and Washington.* Wildlife Habitat Relationships Program, USDA Forest Service Pacific Forest Region.

BATS: SELECTED LITERATURE

Aldridge, H.D.J.N. and L. Rautenbach. 1987. Morphology, echolocation and resource partitioning in insectivorous bats. *Journal of Animal Ecology* 56:763–778.

Barbour, R.W. and W.H. Davis. 1969. *Bats of America*. University Press, Lexington, KY.

Barclay, R.M.R. 1985. A non-commensal maternity roost of the little brown bat (*Myotis lucifugus*). *Journal of Mammalogy* 66(4):782–783.

_____. 1982. Night roosting behaviour of the little brown bat, *Myotis lucifugus*. *Journal of Mammalogy* 63(3):464–474.

Barclay, R.M.R., P.A. Faure and D.R. Farr. 1988. Roosting behaviour and roost selection by migrating silver-haired bats (*Lasionycteris noctivagan*). *Journal of Mammalogy* 69(4):821–825.

Bradbury, S.M., S. Morris and S. McNally, S. 1997. *Bat Survey of the Liard River Watershed in British Columbia: The Lower Liard River and Highway 77 Area.* BC Ministry of Environment, Lands and Parks, Wildlife Branch, Victoria, BC. Unpublished report.

Brigham, R.M. 1991. Flexibility in foraging and roosting behaviour by the big brown bat (*Eptesicus fuscus*). *Canadian Journal of Zoology* 69:117–121.

Christy, R.E. and S.D. West. 1993. *Biology of bats in a Douglas-fir forest*. USDA Forest Service, Portland, OR.

Collard, T.S., S.D. Grindall and R.M. Brigham. 1990. *Identification of the Status and Critical Habitats of Spotted Bat* (Euderma maculatum), *Pallid Bat* (Antrozous pallidus) *and Fringed Bat* (Myotis thysanodes) *in the South Okanagan and Similkameen Valleys, British Columbia*. World Wildlife Canada and BC Ministry of Environment. Unpublished report.

Fenton, M.B. and R.M.R. Barclay. 1980. *Myotis lucifugus*. *Mammalogy Species* 142:1–8.

Fenton, M.B., H.G. Merriam and S.L. Holroyd. 1983. Bats of Kootenay, Glacier, and Mount Revelstoke national parks in Canada: identification by echolocation calls, distribution and biology. *Canadian Journal of Zoology* 61:2503–2508.

Fenton, M.B., C.G. van Zyll de Jong, G.P. Bell, D.B. Campbell and M. Laplante. 1980. Distribution, parturition dates and feeding of bats in south-central British Columbia. *Canadian Field-Naturalist* 94(4):416–420.

Firman, M., M. Getty and R.M.R. Barclay. 1992. Status of Keen's Long-eared Myotis (*Myotis keenii*) in British Columbia. BC Ministry of Environment, Lands and Parks, Wildlife Branch, Victoria, BC. Technical Working Report WR-59.

Fitch, J.H. and K.A. Shump, Jr. 1979. *Myotis keenii. Mammalogy Species* 121:1-3.

Holroyd, S.L., R.M.R. Barclay, L.M. Merk and R.M. Brigham. 1993. *A Survey of the Bat Fauna of the Dry Interior of British Columbia: A Summary by Species with Recommendations for Future Work.* BC Ministry of Environment, Land and Parks, Victoria, BC. Technical Working Report WR 63.

Krutszch, P.H. 1954. Notes on the habits of the bat *Myotis californicus*. *Journal of Mammalogy* 35:539–45.

Kunz, T.H. 1982. Roosting ecology. In *Ecology of Bats*, ed. T.H. Kunz, 1–55. Plenum Press, New York, NY.

_____. 1982. *Lasionycteris noctivagans*. *Mammalogy Species* 172:1–5.

Kurta, A. and R.H. Baker. 1990. *Eptesicus fuscus*. *Mammalogy Species* 356:1–10.

Manning, R.W. and J.K. Jones, Jr. 1989. *Myotis evotis*. *Mammalogy Species* 329:1–5.

Mayle, B.A. 1990. *Habitat Management for Woodland Bats*. For. Comm., Research Information Note 165:1–3.

Nagorsen, D.W. and R.M. Brigham. 1993. *Bats of British Columbia*. Royal British Columbia Museum Handbook, Mammals of British Columbia Vol. 1. University of British Columbia Press, Vancouver, BC.

Nagorsen, D., A.A. Bryant, D. Kerridge, G. Roberts and M.J. Sarell, 1993. Winter bat records for British Columbia. *Northwestern Naturalist* 74:61–66.

Perkins, J.M. and S.P. Cross. 1988. Differential use of some coniferous forest habitats by hoary and silver-haired bats in Oregon. *Murrelet* 69:21–24.

Rainey, W.E., E.D. Pierson, M. Colberg and J.H. Barclay. 1992. *Bats in hollow redwoods: seasonal use and role in nutrient transfer into old growth communities*. Proceedings of the 22nd Annual North American Symposium on Bat Research, Quebec City, PQ.

Rasheed, S.A. and S.L. Holroyd. 1995. *Roosting Habitat and Inventory Assessment of Bats in the Mica Wildlife Compensation Area*. BC Hydro, BC Ministry of Environment, Lands and Parks and Canadian National Park Service. Unpublished report.

Schowalter, D.B. 1980. New records of British Columbia bats. *Syesis* 13:1–3.

Shump, K.A. and A.U. Shump. 1982. *Lasiurus borealis*. *Mammalogy Species* 183:1–6.

_____. 1982. *Lasiurus cinereus*. *Mammalogy Species* 185:1–5.

Thomas, D.W. 1988. The distribution of bats in different ages of Douglas-fir forests. *Journal of Wildlife Management* 52(4):619–696.

Tuttle, M.D. 1988. *America's Neighborhood Bats: Understanding and Learning to Live in Harmony with Them*. University of Texas Press, Austin, TX.

van Zyll de Jong, C.G. 1985. *Handbook of Canadian Mammals Vol. 2: Bats*. National Museum of Natural Science and National Museum of Canada.

van Zyll de Jong, C.G., M.B. Fenton and J.G. Woods. 1980. Occurrences of *Myotis californicus* at Revelstoke and a second record of *Myotis septentrionalis* from British Columbia. *Canadian Field-Naturalist* 94:455–456.

Vonhof, M.J., S. McNalley and A. Yu. 1997. *Roosting Habitat Requirements of Northern Long-eared Bats* (Myotis septentrionalis) *in Northern British Columbia: The Fort Nelson River and Highway 77 Area*. BC Ministry of Environment, Lands and Parks, Fort St. John, BC. Unpublished report.

Warner, R.M. and N.J. Czaplewski. 1984. *Myotis volans*. *Mammalogy Species* 224:1–4.

Wilkenson, L.C., P.F.J. Garcia and R.M.R. Barclay. 1995. *Bat Survey of the Liard River Watershed in Northern British Columbia*. BC Ministry of Environment, Lands and Parks, Victoria, BC.

GREAT BLUE HERON: SELECTED LITERATURE

Butler, R.W. 1992. Great Blue Heron. In *The Birds of North America, No. 25*, eds. A. Poole and F. Gill. Academy of Natural Sciences, Philadelphia, PA, and American Ornithologists' Union, Washington, DC.

Butler, R.W. 1989. Breeding ecology and population trends of the Great Blue Heron (*Ardea herodias fannini*) in the Strait of Georgia. K. Vermeer and R.W. Butler, eds. *The Ecology and Status of Marine and Shoreline Birds in the Strait of Georgia, British Columbia*, 112-117. Canadian Wildlife Service, Delta, BC.

_____. 1991. *A Review of the Biology and Conservation of the Great Blue Heron* (Ardea herodias) *in British Columbia*. Canadian Wildlife Service, Delta, BC. Technical Report Series No. 154.

Forbes, L.S. 1986. The timing and direction of food flights from an inland great blue heron colony. *Canadian Journal of Zoology* 64:667–669.

Forbes, L.S., K. Simpson, J.P. Kelsall and D.R. Flook. 1985. Reproductive success of great blue herons in British Columbia. *Canadian Journal of Zoology* 63:1110–1113.

Hancock, J. and J. Kushlan. 1984. *The Herons Handbook*. Croom Helm, London, UK.

Mark, D.M. 1976. An inventory of great blue heron (*Ardea herodias*) nesting colonies in British Columbia. *Northwest Science* 50:32–41.

MARBLED MURRELET: SELECTED LITERATURE

Carter, H.R. and S.G. Sealy. 1986. Year-round use of coastal lakes by Marbled Murrelets. *Condor* 88:473–477.

Eisenhawer, A.E. and T.E. Reimchen. 1990. Inland flight patterns of marbled murrelets (*Brachyramphus marmoratus*) on the Queen Charlotte Islands, British Columbia. *Canadian Field-Naturalist* 104:439–444.

Harrison, P. 1985. *Seabirds: An Identification Guide*. Houghton Mifflin, Boston, MA.

Kaiser, G.W., H.J. Barclay, A.E. Burger, D. Kangasniemi, D.J. Lindsay, W.T. Munro, W.R. Pollard, R. Redhead, J. Rice and D. Seip. 1994. *National Recovery Plan for the Marbled Murrelet*. Recovery of Nationally Endangered Wildlife Committee, Ottawa, ON. RENEW Report No. 8.

Mahon, T.E., G.W. Kaiser and A.E. Burger. 1992. The role of marbled murrelets in mixed-species feeding flocks in British Columbia. *Wilson Bulletin* 104:738–743.

Nelson, S.K. and S.G. Sealy. 1995. Biology of the marbled murrelet: inland and at sea. *Northwestern Naturalist* 76.

Ralph, C.J., G.L. Hunt, M.G. Raphael and J.F. Piatt. 1995. *Ecology and conservation of the Marbled Murrelet*. USDA Forest Service, Albany, CA. General Technical Report PSW-GTR-152.

Rodway, M.S. 1991. Status and conservation of breeding seabirds in British Columbia. In *Seabird Status and Conservation*, ed. J.P. Croxall, 43–102. ICBP, Cambridge, UK. Technical Publication No. 11.

RAPTORS: SELECTED LITERATURE

Aborn, D.A. 1994. Correlation between raptor and songbird numbers at a migratory stopover site. *Wilson Bulletin* 106:150–154.

Adamcik, R.S. and L.B. Keith. 1978. Regional movements and mortality of great horned owls in relation to snowshoe hare populations. *Canadian Field-Naturalist* 92:228–234.

Anthony, R.G., R.L. Knight, G.T. Allen, B.R. McClelland and J.J. Hodges. 1982. *Habitat use by nesting and roosting bald eagles in the Pacific Northwest*. Transactions of the North American Wildlife and Natural Resources Conference 47:332–342.

Baker, J.C. and R.J. Brooks. 1984. Distribution patterns of raptors in relation to density of meadow voles. *Condor* 86:42–47.

Balda, R.P., B.C., McKnight and C.D. Johnson. 1975. Flammulated owl migration in the southwestern United States. *Wilson Bulletin* 87:520–533.

Balgooyen, T.G. 1976. Behavior and ecology of the American kestrel in the Sierra Nevada of California. *University of California Publications in Zoology* 10:31–86.

Barrows C. 1981. Roost selection by spotted owls: an adaptation to heat stress. *Condor* 83:302–309.

Bechard, M.J., R.L. Knight, D.G. Smith and R.E. Fitzner. 1990. Nest sites and habitats of sympatric hawks (*Buteo* spp.) in Washington. *Journal of Field Ornithology* 61:159–170.

Beebe, F.L. 1974. Field Studies of the Falconiformes of British Columbia. British Columbia Provincial Museum, Victoria, BC. Occasional Paper No. 17.

Bent, A.C. 1938. *Life Histories of North American Birds of Prey.* US National Museum Bulletin 170.

Blackburn, I.R. 1991. *The distribution, habitat selection and status of the northern spotted owl in southwestern British Columbia, 1991.* BC Ministry of Environment, Surrey, BC. Unpublished report.

Block, W.M., M.L. Morrison and M.H. Reiser. 1994. *The Northern Goshawk: Ecology and Management. Cooper Ornithological Society, Lawrence, KS.* Studies in Avian Biology No. 16.

Blood, D.A. and G.W. Anweiler. 1991. *Status of the Bald Eagle in British Columbia.* BC Ministry of Environment, Wildlife Branch, Victoria, BC. Unpublished report.

Bloom, P.H. and S.J. Hawks. 1983. Nest box use and reproductive biology of the American kestrel in Lassen County, California. *Journal of Raptor Research* 17:9–14.

Buchanan, J.B. 1989. Alarm calls, habituation and falcon predation on shorebirds. *Wader Study Group Bulletin* 55:26–29.

Bull, E.L. and J.R. Duncan. 1993. Great Grey Owl. A. Poole and F. Gill, eds. *The Birds of North America, No. 41.* Academy of Natural Sciences, Philadelphia, PA, and American Ornithologists' Union, Washington, DC.

Bull, E.L., A. Wright and M.G. Henjum. 1990. Nesting habitat of flammulated owls in Oregon. *Journal of Raptor Research* 24:52–55.

Burton, J.A. 1984. *Owls of the World: Their Evolution, Structure and Ecology.* Tanager Books, Dover.

Canadian Spotted Owl Recovery Team. 1994. *Management options for the northern spotted owl in British Columbia.* BC Ministry of Environment, Victoria, BC.

Cannings, R.J. 1993. Northern Saw-whet Owl. A. Poole and F. Gill, eds. *The Birds of North America, No. 42.* Academy of Natural Sciences, Philadelphia, PA, and American Ornithologists' Union, Washington, DC.

Carey, A.B., S.P. Horton and B.L. Biswell. 1992. Northern spotted owls: influence of prey base and landscape character. *Ecological Monographs* 62:223–250.

Cooper, J.M. 1990. Bald eagles hunting waterfowl at Delkatla Inlet, Queen Charlotte Islands. Vancouver Natural History Society. *Discovery* 19:94–95.

Clark, W.S. and B.K. Wheeler. 1987. *A Field Guide to Hawks of North America.* Houghlin Mifflin, Boston, MA.

Craighead, J.J. and F.C. Craighead, Jr. 1956. *Hawks, Owls and Wildlife.* Dover, New York, NY.

Crocker-Bedford, D.C. 1990. Goshawk reproduction and forest management. *Wildlife Society Bulletin* 18:262–269.

Dixon, K.R. and T.C. Juelson. 1987. The political economy of the spotted owl. *Ecology* 68:772–776.

Doody, J.S. 1994. Winter roost-site use by female American kestrels (*Falco sparverisus*) in Louisiana. *Journal of Raptor Research* 28:9–12.

Dunbar, D.L., B.P. Booth, E.D. Forsman, A.E. Hetherington and D.J. Wilson. 1991. Status of the spotted owl (*Strix occidentalis*) and barred owl (*Stix varia*) in southwestern British Columbia. *Canadian Field-Naturalist* 105:464–468.

Dunstan, T.C. and B.E. Harrell. 1973. Spatio-temporal relationships between breeding red-tailed hawks and great horned owls in South Dakota. *Journal of Raptor Research* 7:49–54.

Earhart, C.M. and N.K. Johnson. 1970. Size dimorphism and food habits of North American owls. *Condor* 72:251–264.

Ethier, T. 1994. *Survey Methods for Raptors in British Columbia*. Resources Inventory Committee and BC Ministry of Environment, Wildlife Branch, Victoria, BC. Draft manual.

Farr, A. 1987. *Managing Habitat for Bald Eagles in the Fraser Valley of British Columbia: 1986-1987 Observations*. BC Ministry of Environment, Lands and Parks. Unpublished report.

Fielder, P.C. 1982. Food habits of bald eagles along the mid-Columbia River, Washington. *Murrelet* 65:22–25.

Forbes, L.S. and G.W. Kaiser. 1984. Observations of breeding bald eagles in southeastern British Columbia. *Murrelet* 65:22–25.

Forsman, E.D., E.C. Meslow and H.M. Wight. 1984. Distribution and biology of the spotted owl in Oregon. *Wildlife Monographs* 87.

Gieck, C.M. 1991. Artificial nesting structures for bald eagles, ospreys and American kestrels. Pendleton, B.G. and D.L. Krahe, eds. *Proceedings of the Midwest Raptor Management Symposium and Workshop*. National Wildlife Federation, Washington, DC, 215-221. Scientific and Technical Series No. 15.

Glinski, R.L., T.G. Grubb and L.A. Forbis. 1983. *Snag use by selected raptors*. Snag Habitat Management Symposium, 7–9 June 1983, Flagstaff, AZ.

Gutierrez, R.J. and A.B. Carey. 1985. *Ecology and Management of the Spotted Owl in the Pacific Northwest*. USDA Forest Service, General Technical Report PNW-185.

Hamerstrom, F., F.N. Hamerstrom and J. Hart. 1973. Nest boxes: an effective management tool for kestrels. *Journal of Wildlife Management* 37:400–403.

Hansen, R.W. and L.D. Flake. 1995. Ecological relationships between nesting Swainson's and red-tailed hawks in southeastern Idaho. *Journal of Raptor Research* 29:166–171.

Harrison, K.G. 1977. Perch height selection of grassland birds. *Wilson Bulletin* 89:486-487.

Hayward, G.D. and E.O. Garton. 1984. Roost habitat selection by three small forest owls. *Wilson Bulletin* 96:690–692.

Hayward, G.D. and P. Hayward. 1993. Boreal Owl. A. Poole and F. Gill, eds. *The Birds of North America, No. 63*. Academy of Natural Sciences, Philadelphia, PA, and American Ornithologists' Union, Washington, DC.

Hayward, G.D., P.H. Hayward and E.O. Garton. 1993. Ecology of boreal owls in the northern Rocky Mountains, USA. *Wildlife Monographs* 124:1–59.

Hayward, G.D., P.H. Hayward, E.O. Garton and R. Escano. 1987. Revised breeding distribution of the Boreal Owl in the northern Rocky Mountains. *Condor* 89:431–432.

Hayward, G.D. and J. Verner. 1994. *Flammulated, Boreal and Great Grey Owls in the United States: A Technical Conservation Assessment.* USDA Forest Service, Fort Collins, CO. General Technical Report RM-253.

Hodges, J.I., E.L. Boeker and A.J. Hansen. 1987. Movements of radio-tagged bald eagles (*Haliaeetus leucocephalus*) in and from southeastern Alaska. *Canadian Field Naturalist* 101:136–140.

Hunt, W.G., J.M. Jenkins, R.E. Jackman, C.G. Thelander and A.T. Gerstell. 1992. Foraging ecology of bald eagles on a regulated river. *Journal of Raptor Research* 26:243–256.

Hunt, W.G., B.S. Johnson and R.E. Jackman. 1992. Carrying capacity for bald eagles wintering along a northwestern river. *Journal of Raptor Research* 26:49–60.

Janes, S.W. 1984. Influences of territory composition and interspecific competition on red-tailed hawk reproductive success. *Ecology* 65:862–870.

_____. 1984. Fidelity to breeding territory in a population of red-tailed hawks. *Condor* 86:200–203.

Johnsgard, P. 1988. *Owls of North America.* Smithsonian Institution Press, Washington, DC.

Johnson, D.R. 1989. Body size of northern goshawks on coastal islands of British Columbia. *Wilson Bulletin* 101:637–639.

Lamberson, R.H., R. McKelvey, B.R. Noon and C. Voss. 1992. A dynamic analysis of northern spotted owl viability in a fragmented landscape. *Biology Conservation* 6:505–512.

Luttich, S.N., L.B. Keith and J.B. Stephenson. 1971. Population dynamics of the red-tailed hawk (*Buteo jamaicensis*) at Rochester, Alberta. *Auk* 88:75–87.

Marshall, D.B. 1992. *Threatened and Sensitive Wildlife of Oregon's Forest and Woodlands.* Audubon Society of Portland, Portland, OR.

McCallum, D.A. 1994. Flammulated Owl. A. Poole and F. Gill, eds. *The Birds of North America, No. 93.* Academy of Natural Sciences, Philadelphia, PA, and American Ornithologists' Union, Washington, DC.

McInvaille, W.B. and L.B . Keith. 1974. Predator-prey relationships and breeding biology of the great horned owl and red-tailed hawk in central Alberta. *Canadian Field-Naturalist* 88:1–20.

Moore, K.R. and C.J. Henny. 1983. Nest site characteristics of three coexisting accipiter hawks in northeastern Oregon. *Journal of Raptor Research* 17:65–76.

Mueller, H.C. 1977. Prey selection in the American kestrel: experiments with two species of prey. *American Naturalist* 111:25–29.

Nero, R.W. 1980. *The Great Grey Owl: Phantom of the Northern Forest.* Smithsonian University Press, Washington, DC.

Nero, R.W., R.J. Clark, R.J. Knapton and R.H. Hamre, eds. n.d. *Biology and Conservation of Northern Forest Owls.* USDA Forest Service, Fort Collins, CO. General Technical Report RM-142.

Newton, I. 1976. Population limitation in diurnal raptors. *Canadian Field-Naturalist* 90:274–300.

Nicholls, T.H. and D.W. Warner. 1972. Barred owl habitat use as determined by radiotelemetry. *Journal of Wildlife Management* 36:213–224.

Poole, A.F. 1985. Courtship feeding and osprey reproduction. *Auk* 102:479–492.

_____. 1989. *Ospreys: A natural and Unnatural History*. Cambridge University Press, Cambridge, NY.

Preston, C.R. and R.D. Beane. 1993. Red-tailed Hawk. A. Poole and F. Gill, eds. *The Birds of North America, No. 52*. Academy of Natural Sciences, Philadelphia, PA, and American Ornithologists' Union, Washington, DC.

Reynolds, R.T. 1983. *Management of Western Coniferous Forest Habitat for Nesting Accipiter Hawks*. USDA Forest Service, Fort Collins, CO. General Technical Report RM-102.

Reynolds, R.T., R.T. Graham, M.H. Reiser; R.L. Bassett, P.L. Kennedy, D.A. Boyce, G. Goodwin, R. Smith and E.L. Fisher. 1992. *Management Recommendations for the Northern Goshawk in the Southwestern United States*. USDA Forest Service, Fort Collins, CO. General Technical Report RM-217.

Reynolds, R.T. and E.C. Meslow. 1984. Partitioning of food and niche characteristics of coexisting accipiter during breeding. *Auk* 101:761–779.

Reynolds, R.T., E.C. Meslow and H.M. Wight. 1982. Nesting habitat of coexisting accipiter in Oregon. *Journal of Wildlife Management* 46:124–138.

Runyan, C.S. 1987. Location and density of nests of the red-tailed hawk, *Buteo jamaicensis*, in Richmond, British Columbia. *Canadian Field Naturalist* 101:415–418.

Schmutz, J.K., S.M. Schmutz and D.A. Boag. 1980. Coexistence of three species of hawks (*Buteo* spp.) in the prairie-parkland ecotone. *Canadian Journal of Zoology* 58:1075–1089.

Schnell, G.D. 1968. Different habitat utilization by wintering rough-legged and red-tailed hawks. *Condor* 70:373–377.

Shuster, W.C. 1980. Northern goshawk nest site requirements in the Colorado Rockies. *Western Birds* 11:89–96.

Smith, D.G., C.R. Wilson and H.H. Frost. 1972. The biology of the American kestrel in central Utah. *Southwestern Naturalist* 17:73–83.

Speiser, R. 1990. Nest site characteristics of red-tailed hawks in western Washington. *Northwestern Naturalist* 71:95–97.

Spotted Owl Management Inter-agency Team. 1997. *Spotted Owl Management Plan*. Province of BC.

Stalmaster, M.V. and J.A. Gessaman. 1984. Ecological energetics and foraging behavior of overwintering bald eagles. *Ecological Monographs* 54:407–428.

Stalmaster, M.V. and J.R. Newman, 1978. Behavioral responses of wintering bald eagles to human activity. *Journal of Wildlife Management* 42:506–513.

Stalmaster, M.V. 1980. Salmon carrion as a winter food source for red-tailed hawks. *Murrelet* 61:43–44.

Steeger, C., H. Esselink and R.C. Ydenberg. 1992. Comparative feeding ecology and reproductive performance of ospreys in different habitats of southeastern BC. *Canadian Journal of Zoology* 70:470–475.

Steenhof, K. and J.M. Brown. 1978. *Management of Wintering Bald Eagles*. USDI Fish and Wildlife Service, Washington, DC. FWS/OBS-78/79.

Stinson, C.H. 1980. Weather-dependent foraging success and sibling aggression in red-tailed hawks in central Washington. *Condor* 82:76–80.

St. John, D. 1991. *The distribution of the flammulated owl* (Otus flammeolus) *in the south Okanagan*. BC Ministry of Environment, Penticton, BC. Unpublished report.

Sullivan, T.M. 1992. Populations, distribution and habitat requirements of birds of prey. R.W. Butler. ed. *Abundance, Distribution and Conservation of Birds in the Vicinity of Boundary Bay, British Columbia*, 86–108. Canadian Wildlife Service, Delta, BC.

Swengel, S.R. and A.B. Swengel. 1992. Roosts of northern saw-whet owls in southern Wisconsin. *Condor* 94:699–706.

Szuba, K. and P. Bell. 1991. *Hawk Guide for Ministry of Natural Resources Field Personnel*. Ontario Ministry of Natural Resources, Wildlife Policy Branch.

Titus, K. and J.A. Mosher. 1981. Nest-site habitat selected by woodland hawks in the central Appalachians. *Auk* 98:270–281.

Toland, B.R. and W.H. Elder. 1987. Influence of nest-box placement and density on abundance and productivity of American kestrels in central Missouri. *Wilson Bulletin* 99:712–717.

Van Daele, L.G. and H.A. Van Daele. 1982. Factors affecting the productivity of ospreys nesting in west-central Idaho. *Condor* 84:292–299.

van Woudenberg, A.M. 1992. *Integrated Management of Flammulated Owl Breeding Habitat and Timber Harvest in British Columbia*. M.Sc. Thesis, University of British Columbia, Vancouver, BC.

Varland, D.E., E.E. Klaas and T.M. Loughin. 1993. Use of habitat and perches, causes of mortality and time until dispersal in post-fledging American kestrels. *Journal of Field Ornithology* 64:169–178.

Wheeler, A.H. 1992. Reproductive parameters for free ranging American kestrels (*Falco sparverius*) using next boxes in Montana and Wyoming. *Journal of Raptor Research* 26:6–9.

TERRESTRIAL MAMMALS: SELECTED LITERATURE

Akenson, J.J. and M.B. Henjum. 1994. Black bear den site selection in the Starkey study area. Blue Mountains Natural Resources Institute. *Natural Resource News* 4(2):1–2.

Allen, A.W. 1982. *Habitat suitability index models: Marten*. USDI Fish and Wildlife Service. Habitat Suitability Index (HSI) Series.FWS/OBS-82/10.11.

_____. 1983. *Habitat suitability index models: Fisher*. USDI Fish and Wildlife Service. Habitat Suitability Index (HSI) Series. FWS/OBS-82/10.45.

Baker, J.M. 1992. *Habitat Use and Spatial Organization of Pine Marten on Southern Vancouver Island, British Columbia*. M.Sc. Thesis, Simon Fraser University, Burnaby, BC.

Banci, V. 1989. *A Fisher Management Strategy for British Columbia*. BC Ministry of Environment, Victoria, BC. Wildlife Bulletin B-63.

British Columbia Ministry of Environment, Lands and Parks. 1994. *Maintaining Marten Habitat in Managed Forests*. Fish and Wildlife Branch, Thompson Nicola Region and Wildlife Branch, Victoria, BC.

Burt, W.H. and R.P. Grossenheider. 1976. *A Field Guide to the Mammals*. Third edition. Houghton Mifflin Co., Boston, MA.

Buskirk, S.W., A.S. Harestad, M.G. Raphael and R.A. Powell. 1994. *Martens, Sables, and Fishers: Biology and Conservation*. Comstock Publishing, Ithaca, NY.

Corn, J.G. and M.G. Raphael. 1992. Habitat characteristics at marten subnivean access sites. *Journal of Wildlife Management* 56(3):442–448.

Cowan, I. and C.J. Guiguet. 1965. *The Mammals of British Columbia*. British Columbia Provincial Museum, Victoria, BC. Handbook 11.

Hall, R.E. 1981. *The Mammals of North America. Volume 1 and 2.* Second edition. John Wiley and Sons, New York, NY.

Jonkel, C.J. and I. M. Cowan. 1971. The black bear in the spruce-fir forests. In *Wildlife Society*, ed. L.A. Krumholz. Wildlife Monographs.

Koehler, G.M., J.A. Blakesley and T.W. Koehler. 1990. Marten use of successional forest stages during winter in north-central Washington. *Northwest Naturalist* 71:1–4.

Lindzey, F.G. and C.E. Meslow. 1976. Characteristics of black bear dens on Long Island, Washington. *Northwest Science* 50(4):236–242.

Lofroth, E.C. 1993. *Scale dependent analyses of habitat selection by marten in the Subboreal Spruce biogeoclimatic zone, British Columbia.* M.Sc. Thesis, Simon Fraser University, Burnaby, BC.

Lofroth, E.C. and V. Banci. 1990. *Marten Habitat Suitability Research Project: Working Plan.* BC Ministry of Environment, Victoria, BC. Wildlife Working Report WR-50.

Lofroth, E.C. and J.D. Steventon. 1990. Managing for marten winter habitat in interior forests of British Columbia. A. Chambers, ed. *Wildlife Forestry Symposium: A Workshop on Resource Integration for Wildlife and Forest Manager*, 66-76. FRDA 160.

Loucks, D.M., H.C. Black, M.L. Roush and S.R. Radosevich. 1990. *Assessment and Management of Animal Damage in Pacific Northwest Forests: An Annotated Bibliography.* USDA Forest Service, Portland, OR. General Technical Report PNW-GTR-262.

Maser, C., B.R. Mate, J.F. Franklin and C.T. Dyrness. 1981. *Natural History of Oregon Coast Mammals.* USDA Forest Service, Portland, OR. PNW-133.

Morley, R.A. and J.C. Zasada. 1984. Den tree use and movements of northern flying squirrels in interior Alaska and implications for forest management. W.R. Meehan, T.R. Merrell, Jr. and T.A. Hanley, eds. *Proceedings of a Symposium on Fish and Wildlife Relationships in Old Growth Forests, 12-15 April 1982, Juneau, Alaska*, 351–356. American Institute of Fish. Res. Biology, Morehead City, NC.

Nettleton, H.I. 1957. Wood rats damage young Douglas-fir. *Journal of Forestry* 55(11):845.

Novak, M., J.A. Baker, M.E. Obbard and B. Malloch, eds. 1987. *Wild Furbearer Management and Conservation in North America.* Ontario Ministry of Natural Resources.

Ruggiero, L.F., K.B. Aubry, S.W. Buskirk, L.J. Lyon and W.J. Zielinski, eds. 1994. *The Scientific Basis for Conserving Forest Carnivores: American Marten, Fisher, Lynx and Wolverine in the Western United States.* USDA Forest Service, Rocky Mountain Forest and Range Experimental Station. General Technical Report RM-254.

Stevens, V. 1993. *Wildlife Diversity in British Columbia: Distribution and Habitat Use in Biogeoclimatic Zones.* BC Ministry of Environment, Habitat Protection Branch, Victoria, BC. Draft.

Walters, B.C. 1991. Small mammals in subalpine old growth forest and clearcuts. *Northwest Science* 65(1):27–31.

Weir, R.D. 1994. *Diet, Spatial Organization and Habitat Relationships of Fishers in South-central British Columbia.* M.Sc. Thesis, Simon Fraser University, Burnaby, BC.

Witt, J.W. 1992. Home range and density estimates for the northern flying squirrel, *Glaucomys sabrinus*, in western Oregon. *Journal of Mammalogy* 73(4): 921–929.

Woods, S.E. 1980. *The Squirrels of Canada.* National Museum of Natural Sciences and National Museums of Canada, Ottawa, ON.

TREES: SELECTED LITERATURE

Arno, S.F. and R.P. Hammerly. 1977. *Northwest Trees: Identifying and Understanding the Region's Native Trees.* The Mountaineers, Seattle, WA.

Brockman, F.C., H.S. Sim and R. Merrilees. 1968. *Trees of North America: A Field Guide to the Major Native and Introduced Species North of Mexico.* Goden Press, New York, NY.

Lyons, C. and B. Merilees. 1995. *Trees, Shrubs and Flowers to Know in British Columbia and Washington.* Lone Pine Publishing, Edmonton, AB.

Pojar J. and A. MacKinnon. 1994. *Plants of Coastal British Columbia.* Lone Pine Publishing, Edmonton, AB.

United States Department of Agriculture Forest Service. 1990. *Silvics of North America Vol. 1: Conifers, and Vol. 2: Hardwoods.* Agriculture Handbook 654.

VAUX'S SWIFT AND INSECTIVOROUS PERCHING BIRDS: SELECTED LITERATURE

Adams, E.M. and M.L. Morrison. 1993. Effects of forest stand structure and composition on red-breasted nuthatches and brown creepers. *Journal of Wildlife Management* 57:616–629.

Baldwin, P.H. and N.K. Zaczkowski. 1963. Breeding biology of the Vaux's swift. *Condor* 65:400–406.

Belle-Isles, J.C. and J. Picman. 1986. Nest losses and nest site preferences in house wrens. *Condor* 8:483–486.

Bock, C.E. and D.C. Fleck. 1995. Avian response to nest box addition in two forests of the Colorado Front Range. *Journal of Field Ornithology* 66:352–362.

Bull, E.L. 1991. Summer roosts and roosting behavior of Vaux's Swifts in old growth forests. *Northwestern Naturalist* 72:78–82.

Bull, E.L. and R.C. Beckwith. 1993. Diet and foraging behavior of Vaux's Swifts in northeastern Oregon. *Condor* 95:1016–1023.

Bull, E.L. and C.T. Collins. 1993. Vaux's Swift. A. Poole and F. Gill, eds. *The Birds of North America, No. 77.* Academy of Natural Sciences, Philadelphia, PA, and American Ornithologists' Union, Washington, DC.

Bull, E.L. and H.D. Cooper. 1991. Vaux's Swift nests in hollow trees. *Western Birds* 22:85–91.

Bull, E.L. and J.E. Hohmann. 1992. The association between Vaux's swifts and old growth forests in northeastern Oregon. *Western Birds* 24:38–42.

Cooper, J.M. 1991. Vaux's Swifts visit Duncan home. *Victoria Naturalist* 47.5:5.

Davis, C.M. 1978. A nesting study of the brown creeper. *Living Bird* 17:237–263.

De Steven, D. 1980. Clutch size, breeding success and parental survival in the tree swallow (*Iridoprocne bicolor*). *Evolution* 34:278–291.

Erskine, A.J. and W.D. McLaren. 1979. Man's influence on potential nesting sites and populations of swallows in Canada. *Canadian Field Naturalist* 93:371–377.

Finch, D.M. 1990. Effects of predation and competitor interference on nesting success of house wrens and tree swallows. *Condor* 92:674–687.

Franzreb, K.E. 1985. Foraging ecology of brown creepers in a mixed-conifer forest. *Journal of Field Ornithology* 56:9–16.

Grubb, T.C., Jr. and C.L. Bronson. 1995. Artificial snags as nesting sites for chickadees. *Condor* 97:1067–1070.

Grubb, T.C., Jr. and T.A. Waite. 1987. Caching by red-breasted nuthatches. *Wilson Bulletin* 99:696–699.

Guntert, M., D.B. Hay and R.P. Balda. 1967. *Communal roosting in the pygmy nuthatch: a winter survival strategy.* Proceedings of the 14th International Ornithology Congress:1964–1972.

Herlugson, C.J. 1981. Nest site selection in mountain bluebirds. *Condor* 83:252–255.

Hill, B.G. and M.R. Lein. 1988. Ecological relationships of sympatric black-capped and mountain chickadees in southwestern Alberta. *Condor* 90:875–884.

_____. 1989. Territory overlap and habitat use of sympatric chickadees. *Auk* 106:645–652.

Johnson, L.S. and L.H. Kermott. 1991. Effect of nest-site supplementation on polygynous behavior in the house wren (*Troglodytes aedon*). *Condor* 93:784–787.

_____. 1994. Nesting success of cavity-nesting birds using natural cavities. *Journal of Field Ornithology* 65:36–51.

Keller, M.E. and S.H. Anderson. 1992. Avian use of habitat configurations created by forest cutting in southwestern Wyoming. *Condor* 94:55–65.

Kilham, L. 1968. Reproductive behavior of white-breasted nuthatches. I. Distraction display, bill-sweeping and nest hole defense. *Auk* 85:477–492.

_____. 1971. Roosting habits of white-breasted nuthatches. *Condor* 73:113–114.

_____. 1972. Reproductive behavior of white-breasted nuthatches. II. Courtship. *Auk* 89:115–129.

Kroodsma, D.E. 1973. Coexistence of Bewick's wrens and house wrens in Oregon. *Auk* 90:341–352.

Lima, S.L. and R.M. Lee III. 1993. Food caching and its possible origin in the brown creeper. *Condor* 95:483–484.

Mariani, J.M. and D.A. Manuwal. 1990. Factors influencing brown creeper (*Certhia americana*) abundance patterns in the southern Washington Cascade Range. *Studies in Avian Biology* 13:53–57.

McEllin, S.M. 1979. Population demographies, spacing, and foraging behaviors of white-breasted and pygmy nuthatches in ponderosa pine habitat. *The Role of Insectivorous Birds in Forest Ecosystems*, 301-32. Academic Press.

McLaren, M.A. 1975. Breeding biology of the boreal chickadee. *Wilson Bulletin* 87:344–354.

Pogue, D.W. and G.D. Schnell. 1994. Habitat characterization of secondary cavity-nesting birds in Oklahoma. *Wilson Bulletin* 106:203–226.

Power, H.W. 1980. The foraging behavior of mountain bluebirds with emphasis on sexual foraging differences. *Ornithology Monographs* 28.

Power, H.W. 1966. Biology of the mountain bluebird in Montana. *Condor* 68:351–371.

Pribil, S. and J. Picman. 1991. Why house wrens destroy clutches of other birds: a support for the nest site competition hypothesis. *Condor* 93:184–185.

Rendell, W.B. and R.J. Robertson. 1989. Nest-site characteristics, reproductive success and cavity availability for tree swallows breeding in natural cavities. *Condor* 91:875–885.

_____. 1990. Influence of forest edge on nest-site selection by tree swallows. *Wilson Bulletin* 102:634–664.

Robertson, R.J., B.J. Stutchberry and R.R. Cohen. 1992. Tree Swallow. A. Poole and F. Gill, eds. The *Birds of North America, No. 11.* Academy of Natural Sciences, Philadelphia, PA, and American Ornithologists' Union, Washington, DC.

Robinson, K.D. and J.T. Rotenberry. 1991. Clutch size and reproductive success of house wrens rearing natural and manipulated broods. *Auk* 108:277–284.

Smith, S.M. 1974. Nest-site selection in black-capped chickadees. *Condor* 76:478–479.

_____. 1991. *The Black-capped Chickadee: Behavioral Ecology and Natural History.* Cornell University Press, Ithaca, NY.

_____. 1993. Black-capped Chickadee. A. Poole and F. Gill, eds. *The Birds of North America, No. 39.* Academy of Natural Sciences, Philadelphia, PA, and American Ornithologists' Union, Washington, DC.

Sydeman, W.J., M. Guntert and R.P. Balda. 1988. Annual reproductive yield in the cooperative pygmy nuthatch (*Sitta pygmaea*). Auk 105:70–77.

WATERFOWL: SELECTED LITERATURE

Bellrose, F.C. 1980. *Ducks, Geese and Swans of North America.* Stackpole Books, Harrisburg, PA.

Bellrose, F.C. and D.J. Holm. 1994. *Ecology and Management of the Wood Duck.* Stackpole Books, Mechanicsburg, PA.

Boyd, W.S., J.P.L. Savard and G.E.J. Smith. 1989. *Relationships between Aquatic Birds and Wetland Characteristics in the Aspen Parkland, Central British Columbia.* Canadian Wildlife Service, Delta, BC. Technical Report Series No. 70.

Eadie, J.M. and G. Gauthier. 1985. Prospecting for nest sites by cavity-nesting ducks of the genus Bucephala. *Condor* 87:528–534.

Savard, J.P.L. 1991. *Waterfowl in the Aspen Parkland of Central British Columbia. Canadian Wildlife Service, Delta, BC.* Technical Report Series No. 132.

Savard, J.P.L. 1984. Territorial Behaviour of Common Goldeneye, Barrow's Goldeneye and Bufflehead in Areas of Sympatry. *Ornis Scand.* 15:211–216.

Vermeer, K. and R.W. Butler, eds. *The Ecology and Status of Marine and Shoreline Birds in the Strait of Georgia, British Columbia.* Canadian Wildlife Service, Delta, BC.

Zicus, M.C. 1990. Nesting biology of hooded mergansers using nest boxes. *Journal of Wildlife Management* 64:637–643.

WOODPECKERS: SELECTED LITERATURE

Aubrey, K.B. and C.M. Raley. 2002. *The Pileated Woodpecker as a Keystone Habitat Modifier in the Pacific Northwest.* USDA Forest Service, Pacific Northwest Research Station, Olympia, WA. General Technical Report PSW-GTR-181.

Bent, A.C. 1964. *Life Histories of North American Woodpeckers.* Dover Publications, New York, NY.

Bock, C.E., M. Raphael and J.H. Bock. 1978. Changing avian community structure during early post-fire succession in the Sierra Nevada. *Wilson Bulletin* 89:119–123.

Bull, E.L. and R.S. Holthausen. 1993. Habitat use and management of pileated woodpeckers in northeastern Oregon. *Journal of Wildlife Management* 57:335–345.

Bull, E.L. and J.A. Jackson. 1995. Pileated Woodpecker. A. Poole and F. Gill, eds. The *Birds of North America, No. 148.* Academy of Natural Sciences, Philadelphia, PA, and American Ornithologists' Union, Washington, DC.

Bull, E.L., S.R. Peterson and J.W. Thomas. 1986. *Resource Partitioning Among Woodpeckers in Northeastern Oregon.* USDA Forest Service, LaGrande, OR. Research Note PNW-444.

Cannings, R.J. 1991. *Status Report on the White-headed Woodpecker* Picoides albolarvatus. BC Ministry of Environment, Wildlife Branch, Victoria, BC. Unpublished report.

Carlson, A. and G. Aulen. 1990. *Conservation and Management of Woodpecker Populations.* Swedish University of Agricultural Sciences, Department of Wildlife Ecology, Uppsala, Sweden. Report 17.

Conner, R.N., S.D. Jones and G.D. Jones. 1994. Snag condition and woodpecker foraging ecology in a bottomland hardwood forest. *Wilson Bulletin* 106:242–257.

Conway, C.J. and T.E. Martin. 1993. Habitat suitability for Williamson's sapsuckers in mixed-conifer forests. *Journal of Wildlife Management* 57:322–328.

Cooper, J.M. 1995. *Status of the Williamson's Sapsucker in British Columbia.* Ministry of Environment, Wildlife Branch, Victoria, BC. Wildlife Working Report No. WR-69.

Crockett, A.B. and H.H. Hadow. 1975. Nest site selection by Williamson's and rednaped sapsuckers. *Condor* 77:365–368.

Crockett, A.B. and P.L. Hansley. 1977. Coition, nesting, and postfledging behaviour of Williamson's sapsucker in Colorado. *Living Bird* 16:7–19.

Daily, G.C. 1993. Heartwood decay and vertical distribution of red-naped sapsucker nest cavities. *Wilson Bulletin* 105:674–679.

Daily, G.C., P.R. Ehrlich and N.M. Haddad. 1993. *Double keystone species in a keystone species complex.* Proceedings of the National Academy of Science USA 90:592-594.

Ehrlich, P.R. and G.C. Daily. 1988. Red-naped sapsuckers feeding at willow: possible keystone herbivores. *American Birds* 42:357–365.

Guiguet, C.J. 1970. *Birds of British Columbia: (1) Woodpeckers (2) Crows and their allies.* British Columbia Provincial Museum, Victoria, BC. Handbook No. 6.

Harestad, A.S. and D.G. Keisker. 1989. Nest tree use by primary cavity-nesting birds in south-central British Columbia. *Canadian Journal of Zoology* 67:1067–1073.

Ingold, D.J. 1994. Influence of nest-site competition between European starlings and woodpeckers. *Wilson Bulletin* 106:227–241.

Keisker, D.G. 1987. *Nest tree selection by primary cavity-nesting birds in south-central British Columbia.* BC Ministry of Environment, Wildlife Branch, Victoria, BC. Wildlife Report No. R-13.

Kirk, D.A. and B.J. Naylor, 1996. *Habitat requirements of the Pileated Woodpecker* (Drycocpus pileatus) *with Special Reference to Ontario.* Southern Central Science and Technology Technical Bulletin No 46.

Koplin, J.R. 1969. The numerical response of woodpeckers to insect prey in a subalpine forest in Colorado. *Condor* 71:436–438.

Lawrence, L. de K. 1967. A Comparative Life-history Study of Four Species of Woodpeckers. American Ornithologists' Union, Lawrence, KS. *Ornithological Monographs* No. 5.

Mannan, R.W., E.C. Meslow and H.M. Wight. 1980. Use of snags by birds in Douglas-fir forests, western Oregon. *Journal of Wildlife Management* 44:787–797.

Naylor, B.J., J.B. Baker, J.A. Hogg, D.M. McNicol and W.R. Watt. 1996. *Forest Management Guidelines for the Provision of Pileated Woodpecker Habitat.* Ontario Ministry of Natural Resources, Forest Management Branch.

Preston, A. 1990. *Canyon Wren, Sage Thrasher, White-headed Woodpecker, Grey Flycatcher and Grasshopper Sparrows in the south Okanagan.* BC Ministry of Environment, Wildlife Branch, Penticton, BC. Unpublished report.

Scott, V.E., J.A. Whelan and P.L. Svoboda. 1980. Cavity-nesting birds and forest management. R.M. DeGraff and N.G. Tilghman, eds. *Management of Western Forests and Grasslands for Nongame Birds*, 311-324. USDA Forest Service, Ogden, UT. General Technical Report INT-86.

Siddle, C. and G. Davidson. 1991. *Status of the Lewis' Woodpecker* (Melanerpes lewis) *in British Columbia.* BC Ministry of Environment, Wildlife Branch, Victoria, BC. Unpublished report.

Smith, K.G. 1982. On habitat selection of Williamson's and "red-naped" yellow-bellied sapsuckers. *Southwestern Naturalist* 27:464–466.

Sousa, P.J. 1983. *Habitat Suitability Index Models: Williamson's Sapsucker.* US Fish and Wildlife Service, Washington, DC. Biology Report 82(10.47).

Stallcup, P.L. 1968. Spatio-temporal relationships of nuthatches and woodpeckers in ponderosa pine forests of Colorado. *Journal of Ecology* 49:831–843.

Steeger, C., M. Machmer and E. Walters. n.d. *Ecology and Management of Woodpeckers and Wildlife Trees in British Columbia.* Environment Canada, Fraser River Action Plan, Delta, BC.

Tate, J., Jr. 1973. Methods and annual sequence of foraging by the sapsucker. *Auk* 90:840–856.

Tobalske, B.W. 1992. Evaluating habitat suitability using relative abundance and fledging success of red-naped sapsuckers. *Condor* 94:550–553.

Villard, P. and C.W. Beninger. 1993. Foraging behaviour of male black-backed and hairy woodpeckers in a forest burn. *Journal of Field Ornithology* 64:71–76.

Weber, W.C. and S.R. Cannings. 1976. The white-headed woodpecker (*Dendrocopus albolarvatus*) in British Columbia. *Syesis* 9:215–220.

Yom-Tov, Y. and A. Ar. 1993. Incubation and fledging durations of woodpeckers. *Condor* 95:282–287.

Zarnowitz, J.E. and D.A. Manuwal. 1985. The effects of forest management on cavity-nesting birds in northwestern Washington. *Journal of Wildlife Management* 49:255–263.

Indexes

Page numbers in *italics* refer to figures, maps and tables.

Page numbers in **boldface** type refer to detailed accounts for tree and animal species.

C

About the Authors

MIKE FENGER
Professional Forester • Mike Fenger and Associates Ltd.
Following his graduation from the School of Forestry at the University of British Columbia, Mike worked for three decades as a forest biodiversity specialist, most recently with the Biodiversity Branch of the Ministry of Water, Land and Air Protection. His experience encompasses protected areas design, old-growth conservation, habitat surveys and modelling, ecological restoration, environmental impact and risk assessment, forest policy, integrated resource planning and training, and he is a long-time member of the Wildlife Tree Committee of British Columbia. Now in private practice, Mike has two daughters and a son and lives in Victoria with his wife.

TODD MANNING
Habitat Forester, Wildlife Ecologist and Arborist • Manning, Cooper and Associates Ltd.
Todd is a professional biologist, certified arborist and professional forester with a Bachelor of Science in environmental biology, a Bachelor of Education in science education from the University of Calgary and a combined master's degree in wildlife ecology and natural resources extension from the University of Victoria. Todd's consulting work involves mostly forestry-wildlife interactions, partial-cutting systems, the assessment of wildlife trees and dangerous trees and methods for maintaining or enhancing wildlife habitat in forestry operations. Todd was the coordinator of the Wildlife Tree Committee of British Columbia from 1991 to 2005. He lives with his wife and two sons in Metchosin.

JOHN COOPER
Wildlife Biologist • Manning, Cooper and Associates Ltd.
John is a consulting professional biologist with a bachelor's degree in vertebrate zoology from the University of British Columbia and a master's in biology from the University of Victoria. He specializes in ornithology, wildlife biodiversity studies and environmental impact assessments. As a biologist working throughout British Columbia for 27 years, he has produced or contributed to more than 140 books, scientific papers, technical reports and popular articles on wildlife. In 2001, he and his co-authors completed *The Birds of British Columbia*, a four-volume, 20-year compilation covering all the province's bird species. John's interest in birds and wildlife was inspired by his parents and several special friends who showed him how exciting it was to look for something and find it.

WART GUY
Biologist • B.C. Ministry of Environment

Educated at the University of Victoria and Simon Fraser University, Stewart has worked as a naturalist, teacher and professional biologist in British Columbia for the last 26 years. He is currently the project manager for wildlife conservation planning in the Biodiversity Branch of the Ministry of Environment. His many years of involvement in wildlife tree management have been as a consultant, instructor and member of the Wildlife Tree Committee of British Columbia. Stewart lives in Victoria with his wife and three boys.

PETER BRADFORD
Professional Forester • B.C. Forest Service

Peter graduated from the University of British Columbia with a degree in forestry in 1987. He worked as a field forester, mostly on Vancouver Island and in southwestern B.C., before moving to Victoria to develop forest policy, extension programs and training related to silvicultural systems and stand-level biodiversity. More recently, he has been involved in evaluating the effectiveness of forest management policies. Peter is an active member of the Wildlife Tree Committee of British Columbia. He lives in Victoria with his wife and daughter.

(Left to right) Stewart Guy, Peter Bradford, Mike Fenger, Todd Manning, John Cooper